RESIST OR SERVE

THE OFFICIAL GUIDE TO

THE FILES™

CREATED BY
Chris Carter

WRITTEN BY
Andy Meisler

HarperEntertainment
A Division of HarperCollinsPublishers

 HarperEntertainment

A Division of HarperCollins*Publishers*

10 East 53rd Street, New York, N.Y. 10022-5299

HarperEntertainment books may be purchased for educational,
business, or sales promotional use. For information, please write:
Special Markets Department, HarperCollinsPublishers
10 East 53rd Street, New York, NY 10022-5299.

ISBN 0-06-107309-1

HarperCollins ®, ▟ ®, and HarperEntertainment ®
are trademarks of HarperCollins*Publishers* Inc.

First printing: January 1999

Printed in the United States of America

Front cover photograph courtesy of Fox Broadcasting Company

Cover Design: CARL GALIAN

Interior Design: MURPHY FOGELNEST

Library of Congress Cataloging-in-Publication Data
is on file with the publisher.

Visit HarperEntertainment on the World Wide Web at
http://www.harpercollins.com

❖ 10 9 8 7 6 5 4 3 2 1

Once again
        for the first time:
for Emily Meisler

acknowlegments

**For the second year in succession,
the members of the *X-Files* team made
an overwrought and underdressed outsider
feel welcome. Friends and neighbors
played major supporting roles, as well.**

Many thanks to:

Gary Allen, Steve Allen, Val Arntzen,
Laverne Basham, Anji Bemben, Sean Benbow,
Tom Braidwood, Heike Brandstatter,
Jaap Broeker, Al Campbell, Jodi Clancy,
Mark Currie, Kristine Dawson, Brett Dowler,
Tracy Elofson, Briton Erwin, Michelle Fazekas,
Rick Fearon, J. P. Finn, Chuck Forsch, Ron French,
David Gauthier, William Gibson, Vince Gilligan,
Sarah Goldstein, Bob Goodwin, Louisa Gradnitzer,
Jeff Gulka, Nigel Habgood, Dean Haglund,
Ken Hawryliw, Shirley Inget, Laurie Kallsen-
George, Toby Lindala, Greg Loewen, Pearl Louie,
Kate Luyben, Tom Maddux, Rob Maier,
Kim Manners, Brian Markinson, Coreen Mayrs,
Steven Melnick, Marty McInally, Rick Millikan,
Richard Miller, Tim Minear, David Moreland,
Graeme Murray, Lori Jo Nemhauser, Vivien Nishi,
Kim Nordlinger, Shannon Peterson, Todd Pittson,
Paul Rabwin, Joel Ransom, Bob Roe, Willy Ross,
Forest Sala, Joanne Service, John Shiban,
Francine and Scott Sprigel, Mark Snow,
Frank Spotnitz, Patrick Stark, Anita Truelove,
Tracey Warren, Michael Williamson,
Stacy Wise, and Chandra Years.

Guidance and inspiration continue to
emanate from Mary Astadourian and Chris Carter.
Caitlin Blasdell is an editor without peer;
Maureen and Eric Lasher
are the best agents I'll ever have.

ABOUT THE AUTHOR

Andy Meisler writes about television
for the *New York Times* and several other
publications. He is the author of *I Want To
Believe: The Official Guide to The X-Files*
as well as the co-author of *The Secret Life
of Cyndy Garvey* with Cynthia Garvey and
*I Am Roe: My Life, Roe v. Wade, and
Freedom of Choice* with Norma McCorvey.
He lives with his wife in Los Angeles.

contents

the fifth season:

Here is one way to look at television:
as a vast, mind-numbing conspiracy
to dull your brain and steal your soul.
Here is another way to look at television:
as a marvel of humanity tied to technology that,
at its best, can bind us together by tapping into
our deepest thoughts and feelings. And sometimes—
but only very rarely—a single show can tip
the balance in television's favor.

SUCH A SHOW IS *THE X-FILES.* For five years—an eternity by pop cultural standards—this ground-breaking program has continued to burrow deeply into our collective psyche. It has also continued to attract new viewers, keep its old ones, and spark fevered debate and discussion wherever it airs. Which is nearly everywhere.

The X-Files has done this because the people behind the show, particularly its creator and executive producer Chris Carter, have managed to cleave to the basic principles that make the show work, all the while issuing challenges to themselves and their viewers, as well as to the series's principal characters.

By now nearly everyone in the known world knows that the series—a Sunday night fixture on the Fox Network—is the ongoing saga of Fox Mulder (played by David Duchovny) and Dana Scully (played by Gillian Anderson), two FBI agents assigned to an odd corner of their massive investigative agency. Tasked to investigate paranormal and other inexplicable phenomena, they are driven—not primarily by duty or ambition, but by the complicated imperatives of their needs, hopes, and fears—toward the ragged margins of human understanding.

Mulder and Scully are intimate partners, but not lovers. Mulder is the rebel, the dreamer, the lone wolf to whom authority—and the official version—is not to be trusted. Scully, a doctor as well as an agent, is a scientist, a rationalist, a straight arrow whose skeptical demeanor conceals depths of not-always-welcome feelings and desires. Over the past five seasons the pair have encountered more than their share of monsters, aliens, criminals, psychopaths, and earthbound arch-conspirators.

Their dangerous investigations yield much information, but never any final answers, nor the closure so beloved of TV producers and network executives everywhere.

Unlike almost every other dramatic series, the tone and mood of each episode vary wildly. The show is divided into "stand-alone" and "mythological" episodes: the former self-contained and complete in one hour; the latter part of a continuous unraveling of a complex conspiracy involving extraterrestrials and a ruthless shadow government known as The Syndicate (its prime manifestation a sinister manipulator known only as the Cigarette-Smoking Man).

These are the rough parameters of the show. But to make things even more complicated—and ultimately intriguing—*The X-Files* that became a cult hit in 1993, and a worldwide sensation two years later, is not *The X-Files* that exists today. In the past few seasons the plots have become more convoluted; the threats the agents face more sinister; the departures from TV-drama formula more radical; the relationship between Mulder and Scully deeper and ever more problematic.

in just the past year viewers have—among other things—been led backward in time and introduced to a freshly minted *X-Files* prehistory; seen an episode, shot in black-and-white, that flirted with surrealism; digested larger chunks of disturbing information and dire end-of-everything-we-hold-sacred prophecy than ever before; laughed not just *with* the heroic Mulder and Scully, but *at* them; and, perhaps most startling, watched them question their bedrock principles and set themselves adrift on a journey of self-exploration.

To be precise, during the 1997–1998 season, Fox Mulder became a disillusioned skeptic, and Dana Scully flirted with spiritualism and a belief in the paranormal. Who would have thought it? Perhaps not even Chris Carter.

"The truth is," says the forty-one-year-old ex-journalist and magazine editor during an interview early in the fifth season, "as much as we plan things out, things have taken a life of their own."

"It's the most amazing thing!" he adds quickly, smiling. "Actually, it makes me a little giddy, because the show has taken its own path. All of sudden, things are being dictated by the stories we have told before. All the elements are coming together with a crystalline beauty, and in ways that constantly surprise me."

At the same time, as longtime Carterologists are well aware, the ruler of the X-Files empire doesn't let his trips beyond the margins distract him from his basic purpose.

"It all comes down to telling a good story," says Carter, in another interview held during the summer of 1998. "You just have to have a fundamental ability to tell that story, and it has everything to do with reading and reference and what's going on in the world and nothing to do with all the money that's being thrown around in this medium."

Whatever the precise formula, Carter must be doing something right. During the 1997–1998 season *The X-Files* was once again the highest-rated program on the Fox Network. Among the demographic groups that advertisers crave most—adults 18–49 and adults 25–54—it was the fifth highest-rated program on American television, the second highest drama, and the easy winner of it's key 9 P.M. Sunday time slot.

The show also continued to do extremely well in weekend syndication and as a five-nights-a-week fixture on Fox's FX cable network. Internationally, *The X-Files* reached near-ubiquity; its strength mirroring the growth of alternative cable and satellite outlets in countries that formerly offered few viewing choices. Hard-core fan support was reflected in the explosive sales of X-Files related merchandise like books, clothing, CD-ROMS, and even Barbie dolls. During the spring of 1998 more than 55,000 fans attended the official *X-Files* Expos—featuring personal appearances by the show's stars and producers—in ten cities across the U.S.

On another related front, the Hollywood television communities esteem for *The X-Files* can be demonstrated with another significant statistic: On July 23, 1998, the show received sixteen Emmy nominations including nominations for its two lead actors and for best writing, best directing, and best drama. That tied it with NBC's megahit *ER* for most nominations by a network series.

What these facts and figures don't indicate, though, are the unique challenges—from both within and without—that were encountered and, for the most part, overcome by the *X-Files* team this season. The most visible hurdle: Two seasons ago, Fox and Chris Carter decided to make the *X-Files* movie, designed to be enjoyably comprehensible to moviegoers who, for some incomprehensible reason, had never seen *The X-Files*, and a narrative suspension bridge between Seasons Five and Six.

The $60 million feature was shot during the summer of 1997, necessitating both a nail-biting delay in the start of filming the fifth season and a painstaking planning process to make sure that the episodes of Season Five—written and produced, of course, *after* the film—led properly into the feature and the season beyond.

Some of the problems involved in pulling this off were tricky. The lead actors—sworn to secrecy, as was everyone involved the plot of the *X-Files* movie—had to deal throughout the year with the unprecedented and fairly dangerous knowledge of where their trials and tribulations were going to ultimately lead them.

"It was hard to start off the season knowing what we knew in the movie," says Gillian Anderson. "Ultimately, we had to forget all that and just make sense of each new episode individually."

add to all this a major casting disaster (see p. 97); some significant weather woes (see p.59); the fact that movie post-production and re-shooting competed for Chris Carter's attention throughout the entire season; an unprecedented decision to farm out a script each to William Gibson and Stephen King, two world-class—but inexperienced in the ways of *The X-Files*—writers. And then there was what sportswriters like to call a "distraction." A big one.

In 1993—partly for reasons of economics, partly because of the variety of exterior locations available there—Chris Carter and Fox Television shot the *X-Files* pilot in Vancouver, British Columbia. When the series was picked up, all subsequent episodes and seasons were filmed there even as the show continued to be written and edited on the Fox movie lot in Los Angeles.

The advantages to this arrangement: magnificent scenery and an "interesting" climate that helped to give *The X-Files* a "look" all its own; a depressed Canadian dollar that stretched farther for U.S.-based productions; and—most importantly—a magnificently talented and hard-working crew that quickly proved to be the cream of Vancouver's burgeoning film and television community.

The disadvantages: sometimes-unwieldy communications between north and south; an international commute between Los Angeles and Vancouver; and the fact that the show's American stars were required to live in Vancouver ten months of the year, far away from their homes and from the main focus of the U.S. entertainment industry.

When *The X-Files* became an international hit for Fox, Vancouver's cost savings became less important. After completing filming for Season Four, and marrying Los Angeles–based actress Tea Leoni, David Duchovny began expressing publicly (as to a lesser extent, did his co-star Gillian Anderson) a desire that the show be filmed, as was the *X-Files* movie, in Southern California.

Before the start of Season Five, Duchovny renewed his contract for two additional years with the provision that if the series continued to be filmed in Vancouver beyond 1997–1998 he could opt to appear in only eight episodes per season. It was announced that the situation was being reevaluated. And that was how the fifth season—with plans to produce 22 ambitious episodes—began.

"It's been a very demanding year so far," said Vancouver-based executive producer Robert Goodwin, on a rainy day (with "sunny breaks," say the local TV weathermen) in February 1998. "The most difficult year, I think, from a production point of view."

The weary-looking Goodwin added that difficult cast scheduling problems—because of other commitments recurring actors like Laurie Holden (Marita Cavarrubias) was frequently unavailable—meant that portions of two and even three episodes had to be shot simultaneously and complex feats of scene-juggling were often necessary. Add to this all the other logistical problems—and Chris Carter's golden rule that new ground must be broken practically every week—and it's easy to see why second (and occasionally, third and even fourth) film units were constantly in motion. Why in late fall the network order was cut to twenty episodes (the hole was partly filled with an L.A.–produced documentary special, *Inside* The X-Files, that aired February 1). And why the budget for an average episode crept past the truly astonishing figure of $2.5 million.

But to all this most of the Canadian *X-Files* veterans ultimately had the same response: "What else is new?"

Most of the longtimers had developed a quiet pride in their series's groundbreaking tradition, and by Season Five were accustomed to making the impossible look routine.

To the experienced eye, there were some subtle changes—the show's North Vancouver headquarters, for instance, had for some obscure business reason, changed its name from North Shore Studios to Lion's Gate Studios—but since Season Four there had been little staff turnover.

Before the start of each episode, thirty or forty mostly familiar faces jammed into the production office's cramped conference room for production meetings (all were attended this year by Chris Carter). Some of the cars in the adjacent lot sported an impressive line of pastel *X-Files* parking stickers on their windows. Fox Mulder's pet fish still swam happily in their aquarium on a table in set decorator Shirley Inget's office. Several "Chinga" dolls, in various stages of disassembly, rested comfortably in props master Ken Hawryliw's department.

The in-house collection of odd *X-Files* memorabilia behind the receptionist's desk had expanded. It now included a bottle of *X-Files* wine ("This uniquely blended wine," read the label, "is inspired by the spirit of compromise in order to control disagreements as to which fine wine to serve with a episode of *The X-Files*"); a plush alien wearing a crocheted sweater; a bootleg Dana Scully commemorative plate; and a vaguely molar-shaped extraterrestrial wearing a shirt that read "The Tooth Is Out There."

Taped to a wall in the front office was a letter from a North Dakota–based fan describing plans for her *X-Files* wedding ("We will use the *X-Files* theme as our wedding march, and FBI passes instead of corsages"). In a box on the other side of the receptionist's desk, as always, were the daily call sheets—long photocopied forms containing every conceivable detail of that day's shooting schedule—attached to elaborate maps giving directions to the first and second units' shooting sites.

On another rainy day in mid-February one such map lead to Children's Hospital in Vancouver. Inside an unused corridor, filming was proceeding for the season's fourteenth episode, "The Red and the Black." Inside a nearby stairwell was taped a notice informing the hospital staff of the filming. "We love *The X-Files*," somebody had scrawled across it. "We hope it stays."

Staying focused was perhaps a touch easier at the show's Southern California home base where, as it had been since the beginning, the show was written, partly cast, edited, and painstakingly revised and polished for broadcast. A few new faces—junior staff writers and editors, mostly—worked feverishly alongside the veterans. All were ensconced, as always, inside the ramshackle bungalows and office buildings *The X-Files* occupies on the Fox lot.

The Fox Studio's multimillion dollar expansion and renovation project—now in its second full year—continued to have no effect whatsoever on *X-Files* working conditions, except to make visitor parking more difficult and increase the ambient noise level considerably.

Frequent visitors to Building 49, the site of Chris Carter's office and headquarters of his production company, Ten Thirteen, noticed some subtle changes from previous years including heightened security, particularly concerning the carefully numbered and photocopy-proofed pages of the top secret movie script; urgent meetings, screening sessions, and whispered conversations regarding the movie's crucial post-production process; and many more meetings concerning merchandising, special events (particularly the ten-city *X-Files* Expo Tour) and publicity (by the time it premiered in June, the *X-Files* movie spawned cover stories in no less than thirty-three separate magazines).

However, the most crucial business of all—planning the general direction of the *X-Files* season, then turning action, emotion, and suspense into script pages—went on in the usual manner; in brainbusting story meetings and during long hours in front of the computer screen. Even the most subtle and complex seasonal "through line"—the changes in Mulder and Scully's shifting belief systems—were taken, for the most part, in stride.

"That happened because David is always looking for something to do with his character," explained Chris Carter. "He asked us to change it. And we hadn't figured out how to do that without it creating a very big detour in the show that would slow down the kind of story telling we do.

"So one day I thought why not take everything away from him? Take away all his hopes, and give them back to him slowly? And at the same time play with Gillian's character, make Scully suddenly start to develop and confront new spiritual aspects of her life. And then, watch those characters really change places and then come back to where they started."

But as Carter and his *X-Files* colleagues know, there were other even more important changes to be considered. As the shooting season entered its final months, with no decision yet made on moving the show to Los Angeles, rumors began to swirl—especially among the Vancouver crew members—about the future of *The X-Files*. Of particular interest was the casting of actor Chris Owens as a new recurring character, FBI Agent Jeffrey Spender—a sort of anti-Mulder figure with nebulous ties to the Cigarette-Smoking Man and to past and present alien abductions.

Is Spender being groomed as a replacement for Mulder? Is he a projected part-time substitute if the show remains in Vancouver and Duchovny elects to cut back his commitment to the show? Or is he simply a red herring, a bit of fan interest-piquing disinformation, a totally irrelevant plot-driven development?

By late winter, even the individuals most intimately involved appeared to grow weary of the speculation. "To tell you the truth," said a prominent member of the Vancouver crew, "I've worked so hard here and given so much to this great show—done things I could never even imagine doing before I started—that sometimes I feel used up. If the show leaves for L.A., it may be the best chance I'll get to stop and reflect; to relax and do other things for a while."

On Friday, March 28, Chris Carter flew to Vancouver; talked to each department head individually; and told him or her, sadly, that he had hoped there would be some alternative but that *The X-Files* would be moving to Los Angeles for the start of it's sixth season.

Afterward, Carter walked the short distance to the sound stage where the show was being filmed. He gathered the cast and crew around him, and started to read a prepared announcement giving the financial and logistical reasons for the move. He started to thank the Vancouver-based crew for their five years of effort. But before he could finish getting the words out he was overwhelmed by emotion—as were many of the talented artists and technicians listening to him. The *X-Files*'s creator could not go on. Everyone silently let the news sink in.

"In the end I think everyone basically was relieved," recalls Vancouver-based producer J. P. Finn. "Because now that we had the word officially, we could all of go on and plan our lives. In fact, in a way we were sort of elated because the end was in sight, and it was still okay, and in a little while we could relax and relish all our good work."

With much of the tension eased, work continued on the remaining episodes of the season. Even before their *X-Files* tenure was over, many crew members had jobs lined up on other productions, frequently—befitting the *X-Files*'s status as Vancouver's most prestigious TV series—at a higher level than they had occupied previously. On Saturday, April 25, the *X-Files*'s Vancouver wrap party—one of the hottest tickets in town—was held at the Pacific Space Center, Vancouver's main planetarium and science center, and was a mammoth, rollicking success. Dancing, imbibing, and high-decibel recollecting continued well into the morning.

On Tuesday, April 28, David Duchovny filmed his final scene and, after posing for many group snapshots and handing out his farewell gifts—autographed basketballs—to each one of his Vancouver coworkers, left for Los Angeles.

The next day the cast and crew gathered at Riverview Hospital, in the Vancouver suburb of Coquitlam, for the fifth season's final day of principal photography. A strenuous—in fact, nearly impossible—schedule was laid out on the call sheet: nine scenes; eight separate camera setups; and a work day that would last from mid-morning to midnight and beyond.

No matter. The work began at an unflagging pace. In the large circus of trucks and other production vehicles gathered in the hospital parking lot, crew members tended to the actors and hustled large pieces of equipment to wherever they were needed.

From the big generator truck, thick black power cables snaked into obscure, odd-shaped corners of the hospital, where—as director Bob Goodwin controlled things from his seat next to the video monitor—the *X-Files* team endeavored to simultaneously race the clock, do justice to Chris Carter's script, and put the finishing touches on the 1997–1998 season.

"Quiet, people!" scolded assistant director Tom Braidwood, whenever ambient chatter threatened to get out of hand. "We've got work to do!"

As the day wore on, though, and the workload dropped slightly, the *X-File*rs began to gather quietly in small groups exchanging addresses, signing scrapbooks and T-shirts, posing for quick pictures. Chris Carter, his own work finished for the day, joined them outside the hospital and was quickly surrounded by groups of smiling coworkers. He laughed and reminisced with them all.

At around 7 P.M. something extraordinary happened: Dozens of people from the show's production office, many of whom rarely if ever set foot on location, began to arrive at Riverview. They joined perhaps eighty of their friends and coworkers in squeezing into the corridors surrounding an unused hospital storage room, where the set for the Lone Gunmen's office had been erected.

This was Gillian Anderson's final scene: a serio-comic passage in "The End" (5X20) in which Dana Scully asks Frohike, Langly, and Byers—who are dressed in their p.j.s, bathrobes, and (in Frohike's case) bunny slippers—to help her solve yet one more unsolvable mystery.

"Action!" said Bob Goodwin, his wife Sheila Larken (who plays Scully's mother in the series) sitting besides him. Chris Carter stood nearby, watching intently.

The filming proceeded with Anderson perhaps a bit more tense and emotional than the scene required. Several dozen camera angles, nervous flubs, makeup touch-ups, and alternate line readings later, Goodwin announced that he was satisfied.

"Okay, cut! Print it!" he said.

The set was silent for a moment until a stunned realization set in. In a few moments Anderson was to leave the set for the last time; in a few hours she would leave for Los Angeles. In a month and a half the *X-Files* movie would premiere. In just three months, filming for the sixth season—with a new crew, new plot lines, new challenges, and new triumphs—would begin.

The moment passed. The onlookers burst into applause; Anderson nearly burst into tears; the actress asked her friends to gather around her.

From a large cardboard box she held up a bathrobe inscribed GOODNIGHT EVERYBODY. I LOVE YOU—FOREVER. G.A. She invited everyone to visit her trailer, say their farewells, and pick up their own commemorative copy—their gift from her—afterward.

More applause. The actress fought to maintain her composure. And lost.

"I wish there was something that could express the way I love you all," she said, her eyes shining and her voice breaking. "You made it all so special. I will miss you all so much."

X
the episodes

unusual

In an important chunk
of *X-Files* pre-history,
up-and-coming
FBI agent Mulder
crosses paths with
an unlikely trio
of eccentrics; pursues
a beautiful alleged
terrorist; and gets
a searing glimpse
into his own future.

EPISODE: 5X01
FIRST AIRED: November 16, 1997
EDITOR: Lynne Willingham
WRITTEN BY: Vince Gilligan
DIRECTED BY: Kim Manners

GUEST STARS:
Dean Haglund (Langly)
Tom Braidwood (Frohike)
Bruce Harwood (Byers)
Richard Belzer (Detective John Munch)
Signy Coleman (Susanne Modeski)
Steven Williams (X)
Ken Hawryliw (Ken Hawryliw)
Chris Nelson Norris (SWAT
Lieutenant)
Stuart O'Connell (First SWAT cop)
Eric Knight (Hacker Dude)
Harrison Coe (First Suit—stunts)
Brad Loree (Second Suit—stunts)
Paul Anderson (City Cop)
Bob Boyd (Booking Sergeant)
Glenn Williams (Officer)
Peter Taraviras (Officer)

PRINCIPAL SETTING:
Baltimore, Maryland

The **year is 1989.** At Fells
Point Industrial Park in Baltimore,
a police van disgorges a squad of
SWAT cops. They surround a warehouse
with guns drawn.

"What do you know?" asks a SWAT
lieutenant, hunkered down next to a
uniformed city cop.

"We got reports of at least a dozen
shots fired," says the cop. "Front door
looks like it's been jimmied, but the alarm
wasn't tripped."

"You see anybody come out?" asks
the lieutenant

"Not a soul. Whoever it is, they're
still in there."

Their rifle-mounted flashlights stabbing
into the darkness, the SWAT cops stealthily enter the warehouse. The place is filled
with stacked wooden pallets.

"Lieutenant! Over here! Looks like
someone got hit!" says a cop.

Another one shines his light beam onto
a pool of blood on the floor.

"So where'd he go?" asks the
lieutenant.

No answer. "Stay low. Keep looking,"
he adds.

The men move off. The lieutenant
searches his own area—and hears a faint
groan. It seems to be a man's voice,
coming from a large cardboard box.
The lieutenant calls for backup and,
gun aimed toward the sound, approaches
the box. He lifts the top flap. Inside is a
naked man, curled into a fetal position.

"They're here," moans the man.

"Who's here?" asks the lieutenant.
He signals his men to keep searching.

They creep toward a large wooden gate
and lift it cautiously. Three men break
from cover and try to escape.

"Stop! Police!" shouts the cop.

The men don't get far. One of them,
the shortest, trips over his own feet and
lands with a thud. The other two stop
dead— their backs to their pursuers—
and raise their hands.

suspects

"Don't shoot!" says one of the perpetrators still standing.

"Turn around slowly!" screams the cop.

"We didn't do it," says the other standee.

"Do what?" asks the cop.

"Uh, whatever," replies the short guy, struggling back to his feet.

The cop shouts for them to all lay face down on the floor. All do so with alacrity. The SWAT team moves quickly to cuff the miserable trio.

In the commotion the naked man has been temporarily forgotten. He again begins to moan, incoherently at first. His moaning turns into shouting, and his words become intelligible.

"They're here. They're here! THEY'RE HERE!" he screams.

He lifts his head. He is a sweaty, pale-faced man, apparently insane, or frightened to the point of insanity. He is Fox Mulder.

In the Baltimore Police Department Homicide lockup, one of the three clothed intruders—the man we've previously seen as Byers, Mulder's present-day crony—is leaning against the cell door and staring despondently at his hands. They are stained with fingerprint ink. Behind him, in T-shirt and horn rims—full computer nerd regalia—is the man we know as Langly.

"We're screwed," says Langly. He turns to the third jailbird, sitting next to him.

"Thank you so much for getting me involved in this, Doohicky," he adds.

"*Frohike*, you hippie jerk," says his hydrant-shaped companion.

"Doohickey!" shouts Langly.

Frohike rises and walks slowly toward him. "You know, with that long blond hair, you'll be the first one in here that gets traded for cigarettes. I'm gonna be laughing my ass off."

"Oh, yeah?" says Byers, staring menacingly down toward Frohike's bald spot. "You wanna cha-cha?"

"Anytime, any place!" says Frohike.

Byers turns to face them. "Both of you relax!!" he says in his high-pitched voice.

This stops Langly and Frohike, who are squaring off. Instead, they turn their anger to Byers.

"Shut up, narc!" says Langly.

"It's your fault we're here!" says Frohike.

This silences the downcast Byers. A steel door clangs open and all three glance toward the sound.

"You! In the suit!" says the harsh voice of an unseen male. "You first!"

In a darkened police interrogation room Byers sits facing the harsh-voiced man, who introduces himself.

"Detective Munch, Baltimore Homicide," says the cop.

"Did they find her?" says Byers.

"And a good evening to *you*," replies Munch, sarcastically. He adds, "Sorry. No sign of your mystery lady."

"She is real," says Byers. "The FBI man saw her."

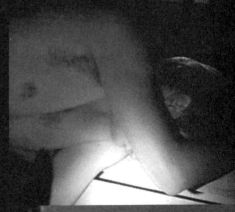

"Yeah, well. Special Agent . . ." Munch looks down at a file. ". . . *Mulder* is currently being held in five-point restraints and jabbering like a monkey. And the FBI's not talking, either."

He adds, "So what I'm looking at here is a warehouse break-in, but with nothing stolen. A shoot-out with no guns. Lots of blood but no bodies. And an FBI agent who likes to pull off all his clothes and talk about space aliens.

"Fill me in," Munch continues, clicking his ball-point, "from the top."

Byers nods and takes a deep breath. He says that his name is John Fitzgerald Byers, born November 22, 1963.

"Seriously?" says Munch.

"I was named after JFK. Before the assassination, my parents were going to call me 'Bertram.'"

"Lucky you. Occupation?"

Byers tells Munch that he is a public affairs officer for the Federal Communications Commission. In that capacity he was attending the computer and electronics show at the Baltimore Convention Center.

"It was," says Byers, "where this whole thing started just this morning."

That morning a serene and carefree Byers—wearing a button on his lapel reading WE'RE YOUR FCC—looks out from his booth at the convention center. Byers the murder suspect narrates the flashback:

"We at the FCC enjoy forging positive ties with the American public. It's our way of saying 'communication' is just another word for 'sharing.'"

Back at the convention, Byers smiles and offers a complimentary button to several grungy-looking passersby.

"Hi, guys. Like a button?" he says.

"Up yours, narc," says the hacker. In hindsight:

"Of course, some people don't see it like that."

In fact, everyone is avoiding his booth. Byers sighs and looks around the hall. Something immediately catches his attention. To wit:

"At any rate, that was where I first saw her."

Down the line of computer exhibits walks

a striking blond woman, wearing sunglasses indoors. She stops in front of Byers's booth and tips down her sunglasses to get a better view. Her eyes reflect a faint fear. Langly stands transfixed.

"Would you like a b-button?" he stammers.

The woman starts to speak, then decides against it. She turns and continues down the hall. Byers watches her go, and agonizes for a moment

"I'm still not sure why I did what I did next. It was so unlike me. There was just something about her."

Langly turns to his fellow FCC man, Ken Hawryliw, who has been sitting at a computer at the back of the booth the whole time. Ken is engrossed in a primitive video game on a 286 computer.

"Ken? I'm going to take a short break, okay?" says Byers.

"Whatever," says Ken, eyes glued to the monitor.

Byers ducks out through the curtain at the back of the booth and "surreptitiously" trails the blonde mystery woman. His quarry pauses briefly to look around her.

"Hello, pretty lady!" says a male voice.

It is Frohike, proudly manning his own booth.

He says, "Picture this: crystal clear television—33 channels worth—with *no* monthly cable bill!"

"Excuse me?" says the woman.

"Now!" says Frohike. "I know what you're thinking: 'Melvin, are you out of your mind? No cable bill?' But that's exactly what I'm saying. And I'm talking premium channels here, too. You got your HBO, you got your Cinemax, you got your Showtime—" He holds up a cheesy-looking cable descrambler box. "—all courtesy of this modestly priced marvel designed and built by the Frohike Electronics Corporation."

"Now, *there's* a name that inspires consumer confidence," says a sarcastic voice from the next booth.

The woman, baffled by Frohike's pitch, turns to listen. Frohike's face darkens. He smacks the curtain that separates him from the booth next door.

"Shut up, punk!" he hisses.

The curtain flies open, and the long-haired Langly emerges.

"Hey, lady!" says Langly. "If you wanna watch *Matlock* with Andy Griffith all blue and squiggly, go right ahead and buy from this guy. But if you want quality bootleg cable, you talk to me."

Frohike glares at his competitor. They launch into a spirited argument about—among other things—"co-ax loss" and the incendiary tendencies of their respective devices. The mystery woman turns and walks away, trailed by Byers. The two cable pirates spot him.

"Ahh-NARC!" says Langly, under cover of a fake sneeze.

Byers ignores this. He follows the woman around a corner; she doubles back suddenly and collides head-on with him. Her purse flies open and her belongings spill out, among them a photograph of a little girl, age two or three. Byers picks up the picture and hands it to her.

"She's very cute," he says shyly.

"Yes, she is," she says. She begins to move away.

Byers screws up his courage.

"Wait!" he says, startled by his own forwardness. "Um, uh, you just look like you could use some help."

At a snack bar table off the convention floor Byers and the woman sit facing each other. The photo of the little girl lies face up between them.

"Her father took her from you?" says Byers.

"My former boyfriend," says the woman. "It's a long story. Basically, I got involved with a man who turned out to be a complete psychotic."

She explains that they were only together a few months; that he left her when she was pregnant; but that he came back and took their daughter six months ago.

"That's terrible!" says Byers. "Did you call the police?"

"Oh, yeah," she says. "The police, and then private investigators. They were all surprisingly unhelpful."

She adds that she has only two leads: the first one that her ex-boyfriend is in the Baltimore area; the second a torn piece of paper with the words ARPANET/WHTCORPS written on it.

"This is why I'm here today," she says. "This has something to do with computers, right? The Internet?"

"Actually, the Arpanet," says Byers. "is a government network created by the Defense Advanced Research Projects Agency. You can access it through the Internet, though."

He adds, "If you want, I can go online and try to find it for you. By the way, my name's John."

"Holly. Nice to meet you," says the woman.

Byers smiles and taps an empty sugar packet on the table. It says HOLLY SUGAR.

"Holly. Just like the sugar," he says.

A few minutes later at the FCC booth Ken Hawryliw is still engrossed in his video game. Byers asks him again to take a short break.

"Whatever," says Ken.

Byers sits at the keyboard and types a few commands. The Internet connection comes up. As this is 1989, things look primitive—no graphics or animation. Byers types the "whtcorps" address.

"So, your ex-boyfriend is into computers?" says Byers, hopefully.

"I don't really know. I really know very little about him, except that he's psychotic."

Byers nods. The computer beeps, and a stark, strictly functional home page appears. It says DEFENSE DATA NETWORK—PROJECT WHITECORPS—LEVEL 8+ DOD EYES ONLY. Near the bottom of the screen the word PASSCODE appears next to a blinking prompt.

Byers gulps with amazement and some fright. "Somehow this kicked us into the Defense Data Network," he says. He turns to Holly. "I'm sorry, I think this is the end of the line."

Holly eyes him with a look of pure seductive innocence. "Isn't this something you could—how do you say it? Hack into?"

Byers is aghast. "*Hack* into? No!" he says.

Holly shoots him a sad look.

"I mean, technically, yes," he whispers nervously. "I probably could. But this belongs to the Department of Defense. This is a secured site. I mean, I work for the FCC. This is the kind of thing we're trying to stop!"

Holly considers this, then nods sadly.

"Thank you, John," she says, finally. "I do appreciate your time."

She smiles faintly, then turns. Byers, agonized, watches her prepare to disappear from his life.

"Wait!" he says, steeling himself. "You didn't see this."

Byers types at lightning speed. After a second or two, VALID ENTRY CODE appears. He's in.

"What did you do?" asks Holly.

"Oh, it's a government system," he says. "I know a couple of 'loginout' tricks with VMS Version Give, and, uh—oh, never mind."

Holly pulls up a chair and sits next to him. "Can you look up Susanne Modeski?" she says. "That's my daughter."

Byers types in the name. The word DOWNLOADING appears and reams of apparent gibberish begin to scroll down the screen. Byers is shocked anew.

"It's an encrypted file!" he says.

"Can you decode it?" says Holly, coolly.

"I'd need some help."

"Can you print it out for me?"

Byers nods distractedly, stabs a few buttons, and a nearby tractor-feed printer begins churning out pages. Holly starts pulling them from the machine, then stops and glances around her. Her eyes widen, and she rushes to Byers's side.

"Hide!" she says, pulling him through the curtains and out of the booth.

"What?" says Byers.

"My ex-boyfriend is out there!"

"The psychotic?"

"He must have tracked me here," Holly whispers. "He's looking for me, damnit!"

Holly peers back through the curtains. On the convention floor stands a man wearing a suit and a quizzical expression. He is standing about twenty feet away. It is Fox Mulder.

A few minutes later the FBI agent—still looking—passes in front of Frohike's booth. A sign on Langly's booth next door reads BACK IN TWO HOURS.

Frohike says to Mulder, "You look like a gentleman who'd appreciate 33 channels of crystal clear television!"

"No thanks, handsome," says Mulder, without missing a beat.

"A man of distinction!" says Frohike, to the retreating G-man. Then, under his breath, "Punk-ass!"

Holly ducks into Frohike's booth through the back curtain, pleasantly surprising him.

"Well, hello, pretty lady!" he says.

She closes the front curtains for privacy.

"Oh yeah!" says Frohike, delighted—until he spots Byers entering the booth, also.

"What's with the narc?" he asks Holly, dismayed.

Flash forward to the police interrogation room: Byers still sits at the table, Detective Munch paces back and forth, apparently in some distress, behind him.

"It was at this point that we enlisted the help of one Melvin Frohike, Computer Hacker. We proceeded to tell him the whole story. I hoped he could assist me in deciphering the encrypted file. It was at this point, however, that Mr. Frohike raised an interesting question."

"I don't understand. Why don't you just kick this guy's ass?" asks Frohike, glancing at Holly's printouts back at the booth.

"What?" says Byers, incredulous.

"No!" says Holly, frantically. "I just want these pages decoded. Can you do that?"

"Sure, baby," says Frohike, suavely. "My kung fu is the best. But it could take hours. I say cut to the chase! If pretty boy out there can tell us where your daughter is, we just need to go beat it out of him!"

"No!" says Holly. "Bad idea. He's dangerous."

"Lady, I'm dangerous," says Frohike. This does not get the desired reaction.

"Oh, all right," concedes Frohike. "So we'll just follow him. For all we know he's got the girl here somewhere. We'll stay back a ways. Just wait here for us."

Frohike grabs Byers's arm. "C'mon, FCC," he says.

The duo trails Mulder—with dogged incompetence—as he questions various exhibitors on the convention floor. As a "disguise" Frohike wears a crude virtual reality visor on his head.

"This dude doesn't look so tough," says Frohike. Then, after seeing Mulder glance back curiously at him. "Act casual!"

They trail Mulder past a booth selling "high-tech electronic alien detectors"—THEY'RE HERE! reads its sign—into a spartan service area behind the floor. Frohike and Byers creep down the semi-dark corridor. Mulder emerges from an alcove and confronts them.

"What's up, fellas?" he says, not unkindly. "You lookin' for somebody?"

"Just, um, the bathroom," says Byers.

"I don't think it's down here," says the agent. He glances at Byers's lapel button. "Hey, you with the FCC?"

"What's it to ya?" says Frohike.

Mulder stares at the little man for a second. "I think we share the same credit union."

He pulls out his shiny new Bureau ID. "Special Agent Mulder. I'm with the Federal Bureau of Investigation. I was hoping maybe you could help me. I was looking for a girl."

He holds up a mug shot of Holly.

"Sorry," says Frohike.

"What'd she do?" says Byers.

Mulder says, "What's it to you?" Then softening, "Thanks guys, all right?"

WANTED
STATISTICS
Wanted on suspicion of
MURDER, SABOTAGE,
INTERSTATE FLIGHT, TERRORIST ACT
AGAINST THE UNITED STATES GOVERN
Employee at the Army Advanced Weapons F
Whitestone, New Mexico

Modeski, Susanne
ID : 0267 - 1287

Responsible for the bombing of an AAW lab
which killed four employees. Also the death o
Military Police Officer who tried to detain the s
at the facility gate.

A phone rings. Mulder reaches into his jacket and pulls out a huge, Paleozoic-era cell phone.

"Yeah, Mulder. Oh, hi, Reggie!" he says.

Frohike and Byers take the opportunity to depart rapidly. Astounded that Holly's "boyfriend" is an FBI agent, they return to the convention floor and discover that she has disappeared. Ken, however, is being hauled away by a posse of military policemen.

"I don't understand," says the hand-cuffed government worker. "All I did was play Dig Dug."

The MPs are unconvinced. "I didn't

hack into anyone's computer," protests Ken. "Seriously, guys. I've got, like, circulatory problems. I have a tendency to fall down a lot."

"Wait!" says Byers guiltily, calling after them. "It was me!"

Frohike grabs hold of him and pulls him aside.

"What're you doing?" he says, angrily.

"I hacked into that computer. It was me!"

"So you're going to turn yourself in?" says Frohike, scornfully. "Are you crazy? A hacker never turns himself in."

He adds, "Listen, whatever the hell is going on around here, it's big. And your lady friend is somehow at the center of it all."

"She needs my help," says Byers. "How can we learn what's going on?"

Frohike says, "The FBI are looking for her. Hack into the FBI mainframe. I know just the guy who can do it."

"You're talking about a premeditated crime against the United States government!"

Hey," says Frohike, with mock surprise, "your second one today!"

He plucks the FCC button off Byers's lapel, then tosses it aside.

"Welcome to the dark side," he says.

In a smoke-filled hotel room a group of pale-faced computer nerds, engaged in a high-stakes game, sit around a table. All are solemn, nervous except for Langly, who presides, Cincinnati Kid–style.

"Okay, ladies!" he says, sneering. "Who's down for fifty? Fifty bucks. Anyone? Aw, man. My diaper-wearing granny'd bet fifty. Hah! There's no game here."

A guy named Eric, a hacker with a pathetically scrawny mustache, speaks up. "All right. Fifty."

Langly is pleased. "Elron the Druid bets fifty!" he says. "Cash only, Elron! I don't take no personal checks from 'The Bank of Middle Earth.'"

He shakes a twenty-sided die over his head, then blows on it. He is, of course, presiding over a red-hot game of Dungeons and Dragons.

"C'mon, natural twenty!" he says. "Daddy needs a new Sword of Wounding!"

Byers and Frohike appear in the doorway. Langly spots them and rushes over to Frohike, furious.

"What's the big idea bringing the narc in here?" he says.

"Me and the narc have a proposition for you," he replies.

"What proposition?"

Frohike leans forward, then whispers, "The coolest hack in the world."

Langly is intrigued. From the back of the room, Eric the Hacker Dude stands and calls out to him.

"Lord Manhammer?" he says.

Langly ignores him, and stares at Frohike. "Say it," he says.

Frohike stares back defiantly.

"Say it," says Langly.

In obvious pain, Frohike swallows his pride. He gazes down at his shoes.

"Your kung fu is the best," he says, finally.

Langly simply stares at him, deadpan, for a second, then smiles.

In the hotel room later that night Langly sits at the controls of a home-built, science fair-ish contraption of exposed circuit boards, wires, and blinking lights. Frohike and Byers look on.

"What does this do?" says the FCC man.

"It's a loop line shunt," says Langly. "Anyone who tries to trace us'll get bounced around by C&P's call-forwarding software. My personal invention."

Byers stares, heartsick, at the illegal contraption.

"Oh, God. I'm gonna get fired. I'm gonna go to jail. I deserve to go to jail."

"Shut up, already!" says Frohike. Then, to Byers, "What do you need me to do?"

"Just watch and learn," brags Langly, typing away at his keyboard. "Bingo!"

The words ACCESS GRANTED appear on the FBI's crude homepage. Langly smirks up at Byers. "Government hacks are a snap," he says. "Last week I got into the Maryland DMV. Changed my endorsement so I could handicap park."

Byers looks down at him, appalled.

"I got tinnitus," says the hacker, defensively.

Byers types Mulder's name. Immediately, the agent's photo and vital statistics appear on the screen.

"Fox William Mulder," reads Frohike. "Born 10/13/61. Degree in psychology from Oxford University. Top of his class at Quantico. Commendations out the yin-yang. Currently attached to Violent Crimes Unit. Single."

He stares at Byers. "Nothing in here about him being a psycho, or having a daughter."

Byers asks Langly to type in Holly Modeski. Nothing. Then he asks for Susanne Modeski.

To their amazement, a mug shot of the woman we know as Holly appears immediately on the screen. Next to it, in bold letters, appear the words WANTED ON SUSPICION OF MURDER, SABOTAGE, INTERSTATE FLIGHT, TERRORIST ACTS AGAINST THE UNITED STATES GOVERNMENT.

There's more. They learn that Susanne Modeski was an employee at the Army Advanced Weapons Facility at Whitestone, New Mexico, and that she blew up one of their labs, killing four people.

Frohike reads, "Subject Modeski is considered unstable and delusional. Intellectually brilliant, yet prone to con-fabulation and fits of violent behavior."

Langly chimes in. "Psychotic and profoundly dangerous."

Frohike: "Armed and extremely dangerous. Do not approach. Call immediately for backup."

Wide-eyed, the two hackers turn to Byers, who appears to be in shock. Then there is a faint click. The hotel door handle turns and Susanne Modeski enters. Her eyes are wide open and her expression is blank.

"You've been reading about me," she says.

The three men have retreated nervously into a corner. The woman turns to face them, then takes a deep breath.

"My name is Susanne Modeski," she says, a tremble in her voice. "I am— I was—an organic chemist for the Advanced Weapons Facility. But I never blew up any lab. And I certainly never killed anybody. All I did was try to quit."

Her voice softens. "I didn't have a job you can just quit."

Modeski admits that she doesn't have a daughter, and that the picture she showed Byers was bogus. "But I desperately needed your help."

"For what, exactly?" asks Byers.

Modeski pulls the printout of the encoded file from her purse. "To get this," she says. "I still need it deciphered. This has everything in it I need to expose the United States government's plot against its own people. One I unwittingly helped to forward by developing ergotamine-histamine gas."

"The Ergotamine?" says Langly.

"E-H for short. It's an aerosolized gas. In small does, it causes paranoia and anxiety in it's subjects."

"Paranoia. Gotcha," says Frohike, his voice dripping disbelief.

Modeski's anxiety level rises. "It's water soluble and leaves no trace. Secret forces within the government plan to test this gas on the American people! Right here in Baltimore! I am not making this up!"

Everyone remains unconvinced, to put it mildly. Modeski redoubles her efforts.

"Nobody's safe!" she says. "I mean, look what they did to JFK."

"Uh, what did they do to JFK?" says Byers.

"Dallas? 1963? *Hello?* They want to control every aspect of our lives! From the cradle to the grave! They practically do already! I'll prove it to you. Just help me decipher this."

She holds up the printout, accidentally bumping her purse. A small silver pistol tumbles out. The boys' eyes widen.

"What do you say, guys?" she says.

Byers's interrogation room narration continues:

"Of course, at that point we didn't feel like we had much choice."

In the darkened convention center Modeski and the boys scurry stealthily around a supercomputer exhibit, rejiggering a massive processor to translate the encrypted files. Frohike sits at its keyboard and runs a cursor over the raw code. A translation appears immediately at the bottom of the screen.

Nervously, Byers reads it. "The surprise defection of Dr. Susanne Modeski," he says, "is a blow to the program—though not a fatal one. The timetable remains unchanged. The first EBO will occur in the Baltimore-Washington area within one week's time."

Langly turns to Modeski. "What's an EBO?" he asks.

"Engineered Biological Operation," says Modeski. "Toxic organic agents used on humans."

Byers reads on:

"Security risks are being attenuated. Dr. Modeski's team has been processed, and plausible denial constructed."

Modeski says, "Which is another way of saying that they've murdered my research associates and placed the blame on me. Understand?"

Her companions' eyes shine with fear. In the silence, Modeski leans forward and stares at the screen.

"Wait," she says. "Here it is. 'E-H product is presently warehoused at 204 Fells Point Road, lot number A-9000, awaiting EBO.' This is it!"

Byers reads, "Subject Modeski currently monitored around the clock. Covert electronics installed per Dr. Michael Kilbourne, 11/6/88.

"Who's Dr. Michael Kilbourne?"

It's now Modeski's turn to be shocked. "My dentist," she says. "Excuse me."

She chooses a pair of pliers from Frohike's toll kit and retreats into a nearby restroom. A few moments later the men, worried, go inside after her. Modeski is standing by the sink, in obvious pain. She holds up the pliers.

"Look at it! Look at it!" she groans.

Gripped by the pliers is a bloody molar. They retreat to the hotel room, and look at it through a magnifying glass. Inside the molar is a tiny wire, extending from a miniature circuit board.

Byers turns to Modeski, sitting in a nearby chair holding a Ziploc bag of ice to her jaw. "What's the address of that warehouse?" he says.

Back in the police interrogation room Detective Munch stares stone-faced at Byers. "Where's the tooth?" he says.

Says Byers, "We flushed it. We were afraid it would give away our location."

Munch says nothing, just continues to stare.

"So," says Byers, after a couple of uncomfortable seconds, "we broke into the warehouse."

At the warehouse Byers's flashlight beam sweeps over a label affixed to a carton. It reads A–9000. Modeski tears at the cardboard with her bare fingers until Frohike hands her his pocketknife. She slashes open the container. It is filled with dozens of individually packaged asthma inhalers.

"This is how they plan on distributing the gas," says Modeski. "This is their 'random test'! Now we've got proof."

She begins pulling out packages to stuff into her purse, until a voice behind them rings out.

"Stay where you are! I'm a federal agent!"

They turn and see Mulder step out of the shadows. In one hand is his pistol. In the other is his FBI badge.

"Susanne Modeski," says Mulder, "you are under arrest for the murder of four people at Whitestone Army base!"

Modeski gasps. Frohike, Byers, and Langly protest her innocence.

"You three are under arrest also!" says Mulder. "Ma'am, stay where you are! You three get down on the floor, now! Ma'am, stop moving! I'm not going to ask you again!"

At that moment the sound of footsteps are heard. Everybody turns to look in their direction. Two grim-faced, dark-suited men enter. They approach Modeski.

"Dr. Modeski," says one of them, "please come with us."

Mulder is confused. He pulls out his badge again.

"Federal agent! Identify yourself!" he shouts.

The two men ignore him. Mulder raises his pistol and demands again that they identify themselves. The strangers glance at each other briefly, pull out automatic pistols, sweep past Susanne, and begin firing at Mulder, who leaps for his life behind the boxes marked A–9000. Byers, Frohike, and Langly—already on the floor—scatter like rabbits.

A short, sharp firefight begins. The gunmen's bullets rip into the boxes shielding Mulder. The inhalers inside them burst and splatter their contents onto the agent. The fluid has a quick effect: Mulder's eyes snap wide open with fear. He drops his gun and claws at his shirt collar, struggling for breath. He drops flat on his back, muttering incoherently. The two men advance on Mulder, shove fresh clips into their weapons, and aim for his head.

Two shots ring out. The gunmen fall alongside their intended target.

Susanne Modeski stands behind them, her pistol smoking. She drops it to the floor, gazes down at Mulder, and exits. Frohike, Byers, and Langly creep timorously, toward the spot where the gunmen and the naked Mulder lie. A loading dock door raises with a metallic clatter. A gaggle of men in gas masks and protective clothing enter.

One of the men takes a quick reading on a portable air analyzer. Satisfied, he removes his mask. The others follow his lead.

Another man enters, this one dapperly suited. He is clearly in charge; his underlings part to let him pass. He walks directly to Mulder and gazes down at the babbling man.

"Sanitize it," he says, curtly. He is X (last seen in 4X01).

Frohike, Byers, and Langly—clearly in shock—stare wide-eyed at the terrifying scene. X turns and gazes coldly at the three civilians. The workmen swing into action, efficiently removing all traces of the gunfight and the E-H gas.

Mulder, still naked, drags himself along the floor and into a corner. He opens his eyes and sees a number of gray, elongated aliens in place of the workmen.

"They're here," moans Mulder.

The cleanup continues. The two gunmen are stuffed into body bags. One of them jolts awake suddenly, startling Byers, Frohike, and Langly.

"I'm still alive," gasps the wounded man.

X stares down at him dispassionately. Someone else zips up the body bag and it is dragged away. This fresh horror finally unfreezes Langly.

"W-who are you people?" he says.

He receives no response. He and his companions scatter as a forklift bears down on them. Amidst the highly organized—but wordless—operation, X stoops down, picks up Modeski's pistol, and examines it.

Byers approaches him. "What authority do you have to do this?" he demands.

"Shut up, Byers!" says Langly.

X walks past Langly, Susanne's pistol dangling from his hand. He walks slowly to where Mulder is cowering. A workman steps up next to X.

"Bag him?" he asks his superior.

X studies Mulder with guarded interest. "No one touches this man," he says in a deep, even voice.

Incredibly, Byers continues to beard the dangerous stranger. "Why are you doing this?" he demands. X turns, finally, to face him.

Byers plunges ahead. "You people framed Susanne Modeski. You plan to test that chemical on an unwitting public. Why? For what possible reason?"

To his companions' horror, the FCC man summons up new reservoirs of indignation or perhaps bravery, or insanity.

"Who gives you the authority?" he demands.

"Byers, shut up!" hisses Frohike.

As Byers says his piece, a couple of workmen stop what they're doing and wander over. X considers, then turns to them.

"No bags," he says.

The workmen nod, understanding. One of them clamps a hand to Byers's shoulder and pushes him to his knees. Frohike and Langly get the same treatment. X checks Susanne's pistol—three more bullets. The workmen leave. X steps behind the three kneeling men, aims the gun at the back of Byers' neck, and cocks the hammer with a loud click.

Byers realizes that his last moments have arrived. Eyes wide open, he holds his head high with an amazing display of courage. X pulls the trigger, and the hammer falls on an empty chamber.

"Behave yourselves," says X, curtly.

He turns to leave. Byers regains his wits—and believe it or not—is still angry.

"That's it?" he shouts. "You're just trying to intimidate us? To scare us, so we'll keep quiet!?"

Frohike turns to him with gritted teeth. "Byers, I swear to God, I'll shoot you myself!"

Byers ignores him.

"It's all true what Susanne said about you people, isn't it?" he says. "About John F. Kennedy? Dallas?"

This last outburst seems to capture X's attention. He stops, looks straight at Byers, and says coolly, "I heard it was a lone gunman."

From somewhere nearby, sirens wail. X exits the warehouse unhurriedly, ducks into the

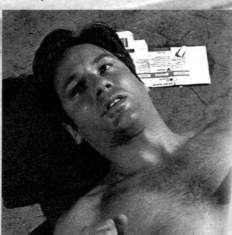

backseat of a black limousine, and is driven away.

A last glimpse of Byers and Munch in the interrogation room:

"And that was the last we saw of them," says Byers. "Almost immediately, the police got there. We panicked and hid. You know the rest."

Byers awaits a response from the detective, who stares at him for a moment, then erupts. "Do I look like Geraldo to you? Don't lie to me like I was Geraldo. I'm not Geraldo!"

Later that night Byers tosses and turns on his jail cell cot. Frohike and Langly are having a similarly bad night.

"Oh, man," groans Langly, rising from a troubled sleep. "It's not all a bad dream. I am in hell!"

"*Women,*" moans Frohike.

"Ain't it the truth," amens Langly.

Byers hauls himself up to a seated position. "What do you mean, 'women'?" he says, indignantly.

Langly says, "You know exactly what he means. Your molar-pullin' girlfriend roped us in and left us swinging in the breeze."

Frohike adds, "Look, she *is* hot, but you've gotta admit we're here because of her."

Byers stiffens. "I'm here because I wanted to learn the truth. I assumed the same went for you. Susanne opened my eyes to it. She doesn't owe me anything."

His voice softens. "If there was some way I could help her still, I'd be there in a second."

Frohike and Langly fall silent, chastened. Munch enters the lockup area and, with a clang, opens their cell door.

He says, "Apparently, Agent Mulder came to and verified your warehouse story—at least what little he seems to recall of it. Three cheers for the FBI. You're free to go. Go!"

The three ex-prisoners file out.

"Here's a tip," adds Munch. "Aluminum foil. It makes a lovely hat, and it blocks out the government's mind control rays. It'll keep you guys out of trouble."

As the boys are being processed for release, an officer tells Munch that Mulder's car—reported as stolen—has been located at the train station. Munch nods, takes one last look at the Lone Gunmen, and walks away. Byers rounds up his colleagues for a quick conference.

"Susanne must have taken Mulder's car last night," he says. "She left it at the train station."

"So?" says Langly.

"Maybe we can catch up with her," says Byers, excitedly.

"Where?" says Frohike. "She took a train."

Byers whispers, "She's too smart for that. Don't you see? She just wants to throw them off."

Langly thinks hard, then says, "She said she wanted to go public."

Frohike picks up his thread. "The Baltimore *Guardian*," he says, "is only a couple of blocks down from the train station."

Susanne Modeski emerges from the downtown office building headquarters of the Baltimore *Guardian*. She walks briskly down a busy street.

"Susanne!" shouts Byers.

He runs to her side. Frohike and Langly, knocking down unlucky pedestrians in their path, follow suit. Doffing her sunglasses, Susanne stares passionately, for just a moment, into Byers's eyes.

"John," she says, "they didn't believe my story. Not a word of it. Who in their right mind would?"

"What are you going to do now?" asks Frohike.

"Try other newspapers. TV stations. Not give up. Keep trying to find people who'll listen. People like you."

"I appreciate what you did for me—all three of you," she says. She's talking to all three, but her look favors Byers.

Byers says, "We still want to help." Susanne smiles, nods, and kisses Byers chastely on the lips.

"You already have," she says.

Fifteen feet away, a corner pay phone begins to ring. All four turn toward it.

"Guys . . . ?" says Langly, warningly.

Susanne turns back to the men. "No matter how paranoid you are, you're not paranoid enough."

She dons her sunglasses and begins moving away, quickly. "Tell the truth!" she says. "Reach as many people as you can with it. That's your weapon!"

She is hurrying away now, breaking into a run. A black Lincoln Town Car pulls out of an alley and screeches to a halt in front of her. Two dark-suited men emerge and hustle her into the back seat.

"Susanne!" yells Byers, running toward the spot.

The Town Car pulls away. In the backseat on the curb side, just visible through the opened window, sits X. The tinted glass rises in its frame and then he is gone.

Back at the now-concluded electronics convention, Byers, Frohike, and Langly sit dejectedly in the partially dismantled FCC booth. Footsteps click toward them. The boys look over their shoulders curiously, then stand. It is Mulder.

"Feeling better?" asks Frohike.

"Yeah, I am. Thank you," says the FBI agent, slowly. "I just, um, I have these weird ideas in my head that I can't seem to shake."

"What kind of ideas?" asks Frohike.

"Weird ones," repeats Mulder.

Langly looks at him curiously. "You gonna bust us?"

"I'm not sure yet. I just talked to my ASAC and he tells me that Dr. Susanne Modeski is no longer wanted by the FBI. She's still missing, but the case is suddenly closed."

He adds, "What I need from you guys is to tell me what the hell happened last night."

Byers, who seems to have been profoundly transformed by his experience, nods. "You want the truth?" he asks.

"Yeah, I want the truth," says Mulder.

Byers glances at Langly and Frohike, then faces Mulder.

"You might want to sit down," he says. "This is going to take a while."

back story:

For those who've just joined us, a recap:

John Fitzgerald Byers, the Bob Newhart-esqe conspiracy theorist, is played by Canadian actor Bruce Harwood. Hippie/techno-nerd Ringo Langly is stand-up comedian Dean Haglund; and lecherous Smurf-like Melvin Frohike is actually *X-Files* first assistant director Tom Braidwood. Since their initial appearance in "E.B.E." (1X16), the Lone Gunmen have become extremely popular recurring

characters. Which is not to say, however, that under normal circumstances they would be chosen as the mainstays of an entire episode.

But circumstances at the start of the fifth season were far from normal. In order to have a fighting chance to complete the show's network episode order, production in Vancouver *had* to start by the final week of August 1997. Unfortunately, series stars David Duchovny and Gillian Anderson, still filming the *X-Files* movie, were tied up in Southern California until the beginning of September.

So a "Lone Gunmen episode"— begun on August 20; completed with the few scenes including Special Agent Fox Mulder several weeks later; then aired as the third show of the new season—it was. Whether attainable or not, the producers' obvious intention was to alleviate the absence of the show's two stars with the cult appeal of the three auxiliary characters. Supervising producer Vince Gilligan was asked to write the episode.

"We talked about it quite a bit at the end of Season Four," says Gilligan. "I felt flattered that they offered it to me, and I also thought 'How the hell am I going to do this?' Then I came up with an entire story. And ended up throwing the whole thing out."

Gilligan's first Lone Gunmen plotline, set in the present, revolved around nanotechnology: the emerging science of creating very small, very clever machines.

"I pitched it to Chris," he says, "and as I was pitching it to him he got more and more quiet and I got more and more nervous. I think the story had a lot of interesting, cool moments in it. But at the end Chris said, and rightly so, 'This may be our one and only chance for an episode with just the Lone Gunmen, and I don't think you're making the most of it.'

"I was sort of bummed out, yet in my heart I knew he was right. And then Chris said to me, 'Why don't you show us how those guys met?' And that sort of sparked something. And then it came together fairly quickly after that, I recall."

Back at the drawing board, Gilligan proceeded to "reverse engineer" the Gunmen's backgrounds, and when these were set, he extrapolated their first meeting with Mulder. "What came to me early on was these guys had to live not too far from D.C. With that in mind, I figured that Baltimore was only thirty or forty-five minutes up the road.

"Then came the interesting *Homicide* crossover. When I was ten or fifteen pages into the script I realized that the whole episode was framed around Byers telling his story to a Baltimore homicide detective. So I figured 'What the heck? *Homicide*'s a great show, so why not try to get Richard Belzer to play his Detective Munch character?"

Gilligan's first movie, *Wilder Napalm*, was produced by Mark Johnson, a former partner of *Homicide* co-creator Barry Levinson. Levinson put Gilligan in touch with Tom Fontana, the NBC show's executive producer.

"Tom Fontana is a great guy," says Gilligan, "and he couldn't have been more helpful. NBC was great about it and Fox was real happy, too. Only the lawyers were a little nervous. For a while, they kept calling me up and saying, 'Uh, are you *sure* you have permission from NBC?' And I kept saying to them, 'Uh, that's what the guy said.'" (For the record, according to L.A. casting director Rick Millikan, the trans-network crossover went off without a hitch.)

Some other significant creative contributions: While filming his scenes in "Unusual Suspects," David Duchovny insisted on wearing a wedding ring; thus adding a tantalizing clue to his background that will be explained—maybe—in the future.

Props master Ken Hawryliw scoured the pharmaceutical supply warehouses of North America to obtain what he firmly believes is the world's largest collection of empty asthma inhalers; special effects coordinator David Gauthier then rigged a fair number of them to explode and spew gas during the climactic gun battle.

In order to roll back the clock to 1989, makeup artist Laverne Basham did a more thorough job covering over the Gunmen's wrinkles and under-eye circles than usual; hair stylist Anji Bemben removed some of the gray in their hair and beards as well as temporarily restoring Fox Mulder's Season One hairstyle. In Los Angeles, producer

Paul Rabwin tracked down the Japanese copyright owners of the "classic" video game Dig Dug and obtained their delighted permission to use it on *The X-Files*.

As for the Gunmen themselves— who were told of their promotion while filming their small parts in the *X-Files* movie—they learned quite a bit about their characters—and themselves—during the production. "What we read in the script wasn't really our origins as we'd imagined it," says Dean Haglund. "I'd thought we were all in a university garage band together or something. Bruce thought he was a photocopier repairman."

Normally, adds Haglund, while working on location he and Harwood share a small trailer. "So we sit and chat and stuff," he says, "and Tom comes over and hangs out. There's never any question of saying, 'Damnit! We want our own trailer!'

"But the funny thing is, during *this* episode my agent called me up and said, 'Do you want me to fight it out for you?' I thought a minute, then told him, 'Nah, it's cool here with just one for the three of us.'"

Ⓧ

Susanne Modeski owes her alias to Vince Gilligan's girlfriend, Holly Rice. "I try to get her into every show I write," he says. Other mentions include "Pusher" (3X17) and "Folie a Deux" (5X19).

Ⓧ

Props master Ken Hawryliw, a former acting student, made his *X-Files* debut playing "himself" in 5X01. He wore his own clothes on camera—and in real life is known to say "Whatever!" quite frequently.

Ⓧ

Eric Knight, who played Eric the Hacker Dude, is David Duchovny's personal assistant.

Ⓧ

5X01 marks the popular character X's first flashback appearance since he was killed in "Herrenvolk" (4X01).

redux all lies

After faking his own
suicide to shake off
Syndicate and
        FBI surveillance,
Mulder secretly
searches for the cause of—
and cure for— Scully's
terminal cancer.

EPISODE: 5X02
FIRST AIRED: November 2, 1997
EDITOR: Heather MacDougall
WRITTEN BY: Chris Carter
DIRECTED BY: R. W. Goodwin

GUEST STARS:
Mitch Pileggi
(AD Walter Skinner)

William B. Davis
(The Cigarette-Smoking Man)

John Finn (Michael Kritschgau)
Steve Makaj (Scott Ostelhoff)
Ken Camroux (Senior Agent)

Charles Cioffi
(Section Chief Scott Blevins)

Barry W. Levy (Vitagliano)
Don S. Williams (Elder)
Bruce Harwood (Byers)
Tom Braidwood (Frohike)
Dean Haglund (Langly)
Julie Arkos (Holly)
John D. Sampson (Sentry)

PRINCIPAL SETTINGS:
Washington, D.C.; Alexandria
and Sethsburg, Virginia

In a brief flashback to 4X24 ("Gethsemane"), Mulder is seated on the sofa in his apartment, staring intently at the TV screen. A video-tape of the 1972 conference on the possibility of extraterrestrial life is playing. Mulder is racked with guilt over Scully's illness and his own dashed hopes over the revelation that the alien body he discovered was a fake. Everything he's believed in and worked to prove has been revealed to be false.

The action moves forward: Mulder reaches for his weapon, checks that it is loaded, and turns off the television. His telephone rings. It is Kritschgau, the Defense Department operative who has previously told him that he, Scully, and the X-Files were pawns in a massive program of government deception. Kritschgau implies obliquely that he has more information for Mulder.

Mulder will have none of this. "Did they give Agent Scully this disease?" he demands. "Did they do this because of me?"

"They may be listening, Agent Mulder," cautions Kritschgau. "They may be watching everything you do and say."

Mulder glances upward and spots a dark pinhole next to a light fixture on the ceiling.

Somewhere nearby, a shadowy figure is looking at a video monitor. The door to this location bursts open and Mulder, gun in hand, pushes through. He confronts Scott Ostelhoff, the man whose shotgun pistol silenced over half a dozen men in the previous episode, and who is lighting flash paper that he has tossed into a metal wastebasket.

"Back away!" shouts Mulder, overturning the wastebasket and trying to stamp out the fire with his foot. Ostelhoff lunges for his shotgun pistol. One shot rings out.

Later that night, a weary Scully enters her darkened Washington apartment and begins to take off her clothes.

"Keep going, FBI woman," says Mulder, who has been lying in wait for her.

After Scully recovers from her shock, Mulder shows her Ostelhoff's government ID card. He tells her these facts: his apartment had been under surveillance for at least two months; Ostelhoff, like Kritschgau, worked for the Department of Defense; the assassin is now dead from "a bullet wound to the face"; Mulder has reported the death to no one; and, since phone records he found in Ostelhoff's apartment included at least a dozen calls to the FBI telephone exchange, the Bureau is somehow connected to the hoax described by Kritschgau.

"How long has this been going on?" asks Scully.

"Maybe since the beginning," says Mulder. "Since you joined me on the X-Files."

Scully says, "That would mean that for four years we've been nothing more than pawns in a game. That it was a lie from the start." She blinks away tears of anger and frustration.

"These men," she adds, "you give them your trust. You're supposed to trust them with your life."

"There are those who are to be trusted," says Mulder. "What I want to know is who among them is not. But I won't let this treason prosper. Not if they've done this to you."

"We can't go to the Bureau making these accusations," says Scully.

"No," says Mulder. "But as they lie to us, we can lie to them. A lie to find the truth."

On a laboratory workbench, an unseen scientist performs an unspecified test, placing drops of clear liquid into a segmented glass container.

Another flashback from 4X24: It is early the next morning in Mulder's apartment, which is swarming with uniformed officers, detectives, and forensic technicians. Scully enters, flashes her FBI ID, and pushes her way through the crowd. An Arlington PD detective named Rempulski greets her grimly. He leads her to a sheet-covered body lying facedown between the couch and the coffee table and lifts a corner of the sheet.

"Is it him?" he asks.

"Yeah," whispers Scully.

Back to 5X02: In the hallway outside Mulder's apartment, Scully is intercepted by AD Skinner. She confirms her "identification" of Mulder. Skinner tells Scully that Section Chief Blevins, the man who originally assigned her to the X-Files, wants to talk to her.

"He believes you have information you haven't come forward with," says Skinner, who appears to have some unanswered questions himself.

At the Defense Department's Advanced Research Project Agency facility—where Scully tracked down Kritschgau in 4X24—Mulder walks through the main lobby and enters a secure area by swiping a ID card through the guard gate.

At FBI headquarters later that day, Scully enters Blevins's office. Skinner enters behind her. A senior FBI agent—who was also with Blevins in the pilot episode—is also in the room.

"From all reports," says Blevins to Scully, "your work on the X-Files brought you very close to Agent Mulder."

"Yes, sir," says Scully.

Blevins says, "There are those in the Bureau who believe that you came to share his belief in the paranormal, and in the existence of extraterrestrial life."

"No sir," says Scully. "That couldn't be further from the truth."

Blevins tells Scully that she is being questioned because the FBI has learned that a Department of Defense employee had contacted her and passed her classified information shortly before Mulder's "accident."

"He had information about the discovery of what Agent Mulder believed was an alien corpse," says Scully. "He said the body was part of a hoax."

"He provided evidence of this?" says Blevins.

"He provided us with no hard evidence," says Scully unconvincingly.

Blevins presses Scully for the informant's name. Scully remains silent. Blevins tells her that she will have to reveal whatever she's withholding at a special FBI panel he has convened for that evening. Scully still says nothing.

Skinner stands and pulls a surveillance photo from a manila envelope.

"Is this the man? Michael Kritschgau?" he asks accusingly.

"Yes," says Scully reluctantly.

At the DARPA facility, Kritschgau intercepts Mulder among a morning crush of employees. "How did you get in here? You can't bypass security," asks the astonished DOD man.

"You can with the Card," says Mulder, showing him Ostelhoff's identification.

"Put that away. Put it away!" says Kritschgau frantically.

Mulder coolly pockets the card. "You knew my apartment was being surveilled," says Mulder. "How?"

An extremely nervous Kritschgau hustles Mulder into his office. He tells Mulder that he was followed from Mulder's apartment after their first meeting. Mulder tells him that Ostelhoff had had contact with someone at the FBI. Kritschgau asks how he got Ostelhoff's card.

"I found it on a dead man," says Mulder.

Understanding exactly what the agent means by this, Kritschgau tells Mulder that Ostelhoff's ID gives him top-security clearance.

"You have access to everything, Mr. Mulder," he says. "Things I don't. Things I can only tell you about."

"I need to know who did this to Scully," says Mulder.

Kritschgau says, "What you can have—what you may find—is so much more than that. What you want most desperately of all."

"The cure for Scully's cancer?"

Kritschgau nods, then asks Mulder who else knows that Ostelhoff is dead.

"Only Agent Scully," says Mulder.

"Then you have only until they learn what's happened to him. If they run a scan on his card, they'll know you're inside."

Later that morning, someone picks the lock on Mulder's apartment. The door swings open and the Cigarette-Smoking Man steps inside. He appears shaken. He looks sadly at the tape outline of a body on the floor and gazes at an old framed photograph of young Mulder and his sister Samantha. A beam of light hitting the floor leads his eye to the ceiling. He spots the pinhole for the surveillance camera— and seems genuinely surprised.

On the laboratory bench we've seen previously, the unseen scientist removes a drop of liquid from the segmented vessel, places it into a petri dish, and places it under an electron microscope. A single cell floats in the pinkish media.

In the X-Files office at FBI headquarters, Scully picks up the phone, reaches a woman—Holly (seen previously in "Pusher" [3X17])—in the Bureau's communications unit, gives her the dates and times of Ostelhoff's calls to the FBI exchange, and asks her to trace them internally.

"I've got five calls," says Holly, "matching those times and dates to an executive level extension."

"Whose?" says Scully.

"It's a branch extension. It could be anyone at that level."

"Would Assistant Director Skinner be on that branch extension?" asks Scully.

"Yes," says Holly.

Scully hangs up the phone. It rings immediately, startling her. It is the paleoclimatologist Vitagliano (from "Gethsemane" [4X24]), who reminds her that she had asked him to examine the ice-core samples gathered near the alien burial site.

"Right. I'm sorry I haven't gotten back to you," says Scully.

"I think you might want to come to the lab," says the scientist. "There's something I know you're going to want to see for yourself."

At the DARPA facility, Kritschgau leads Mulder out of his office and toward an even higher-security area.

"What am I looking for?" asks Mulder.

"Level Four is a biological quarantine wing," says Kritschgau. "It houses a series of labs and medical facilities, and an elaborate system for the storage of mass quantities of DNA."

"DNA from whom?" asks Mulder.

"Virtually every American born since 1945. Every immigrant, every indigenous person who's ever given blood or tissue to a government doctor."

Mulder realizes the significance of this immediately. As Kritschgau leads the shaken agent toward Level Four, he explains what he knows about the project. This is his explanation:

"This is the hoax into which you have been drawn. The roots go back fifty years, to the end of World War II. Playing on a virulent national appetite for bogus revelation and a public newly fearful of something called the atom bomb, the U.S. military command began to fan the flames of what were being called 'flying saucer stories.' There are truths which can kill a nation, Agent Mulder, and the military needed something to deflect attention away from its arms strategy: global domination through the capability of total enemy annihilation. The nuclear card was fine as long as we alone could play it, but pointed back at us the generals and politicos knew what they couldn't win was a public relations war.

"Those photos of Nagasaki and

Hiroshima were not faces Americans wanted to see in the mirror. Oppenheimer knew it, of course, but we silenced him. When the Russians developed the bomb, the fear in the military was not for safety at home, but for armistice and treaties. The business of America isn't business, Agent Mulder. It's war. Since Antietam, nothing has driven the economy faster.

"We need a reason to keep spending money, and when there wasn't a war to justify it, we called it war anyway. The Cold War was essentially a fifty-year public-relations battle. A pitched game of chicken against an enemy we did not much more than call names. The Communists called us a few names, too. 'We will bury you,' Khrushchev said, and the public believed it. After what McCarthy had done to the country, they ate it with a big spoon. We squared off a few times, in Korea and Vietnam. But nobody dropped the bomb. Nobody dared."

Mulder interrupts him. "What's any of that have to do with flying saucers?" he asks.

Kritschgau continues: "The military saw a good thing in '47 when the Roswell story broke. The more we denied it, the more people believed it was true. Aliens had landed—a made-to-order cover story for generals looking to develop the national war chest. They opened official investigations, with names like Grudge and Twinkle, Project Blue Book and Majestic 12. They brought in college professors and congressmen and fed them enough bogus facts, enough fuzzy photos and eyewitness accounts, that they believed it, too. They even hooked Doug MacArthur, for God's sake.

"I can't tell you how fortuitous the timing of it all was. Do you know when the first supersonic flight was, Agent Mulder? 1947. Soon every experimental aircraft being flown was a UFO sighting. And when the abduction stories started up, it was too perfect. We'd almost gotten caught in Korea. An ambitious misstep. China and the Soviets knew it. The UN got all worked up about it."

Mulder looks at Kritschgau. "Germ warfare," he says finally.

"We were accused of using it on the Koreans."

Kritschgau nods. "It was developmental then," he says. "Nothing like what we or the Russians have now. The bioweapons used in the Gulf War are so ingenious as to be almost undetectable. Developed right here in this very building."

Mulder says, "Then all these accounts of abductions—you're saying they've all been lies?"

"Not lies, exactly," says Kritschgau. "But unsuspecting citizens taken and tested. A classified military project above top secret. And still ongoing."

"But I've seen aliens. I've witnessed these things," says Mulder.

Kritschgau, leading Mulder into an elevator, says, "You've seen what they've wanted you to see."

"Then why a hoax?" asks Mulder.

"The body you found is so good, so believable, that only a directed scientific examination would have proven the fraud."

Mulder says, "Scully would have known."

"The timing of the hoax," replies Kritschgau, "was planned so that Agent Scully wouldn't be alive to do an examination."

The elevator door opens, but Mulder blocks Kritschgau's path. "You went along with all this," says the agent accusingly.

"I've paid the price, Agent Mulder. When my son came home from the Gulf War, it was my retribution. I'm helping you now, but not unselfishly."

"You believe there's a cure for him in there, too," says Mulder.

Kritschgau says, "I have to think there is."

Mulder and Kritschgau arrive at a security door to Level Four. Mulder swipes his card through a reader, the door opens, and he walks through. Kritschgau turns and heads back. He is accosted by two armed sentries.

"DOD is detaining you for questioning," says one of them. "Would you come with us, Mr. Kritschgau, sir?"

At an otherwise empty racetrack, the

Elder sits in a box in the grandstand and watches a horse and rider complete their workout. In a seat just a short distance away, another man sits quietly.

The Cigarette-Smoking Man arrives, takes a seat next to the Elder, and complains bitterly that he hadn't been informed of Ostelhoff's surveillance of Mulder. He asks if the operation was run out of the Defense Department. The Elder coolly disclaims all knowledge of the project. They both know that he is lying.

"I've always kept Mulder in check," says the Cigarette-Smoking Man. "I put this whole thing together. I created Mulder."

"Agent Mulder is dead," says the Elder flatly.

"You know that for a fact?" challenges the Cigarette-Smoking Man.

"Our FBI source confirmed it this morning. Mulder killed himself," says the Elder.

He adds, "Mulder was an asset. But without his partner, you may have underestimated his fragility."

The Cigarette-Smoking Man replies, "I never underestimated Mulder. I still don't."

At the American University paleoclimatology lab, Dr. Vitagliano tells Scully that he's finished testing the cells in the ice-core sample. He reports that the cells were unclassifiable—neither plant nor animal—and that he placed them in a nutrient media. The cells began to divide.

"But they didn't just multiply," adds Vitagliano. "They began to go through the stages of morula, blastula, gastrula—"

"They began somatic development," says Scully, astonished.

Vitagliano nods, rises from his chair, and leads Scully to his microscope. She peers at the rudimentary creature.

"The beginning of a life-form," says Vitagliano. "Growing into what, I don't know."

Inside the DARPA research facility, Mulder cautiously explores a Level Four corridor—until he spots the two sentries

searching frantically for him. He picks the lock of a door leading off the hallway, enters a dark room, and waits there until his pursuers are safely past. He flips a light switch. The room is filled with metal hospital gurneys, lined in rows. On each gurney is an alien body, exactly like the one found in the ice cave in 4X24. A strobing light begins to illuminate the room. It is flashing through a small, square window on a door at the far side of the room. Mulder opens the door, which leads to a long, dark corridor. The strobing light is emitting from another door at its far end. Mulder walks toward it.

At the American University lab, Vitagliano is drawing blood from Scully's arm. He tells her that he's not sure what she's asking him to do.

"I want you to do a Southern Blot, to run the culture you've shown me against my own DNA," says Scully. "You said when you looked at the unclassified cells under the EM they were full of virus."

"Right," says Vitagliano. "What are you looking for?"

"A match. And I need it before seven."

"Tonight? Not going to happen," says Vitagliano.

"It's got to happen," says Scully. "Everything in my life depends upon it."

Scully turns and looks toward the window in the lab door. Skinner is peering through at her. She quickly exits the lab in pursuit, but the assistant director is gone. She turns a corner in the corridor—and finds herself face-to-face with him.

"You followed me here. Why are you following me?" asks Scully. "Is this more dirty work you're doing for the DOD?"

Skinner says, "Why don't you tell me something, Agent Scully? Why don't you tell me what you're doing here?"

Suspicious of Skinner's ultimate allegiance, Scully discloses nothing.

"Your lie is on the record, Agent Scully," says Skinner.

"And yours?" says Scully.

"On my desk," says Skinner, "I have the pathology and forensics reports for the body found in Agent Mulder's apartment."

He adds, "You have to answer for yourself in five hours. As you compound the lies, you compound the consequences for them."

Scully says, "All lies lead to the truth, don't they?"

"And what about your lie?" replies Skinner. "What does it lead to?"

Inside DARPA Level Four, Mulder puts his face to the window. On the other side

of the door is an operating theater; a woman lies on an operating table, eyes open. Her hands and feet are bound down with Velcro cuffs. A hose protrudes out of her greatly expanded abdomen. Suspended over her is a lighting grid, from which an intense blue geometric pattern of light is projected.

Mulder moves away from the door, heading back into the hall from which he spotted the sentries. He enters a long, seemingly endless tunnel, which finally ends at an emergency evacuation door. Mulder swipes his card and enters a warehouse—which appears to be the repository for all the alien-related odds and ends that the Cigarette-Smoking Man has taken from Mulder over the years. At one end of the building are floor-to-ceiling cabinets filled with small drawers. Index cards labeled alphabetically are attached to each drawer; Mulder finds the ones that start with the letter "S."

Reaching for the handle on one of them, he pulls it out as far as it goes, revealing a series of small index cards, which he begins to finger through rapidly. He draws out one card.

It reads DANA KATHERINE SCULLY.

At the American University lab, Scully, wearing gloves and goggles, performs a Southern Blot: a complicated test designed to isolate DNA—the genetic building blocks of life—from blood. The test has several steps; after finishing them, Scully places tiny samples of her DNA in gel-filled glass containers.

At the DARPA facility, Mulder looks at Scully's index card, which is covered with several lines of letters and numbers. In the bottom right-hand corner is an index number that begins with the letters SEP. Mulder opens another drawer and finds the card that reads MICHAEL LEE KRITSCHGAU. The card behind it reads MICHAEL LEE KRITSCHGAU, JR. That card is empty except for the name on the top.

In a photographic dark room, Scully shines a UV light on her genetic material, which reacts by glowing a fluorescent pink. She lays a special paper towel atop the gel, onto which she soaks blue dye. Scully takes the paper off the gel, placing it in a liquid-filled Ziploc baggie. To the liquid in the baggie Scully adds more liquid poured from a test tube. She takes the paper from the baggie, carefully placing it on a piece of X-ray film.

Mulder moves through a different part of the DARPA warehouse; it is stacked with cardboard boxes floor to ceiling. He finds a box with the same index number as on Scully's card. Inside it is a series of small metallic vials, arranged in a special holder.

In the dark room Scully removes the paper from the X-ray film. It is 6:37 P.M. Dr. Vitagliano enters just as Scully turns on a white-light spot lamp. We see the X-ray film has a series of black strip lanes on it.

"There it is," says Scully, eyeing a pair of lanes not like any of the others, because they are paired. "My DNA hybridized with the viral DNA from the cell culture."

"Yes," says Vitagliano, amazed. "But that means that the material in the ice-core sample—you'd have to have DNA from the unclassified chimera cells in your own body."

"I know," says Scully gravely.

"But how? And how did you know?"

"I believe I was exposed to this materi-

al," says Scully. "And it is responsible for giving me a serious illness."

"What kind of illness?"

"One which cannot be cured."

In the DARPA warehouse, Mulder lifts a vial out of its holder. He looks carefully at it, considering the life-giving substance that might be contained inside. At 7:07 P.M., he leaves the warehouse.

Another flashback—this time with small but significant additions— to "Gethsemane" (4X24): In a large conference room at FBI headquarters, a high-level investigative committee, chaired by Section Chief Scott Blevins, is assembled. Scully enters and is asked by Blevins to take her seat. She does so.

"Agent Scully, we've had a brief discussion," says Blevins. "But will you restate the matter we're here to put to rest?"

"Yes, sir," says Scully.

She braces herself, and—without referring to notes—begins:

"Four years ago," she says, "Section Chief Blevins assigned me to a project you know as the X-Files. As I am a medical doctor with a background in hard science, my job was to provide an analytical perspective on the work of Special Agent Fox Mulder, whose investigations were fueled by a personal belief that his sister had been abducted by aliens when he was twelve."

In the DARPA facility, Mulder retraces his steps through the Level Four facility. He scans the area carefully, looking for the two sentries who pursued him earlier.

In the FBI star chamber, Scully's voice begins to waver. "I come here today, four years later, to report on the illegitimacy of Agent Mulder's work," she says. "That it is my scientific opinion that he became, over the course of these years, a victim. A victim of his own false hopes—and of his belief in the biggest of lies."

Mulder reaches the security door. A light on the device is red. He swipes his ID card. The red light goes out—and comes back on again.

Scully says, "Recent events have shed new light on the factual and physical evidence that would serve to prove the existence of extraterrestrial life— which is the foundation of Agent Mulder's consuming devotion to his work."

She adds, "I am here today to expose this lie, to show the mechanism of the deception that drew him, and me, into it, and to expose Agent Mulder's work for what it is. And what it was."

The Senior Agent, last seen in Blevins's office, addresses Scully: "You were contacted by a man who claimed he worked for the Defense Department," he says. "A Michael Kritschgau. Who told you Mulder was taken in by a hoax. By a body found in the Yukon."

Scully replies, "They had managed the frozen corpse by helicopter down the side of the mountain, and across the Canadian border in a refrigerated truck. After conducting a limited physical examination, Agent Mulder was ready to believe that the body was that of an extraterrestrial biological entity. That he had finally found the proof which had eluded him. Which would confirm not only the existence of alien life, but of his sister Samantha's abduction."

Blevins says, "But this man Kritschgau had convinced you otherwise. How?"

Scully says, "He told me a story which detailed point by point the systematic way in which Agent Mulder had been deceived and used. And how I, as his partner, had been led down the same path. Losing a family member due to my allegiance, and contracting a fatal disease which I was being told was being engineered by the men who were responsible for Agent Mulder's deception."

"Were you able to convince Agent Mulder of these facts?" asks Blevins.

At the DARPA facility, Mulder swipes his card again—with the same results.

In the FBI conference room, Scully continues her report. "What I couldn't tell Agent Mulder," she says, "what I had only just learned

myself, was that the cancer which had been diagnosed in me several months earlier had metastasized."

Mulder reaches down and tries the door, but it is locked. He turns back to see the two sentries rounding the corner in the background, moving quickly toward him.

Scully says, "And the doctors told me short of a miracle it would continue to aggressively invade my body, advancing faster each day toward the inevitable."

The sentries continue to advance upon Mulder.

Scully says, "These facts—these revelations—once learned were devastating to Agent Mulder. Early this morning," she says, "I got a call from the police asking me to come to Agent Mulder's apartment. The detective asked me—he needed me to identify a body."

She can not go on.

"Agent Scully?" says Blevins softly.

Scully's voice trembles as she forces herself to finish her report. She says, "Agent Mulder died late last night— of an apparent self-inflicted gunshot wound to the head."

Scully looks up from the table and sees Skinner entering the room with a file folder in his hand. Their eyes meet. He levels her with a judgmental gaze.

At the DARPA facility, a desperate Mulder, the sentries bearing down on him, swipes his card a third time. The light turns green and the door pops open. Mulder escapes into the crowded central facility.

The Cigarette-Smoking Man, taking a drag, is standing nearby behind two seated sentries.

"It's okay," he says, with a thin smile. "Let him go."

In the FBI star chamber, Skinner, having caught Scully in a lie, stares her down. She turns away.

"Agent Scully," says Blevins. "Those

accusations that you made that you were given a disease—these are extremely serious charges."

"Yes, sir," says Scully, holding up a file folder. "But I have proof. Of the men behind this. Of the lies I believed."

She pulls the X-ray film from her folder, stands, and declares angrily, "What I have here is proof undeniable that the men who gave me this disease were also behind the hoax. A plot designed to lead to Agent Mulder's demise—and my own. Planned and executed by someone in this room."

The conference room erupts in alarm and confusion.

Scully continues, "What I have in my hand is scientific evidence—"

Several drops of blood fall on the X-ray film. They are from Scully's nose. She dabs at her nose with her finger, then suddenly gets woozy. She begins to fall. Skinner leaps forward and catches her.

"You—" says Scully.

"Somebody get a doctor," says Skinner.

In another location, somebody is pouring a small amount of liquid from the metallic vial that Mulder had procured into a complicated scientific instrument—a mass spectrometer. It is Byers. The other Lone Gunmen—Frohike and Langly—are with him. Mulder also watches the procedure intently.

The instrument's meters and readouts flash. Byers looks away, catching the eyes of Frohike and Langly.

"What? What is it?" says Mulder.

Byers can hardly bring himself to speak.

"It's deionized water," he says finally. "Nothing more than that."

to be continued...

back story:

In most uses, the word *redux* (pronounced i-DUCKS) means "brought back, revived, estored" (as in: "Albert Gore is Hubert Humphrey edux."). But it also has a specialized medical meaning, indicating the return of an organ or organism to a healthy state.

Both definitions work fine in describing "Redux" (5X02) and "Redux II" (5X03), the last two-thirds of a trilogy begun with "Gethsemane" 4X24). In that final episode of the fourth season, a stoic and determinedly rational Scully battles terminal cancer, while a single-minded and nearly desperate Mulder pursues some not-exactly-rock-solid evidence of extraterrestrial life. By the end of the cliffhanger Mulder is a disillusioned, self-doubting skeptic and Scully has launched herself into a searing spiritual journey.

By the end of 5X03 the entire series has been relaunched and sent spinning off, quite suddenly, in a startling new direction. Scully's cancer has been "cured"; Mulder's alien sighting has been debunked; and much of the evidence the team has gathered is revealed to be tainted.

Leading directly from these plot twists is Mulder's season-long bout of disillusionment, which in turn leads toward the climactic developments of the post–Season Five *X-Files* feature film.

"We wanted to tie up a lot of loose ends from the past season, and play the idea that the conspiracy is a hoax and that it had been done to hide various terrestrial and temporal misdeeds," says Chris Carter, who wrote all three episodes.

"I think the 'Redux' shows are most interesting for Mulder's switch in character," says co–executive producer Frank Spotnitz.

Maybe so, but judging from a considerable amount of fan and TV industry reaction, one of the most attention-getting aspects of the episodes was Mulder and Scully's intensified and somewhat more sharply defined feelings for each other—a development that will resonate through the fifth season, but that, true to form, will scarcely be mentioned again. Another major event—the alleged death of The Cigarette-Smoking Man, an increasingly important character in past seasons—set off an even larger wave of head-scratching and anguished speculation.

As for the Vancouver-based cast and crew, 5X02 and 5X03 are remembered as early-season tests of patience and ingenuity and for a number of slight disappointments along the way.

"Even though this wasn't technically our first show of the season, I think there were some cobwebs," says Carter, citing some disappointment with the lighting and the two montage sequences showing Scully's Southern Blot DNA and the archival-footage history of the Cold

More successful were several less-unprecedented exercises in production overkill. For instance:

Ⓧ

For the pivotal scene in the Level Four DARPA facility, production designer Graeme Murray, construction coordinator Rob Maier, and set decorator Shirley Inget teamed up to conceive and build the mammoth wood-and-stainless steel cabinets that hold the microchip-bearing test tubes. "There were ten thousand drawers," says Inget, "so we had to set up a production line to type up ten thousand labels. We had to custom-order ten thousand identical drawer pulls, and we had several little men on several big ladders with several little screw guns. Afterward, we realized we didn't have space to store the drawer pulls. So they probably all ended up in the Dumpster."

Ⓧ

Given the assignment to create a specialized holder for Scully's microchip, props master Ken Hawryliw designed one and had it custom-built out of nickel-plated stainless steel. The card-operated security gate was also built from scratch.

Ⓧ

Casting directors Rick Millikan (Los Angeles) and Coreen Mayrs (Vancouver) assembled an unusually large and varied collection of infrequently recurring actors, including John Finn (Kritschgau); Megan Leitch (Samantha Mulder); Pat Skipper (Bill Scully, Jr.); and Charles Cioffi (Section Chief Blevins).

Ⓧ

Using her usual panoply of camera and post-production tricks, visual effects supervisor Laurie Kallsen-George turned twenty of makeup and special effects master Toby Lindala's gelatin alien bodies into five times that many for the warehouse scene.

Ⓧ

By eliminating all lip color; applying shading to hollow out her cheeks; and mixing a little gray into her face powder, makeup artist Laverne Basham gave Gillian Anderson the proper death's door appearance for her later hospital scenes. "She's pretty thin already, so we didn't have to do much to change her look there," says Basham.

Ⓧ

In fact, even the pickiest of in-house critics think that by the end of "Redux II" the season was truly up to speed.

Ⓧ

Frank Spotnitz says, " 'Redux II' is one of my favorite episodes. I think the story has a crystal purity and clarity, and it just comes to a perfect point for me."

Ⓧ

Chris Carter says, "I think that 'Redux II' is one of the best episodes we've ever done."

Ⓧ

Gillian Anderson says, firmly, "I thought it was a terrific episode, especially the scenes in the hearing room, and the whole progression of Scully praying. How it was written and shot and how it was edited. Fabulous."

redux II

While Scully, dying from cancer,
undergoes the desperate treatment
her partner has stolen for her,
Mulder penetrates the inner circle
of the Syndicate-FBI conspiracy.
He finds many of the truths that
have long eluded him—as well as
disillusionment, despair, and danger.

EPISODE: 5X03
FIRST AIRED: November 9, 1997
EDITOR: Lynne Willingham
WRITTEN BY: Chris Carter
DIRECTED BY: Kim Manners

GUEST STARS:

Mitch Pileggi (AD Walter Skinner)

William B. Davis
(The Cigarette-Smoking Man)

Ken Camroux (Senior Agent)

Charles Cioffi
(Section Chief Scott Blevins)

Don S. Williams (Elder)
Megan Leitch (Samantha Mulder)
Bruce Harwood (Byers)
Tom Braidwood (Frohike)
Dean Haglund (Langly)
Sheila Larken (Mrs. Scully)
Pat Skipper (Bill Scully, Jr.)
John Finn (Michael Kritschgau)
Robert Wright (Dr. Zuckerman)
Arnie Walter (Father McCue)
Willy Ross (Quiet Willy)
Brent Shepard (Doctor)
Erin Fitzgerald (Waitress)
Catherine Barroll (Secretary)

PRINCIPAL SETTING:
Washington, D.C.

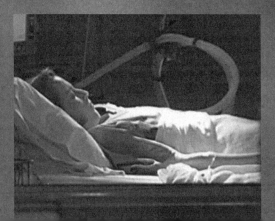

It is 5:13 in the morning

at the emergency medical unit of Trinity Hospital in Washington. Fox Mulder storms in, asks directions to Dana Scully's room, and raises hell when the information is not immediately forthcoming. An intimidated doctor tells him that Scully is in the ICU; Mulder is about to go there when Walter Skinner—accompanied by other FBI agents—arrives. Mulder brushes past Skinner, who in "Redux" (5X02) he suspected might be part of the FBI–Defense Department conspiracy. The assistant director turns and pursues him.

"Moving well for a dead man," says Skinner.

"Yeah," says Mulder, curtly.

"You've got a lot to answer for, Agent Mulder," says Skinner.

Mulder doesn't respond. He enters the ICU and, looking through a large window, spots Scully lying in a bed. She is hooked up to a ventilator.

"What happened to her?" says Mulder.

Skinner says, "She went into hypovolemic shock. She's lost a lot of blood."

"Due to what?" asks Mulder. Skinner does not answer.

"*Due to what?*"

"She's dying," says Skinner, finally. "Let's go."

"I'm staying here," says Mulder.

Skinner says, "There's nothing you can do for her."

He takes Mulder's arm. Mulder pulls away angrily and starts toward the door leading into Scully's room.

"Get the hell away from me!" says Mulder. But Skinner restrains him, surprising Mulder with his force.

"I don't want to have to arrest you," says Skinner.

"Let me go, damnit!"

But Skinner doesn't let him go. Mulder struggles to escape. The other agents appear and look through the window at the two struggling men. They enter, help

Skinner wrestle Mulder under control, and drag him back into the hallway. The anguished Mulder turns his head to get a last glimpse of his unconscious partner.

Mulder is escorted, more or less forcibly, to the FBI office of Section Chief Blevins. Skinner is also present, as is the Senior Agent from the similar scene in 5X02 in which Blevins questioned Scully.

Blevins smoothly tells Mulder that the revelation that he is still alive "reshapes" the investigation into the murder in Mulder's apartment building. He asks the agent to help them identify the dead man. Mulder remains silent.

"Agent Mulder," says Blevins. "We're here informally to give you the chance to help yourself."

"Help myself how?" asks Mulder.

"By allowing any facts or details which might serve to let us go ahead with this inquiry in a more informed matter."

"That helps you," replies Mulder. "How's it help me?"

Under Skinner's accusatory gaze, Mulder continues treating Blevins's questions with scorn.

"Agent Scully lied to us," says Blevins. "Why?"

No answer.

"Who is protecting whom?" asks the section chief.

Silence.

"Your choice is your own," says Blevins, "but your failure to answer will reflect poorly on the record in a formal inquiry."

"Are we finished here, then?" says Mulder curtly.

He gets up and leaves the room. Skinner also exits and intercepts him in the hall. Surprisingly, he tells Mulder to continue withholding information from his superiors.

"Thanks, buddy," says Mulder sarcastically.

"Right now you need a buddy," says Skinner. "You need any help you can get."

Mulder says, "You should have men-

tioned it down at the hospital when you were hauling my ass off."

"I saved your ass, Agent Mulder," says Skinner.

The AD adds, in an angry whisper, "I've been withholding forensic evidence about the body on your apartment floor. Until you showed up last night, I was the one keeping your secret. I had no choice but to bring you in. Scully'll verify all that."

"That's a good place to lay it," he says with a thin smile. "Considering her condition."

"You want me to lay it where it belongs, Agent Mulder? Pathology turned up two gunshot wounds on the dead man in your apartment. One fired point blank through the left temple with a handgun. The second a post-mortem wound to the face to remove the man's identity. I'd be happy to verify the ballistics on the first shot."

Mulder is cornered, and he knows it. "How can you help me?" he asks.

"Tell me why Scully lied for you," says Skinner.

Mulder tells him that her disease was given to her by a mole inside the FBI.

"Who?" asks Skinner.

Mulder says dejectedly, "I failed to find out. I failed in all respects."

Skinner nods, relieved. "You don't want to forget who your friends are,

Agent Mulder," he says. "To remember who you can trust."

At the same racetrack at which he was seen in 5X02, the Elder—accompanied by the silent man, whose name is Quiet Willy, who we'd also seen there before—watches a televised congressional hearing on the ethics of human cloning. The Cigarette-Smoking Man arrives.

"Mulder is alive," says the Elder.

The Cigarette-Smoking Man nods, unable to hide his satisfaction at the news. "As I said, he is not to be underestimated."

"Yes. As you said," says the Elder. "Though I hear he has you to thank, in some part, for his new freedom."

"Yes," says the Cigarette-Smoking Man.

The Elder says sternly, "We're too vulnerable. Our man in the FBI is exposed. Now we have even further risk to the project. What Mulder may have seen would expose our plans."

The Cigarette-Smoking Man says, "What Mulder saw only serves us, only serves to insure our plans."

The Elder stares at his underling with obdurate disbelief.

The Cigarette-Smoking Man adds, "Mulder is in trouble. He needs help. We can give it to him."

"In exchange for?"

"His new loyalty. To us."

The Elder gives the Cigarette-Smoking Man the same stone-faced look as before.

"As I've said all along," adds the Cigarette-Smoking Man, "he's so much more valuable to us alive."

He turns and walks away, watched for several moments by the Elder. Then the Elder looks toward his silent associate.

"You can proceed now," he says. The other man nods.

At the hospital, Scully, her condition somewhat improved, has been moved from the ICU into a regular room. Mulder arrives and tells his partner that he is going to testify to everything he knows about the FBI–Defense Department conspiracy. Scully warns him that if he does so, Skinner will reveal his forensic evidence.

"Mulder, Skinner is dirty," she says. "He's not your friend."

"I don't believe that," says Mulder.

Scully says, "If you testify, he's going to use it to ruin you. He's been in a position to know everything. Everything we've done for the last four years."

Mulder insists that the evidence he's gathered will expose the conspiracy no matter what any of the conspirators do or say.

"You've got to be sure," says Scully. "If you can't bury them absolutely, they're going to bury you. They'll make you into a murderer with an unbelievable alibi."

Mulder says, "If I don't testify now, Scully, they'll begin to bury the truth."

Scully squeezes his hand tightly, nodding. "Then you've got to lay it on me," she says. "Tell them I killed that man."

"Scully. I can't," says Mulder.

"You can," says Scully. "If I can save you, then let me. Let me at least give what's happened to me some meaning."

Mulder shakes his head. As he does so, Scully's mother enters. She sees his hands in hers; he greets her awkwardly and leaves. Scully's older brother, whom we've seen in "Gethsemane" (4X24) but whom Mulder has never before met, greets the agent in the hospital corridor.

"Mr. Mulder," says Bill Scully, Jr. "I know something about you—what Dana's been through with you. Leave the work away from here, okay? Let her die with dignity."

Without waiting for Mulder's reply, he turns and walks into his sister's room.

In a stairwell at the top of a multi-storied parking structure, a door opens and Quiet Willy enters. He is carrying a molded fiberglass suitcase; he opens it, revealing a disassembled sniper's rifle.

Mulder leaves the hospital the way he came in. As he does so, he sees the Cigarette-Smoking Man heading toward Scully's room.

"Please tell me you're here for severe chest pains," says Mulder, blocking the other man's path.

The Cigarette-Smoking Man says, "You should be glad for why I'm here. To pay you some respect—"

"Go to hell," says Mulder.

"—for your cleverness and resource. What you've managed to do for Scully."

"What are you talking about?"

"Breaching the security at the Defense Department facility. Finding the cure for her disease."

Mulder says, "What I found was useless."

"On the contrary," says the Cigarette-Smoking Man. "It is essential to her survival."

At a workbench we've seen before, Mulder pours the last of the deionized water out of the metallic vial he liberated in 5X02. To the astonishment of Mulder and the three Lone Gunmen gathered around him, a tiny microchip remains inside.

"This is the cure for cancer?" says Frohike.

"For Scully it may be," says Mulder.

"How?" asks Byers.

Mulder says, "Some time after her abduction, she found a small metallic chip implanted subcutaneously on her neck. Not long after she had it removed her cancer developed."

Langly says, "I know you're preaching to the choir here, Mulder—but I've never heard of such a thing."

"Scully met a group of women, all with similar abduction stories," explains Mulder. "Each had a chip removed from her neck. And all died from cancer."

The following day, the FBI investigative committee has reconvened. The witness is Michael Kritschgau. Under questioning from Blevins, he admits that he came to Mulder and Scully and gave them classified information shortly before Scott Ostelhoff's death.

"What motivated this?" asks the section chief.

Kritschgau says, "My knowledge of government involvement in a conspiracy against the American people."

This causes a minor commotion in the star chamber. The Senior Agent cuts in. "Before we get into any specifics on that subject," he says, "I'd like to ask you a more pointed question. Do you know who killed Scott Ostelhoff?"

"No, I don't," says Kritschgau, after a long pause.

Blevins asks, "Are you aware of any connection between his death and Agents Mulder and Scully?"

"No," he answers. "I'm aware of one death in connection, though. My son, who died this morning."

Kritschgau fights back his emotions. He's given a moment to recover. The Senior Agent asks the next question.

"Mr. Kritschgau—you are employed by the Department of Defense, is that correct?"

"Technically," says Kritschgau.

He pauses again, then adds, "Part of my remuneration has come from another source. A congressional lobbying firm. Something called Roush."

Skinner speaks up for the first time. "Roush? Any idea what that is?" he says.

"No sir," says Kritschgau. Blevins and the Senior Agent exchange glances.

In Scully's hospital room, Mulder tries vehemently to convince Mrs. Scully and Bill Scully that implanting the stolen microchip in her body is worth a try. Scully's oncologist, a Dr. Zuckerman, watches silently.

"This is crazy. Just crazy," Bill Scully tells Mulder.

"Crazy in what sense?" replies Mulder. "That it might save your sister's life?"

Bill Scully says, "You're not a doctor. You've got no place even suggesting this science fiction."

Mulder turns to Zuckerman. "Would she have to stop with her conventional treatment?" he asks.

"To be honest," says Zuckerman, "at this point the only approach I have left with her particular cancer is quite unconventional."

All eyes are on Scully as she fingers the metallic vial.

"I'd like to try this," she says. She holds out the vial to Zuckerman. He steps over and takes it from her.

"I don't suppose it came with instructions," he says with mock consternation. Scully smiles at him.

In the stairwell, Quiet Willy meticulously assembles his sniper's rifle. He then affixes a small laser sight; loads several rounds of ammunition; sights down the barrel; and checks his watch.

In the corridor outside Scully's room, Mulder sits alone. Bill Scully emerges and walks past him, then stops. He retraces his steps.

"You really believe this crap, don't you?" he says.

"What crap is that?" says Mulder.

Bill Scully stares at Mulder, then shakes his head. "She's your big defender. But I think the truth is, she just doesn't want to disappoint you."

"If it works," says Mulder, "I don't care what you think she thinks."

"You're a real piece of work. You know that, Mr. Mulder?"

"Why?" says Mulder. "Because I'm not playing by your rules? Because I'm not part of the family tragedy?"

"You're the reason for it," says Bill Scully, flatly. He adds, "I've already lost one sister to this quest you're on. Now I'm losing another. Has it been worth it? I mean, for you. Have you found what you've been looking for?"

For a few horrible moments, Mulder doesn't answer. "No," he says finally.

"No? You know how that makes me feel?"

Mulder says painfully, "In a way I do. I lost someone very close to me—a sister. And then my father. Because of the things I've been looking for."

"These what? Little green aliens?" says Bill Scully.

"I don't know anymore," says Mulder, miserable.

Bill Scully stares at Mulder, who seems to have lost all the fight in him.

"You're one sorry sonofabitch," says Scully's brother. "Not a whole lot more to say."

Mulder watches him round the corner, then sits by himself for several painful moments. His cell phone rings.

"How's our patient?" says a voice Mulder knows only too well. "You did find the chip, didn't you?"

"Yes," says Mulder.

The Cigarette-Smoking Man says, "I can imagine there was some question to its medical value."

"There still is."

"So I have yet to earn your trust, in spite of my gesture."

"You could say that."

"Well," says the Cigarette-Smoking Man, "I have something else to offer you. To cement our bond."

"Gonna take a lot of cement," says Mulder.

"I've arranged a meeting I think you'll want to be at, Mr. Mulder," the Cigarette-Smoking Man replies.

In a small diner that night, Mulder sits with a coffee cup in front of him, watching the waitress. Her arms laden with condiment bottles, she walks over to where he sits.

"Tabasco. Cures anything," she says.

"I'll keep that in mind," says Mulder.

Just after 9:30 a car, headlights blazing, pulls up in front. Two people are seated in the front seat; they remain inside with the motor running. Curious, Mulder stands and looks outside through the window. The headlights are finally turned off and Mulder recognizes the occupants immediately: they are the Cigarette-Smoking Man and a grown woman—last seen in "End Game," (2X17)—in the passenger seat.

"You know them or something?" asks the waitress.

"Yeah. I think that's my sister," says Mulder.

Mulder leaves the diner and walks toward the car. It is indeed Samantha Mulder. With tears in her eyes, she exits and joins her brother.

She is the first to speak. "I was afraid I'd never see you again," she says. "He always told me something had happened to you that night."

"Who?" says Mulder. "Who told you that?"

"My father," says Samantha. She gestures toward the Cigarette-Smoking Man sitting behind the wheel.

In the diner later that night, Samantha and Mulder sit facing one another.

"I never really knew what happened," says Samantha. "I could never put the memories all back together, but as much as I tried to remember, I tried more to forget."

"Why?" asks Mulder, stunned.

"I was eight years old," says Samantha. "I was eight years old. I was frightened to death. They told me I was an orphan."

Mulder stares at her as if she were an apparition. Outside, the Cigarette-Smoking Man sits in the car, smoking.

"But you called this man your father," says Mulder.

Samantha says, "Some time later, I don't know how long, my foster parents took me to a hotel room and said I was going to see my father."

"But you knew who your father was."

"I thought I knew. But he told me that it had all been a secret. That he and Mom hadn't told anyone to protect the family."

"And you believe that?" says Mulder incredulously.

Samantha nods and explains that the man who called himself her father was kind to her and that is all she can remember about the night she disappeared.

"You were abducted, Samantha," says Mulder forcefully. "I can help you. I can help you to remember."

"I don't want to, Fox. I don't."

"Then why come here at all?"

"My father told me he'd found you," she says, "and that you wanted to see me very badly—that you'd been looking for me a long time. Is it true?"

"Yes," says Mulder. She reaches out and takes his hand.

"Samantha," says Mulder. "You have to listen to me. What you've been told—what this man has told you—it may not be true."

Samantha refuses to believe him. Mulder asks her to come with him to see their mother. Samantha is surprised that she is still alive, but she shakes her head.

"Why can't you?" asks Mulder.

"This is too much," says Samantha. "I didn't want to come here at all, Fox. I was afraid to see you. I have my own life. I have children of my own."

Mulder begs her to stay with him, or at least tell him where she can be reached. She stands up from the table, then pulls her hand away from his.

"Please let me go," she says, then walks toward the door as Mulder watches helplessly. "Please. I promise you I'll think about it."

In the hospital, Dr. Zuckerman injects Scully with a cancer-fighting substance, flurodeoxy deoxyglucose.

"If you're making any progress," he says. "I'm hoping it might show up on the PET scan."

"You're not holding your breath, though, are you?" says Scully.

Zuckerman looks up at her, unsurprised by the question.

"I'm going after your cancer as aggressively as I know how, Dana," he says patiently. "If I can jump-start your immune system, if I can get your cytolytic cells to recognize your tumor as something to attack, then there's a chance."

Scully says, "My cancer—nasopharyngeal—I'm well aware it has a very poor response to treatment."

"You're doing everything you can," says Zuckerman.

"Am I?"

"And then some," he says ironically.

Scully watches him take the spike out of her arm, then forces herself to say what's on her mind.

"Have you ever witnessed a miracle, Dr. Zuckerman?" she says.

"I don't know that I have. But I've seen people make recoveries, come back from so far gone I can't explain it."

"Isn't that a miracle?"

Zuckerman says, "There was something from my religion I learned as a boy. Whoever destroys a single life is as guilty as though he had destroyed the entire world, and whoever rescues a single life earns as much merit as though he had rescued the entire world. Maybe they are miracles, but I don't dare call them that."

Scully smiles up at him. "Thank you," she says.

Mulder walks down a Washington, D.C., sidewalk. He is in the crosshairs of a rifle sight. Quiet Willy stands at a corner of the parking structure, aiming outward and downward. Mulder reaches a street corner and stands impatiently next to a brick building. He is joined by the Cigarette-Smoking Man, and—still tracked by the assassin—they walk together through a busy Georgetown street.

"What do you want from me?" asks Mulder.

"Want from you?" says the Cigarette-Smoking Man mockingly.

Mulder says, "You give me these things—the only things I've ever wanted. You have no other reason to do this."

"It's true," says the Cigarette-Smoking Man. "No act is completely selfless. But I've come today not to ask, but to offer. To offer you the truth you so desperately sought. About the project, and the men who have conspired to protect it."

Mulder counters that he already knows the truth.

"What have you seen?" says the Cigarette-Smoking Man. "You've seen but scant pieces of the whole."

"What more can you show me?" says Mulder.

The Cigarette-Smoking Man tells him that Kritschgau has lied about the non-existence of extraterrestrial life, that only he can tell Mulder the real story.

"In exchange for what?" asks Mulder.

"Quit the FBI. Come work for me. I can make your problems go away."

"No deal."

The Cigarette-Smoking Man chuckles. "After all I've given to you—"

Mulder erupts in rage. "What have you given me?" he says angrily. "The claim of a cure for Scully. Is she cured? You bring my sister to me, only to take her back. You've given me nothing!"

The Cigarette-Smoking Man says, "What is given can be taken away. I intend to keep my promises. I just need something from you."

The furious Mulder gets right up into the Cigarette-Smoking Man's face. "You murdered my father," he says. "You murdered Scully's sister. And if Scully dies, I will kill you. I'll put you down. I don't care whose father you are."

"You certainly are capable of that, from what I'm told," says the Cigarette-Smoking Man coolly. "I understand you have a hearing tomorrow where you'll have to testify to these murderous impulses of yours."

In the parking structure, Quiet Willy sights his rifle and prepares to shoot. But Mulder and the Cigarette-Smoking Man are so close together that it would be hard to shoot one and not the other. Mulder walks away. The assassin pulls his gun back. He has missed his shot.

In her hospital room, Scully, her condition unchanged, rests on her bed. Her mother enters; she has sent for her, Dana says, to tell her something important. She begins to cry; her mother embraces her.

"I fight and I fight, but I've been so stupid," she says. "I've been so wrong."

"What? What is it?" says Mrs. Scully.

"I've come so far in my life on simple faith," says Scully. "And now when I need it most I push it away."

Scully breaks away from her mother, grasps at the chain around her neck, and pulls out the small Christian cross she wears. "Why do I wear this?" she says. "I'll put something I don't understand on the skin of my neck. I'll subject myself to these crazy treatments. I tell myself I'm doing everything I can, but it's a lie."

"You haven't lost your faith, Dana," says Mrs. Scully.

"But I have, in a way," says Scully. "When you asked Father McCue to dinner [in "Gethsemane," 4X24] to minister to my faith, I just blew him off."

Mrs. Scully tries to calm her.

"I'm not getting better, Mom," says Scully. "My PET scan showed no improvement."

"I know you're afraid, Dana," says her mother. "And I know you're afraid to tell me. But you need to tell someone."

Scully nods.

"He's been praying for you," says Mrs. Scully.

"Father McCue?" says Scully. "Would you call him for me?"

"Of course," says Mrs. Scully, nodding.

In the Syndicate headquarters room that night, the Elder sits watching the congressional hearing. As the TV camera pans the spectators' gallery, it finds Assistant Director Walter Skinner talking to another man. Seeing this, the Elder quickly reaches for his phone and punches in some numbers.

"Turn on your television. Are you watching the hearings? Do you see who's there? Who he's there talking to? He's gathering information. For who?"

Whoever is at the other end replies. The answer is indistinct, but whatever it is, the Elder is not satisfied.

"Our colleague was supposed to have fixed the FBI problem," he says. "You will fix it now, do you understand me? Then I will fix it for good." He hangs up the phone angrily.

In her hospital room that night, Scully is asleep. Mulder enters quietly and stands watching her for a moment, torn over something, debating with himself about waking her to share his thoughts. Then he bends to one knee and lays his head on the side of her bed in quiet, private anguish.

The next day Mulder, depressed and nearly expressionless, enters Blevins's FBI office. The section chief holds up a file folder—the same one that Skinner had brought into the star chamber in 5X02—and tells him that he has forensic evidence indicating he was the man who shot Ostelhoff.

"Where did you get it?" asks Mulder.

"I'm not at liberty to say," says Blevins. "But unless you can offer up someone else who might have fired the kill shot, everything points to you as this man's murderer."

Mulder says nothing.

Blevins says, "Are you prepared to give testimony that you are not the man who fired that shot?"

Mulder ignores this. "Why am I here?" he says.

Blevins tells him accusingly something Mulder already knows: the dead man worked for the Department of Defense.

"This man was spying on me!" says Mulder.

"Do you know for whom?" asks Blevins.

Again Mulder is silent.

Blevins says, "Agent Scully was prepared to name the man at the FBI who was involved in the plot against you and her. We believe she was about to name Assistant Director Walter Skinner—who we've just now learned has been working inside the FBI with a secret agenda."

"I refuse to believe that," says Mulder.

"We have accumulated substantial evidence against him," says Blevins.

"Show it to me."

Blevins does not. Instead, he shifts tactics and offers to exonerate Mulder from murder charges if he names Skinner as the traitor.

"That's what I've called you here to recommend," says Blevins. "As a friend."

Mulder stands up to leave. "I'll see you at the hearing," he says.

At the hospital later that day, a drawn and tired Scully receives her partner. He tells her of his visit the night before; she asks him what he wanted to discuss with her.

"I was lost last night," says Mulder, "but as I stood there I thought I'd found my way. I was offered a deal. A deal that would save my life in a way. And although I'd refused this deal earlier, I left here with my mind made up to take it."

"A deal with who?" says Scully.

"It doesn't matter now. I'm not taking that deal. I'm not taking any deal. Not after this morning."

"What happened this morning?"

Mulder tells Scully about Blevins's promise to clear him if he testifies against Skinner.

"Are you going to name him?" asks Scully.

"No."

"Then they'll prosecute you," says Scully.

Mulder nods. "They have evidence against me," he says. "They know I killed that man."

Scully says, "Even with ballistics evidence, I could still be the shooter—"

Mulder shakes his head. "I can't let you take the blame. Because of your mother, and because I couldn't live with it."

He adds, "To live the lie you have to believe it, like these men who deceive us. Who gave you this disease. We all have our faith, and mine is the truth. I've been looking for it so long I don't know any other way."

Scully regards Mulder with a respectful sadness.

"Why come here," she asks, "if you'd already made up your mind?"

Mulder replies, "I knew you would talk me out of it if I was making a mistake."

She takes his hand and squeezes it tightly. They both turn in reaction to the door opening. It is Father McCue.

"You'll be in my prayers," says Scully to Mulder. Mulder turns away from her and leaves.

In the FBI star chamber later that day, Blevins waits impatiently. The Senior Agent is also present. Skinner sits next to him. Mulder arrives and apologizes for the delay.

"Agent Mulder," says Blevins, "the assembled members of this review panel first convened to address your reported death, only to find out shortly, this report had been a lie. That you were indeed very much alive, and that the body found in your apartment, believed to be yours, was a murder victim—killed with a weapon issued by the FBI and registered to you—"

Mulder interrupts. "Respectfully, sir," he says, "I'd like to set the record straight today—so that the process which you have begun can be completed, and the guilty parties named."

Skinner jumps in and asks for a short adjournment, but Mulder ignores him.

"Go on, Agent Mulder," says Blevins.

This is Mulder's testimony:

"Four years ago, working on an assignment outside the FBI mainstream, I was paired with Special Agent Dana Scully, who I believe was sent to spy on me, to debunk my investigations into the paranormal. That Agent Scully did not follow these orders owes more to her integrity as an investigator, as a scientist, as a person. She's paid greatly for this integrity—"

Blevins jumps in. "Agent Mulder," he says. "Agent Scully lied straight-faced to this panel about your death."

Mulder stops to refute him. "She lied because I asked her to. Because of evidence I had of a conspiracy at work. A conspiracy against the American people—and a conspiracy to destroy the lives of those who might reveal its real purpose."

In the parking garage, Quiet Willy is again at his post. Through his scope he tracks the Cigarette-Smoking Man walking down the street. It's an imperfect shot due to trees, lampposts, and the other people on the street, but the Cigarette-Smoking Man remains in the crosshairs until he disappears into the front entrance of the brick building.

In the hearing room, Mulder continues.

"To conduct experiments on unwitting victims to further a secret agenda for someone within the government, working at a level without restraints of responsibility. Who deceive as they pretend to honor. The price of this betrayal: the lives and reputations of the deceived."

In Scully's room, Father McCue is at her bedside, praying with her.

"Agent Scully is lying in hospital right now, diagnosed with terminal cancer—a victim of these same tests, conducted without her consent or knowledge by these same men, who as they try to cover their tracks, who try to suborn and prosecute those who they've used in the plot. I will now call by name—"

Now the Senior Agent jumps in. "Agent Mulder!" he says. "Did you or did you not shoot the man found dead in your apartment—"

"I will answer that question—" begins Mulder, but the Senior Agent cuts him off.

"Did you shoot Scott Ostelhoff, employee of the Department of Defense—"

"I will answer that question—" repeats Mulder.

In the hospital room, Scully, tears now streaming down her face, continues praying with Father McCue.

Inside his apartment, the Cigarette-Smoking Man exhales a cloud of smoke and studies a photograph. It is of Mulder and his sister Samantha. Through the Cigarette-Smoking Man's open window is the parking structure.

"I will answer that question," says Mulder, "after I name the man responsible for Agent Scully, the same man who directed my apartment be surveilled by the DOD. A man who I want prosecuted for his crimes. Who is sitting in this room as I speak."

"Agent Mulder!" says the Senior Agent. "The section chief has asked you a question. You are going to answer it."

"I can't do that, sir," says Mulder, "because the section chief is the man I am about to name." The room erupts at this announcement.

In the apartment, the Cigarette-Smoking Man is still looking at the photograph. He notices something that causes him alarm—a red laser dot on the center of his chest. He looks up and out the window and sees Quiet Willy firing his weapon.

In the FBI hearing room, Section Chief Blevins is up on his feet, shouting something at Mulder. His words cannot be heard above the din. Mulder sits calmly in his seat. Skinner stares at him. The Senior Agent leaves the room quickly and hurries down an empty corridor.

The photograph of Mulder and Samantha—now blood-spattered and the glass in its frame shattered by a bullet—lies on the floor of the apartment. The Cigarette-Smoking Man lies on his stomach nearby. For a moment, he appears dead; then his eyes blink and his hand reaches out feebly to find the photo. When his hand touches the frame, only then do his eyes close.

Inside Blevins's FBI office, the Senior Agent talks into the phone, his manner urgent, but his words hushed and unintelligible. A panicky-looking Blevins enters; the Senior Agent turns and raises a handgun. A shot rings out; Blevins falls; the Senior Agent steps over his body and exits.

In the hospital corridor, Mulder is sitting outside Scully's room. Skinner appears at the end of the hall, approaches, and with a nod sits down on the bench next to him.

"The Smoking Man is dead," says Skinner.

"How?" asks Mulder.

"Shot through his window."

Skinner hands Mulder the photo of himself with his sister. "Forensics found it at the scene," he says. "We're assuming it's his blood."

"Assuming?" says Mulder, confused.

"No body was found, though there was too much blood loss for anyone to have survived."

Mulder stares at Skinner, unconvinced. He looks back at the photo.

Skinner says, "This afternoon, when you named Blevins. How did you know?"

"I didn't," says Mulder. "I guessed."

"Hell of a guess," says Skinner. "Blevins had been on payroll for four years to a biotechnology company called Roush, which is somehow connected to all this."

"I'm sure whatever connection has already been erased."

Skinner nods. "They're cleaning up, taking everything away."

"Not everything," says Mulder. "Agent Scully's cancer has gone into remission."

Skinner is stunned. "That is unbelievable news," he says after a moment.

"That is the best news I can ever imagine," says Mulder, trying—with limited success—to restrain his emotions.

Skinner asks Mulder what treatment turned her disease around.

"I don't know," says Mulder. "I don't know if we'll ever know."

Skinner says, "Can I see her?"

Mulder nods. "I know she'd like to see you. She's in with her family."

Skinner gets up, moves to the door, and opens it. Inside, Scully is lying in bed, her mother and brother by her side. Dr. Zuckerman and Father McCue are there, too. She sees Skinner and her face beams.

Mulder remains seated, alone. He looks down again at the photograph—at his family photograph—and surrenders to his emotions at last.

back story:

One day late in the summer of 1997, a man operating under an assumed name drove up to a North Vancouver address and entered a small room. Awaiting him inside were *X-Files* creator Chris Carter, director/producer Kim Manners, and casting director Coreen Mayrs.

"My mindset was that of an assassin," recalls the man whom we'll call—for just a little while longer—Willy Ross. "At that moment, I felt I could have killed anyone in there."

Fortunately for everyone concerned, he didn't, and in an astonishingly short time this man was assigned a small but important part in *The X-Files*'s fifth season. "Willy Ross" also introduced a splash of quirkiness and eccentric ambition into an environment where the standards for such qualities are extremely high.

"First of all, I'm not Willy Ross. I'm Steve Allen," says the balding, gray-mustached man chosen to play the part of the wordless killer Quiet Willy—the nerveless apparatchik who finally puts the Cigarette-Smoking Man out of action.

This Steve Allen is not, incidentally, a songwriter or a mystery novelist or married to Jayne Meadows. But we've gotten ahead of ourselves.

Our story of worlds in collision begins in the early 1980s, when Steve Allen—not the first host of *The Tonight Show*, but a young Toronto policeman—was nearing his fifth anniversary with the force.

Despite the fact that a corporate jet once crashed into his patrol sector, the future Syndicate sniper was growing bored with driving around his notably low-crime city. Allen signed up for an improvisational comedy course given by the famed Second City comedy troupe, and after a few classes was invited to join the group's most advanced seminar, a steppingstone to a professional career, in a remote Northern Ontario resort town. But his police duties prevented him from attending.

"So I thought about it for a little while," says Allen, "and a few months before my pension locked in I quit the police force, took my money in a lump sum, and went to Europe for six months."

When Steve Allen returned to Canada he moved to Vancouver and supported himself with a new job: painting murals; usually on the walls of restaurants and young chidren's bedrooms. Several years later, attracted to a comedy course taught by two visiting Texas comedians, he launched another profession part-time.

In 1997 he decided he also wanted to become an actor, and made an appointment to meet with local talent agent Carmela Evangelista. "It was very strange," says Evangelista. "When he came into my office he took out a pen and a little tiny notepad, and kept asking me questions like 'What do you look for in an actor?', as if he were still a cop. Or Detective Columbo.

"And the funny thing was," she says, "the more he just sat there, not really saying much, the more I thought, 'This guy is really an *X-Files* type.'"

The agent also thought that Allen—now Willy Ross professionally, since his real name had already been taken—would have some success auditioning for small cop roles on shows filming around town. No dice.

But here's where fate begins to really step in. Eight abrupt thank you's later, Evangelista sent Steve/Willy—Allen's middle name is William; his father's first name is Ross—to read for the part of an *X-Files* assassin. The part had originally been written for a recurring character, the Gray-Haired Man, played by veteran actor Morris Panych. But Panych had a previous theater commitment and was unavailable.

The script pages Allen/Ross received contained dialogue previously written for the Gray-Haired Man, and he spent most of that night before his audition rehearsing with an actor friend and working himself into the aforementioned homicidal fury. His competitors for the part were a number of accomplished local character actors.

Coreen Mayrs recalls, "I'd prescreened Willy a week or so before—he'd just stuck his head in my office—and I decided to audition him in the middle of the other guys. He was . . . well, different. At the end of the session, Chris turned to me and he said, 'I liked this guy.' And so I told him his name was Willy Ross, and that he'd never really done anything before. And he said, 'That's okay. He can be Quiet Willy.'

"And then we all started to laugh and Kim Manners, who was directing 'Redux,' began announcing to anyone who would listen that 'We've cast Quiet Willy!' And then, everybody wanted to meet Quiet Willy. Quiet Willy became a kind of mysterious enigma around the production office."

Since his part as rewritten had no lines, Ross was able to maintain his enigmatically murderous demeanor ("Never move the jaw.

Always look through the person in front of you.") throughout his multiple stints on the *X-Files* set. True to form, he never once introduced himself to Chris Carter, who directed "Redux II," or revealed to anyone who mattered that he was really Steve Allen.

Still, he says, the role marked a turning point in his life. Since guest-starring as Quiet Willy he's tried out (albeit unsuccessfully) for several more cop roles; cohosted, with William (Cigarette-Smoking Man) Davis, an American Cancer Society benefit; won a nonspeaking part in a Pfizer Pharmaceuticals commercial for Viagra; did stand-up and had a tryout performing a comedy striptease (dressed, at least at first, as an NBA referee) during breaks in the action of Vancouver Grizzlies basketball games. He's even been recognized, by serious *X-Files* fans, in public.

"An *X-Files* fan visiting from Scotland came up to me and asked if he could take my picture," he says. "And then there was this woman who handed me a card with her home phone number. I asked her why. She told me, 'Because ten years ago I saw a spaceship around here, and I'd like to talk to you about it.' It turns out she thought I was really an alien. Have you ever heard anything as strange as that?"

detour

A primeval forest is threatened by encroaching civilization. Its secret inhabitants— fierce predators with glowing red eyes— fight back.

EPISODE: 5X04
FIRST AIRED: November 23, 1997
EDITOR: Casey O Rohrs
WRITTEN BY: Frank Spotnitz
DIRECTED BY: Brett Dowler
GUEST STARS:
Tom Scholte (Michael Sloan)
Tyler Thompson (Louis Asekoff)
Alfred E. Humphreys
(Michael Asekoff)
Simon Longmore (Marty Fox)
Colleen Flynn (Michelle Fazekas)
Merrilyn Gann (Mrs. Asekoff)
Anthony Rapp (Jeff Glaser)
Scott Burkholder (Agent Kinsley)
J. C. Wendel (Agent Stonecypher)
Ian Brown (Trooper #1)
Nicholas Harrison (Trooper #2)
Terry David Reeb (Creature #1)
Axl Aartsen (Creature #2)
PRINCIPAL SETTING:
Leon County, North Florida

In a pristine woodland in the Deep South, two sweaty and mosquito-bitten surveyors prepare to take their measurements. The first one, Michael Sloan, jabs his surveyor's pole into the rich soil. The second, Marty Fox, stands several dozen yards away, peering through a surveyor's transit and fiddling with the eyepiece.

They communicate via walkie-talkie. "Let's shoot this, Marty," says Sloan, impatiently.

The surveyor's pole wavers. "Hold it still, Sloan," says Fox. "Hold it still!"

"I'd like to see you hold it still!" says Sloan, slapping at yet another mosquito. "The sooner they pave over this swamp, the better."

"It's not a swamp," replies his coworker, scornfully. "You're standing in a forest with indigenous plant and animal species you're obviously too ignorant to appreciate. Mark it there and give me another position."

Sloan grits his teeth, marks the spot with a short metal stake, and moves his pole a dozen yards to his left.

"Shoot this one real carefully, Marty," he radios, "because this is where they're gonna put the Blockbuster."

"You're a real moron, you know that?" says Marty.

"Tree hugger," mutters Sloan.

Marty leans down to look through the transit. "You should be sad," he says, "to see the demise of an ecosystem that's been here for thousands of years. We should all be. Gimme four feet to your left."

Sloan radios that he can't do it—that his pole is stuck fast in the ground. He yanks hard, to no avail, then kneels down to see that the pole is mired in a massive, gnarled root. He gingerly presses his fingers into the bark at the base of the pole. They come back smeared with blood.

"This is weird," says Sloan.

Two bright red eyes snap open on the surface of the bark. Through his walkie-talkie Marty hears Sloan scream in terror. He looks through the transit and sees the blur of something being yanked downward. Then Sloan is gone. Completely.

Marty calls his partner's name. Nothing. He sees something moving—what it is, he can't tell—through the tall grass, toward him. Terrified, he turns and runs away from it. He crashes through the forest, frantically waving low-hanging branches away from his face. Panting with fear and exhaustion, he jumps into a depression behind a fallen log and scans the area behind him. There is no sign of what chased him, or what attacked Sloan.

He sighs with relief and runs his fingers over the strange-textured log alongside of him. Two glowing red eyes snap open. Marty is pulled down, screaming, into the earth.

In the same location the next morning a hunting dog, on the scent of game, trots through the woods. It is followed by a twelve-year-old boy, Louis Asekoff. He is trailed by his father, carrying a 12-gauge shotgun. The dog strains at his leash.

"Louis, let Bo do the work," says the father.

Louis lets the dog run ahead. "How's he know how to find a possum?" he asks.

"Shhh," says the father, speaking quietly. "Animals sense things we can't. That's how they survive."

"Is that how Bo knows how to hunt?" says Louis.

"Yeah," says his father. "Our ancestors were hunters, too. But most of us have lost those instincts."

He nods toward his shotgun, adding,

"So now we need a little help."

Louis's eyes wander from his father's to something directly behind him. It is the surveyor's transit, left from the night before. The older man's eyes narrow. Somewhere to the right of them Bo begins to bark frantically. Now Asekoff senses that something is wrong.

"Stay close, Louis," he says.

They move toward the dog. Near a fallen log is a man's jacket. It is covered with blood; swarms of flies buzz over it.

"What is it, Dad?" asks Louis.

His father doesn't answer. Instead, he stares intently at his dog, which is growling at something in the distance.

"Dad?" says Louis.

"Quiet," he replies. "Listen to me. I want you to take Bo and run home." He grimly breaks open his shotgun.

"What's the matter?" asks Louis.

Replies his father, "Run home and don't stop. Understand?"

Frightened now, Louis nods. His father loads two shells into the 12-gauge.

"*Run*, Louis," he whispers.

The boy takes off. When he reaches a clearing he hears a shotgun blast. He turns, looks. Another blast. Bo strains at his leash, barking. Louis hesitates a moment, then pulls the dog back.

"Bo, no!" he says. "C'mon!" Terrified, he turns and runs for home.

On a two-lane highway nearby a rented sedan cruises contentedly. At the wheel is FBI Special Agent Michael Kinsley; riding shotgun is his partner, Carla Stonecypher. She holds a brochure headlined FBI CREATIVE TEAM SEMINAR. In the backseat are Scully and Mulder.

Kinsley says, "Last year was something of a personal revelation. We were doing an exercise called 'Team Builders.' Where we were given two minutes to build a tower out of ordinary office furniture."

Stonecypher adds, "When I stood on Mike's shoulders and put that electric pencil sharpener on top of the pile? We both knew we could never have done it alone."

Mulder leans toward Scully, his expression one of numb horror.

"Kill me now," he murmurs, with conviction.

Scully smiles nervously. It's been a long ride.

"You ever been to one of these teamwork seminars, Agent Scully?" asks Kinsley.

"Um, I think I went to a Constructive Problem Solving Course when I first joined the Bureau," she says.

Stonecypher turns and smiles brightly at her colleague. "Oh!" she says. "Did you play that game where you couldn't use negative words?"

Kinsley adds, "I couldn't believe how hard it was not to use the word 'but'!"

This remark obviously resonates with Mulder. "I'm having the same problem right now!" he says.

This piques Stonecypher's interest.

"Have you ever been to a team seminar, Agent Mulder?" she asks.

"No," says Mulder, his voice dripping regret. "Unfortunately, around this time of year I always develop a severe hemorrhoidal condition."

"Well," says Kinsley, "it builds muscles you didn't even know you had."

"Communication!" says Stonecypher. "That's the key."

Mulder glances at Scully, appealing silently for mercy. Their car reaches a police roadblock and stops.

A state trooper leans in. "Sorry, folks," he says. "It'll be a few minutes."

Mulder yanks open his door handle, exits the car, and walks briskly toward a knot of milling civilians and officers and parked police cruisers.

"Thank you, Jesus," he murmurs.

He takes a deep breath, looks around him distractedly, and is accosted by a distraught-looking woman in her forties.

"Are you from search and rescue?" she asks.

Mulder comes back into focus. "No," he says, staring at her. "I'm just stretching my legs."

His reply makes her even more frantic. "They said they'd have word for us about what happened to my husband. I need somebody to tell me what's going on."

She explains that her husband, Michael, was in the woods teaching his son to shoot, that her son heard shots as he was fleeing the scene, and that the police won't even let her talk to him.

Mulder looks past Mrs. Asekoff and spots Louis; the boy is petting Bo while being questioned by several officers.

"I'll try to find out who's in charge, all right?" he says.

He strides directly into the woods while Stonecypher and Kinsley, waiting with Scully at the car, can only watch.

"Now where's he going?" asks Stonecypher, impatiently. With only an apologetic smile, Scully trails her partner to the crime scene. Kinsley does some wandering of his own: to a large tree stump sawed off and marked with red arrows on its rings indicating milestones of history.

"Hey, Stonecypher! Take a look at this!" he says. "This tree was here twenty years before Ponce de Leon landed."

Stonecypher, however, is less impressed. "We're gonna be late for the wine and cheese reception," she says, sulking.

In the woods Mulder reaches a familiar-looking clearing and is introduced to the search and rescue leader, Officer Michelle Fazekas.

"My name is Fox Mulder. I'm an officer of the FBI," he says. Fazekas isn't overly impressed, either.

"FBI? Who called you guys out?" she asks.

"Nobody. We just got stopped at your roadblock. It sounds like you've had a shooting."

"Shots were reported," she says, "but we have no evidence of anyone being shot."

"Then what do you have evidence of?"

Though she is defensive, and not completely comfortable doing so, Fazekas tells him about the missing survey team, the bloody jacket, and Louis's separation from his father.

"Separated by what?" says Mulder.

"It looks maybe like some kind of animal attack."

"What kind of animal?"

"I'm not sure yet," she says, warily. She adds that she found unidentifiable tracks leading into the woods alongside the surveyors'.

"Couldn't identify as the surveyors'?" says Mulder.

"As man or animal," replies Fazekas.

Scully enters the clearing and beckons impatiently to her partner. Mulder breezily asks her to hold off a minute and asks Fazekas whether she'd been able to track Louis's father.

"I tracked him all the way to where he fired the shot," she says. "The ground's rocky, but from the depressions in the underlying soil I can tell you that he entered the bushes from over there, where I pick up another set of tracks."

She adds, "Two distinctly different set of tracks. And there, from the way the ground's upset, is probably where the man was attacked."

Mulder asks whether there were any other signs of the attack. Fazekas shakes her head.

Mulder says, "You have panther in these woods?"

"There's panther. Bear."

"And these tracks looked like none of them?"

"No, sir." Fazekas's face betrays her concern about the lack of good answers.

"You know a good motel in the area?" asks Mulder.

That night at the Asekoff home— a fairly new tract house on the edge of what once was wilderness—Louis has fallen asleep in his bed while watching the old Claude Rains horror film *The Invisible Man.* His mother, obviously exhausted with worry, enters his room and kisses him gently on the cheek.

She snaps off the video. Louis awakes.

"He's not coming back, is he?" he says.

Mrs. Asekoff forces a smile. "Now, why would you say that?" she says.

"Dad's a good shot. If he'd hit what he was aiming at, he'd be home by now."

His mother wavers, then recovers. "We've got to be brave, Louis," she says. "We've both got to be brave. We'll find out more about it in the morning. Get some sleep now."

She rises and

leaves her son's room, closing the door behind her. Unnoticed by the humans, Bo the dog is staring out a window, whimpering.

In his motel room Mulder is staring at the display on his laptop. It shows, with accompanying text, various wild animals chomping their prey. Scully knocks and enters. She is carrying a tray of cheap white wine; two plastic goblets; and assorted low-rent hors d'oeuvres.

"Who cut the cheese?" asks Mulder.

Scully closes the door behind her. "Since we weren't going to make it to the conference," she says.

"Par-tay!" exclaims Mulder.

Scully adds, mock-seriously, "However, I must remind you that this goes against the Bureau's policy on male and female agents consorting in the same hotel room while on assignment."

"Try any of that Tailhook crap on me, Scully," replies Mulder, "and I'll kick your ass."

Scully smiles and pours the wine into the goblets.

"Pop quiz, Scully," says Mulder. "What animal will attack the strongest, leaving the weakest to escape? The answer is none. From what I see, not one of the more than 4,000 species native to North America takes the strong when the weak is vulnerable."

Scully says, "What does that have to do with anything?"

"I think," says Mulder, "that whatever attacked this kid's father may not have been an ordinary predator."

Scully is puzzled and skeptical. "Mulder, I thought this was just a ploy to get out of the conference."

"I think," says Mulder, "what we stumbled on here might be more than the local authorities realize. The scenario described by the boy sounds to me like a primitive culling technique."

Mulder prepares to depart. "Where are you going?" says Scully.

"There's something I want to check out," he replies.

Scully says, "Mulder, sometimes I think some work on your communications skills wouldn't be such a bad thing."

Mulder smiles, delighted at the thought. "I'll be back soon," he says, "and we'll build a tower of furniture."

At the Asekoff house Bo is now barking frantically through the window. Mrs. Asekoff soothes him, looks out the window, and calls upstairs.

"It's all right, Louis," she says. "You can go to sleep now."

The woman's expression, however, indicates that she is deeply worried. She unlocks the backdoor and lets Bo out. He runs, barking, into the bushes in the backyard. After a moment's hesitation she follows, closing the door behind her.

But the dog has disappeared. Mrs. Asekoff approaches the bushes, calling him. He leaps, snarling at her, and refuses her command to come back inside.

"All right then," she says, irritated. "Stay out the night."

She returns to the door. It is closed and locked. Terrified, she pounds on it.

"Louis! Louis!" she yells.

Louis bolts upright in his bed. Hearing both his mother's cries and her frantic knocking, he throws aside his covers and runs from his room. In the hallway, he hears a floorboard creaking. He turns to see two glowing red eyes staring back at him. Energized by fear, he averts his gaze and runs downstairs, turning back every few seconds to see his pursuer gaining on him. He makes it to the kitchen, dives into a doggie door cut into the rear entrance, and squeezes past the rubber flap—only to be caught by something that pulls him, hard, out the other side.

He screams, loudly.

"What is it, Louis?" says Mulder, grasping him reassuringly.

"It's in the house!" cries the terrified boy.

Later that morning the house is swarming with policemen. Scully enters Louis's room, pulls a cassette out of the VCR, and joins Mulder, Louis, and Mrs. Asekoff in the dining room. She hands Mulder the copy of *The Invisible Man*. He is less than supremely impressed.

"The Invisible Man was invisible," says Mulder. "Louis said he was chased by a creature with glowing red eyes. Let me show you something."

He leads his partner past a strand of

yellow crime scene tape, enters the kitchen, then kneels at the base of the rear door. "Got tracks here," he says. "Here, here, and here. Dried mud against the tile, tracked in from the outside."

"Could be from the dog," says Scully.

"No, no," says Mulder. "You see the ball of the foot here? A large foot, and I count five toes."

"Wait a minute," says Scully. "I thought you said it wasn't human."

"Well, I'm not saying it is. The weight distribution is all wrong. People walk heel to toe. Whatever this thing is, it walks on the ball of its foot."

Scully frowns. "You're putting me on," she says.

Mulder smiles. "No. My dad and I were Indian Guides. I know these things."

With some difficulty, Scully reins in her skepticism. "So," she says, "if it's not a man and not an animal, what the hell is it?"

Michelle Fazekas, the search and rescue leader, joins the agents and confirms Mulder's assessment of the strange footprints.

"Well, whatever it is," says Mulder, "it's attacked three grown men, presumably in broad daylight, disposing of its prey without detection. And it wasn't shy last night about coming out of the woods to try again."

He adds, "What we've got here is a predator with low visibility and a high degree of motivation. And it's got one advantage we don't have: the entire Appalachicola National Forest."

Fazekas looks at Mulder, worried. "Then how do you stop it?" she says.

"By identifying it," says Mulder. "And finding it before it finds something else."

At the edge of the woods that day Mulder and Scully huddle with a young guy, Jeff Glaser, who's holding a device that looks like a notebook computer attached to a radar gun.

"It's called a FLIR for Forward-looking Infra-red," says Glaser. "It was developed for chopper pilots in Vietnam. Detects body heat at three hundred yards."

Mulder gazes down at the gizmo. "It's pretty sophisticated for government issue," he says. A ghostly image appears on the computer screen. It is Fazekas,

who is indeed walking up the road toward them.

"Jeff's our local tech head," she says. "Some people prefer searching with dogs. I prefer another pair of hands if I get in trouble."

She notices Scully talking on her cell phone, and cautions Mulder that phones are useless in the forest. "So stay close. Maintain visual contact. If you get lost, initiate aural contact. That means holler."

They troop off into the deep woods. Scully tells Mulder that the local police suspect a homicidal transient of committing the crimes they're investigating.

"I don't think it's a drifter, Scully," says Mulder. "And I think we may be looking for two individuals."

"Why do you say that?" asks Scully.

"That thing lured the woman out of the house last night to separate her from her son."

"For what purpose?"

"Divide and conquer. If your enemy is greater in numbers than you, you divide and conquer to diminish those numbers."

"What enemy would that be?"

"Encroaching development," says Mulder. "That's what I suspected when I went to check on Louis and his mother."

Scully looks at him quizzically. "You think this is about a housing tract?"

Mulder says, "That survey team was staking out a new hundred thousand acre plot. Civilization is pushing fast into those woods. Something out here is pushing back."

The humans move single file through the forest. Fazekas marks the path they've taken, reaching down every dozen yards or so to place a small white stone. Glaser is next in line, gazing at his FLIR screen. Scully catches up to him.

"Anything?" she says.

"No," says Glaser. "Nothing at all. Not even wildlife."

"Isn't that a little strange?"

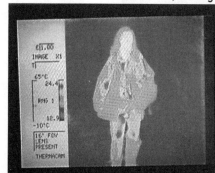

"Yeah. This forest is usually alive with sound. I'm not, like, an expert, but I've never seen it like this before."

Scully looks around warily. "Sure is beautiful, though," she says.

"That's what happens," says Glaser. "People get to looking around. Next thing they know, something eats them."

"What do you think killed those men?" asks Scully.

Glaser shrugs. "Nature is populated," he says, "with creatures either trying to kill something they need to survive, or trying to avoid being killed by something that needs them to survive."

He adds, reciting from memory, "'If we become blinded by the beauty of nature we may fail to see its cruelty and violence.'"

"Walt Whitman?" asks Scully.

"No," says Glaser. "*When Animals Attack*. On the Fox Network."

They press on. Behind them, out of their field of vision, a gnarled white hand reaches up and removes one of the marker stones. Some time later, a blip appears on Glaser's FLIR screen.

"I've got something," says Glaser. "It's about twenty yards ahead."

The searchers stop and huddle around the techie. Fazekas peers down the trail. "Where? I don't see it," she says.

"It's just sitting there," says Glaser.

Still nothing. The white dot veers off the edge of the computer screen.

"It's on the move!" shouts Glaser.

Fazekas breaks into a run, the others following. While Glaser shouts out directions, the group pursues the phantom target single file. Then two dots appear on the screen, moving in opposite directions. The pursuers split up. Fazekas searches in one direction, Scully following. Mulder takes off in the other, Glaser behind him.

"About twenty yards ahead of you!" shouts Glaser, head down and locked on the FLIR screen.

Mulder moves in on that position, gun drawn. He sees nothing.

"Now it's gone," says Glaser, puzzled by this. The screen is blank. "I don't know where it went."

Scully and Fazekas, running blindly through the underbrush, emerge into a clearing where Fazekas inexplicably stops.

"What is it?" says Scully, her own weapon drawn.

"I don't know," says Fazekas, nervously.

Scully goes on red alert. "They're trying to separate us. Pull us away from the others. Let's go back."

Fazekas says nothing but turns and retraces her steps. Scully trails her, covering their retreat. Behind them is an old, gnarled tree. The pattern of the bark resolves itself into a crude face: two glowing red eyes pop open. Fazekas is yanked down out of sight—too fast for anything more than a muffled gasp.

"Michelle!" Scully shouts. There is no reply.

"Mulder! I need help. Mulder!" Her cries echo in the empty forest.

A short while later Mulder—followed by a rattled Glaser—responds to Scully's cries and crash into the clearing where she is standing. There is no sign of Fazekas, either visually or on the FLIR.

"What the hell's happening here?" says Scully.

"They separated us," says Mulder. "That was on purpose. They divided us so that they could go after her. She was in the lead, and presumably the strongest. They pick the strongest first."

He adds that they have to stay where they are and search for Fazekas. This is not exactly an attractive idea to Glaser.

"This is nuts. This is loony tune, man," he says. "We gotta go back, out of these woods before it gets dark."

"You're right," says Mulder, looking him in the eye. "You go back. You leave me the FLIR and go back."

"We've got to go together," protests Glaser, his voice quavering.

"We have to find her," says Mulder.

"If we stay here," says Glaser, "they may not find anyone."

Scully has been unsuccessfully dialing her cell phone throughout this. She gives up and walks over to her partner.

"Mulder, he's right," she says, reluctantly. Mulder looks at her in surprise.

Scully adds, "We weren't prepared for this. We have no way of telling them where we are. We don't have any food. Michelle had our only water. Look, I'd like to find her, too. But I think the risks of that are just way too foolish."

Mulder thinks for a long moment. "All right. We all go, then."

Glaser nods, relieved—until Mulder turns to him.

"You lead the way," he says.

They move off, Glaser carrying the FLIR and scanning the path ahead of them. Scully and Mulder walk a few yards behind.

Scully says, "I don't have much faith this device will do us any good."

Mulder nods. "So far," he says, "all it's done is split us up."

Scully says, "Whatever it was that we were chasing did show up on the screen at first."

"What does that tell us?" asks her partner.

"Nothing."

"Uh-huh."

"Except that we're going in the right direction."

Mulder thinks for a moment. "Maybe," he says, "it can regulate its temperature. You know any other animal that can?"

"Ticks," says Scully. "I've heard that they can halt their metabolism for up to eighteen years, essentially going into suspended animation, until something warm-blooded comes along."

"That's very interesting," says Mulder. "Thirty years ago the town of Point Pleasant, West Virginia, was terrorized for over a year by something. Killing livestock, terrorizing people. Witnesses described them as primitive-looking men with red piercing eyes. They came to be known as 'the mothmen.'"

Scully shoots him a skeptical look.

"I've got an X-File dating back to 1952 on it," he says.

"What would that be filed next to?" says Scully. "'The Cockroach That Ate Cincinnati'?"

Mulder stops, thinks, and pronounces

solemnly, "No. 'The Cockroach That Ate Cincinnati' is in the C's. Mothman's over in the M's".

Just ahead of the agents, Glaser stops walking and stares into the woods. "This isn't the way we came," he says.

He adds that he hasn't seen any of Fazekas's path markers in the past twenty minutes. Mulder counters that that's because he's been staring at the FLIR screen the whole time. Their discussion breaks down into a time- and energy-wasting argument; in the midst of which Scully notices a disturbance in the under-brush: something tearing through it, moving quickly but making no sound.

"Everybody stand still," says Scully. "There's something out there."

"Where?" says Mulder, drawing his gun.

Glaser scans the area with his heat-seeker. "Nothing," he says.

"I saw it," says Scully, leveling her own weapon. "The woods have gone silent again."

Something again bursts out of the underbrush—this time, behind them. They whirl toward the source of the rustling sound.

"I got it! I got it in my screen," says Glaser. "About thirty yards ahead just sitting there."

Mulder moves quickly off—alone—in its direction.

"Mulder?" says Scully.

"This is not a good idea!" bleats Glaser.

"Talk to him, Jeff!" says Scully.

Glaser glances at his screen. "Go to your right!" he yells.

The agent cautiously moves in that direction, going deeper into the brush. He sees nothing, but behind a tree, hidden from his view, a crude face melts into the bark pattern. The heat spot on the FLIR fades to black.

"Mulder, it's not on the screen," says Scully.

Mulder takes a few more cautious steps forward. His attention is drawn to a fallen log on which the crude shape of the creature is barely discernible. It leaps up and runs away through the bush. Mulder levels his gun and fires—once, twice, then three more times. There is no discernible result.

"Scully, I've lost him!" shouts Mulder.

But now his partner sees something rippling through the grass.

"I've got it!" says Scully, firing rapidly in its direction.

Then, silence. "Did you hit it?" asks Mulder, standing nearby.

"I don't know!" says Scully. "It just stopped."

"Where's Glaser?" asks Mulder.

Scully turns quickly to see the panicked civilian running headlong away from them. He reaches a fallen log—and is yanked down out of sight in exactly the same ways as Michelle Fazekas.

Only the two agents are left standing. "How many shots did you fire?" asks Mulder.

"Six. Maybe seven," says Scully.

"That your only clip?"

"Yep."

"Don't fire again," says Mulder, "until you're sure you're going to hit it. It may be trying to expend our advantage."

Scully says, edgily, "What the hell is it, Mulder?"

"I don't know. But whatever it is, it's smarter than us. At least out here."

Mulder turns to face Scully. At that moment he is yanked downward—exactly the same as the three victims before him.

"Mulder!" shouts Scully.

Mulder yells in response. She moves quickly toward the sound and sees him grappling desperately with something on the ground. She fires three shots. Something runs away. Her partner—dazed and bleeding—stares up at her.

That night the stars shine brightly

through the treetops. In a small clearing, Scully struggles to light a small pile of kindling by striking a spark from two small rocks. Nothing doing.

She turns to the injured and shivering Mulder, lying huddled against a log. "You were an Indian Guide," she says. "Help me out here."

"Indian Guide says maybe you should run to the store and get some matches," murmurs Mulder.

"I would," says Scully, abandoning her attempt, "but I left my wallet in the car."

She sits down next to Mulder, pulls out her gun, and removes a bullet from the clip. "If I can separate the shell from the casing," she explains, "maybe I can get the powder to ignite."

"Hmm. And maybe it'll start raining weenies and marshmallows," says Mulder.

Scully says, "Do I detect a hint of negativity?"

"No!" says Mulder. "Yes, actually. Yes."

Scully, still fiddling with her bullet, looks over in his direction. "Mulder, you need to keep warm. Your body's still in shock."

"I was told once that the best way to regenerate body heat," says Mulder, hopefully, "is to crawl naked into a sleeping bag with someone who's already naked."

"Maybe if it rains sleeping bags," she says, "you'll get lucky."

Scully smiles to herself, then thinks for a moment. "Have you ever thought seriously about dying?" she says.

"Yeah, once," says Mulder. "When I was at the Ice Capades."

Scully gives this remark the look of mild disdain it deserves. "When I was fighting my cancer," she continues, "I was angry at the injustice of it. And at its meaninglessness. And then I realized that that was the struggle: to give it meaning. To make sense of it. Like life."

Mulder's expression turns serious. He speaks in a low voice. "I think nature is supremely indifferent to whether we live or die," he says. "And if you're lucky you get seventy-five years. If you're really lucky you get eighty years, and if you're extraordinarily lucky you get to have fifty of those years with a decent head of hair."

Scully chuckles appreciatively.

"I guess it's like Las Vegas," she says. "The house always wins."

Finally, with a small cry of delight, Scully works the slug loose from its casing.

"Go, girl," says Mulder. He continues their metaphysical discussion. "Hey! Who did you identify with when you were a kid? Wilma or Betty?"

"I identified with Betty's bustline," says Scully.

"Yes," says Mulder. "I did, too."

Scully says, "I never could have been married to Barney, though. Kids were cute, though."

"But where," asks Mulder, "are they today?"

He lifts his head to watch Scully sprinkle gunpowder on the pathetic pile of kindling. She strikes the two rocks together. The gunpowder flares up, but only for a brief, spectacular moment. Then it dies out, the fire unlit. Scully turns to her partner.

"Mothmen?" she says, skeptically. "Really?"

"Yeah," says Mulder. "But there seem to be only two of them."

Scully moves over to Mulder, snuggles her warmer body next to his, and wraps her arm around him.

"I don't wanna wrestle," says Mulder.

Scully places his head in her lap.

"One of us has got to stay awake, Scully," he says.

"You sleep, Mulder."

"You get tired," says Mulder, closing his eyes, "you wake me."

"I'm not gonna get tired," says Scully.

Mulder says, "Why don't you sing something?"

"No, Mulder."

"Why don't you sing something. I'll know you're awake."

"Mulder, you don't want me to sing. I can't carry a tune."

"It doesn't matter. Just sing anything."

Silence. Then, Scully sings, "Jeremiah was a bullfrog. Was a good friend of mine. Never understood a single word he said, but I helped him drink his wine."

Scully was correct about her singing abilities.

"Chorus," murmurs Mulder.

"Joy to the world!" sings Scully. "All the boys and girls. Joy to the fishes in the deep blue sea. Joy to you and me."

Mulder falls asleep peacefully. Just outside the cold campground, two glowing red eyes blink open, watching.

The next morning Mulder wakes up to the sounds of the forest. He jerks himself upright when he realizes he is alone. He calls for Scully; she is a few yards away, gathering wild berries.

"I wouldn't go far," he says.

"Mulder," says Scully jauntily, "you haven't left my sight."

She walks back toward her still-sore partner. Mulder averts his eyes for a moment as she is jerked down from below with a muffled whimper.

Mulder looks up to find her gone. "Scully!" he shouts.

He hobbles painfully to the spot from which she disappeared. Scully's voice floats faintly back up to him.

"I'm down here! I fell down a hole!" she says.

Mulder peers down into a small cave sculpted out of the earth. Scully lies on the ground, her face smudged with dirt.

"Are you all right?" says Mulder.

"Yeah," says Scully, grimacing. "I landed on soft dirt. Kind of."

"What's down there?" asks Mulder.

"I don't know," she says. "It's pretty dark." She turns, startled to find herself face-to-face with Michelle Fazekas, who, unconscious or dead, has been lashed upright to a pole.

"I found Michelle," she says.

"Is she alive?"

Scully feels for a pulse. "Not for much longer. Mulder, we have to get her out of here."

Scully looks around her for a way out. She is in some kind of a high-ceilinged chamber, or a network of chambers. Other victims—or perhaps just their corpses—lie all around her. Some distance away, two red eyes blink back at her.

"Mulder," she says, her voice wavering,

"I'm not alone. And I don't have my weapon!"

Mulder drops his own gun down the hole. In the forest behind him the grass starts to ripple. Mulder turns to see this and, weaponless, drops himself down the hole. He falls with a painful thud next to Scully.

Scully keeps Mulder's gun aimed at the creature.

"Mulder, are you okay?" she says, turning slightly.

"Don't mind me," he groans. Then he spots something. "Scully!"

The creature is emerging from the shadows at them. Scully wheels on Mulder's warning and fires three shots in quick succession. On the ground lies the primitive-looking creature. It is not moving, and its eyes are shut.

"There has to be a scientific explanation for this," says Scully.

They cut Michelle Fazekas down from the pole. On it is carved the words AD NOCTUM. They carefully stack the bodies in a pile at the bottom of the hole. The topmost body lies approximately a quarter way up to the hole

"Too bad we don't have any office furniture," says Mulder.

"If they could see us now," replies Scully, wryly.

"Go, team!" adds Mulder. "Twenty more bodies and we win the honey-baked ham."

A faint voice wafts down to them.

"Agent Mulder! Agent Scully!" It is the voice of Agent Kinsley. He peers down into the cave.

"What are you doing down there?" he says.

Mulder and Scully look at each other. For the moment, they are at a loss for words.

Shortly afterward the entrance to the forest is swarming with policemen and paramedics. A barely conscious Michelle Fazekas, hooked up to an IV and covered by a thermal blanket, is carried out on a litter. Michael Asekoff is transported toward an ambulance in a similar fashion.

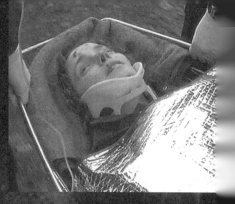

Walking next to him, near tears, are his wife and son. Mrs. Asekoff squeezes her husband's hand as he's loaded inside an ambulance. Then, sobbing with relief, she hugs her son.

Kinsley joins Stonecypher for a final huddle with the local authorities. Then Stonecypher walks over to a tattered and bandaged Mulder, who is gazing at the historically annotated tree stump.

"Well," says Kinsley, "we just got all the thanks while you did all the work."

"No. On the contrary, Agent Kinsley. We would never have gotten involved in this if not for you."

"Really?" says Kinsley, confused.

Before he can figure out this compliment, Mulder points to the marker on the stump indicating Ponce de Leon's arrival in Florida.

Mulder says, "There was something in the cave that Scully fell into. An inscription 'AD NOCTUM.'"

"That's, um, Latin," says Kinsley.

Mulder nods. "Meaning 'into darkness.' The Spanish conquistadors used to carve it into the posts they lashed the natives to. As a warning."

"So who are you saying wrote this?" says Kinsley.

"Ponce de Leon came here four hundred and fifty years ago looking for the Fountain of Youth," says Mulder.

Kinsley thinks for a second, then says incredulously, "You mean, you think that *that* body? The one that Agent Scully shot? No!"

"After four hundred years in the woods," says Mulder, "don't you think that they might have adapted perfectly to their environment."

Kinsley stares at his FBI colleague. "You're making this up," he says.

"Why would I do that?"

"Because you work on the X-Files," says Kinsley. "Because you just want to write off your motel."

Mulder nods understandingly. Agent Stonecypher approaches them to say that Search and Rescue has been unable to find either Jeff Glaser or the second predator.

"I wouldn't be surprised," says Mulder, "if they couldn't find either one of them."

Stonecypher furrows her brow. "Agent Mulder, I'm confused," she says. "Why would they come after the boy in the house that night?"

Mulder replies, "These predators have been in these woods a long, long time. They would have perceived any encroachment on their territory as an enemy, even a little kid like that."

"But that would mean they'd come after any of us who'd been in the woods. Wouldn't it?"

Mulder looks around him. "Where's Agent Scully?" he asks.

"Oh," says Stonecypher, "she got a lift back to the motel to pack up both your things."

"She did? Excuse me," says Mulder. He rushes off to their car, starts it, and drives away.

Kinsley watches him depart, obviously deeply concerned.

"My jacket's in that car," he says, finally.

Back at the motel Scully calmly unlocks her door and lets herself in. She packs up her toiletries, and opens up the closet.

Mulder roars up into the parking lot and runs to her motel room. He calls his partner's name and knocks frantically on the door. Scully sticks her head out of the adjacent room.

"Mulder, what's going on?" she says.

Mulder doesn't say anything. He slumps his shoulders in relief, moves past her into his room, and grabs their suitcases.

"Let's get out of here," he says.

Scully nods, confused. After a last backward glance, Mulder closes the door behind him.

Under the bed, two glowing red eyes appear.

back story:

The farther you stray from civilization, the more capricious—and cruel—the forces of nature can become. Somehow, this familiar-sounding truism was overlooked completely by the men and women behind "Detour."

The result: a waterlogged logistical nightmare.

"Nineteen days of shooting," groans Brett Dowler—who, after three seasons as the *X-Files*'s second-unit director, was getting a coveted first shot at directing an episode all his own. "It rained *every* day—incredible even for Vancouver. Almost every scene was outdoors, on location, in daylight. And since it was already deep into the fall, the days were short. We couldn't roll before eight A.M. or after six in the evening. Add in one hour for lunch and three hours to wrap and you can see what we were up against."

Since the normal shooting time allotted for one episode is only eight days, the long delay in completing "Detour" put severe strains on both the Vancouver-based producers and the L.A.-based post-production team. Actors' schedules were frantically juggled; chunks of first- and second-unit production time were borrowed from other episodes. Director/producer Kim Manners, who had just finished "Redux II," was brought in to back up Dowler, putting in one day as head of the second unit.

Eventually, the company bailed out completely from it's principal location in the Seymour Demonstration Forest in North Vancouver. One of the episode's pivotal scenes, in which Scully and the injured Mulder huddle around their campfire in the forest, was filmed in a hastily built stage set in an enclosed—and dry—sound stage.

"It was frustrating. I was sad," says Dowler. "You can't blame anybody for rain in this city, but still, when it starts turning into money, everybody remembers the holdups when the bills start coming in."

Others have equally vivid memories: such as makeup artist Laverne Basham, who recalls days and days of touching up the actors' moist makeup under umbrellas; sound mixer Michael Williamson, who struggled to keep the sound of rain dripping off nearby leaves out of the dialogue; camera operator Marty McInally, who stumbled into a hole, fell backward, and damaged his equipment while executing a particularly tricky Steadicam shot; and unit production manager Ron French, who discovered one morning that—for some unfathomable reason—someone had stolen $1,500 worth of fake rubber tree bark off a real Vancouver tree specially "dressed" for the occasion.

Frank Spotnitz, the episode's writer, says sheepishly, "I thought I'd come up with a very simple concept. Literally, one that was easy for the props people and all the other departments. It was just, well, *outside*."

The episode had its origins, says *The X-Files*'s co-executive producer, during a recent re-viewing of the film *Deliverance*. He recalls, "The idea of being stranded in a hostile environment is very interesting to me and so is the idea of something moving in the brush that you can't see. I wanted to insert Mulder and Scully into the story in an atypical way. I just ran with that."

In fact, after all the rain delays are wrung out of the equation, most of the people associated with "Detour" consider it a solid early-season episode. Not surprisingly, the most interesting special-effects challenge was provided by Spotnitz's concept of prehensile forest creatures able to disappear into their surroundings.

At first, the idea was to costume specially selected actors—cast from Vancouver's Central American community—in form-fitting "bark suits" that would nearly disappear against the foliage, then be further blended into the background in post-production. Makeup/special effects supervisor Toby Lindala had the bark suits meticulously constructed, but in the end the difficulties were such that most of what we see of the creatures was created electronically.

To computer generate the creatures' glowing red eyes, visual effects supervisor Laurie Kallsen-George blended and modified a number of digitized eyeball images, including those of her family's female half-Labrador retriever, Danny, whom she photographed in her backyard while shining a flashlight in the dog's face.

Other inspired improvisations include the agents' Dilbertian "team builder" exercise, which was contributed by supervising producer Vince Gilligan during the rewrite process. Glaser's FLIR device was actually a Sony Watchman, modified by propmaster Ken Hawryliw and hooked up to an infrared camera.

And Scully sings! In Frank Spotnitz's original draft Dana Scully's campfire song was Hank Williams's "I'm So Lonesome I Could Cry." However, his boss Chris Carter requested something "off the wall and strange"—and the immortal "Joy To The World" was substituted.

"In retrospect, the song was perfect," says Frank Spotnitz. Indeed, Gillian Anderson's rendition made such an impression that she was asked to sing it again—and did so—during a personal appearance at the *X-Files* Expo in New York City last May.

As for Anderson herself, she recalls "Detour" vividly as being "a pain in the butt." She also maintains steadfastly that she remained totally in character throughout it.

"In that scene I sang *intentionally* badly," she says. "In real life I can do a lot better than that."

⊗

Anthony Rapp, who played the nerdy technician Jeff Glaser, is one of the original stars of the Broadway musical *Rent*. He took ten days off from the show to work on *The X-Files*.

⊗

The character Michelle Fazekas was named after co-executive producer Frank Spotnitz's assistant.

The actress who played the part, Colleen Flynn, was best known for playing a young wife who died giving birth in a memorable 1995 episode of *ER*.

christmas carol

While spending the Christmas
holiday with her family, Scully
receives a mysterious phone call.
She is summoned to help a desperately
ill child, whose tragic history is
inexplicably linked to her own.

EPISODE: 5X05
FIRST AIRED: December 7, 1997
EDITOR: Heather MacDougall
WRITTEN BY: Vince Gilligan & John Shiban
& Frank Spotnitz
DIRECTED BY: Peter Markle

GUEST STARS:
Pat Skipper (Bill Scully, Jr.)
Sheila Larken (Mrs. Scully)
Karri Turner (Tara Scully)
John Pyper-Ferguson (Detective Kresge)
Rob Freeman (Marshall Sim)
Lauren Diewold (Emily Sim)
Melinda McGraw (Melissa Scully)
Joey Shea (Young Dana—1968)
Zoë Anderson (Young Dana—1976)
Rebecca Codling (Young Melissa—1976)
Gerard Plunkett (Dr. Ernest Calderon)
Patricia Dahlquist (Susan Chambliss)
Ryan de Boer (Young Bill, Jr.—1968)
Walter Marsh (Pathologist)
Jo-Anne Fernandes (Forensic Technician)
Dan Shea (Deputy)
Gregor Sneddon (FBI Courier)
Eric Breker (Dark-Suited Man #1)
Stephen Mendel (Dark-Suited Man #2)

PRINCIPAL SETTINGS:
San Diego and Chula Vista, California

On a sunlit tabletop

a nativity scene of fine porcelain is lovingly arrayed by Tara Scully, Dana Scully's sister-in-law. Tara is standing in the living room of the San Diego home she shares with her husband, U.S. Navy Lieutenant Commander Bill Scully, Jr. (last seen in 5X03).

The front door opens and Bill Scully, Dana Scully, and their mother enter. Mrs. Scully hugs Tara and exclaims happily over her very pregnant state.

Bill Scully says, "Sorry about the digs, Mom. I know you were hoping like hell you'd never have to spend another night in base housing."

"Are you kidding?" she replies. "This is wonderful."

Scully agrees, although somewhat less enthusiastically. "This is the exact same layout as *our* old house."

"That's the navy for you," says Bill.

"Bill tells me, Mom," says Tara, "that you're going to be sleeping in your old room, and the nursery's going to be Dana and Melissa's room?"

Scully winces slightly at the mention of her murdered older sister. She remains downstairs while the other three go up to their rooms. The phone rings. She calls after her brother, but he is out of earshot. She picks up the receiver.

"Scully residence," she says.

"Dana," says a woman's voice.

"Yes. I'm sorry. Who is this?" says Scully briskly.

"Dana," says the woman, in an urgent whisper. "She needs your help. She needs you, Dana. Go to her."

The line goes dead. "Who is this?" says Scully.

Shaken, she thinks for a second, then quickly clicks the cradle switch and dials another number.

"FBI San Diego," says a female voice at the other end.

Scully identifies herself and gives her FBI badge number. "Can you transfer me to your sound agent, please?" she says. "I'd like to trace the last number that was dialed in to this phone."

In an upscale San Diego neighborhood Bill Scully—his sister sitting next to him in the passenger seat—stops his Cherokee in front of a house swarming with policemen. An ambulance is parked outside. Scully walks through the front door and heads upstairs to the crime scene. She is stopped by a local cop, Detective Kresge.

"Whoa, whoa, who are you?" he says.

"Scully, FBI. Can you tell me what's going on?"

"Uh, no offense, 'Scully, FBI,'" he says defensively, "but what's it to you?"

Scully tells him about the phone call she received.

"When was this?" says Kresge.

"About twenty minutes ago."

The detective's eyes narrow. "I've been here thirty minutes. I guarantee you that no one's called out to you or anybody else. Phone's off the hook."

Scully glances at a hallway table and sees that this is indeed the case. "Please," she says softly, "can you tell me what happened here?"

Kresge stares at Scully for a moment, then leads her into a bathroom. A woman's lifeless arm hangs over the bathtub, which is brimming over with blood. Scully edges closer. A blond woman—dead—reclines in the red-tinged water.

"This is Mrs. Roberta Sim, age forty, suicide. She's been dead at least three hours. You got a call from her? She must have dialed 1–800-THE GREAT BEYOND."

Shaken, Scully pushes her way through the forensic techs to the front porch. Her brother meets her there.

"What's going on?" says Bill Scully. "They're joking about you getting a call from a dead woman."

Scully says, "I thought it was a dead woman, just not the one in there."

"What are you talking about?" says Bill Scully.

"I know it's not possible, Bill," says Scully, shaken, "but it sounded just like her."

"Who?"

"Our sister. Melissa."

A few minutes later Scully, who has

re-entered the house, watches as a policeman replaces the hallway phone on its hook. She peers down a hallway and into a kitchen, where a 40ish man, Marshall Sim, is carrying a little girl on his hip, hugging her protectively.

Scully's gaze is broken by Kresge, who pockets his cell phone as he approaches.

"I don't know what to tell you," he says, in hushed tones. "Pac Bell doesn't confirm that there was an incoming call from this address to your brother's house. From this end, they show no outgoing call. Plus they confirm the phone here's been off the hook for the last three hours."

"What's their explanation?" says Scully.

"A records mix-up," says Kresge. "A software glitch. It's obviously just some kind of mistake. Anyway, I've got to wrap things up. Talk to the husband."

Scully, unconvinced, says nothing.

"Listen," adds Kresge, "weird phone calls aside, this is pretty straightforward. A lot of people check themselves out around Christmas time."

Scully lingers for a few moments, staring sadly at the little girl, until Kresge shuts the kitchen door for privacy.

At Bill Scully's house later that evening the family is gathered in the dining room, sitting down to a festive meal amidst the bright holiday decorations. All are happy and animated, except for Scully, who is plainly troubled. She excuses herself, walks to the hallway telephone, and punches in a familiar number.

The phone rings in Mulder's darkened apartment. Keys jingle outside the front door and Mulder bursts in, dressed in jogging clothes. He picks up the phone just in time.

"Hello? Hello?" he says.

At the other end Scully stands mute, uncertain. Paralyzed.

"Hello?" says Mulder. Scully hangs up the phone, returns to the dining room, and takes her seat.

"Everything okay?" asks her brother.

"Yes," says Scully, a bit too quickly and emphatically, and passes the biscuits.

"Oh. Ow!" exclaims the pregnant Tara.

All at the table look toward her, concerned. "That was a good one!" Tara says with a laugh.

"Was he kicking?" asks Bill, Jr.

"More like kick-boxing!" says Tara. She turns to Mrs. Scully. "You had boys and girls—so which ones kicked more?"

Mrs. Scully smiles warmly and turns to her daughter. "Oh, I had some pretty tough girls," she says.

Tara beams, but it's plain that this line of conversation is making Scully desperately unhappy.

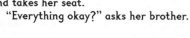

"You know, I can't believe I'm about to say this," says Tara, "but big and fat as I am now, I can't wait to have more." She adds, "This is a baby, our son. It kind of gives everything new meaning. I can't help but think that life before that is somehow less, a prelude."

Scully lowers her head, near tears. Later that evening Scully, still upset, shares the dishwashing chores with her mother.

"Dana, what's the matter?" says Mrs. Scully.

"Nothing," she replies.

Scully stops and, with an effort, turns to face the older woman.

"Mom, I'm very happy for Bill and Tara," she says. She pauses, gathering strength to relate the rest. "Several months ago (in 4X15) I learned—as a result of my abduction, of what they did to me—that I cannot conceive a child."

Mrs. Scully immediately embraces her daughter. "I'm so sorry," she says.

"It's okay," says Scully, tearfully. "I just never realized how much I wanted it, until I couldn't have it."

That night Scully sleeps fitfully in the guest room, already fitted out with a crib and toys for the baby on the way. The door to the room swings open, revealing young Bill, Jr., about eight years old, and young Dana, around four. The room is now decorated as a typical mid-sixties girls' bedroom.

Bill, Jr. is angry at his sister. "Dana, where is it? Where's that rabbit?" he says.

"I'm not telling you!" shouts Dana.

"I'm gonna find that rabbit and *cook* it! I'm gonna turn it into stew!"

"No, you're not!" says Dana, shoving him hard.

"Rabbit stew here I go!" says Bill, Jr.

"You're not gonna find him! *Bill!*"

Little Dana hurries down some rickety stairs into the basement. Looking carefully behind her, she walks into a dark corner and pulls out a steel *Lassie* lunch box. As she opens it her face registers shock. Inside is the pet rabbit, dead, clearly suffocated inside the lunch box. Maggots writhe over its surface. Dana slams the lid shut. Sensing somebody else in the basement, she gazes behind her. On the stairway, gazing back at her, is another little girl. It is the little girl from the Sim house. A strange chirping sound is heard.

Scully is jolted awake. She switches on the lamp on her nightstand. It is 2:21 A.M. She fumbles in her suitcase, pulls out her ringing cell phone, zips up the antenna, and answers it.

"Scully," she says.

"She needs your help," says a familiar woman's voice.

"Who is this?" says Scully. "Why are you doing this?"

"Go to her," says the voice.

The connection is broken. Standing motionless, Scully slowly lowers the phone from her ear.

Sometime later that night, Scully rings the front doorbell of the Sim house. Inside, lights are still on. The door is opened.

"Mr. Sim," says Scully, "I'm very sorry for your loss, and I'm sorry to disturb you at this hour—"

"What do you want?" asks Sim, abruptly.

Scully relates the call she had just received and tells him that again she has traced it to his telephone.

Sim shakes his head impatiently. "I have no earthly idea what you're talking about."

Scully says, urgently, "This is the sec-

ond time today this has happened, and I would really like to get to the bottom of it."

She peers past Sim. Inside the house two dark-suited men converse. They stare at Scully for a second, catching her eye, then resume their discussion. Sim leans forward, blocking her view.

Sim says, "The detective told me. Something about a screwup with the phones."

He adds, with mounting anger, "No one's called you from here. Not earlier today, and certainly not tonight. You can't imagine how bad a day this has been for my daughter and myself."

Scully says, "I understand—"

"Well, if you understand, you'll stop coming around upsetting me with this nonsense. *Please.*"

He shuts the door in Scully's face. She walks back to Bill, Jr.'s Cherokee. From a high window, the little Sim girl gazes down inscrutably, watching her go.

Early the next morning Scully enters a San Diego PD precinct house. She stands in the bullpen area, hesitant. Detective Kresge comes up behind her.

"Scully, FBI!" he says, bemused. "What can I do for you at this ungodly hour?"

Scully says, grimly, "I'd like to see everything you have on the Roberta Sim case."

"The Roberta Sim case," says Kresge, a bit impatiently. "There is no Roberta Sim case. It's a simple suicide. We sorta went through this before, you and I, didn't we?"

Scully is undeterred. "Whatever you wish to call it," she says, "I'd appreciate seeing everything you have."

Kresge stares at Scully as if trying to figure out her strange obsession.

Scully smiles slightly. "In the spirit of the season?" she asks.

A few minutes later Scully opens the box containing the Sim records. Kresge stands by, curious. The FBI agent studies a photo of Mrs. Sim's slashed wrist, then digs deeper into the file.

"So, what are you looking for?" says Kresge. "Can you even tell me?"

Scully keeps reading. "It says here your precinct visited the Sims' before. Two weeks ago—a domestic disturbance call."

CHRISTINE DOB: 11/2/94: BIRTH RECORDS
SEALED PER CALIFORNIA ADOPTION SERVICES.

She picks up her cell phone, calls FBI
headquarters in Washington, and asks to
have the case file on Melissa Scully sent
to her as soon as possible. She hangs up,
removes her glasses, and rubs her eyes
wearily.

In a funeral parlor, in the late 1960s,
young Dana Scully is holding the hand
of a faceless, black-suited adult. He is
leading her down the aisle, through a
group of seated mourners, toward a
silver-handled coffin on a white altar.
Blood-tinged water leaks through the
coffin lid; a bright red puddle blossoms
on the floor directly in front of it.

Young Dana reaches the coffin and
looks down. Blood-tinged water fills it to
the brim. Lying beneath the surface is
Roberta Sim. Her sightless eyes open.

Young Dana, startled, takes a step
back. She turns and looks at the adult
who still holds her hand. It is Marshall
Sim. He turns to her.

"Dana?" he says, in the voice of Bill
Scully.

Scully jolts awake, lifting her head
from the table. Her brother looks down at
her.

"Is this where you stayed the night?"
he says.

"Yeah, some of it," says Scully.

"It's supposed to be a vacation," says
Bill, Jr. "What're you working on that's
so important?"

"Just some unfinished business," says
Scully.

He asks her to join the family
excursion that morning. Scully begs off,
promising to meet them later for lunch.

"All right, lunch," says her brother, his
forced smile registering concern and
irritation. "We'll hold you to that."

At the San Diego precinct house
Kresge looks up from his desk and smiles
wryly.

"Agent Scully," he says, looking at his
watch. "It's been what—four hours? I was
getting worried."

Scully briskly asks to order an autopsy
on Roberta Sim's body. "There's a possibility she was murdered," she says.

Kresge's shoots her a look of pure
skepticism. "What?" he says. "You get
another phone call?"

Kresge says, "We sent a unit because
the neighbors complained they were
screaming at each other. It wasn't a
happy household. Happy people don't kill
themselves."

Scully turns a page and finds something else. "They ran a tox screen?"

Kresge says, "It's just procedure."

Scully tells Kresge that the test turned
up high levels of a drug called sumatriptan.

"It's some kind of new migraine medicine," says Kresge. "Apparently, you take
too much of it and you're wearing a cloud
for a hat. I figured she anesthetized herself, then—"

He mimes cutting his own wrist, and
adds, "We found a bunch of empty sample packets in the bathroom trash. A couple more in her purse."

Scully lifts Roberta's purse from the
evidence box. She pulls out several
unopened sumatriptan samples and then
a portrait of the little girl. She studies it
closely, drawn to the image.

"I'd like to borrow this," she says.

Inside Bill, Jr.'s house later that night,
Scully removes a thick family photo album
from a sideboard. She rustles through the
pages, quickly finding what she's looking
for. It is a picture of her sister, marked
MELISSA IN NAGOYA FARMERS MARKET,
JAPAN 1966.

She pulls out the photograph of the
Sim girl and places it next to Melissa's.
The two little girls are uncannily similar.

Later that day Scully sits at the dining
room table, accessing via modem a database of San Diego birth records. She
types "Sim, Emily," into her laptop. The
reply comes back immediately: SIM, EMILY

Scully brushes this off and tells him that she suspects Marshall Sim of murdering his wife.

"He's got an ironclad alibi," says Kresge. "Mr. Sim was at the doctor's office with his daughter. They were there all morning. We checked."

Scully replies, "I took another look at the police photos this morning. There were no hesitation cuts on Roberta Sim's wrist. Suicide victims seldom make the fatal cut on their first try."

"Seldom, but not always," says Kresge. "Is that all you got?"

"No. Why was the phone off the hook when you got to the Sims' house?"

Kresge says, shrugging, "The wife took it off. I'm guessing she didn't want to be interrupted."

Scully says, leaning toward him, "Your incident report says the husband called the police when he discovered his wife dead. But if the phone was off the hook when you arrived, how did he call you?"

Kresge says, "What are you suggesting?"

"I'm suggesting," says Scully, "that there are questions here that beg further investigation."

At an autopsy bay Scully—observed by a dour, elderly pathologist—pokes around purposely inside Roberta Sim's internal organs.

"Stomach contents," says Scully, "appear to include coffee, whole wheat toast, and cantaloupe. No medicine tablets. Empty packets of sumatriptan succinate were found. But I see no evidence that there were any pills ingested."

The pathologist says, "Obviously they were. Sumatriptan showed up on the tox screen."

"Then why didn't it show up in her stomach?" says Scully.

"It was absorbed into the bloodstream."

"No. I don't believe that the absorption would be that complete. Not that close to her death."

"Then how did the sumatriptan get into her bloodstream, Ms. Scully?"

At the precinct

house Detective Kresge contemplates his FBI colleague wearily.

"A needle puncture," he says.

"On the heel of her right foot," replies Scully, intensely. She adds that it was extremely tiny and easy to miss. "It was meant to be overlooked. I believe that this woman was injected, anaesthetized so she wouldn't fight back, and her suicide was staged."

Kresge turns to the pathologist, who is also present. "What do you think?" he says.

"It's a possibility," admits the doctor, with a shrug. "But then again it's possible that this woman simply stepped on a tack and the rest is simply blue-sky conjecture."

"I say," says Scully, "that it justifies opening a murder investigation."

Late that afternoon a squad of policemen and detectives is making a thorough and highly obtrusive search of Marshall Sim's living room. Sim, extremely agitated, arrives and zeroes in on the person he believes is behind his persecution. He walks quickly to where Scully is standing.

"This is your doing!" he says. "You didn't have the decency to leave me and my daughter alone."

Scully says, coolly, "Mr. Sim, where is you daughter now?"

Sim struggles for control. "She's at a friend's house. Thank God she's not here to see this."

Scully says nothing. A female forensic tech arrives, holding a thin, disposable-type hypodermic needle in a see-through plastic evidence baggie. She tells Kresge that the syringe was found in his trash.

"You got an explanation for this?" says Kresge.

"Yes," says Sim, immediately. "My daughter suffers from a severe form of anemia. She requires daily injections."

Scully replies that they'll check out this alibi. She takes the forensic tech aside, hands her the hypo, and orders the contents analyzed, including a PCR test to determine whose blood is on the needle.

The tech nods and moves off. Momentarily

PRINT   INFO
Records Of Live Birth
San Diego County Department Of Health

SEARCH BY DATE, YEAR, PLACE OF BIRTH OR BY NAME
Click here to see text version
SEARCH

ENTER SIM, EMILY

About This Web Site   Frequently

idle, Scully looks through a dining room window. Something catches her eye: two dark-suited men, whom we recognize as Sim's visitors from the night before, sitting in a gray sedan across the street. One of them realizes they've been spotted. The other man calmly puts the car in gear and drives away.

That night Scully returns to Bill Jr.'s darkened house. She holds a large manila envelope; on the dining room table is another, larger one containing Melissa Scully's FBI file. She opens it and removes a clear plastic sheet with what looks like gray smudges on it. She opens the envelope she came in with; it also contains a PCR print. Scully compares the two by placing one atop the other. The smudges are nearly identical.

"Dana? Are you all right?"

It is Mrs. Scully, who reminds her daughter that it is two in the morning and that, to everyone's disappointment, she missed her lunch date.

Scully looks up, greatly upset, from the PCRs in her hand.

"Mom, sit down," she says.

Struggling to keep her voice under control, she adds, "The woman who committed suicide has an adopted daughter named Emily. I got a sample of Emily's blood and had the lab run a test on her DNA. This is Emily's. This is Melissa's, which we ran during her murder investigation. They match."

Mrs. Scully shakes her head, uncomprehending. "What does that mean, 'they match'?" she says.

"It means," says Scully. "That this little girl—Emily—is Melissa's daughter."

A few moments later Scully is showing her still-stunned mother the photos of young Melissa and Emily Sim. Mrs. Scully protests that many young girls look alike; Scully adds that genetic markers are definitive proof and that the PCR test indicates there is a 60 percent chance that Melissa is

Emily's mother. Mrs. Scully is still skeptical; Scully adds that she's ordered a more definitive test, an RFLP, that will be finished in a couple of days.

"Dana, I'm already sure," says Mrs. Scully, distraught and a little angry. "Your sister never had a baby. She would have told me."

Scully sits close to Mrs. Scully and looks her in the eye. "You remember about four years ago, when Melissa took off?" she says. "She traveled up and down the West Coast. We didn't know where she was half of the time."

Mrs. Scully says, "You think she was pregnant and she didn't want us to know?"

Scully says, whispering urgently, "That was 1994. Emily was born that November. She could have given her up for adoption and none of us would have even known."

Mrs. Scully shakes her head, upset. "Dana, listen to me," she says. "I know what you're going through."

"Mom," says Scully, frowning, "this has nothing to do with what I'm going through."

Mrs. Scully gazes at her daughter sympathetically. "It happened to me," she says. "When your father died, it was a long time before he left me. I saw him in my dreams. The phone would ring, and just for a moment I'd be sure it was his voice.

"And now you're doing the same thing. With Melissa. You're seeing her in this child. But that does not make this child my granddaughter."

Scully turns away from her mother.

Mrs. Scully continues, "We're still connected to them, Dana. Even after they're gone."

That night Scully sleeps fitfully. In a house the same dimensions as Bill Scully's, two teenage girls enter the living room, giggling. One of them is a skinny redhead, around twelve or thirteen, in her nightgown. It is young Dana Scully.

"Look at all the presents!" says Dana.

Her older sister Melissa joins her at the base of the Christmas tree. "This one's for me," says Dana.

"You wish! That's for Billy, you dope!"

Dana picks out a flat, gift-wrapped package. "This is gotta be it!" she says, happily. "It's gotta be *Hotel California*!"

Melissa tells her to pipe down, but Dana is undaunted. She holds up a small box wrapped in red paper.

"I wonder what this is?" she says.

"I don't know," says her sister, "but I got one, too."

Their mother says, "You don't have to shake it, Dana. You can open those now. It's too late."

A younger Mrs. Scully, in bathrobe and slippers, is watching them from the stairway. The girls turn toward her guiltily. But she is smiling. They unwrap their respective presents. They are identical gold crosses.

"Thanks, Mom," says Melissa, genuinely pleased.

Mrs. Scully says, "Your grandmother gave me a cross just like that when I was about your age."

She fastens it around her younger daughter's neck.

"It's pretty," says Dana.

"It means God is with you," says Mrs. Scully. "He'll watch over you wherever you go."

Standing in her mother's place, the adult Dana Scully looks down fondly at her younger self. Young Dana looks back up at her, troubled at the sight. A loud knocking interrupts their moment together.

"Dana?" says Tara Scully.

Her sister-in-law awakens, and raises her head from the pillow.

"Sorry," says Tara. "There's a detective here to see you."

Scully, dressed in T-shirt and jeans, joins an excited Detective Kresge in the kitchen.

"Interesting tidbit on Mr. Sim," he says. "Bank deposits. Large ones. Thirty thousand dollars a pop. Three times in the last eighteen months. All the checks have been made out to his wife. The last one was deposited yesterday. *Apres morte.*"

"Where did the check come from?" says Scully.

"A pharmaceutical firm in Chula Vista," says Kresge.

On an outside walkway at the campus headquarters of Transgen Industries, Scully and Kresge intercept Dr. Ernest Calderon. They identify themselves and tell him of the death of Roberta Sim. A look of tightly controlled shock crosses his face.

"You knew Mrs. Sim?" asks Scully.

Calderon tells her that her daughter Emily is a patient at his clinic.

"What were you treating her for?" asks Scully.

"Ah, she's a subject in one of our clinical trials," says Calderon. "We're developing gene therapies for several blood disorders. She's suffering from a rare type of autoimmune hemolytic anemia. She's a very sick little girl."

Scully asks, "What's her prognosis?"

Calderon is evasive. "I'm afraid I really couldn't say. These are ongoing double-blind trials. It could be years before we have any results."

Kresge asks whether Transgen was paying the Sim family for Emily's participation in the test and if so, how they found her. Calderon admits that large payments were made and says that she was brought to their attention by her father.

"Then why were the checks made out to her mother?" asks Scully.

Calderon answers reluctantly. "Ah, how should I put this? These payments were a gesture of goodwill toward Mrs. Sim. She wasn't completely convinced that our experimental treatment was the way to go."

Scully asks, "She wanted to pull Emily from the program?"

Calderon nods. "She filed the paperwork, but her husband later withdrew it."

Scully begins to put the pieces together. "Dr. Calderon," she says, "did you ever prescribe sumatriptan injections to Emily as part of her treatment?"

"No, no. I prescribed them for the husband, when he mentioned he was suffering from migraines."

At the Sim home later that day Scully watches as Kresge, accompanied by a squad of detectives and patrolmen, places Marshall Sim under arrest for the murder of his wife.

"Are you out of your mind?" shouts Sim.

"Where's Emily?" asks Scully.

She walks to the stairwell and looks up. Emily is standing at the top of the stairs. The girl is stoic, her eyes revealing nothing.

A while later Scully leads Emily by the hand to a waiting van and carefully buckles her into the child seat. Emily reaches up to touch the cross around Scully's neck.

"You like that, huh?" says Scully, gently.

Emily nods. Scully removes the cross from around her own neck and fastens it around the little girl's.

A social worker places her hand on Scully's shoulder. It's time to go.

"I'll see you soon," says Scully. The door is closed, the engine started, and Emily— looking sadly through the window at Scully— is driven away.

At a holiday party in Bill Scully Jr.'s house, several dozen friends and neighbors sip eggnog and converse happily—all except Scully, who sits, deep in thought, in a corner. Her brother notices her.

"Dana, can you give me a hand in the kitchen?" he says.

Scully agrees. They move off into the dining area.

"I need you to tell me what's going on," says Bill Scully. "You're not here, Dana, you're a million miles away. I thought you came here to see the family."

"I did," concedes Scully.

Bill Scully says, impatiently, "Well, I thought that this other thing was

resolved. I thought you caught the guy who murdered that woman."

"We did," says Scully, joylessly.

"Then it's about the girl, isn't it?" says Bill Scully. "Mom told me. You really think that Melissa had a baby?"

"Yes, I do," says Scully.

"That she called you from beyond the grave to tell you that? This sounds like something that partner of yours would say."

His dig angers Scully. "Bill," she says, "it does not matter where that phone call came from. What matters is that there is a little girl who needs my help."

Bill, Jr. says, just as determinedly, "This isn't about any little girl, Dana. It's about you. It's about some emptiness, some void inside yourself that you're trying to fill."

Scully stiffens. "Bill, I don't expect you to understand," she says. "But I am not going to stand here and justify my motives."

They glare at each other. Mrs. Scully approaches them and tells Scully that she has a phone call. It's Detective Kresge.

"Merry Christmas, Agent Scully," he says. "Got a little present for you. Marshall Sim just confessed."

He adds that Sim's signed statement includes an admission that he was in the house at the time of his wife's "suicide."

Scully asks, "What about the witnesses that placed him at the doctor's office at the time of the murder?"

Kresge says, "I guess they were mistaken."

Scully says, coming to another important realization, "Maybe they weren't."

Later that day Scully drives up to the guard gate of the county lockup. She glances to her left and sees the two dark-suited men, in their gray sedan, exiting the facility. She reacts, flinging open her car door and running after them. But it's no use. They're gone. Inside the jail Scully walks quickly with her police escort toward Sim's cell.

"Did they identify themselves?" she asks.

"They said they were his lawyers," says the deputy.

"How long were they here?"

"Ten, fifteen minutes. Tops."

They reach the cell and he peers through the small observation window. Sim is hanging from a crude noose—made out of his pants legs—attached to the top of his bunk bed. The deputy curses, unlocks the door, and struggles to lift Sim up and untie the noose. It is too late.

Later that day a despondent Scully enters the front door of the festively decorated Scully home. A cheery fire blazes in the fireplace.

Bill Scully appears unexpectedly behind Scully, startling her. He notices his sister's mood. "What happened?" he says.

Scully says, "Marshall Sim, Emily's adoptive father, is dead. They made it look like a suicide. Just like his wife."

"My God! Do you know who did it?" says Bill Scully.

"No," whispers Scully.

"Do you think it has something to do with that little girl?"

Scully says, "I think it might."

Bill Scully looks sympathetically at Scully for a moment, then leads his sister to an upstairs bedroom. He retrieves a photograph from a bureau drawer, and hands it to her. It is of Melissa, slim and smiling, in her twenties.

"Look at the date on the back," says Bill.

It reads OCTOBER 7, 1994.

"Does Melissa look pregnant to you in that picture?" he says. "That's about four weeks before the girl was born."

"Bill, that doesn't prove anything," says Scully, agitated. "Melissa didn't have to get pregnant to have a baby. There's in vitro fertilization. There's surrogate motherhood—"

Her brother interrupts her. "Dana, listen to yourself. You're creating this whole scenario to fulfill a dream."

"What dream?"

"To have a child," he says. This hits Scully hard.

"Look, I understand," adds Bill, with a mixture of urgency and compassion. "God

knows Tara and I tried for years. But making this girl into Melissa's daughter is not the way. You're only going to end up hurting yourself."

Scully, defiant, says nothing. The doorbell rings, and her brother answers it. It is the country social worker we've seen previously. Her name is Susan Chambliss.

"It's about the adoption," she says. Scully, who has come to the foyer to greet her, leads her toward the dining room. Bill Scully looks on disapprovingly.

A few minutes later Scully—glancing down at Emily's case file spread out before her—looks as if she's just had her face slapped. She struggles to hide a rush of emotion.

"I don't understand," she says. "I think I have a right to know why you're rejecting my application."

"It's not mine to accept or reject, Dana," says Chambliss, not unkindly. "We only make recommendations to the judge. And at this point, I would advise against you becoming an adoptive parent."

She adds, "You're a single woman who's never been married or had a long term relationship. You're in a high-stress, time-intensive, and dangerous occupation. One that I sense you're deeply committed to and one which would overnight become a secondary priority to the care and well-being of this child. I'm not sure that this is a sacrifice you're prepared to make."

Scully looks up, near tears. "It is one I have given a great deal of thought to," she says. She adds, "To be honest, I've started to question my priorities since I was first diagnosed with cancer. And I feel I've been given a second chance."

She is crying now. "Ever since I was a child I've never allowed myself to get too close to people. I've avoided emotional attachments. Perhaps I've always been so afraid of death and dying that any connection seemed like a bad thing. Something that wouldn't last. But I don't feel that way any more."

Chambliss gazes at Scully for a moment, then speaks.

"I know that you are a trained physician," she says, "and are aware of Emily's medical condition. I want to stress to you, Dana, Emily is a special needs child. According to her doctors, her condition is incurable. She requires constant care, both medical and emotional." She adds, "The good news is, you have first-hand experience of grave illness. The bad news is, you'd have to relive it through the eyes of a child."

Scully tries to wipe away her tears. "I realize that," she says. "And I feel that I am ready."

Chambliss turns away, gathers up her files, and tells Scully that she will review the file and make a final recommendation.

Emotionally drained, Scully sinks down onto the couch in front of the still-crackling fire. A hand reaches out, touching the back of her neck.

"Dana . . ." whispers a woman's voice.

"Melissa?" says Scully.

"You know anybody else who's up?" she replies. It is indeed Scully's sister, looking just as she did on Christmas Eve, 1991.

"I couldn't sleep," says Scully.

Melissa sits down next to her bathrobe-clad sister. She is wearing the same dress as in the photograph. "You worried about Quantico? Or who's going to get the most presents this year?"

Scully says, "I guess I'm afraid of making a big mistake. I could tell Dad sure thinks I am."

"Well," says Melissa, "It's not his life, Dana."

"I know that. But you know what? When I started med school it felt so right. It just seemed that was where I was supposed to be. And then by the time I graduated I knew it was wrong. But now the FBI feels right. What if that's wrong, too?"

Her older sister smiles. "There's no right or wrong," she says. "Life is just a path. Follow your heart and it will take you where you're supposed to go."

Scully says, frowning, "God, you sound like a greeting card." She adds, "I don't believe in fate. I think we have to choose our own path."

Melissa's expression turns serious. "Well, just don't mistake the path with what's really important in life."

"Which is what?"

"The people you're going to meet along the way. You don't know who you will meet when you join the FBI. You don't know how your life is going to change or how you're going to change the lives of others."

Melissa gazes warmly at her little sister.

"Hey! Good morning!" says Tara Scully.

She walks over to Scully, who has been sleeping on the couch, and wishes her a Merry Christmas. Bill Scully and Mrs. Scully follow suit.

"She was always first up on Christmas morning," says Bill, Jr. "Couldn't wait to get at those presents."

As they begin to dig into their holiday treasure trove the doorbell rings. It is an FBI courier with a package for Scully. She signs for it and wishes him a happy holiday, too.

Inside the envelope is a sheaf of documents, including an FBI memo, in an official file. Scully looks through them quickly. Her face registers dull shock. Seeing her, the others in the dining room fall silent.

"What is it?" says Mrs. Scully.

"It's the DNA tests on Emily Sim's blood," says Scully.

"What does it say?" asks Bill Scully.

"It says definitively," says Scully, "that Melissa's not Emily's mother, but that they found striking genetic similarities between Emily and Melissa. So many," she adds, "that they ran a test against another sample that they already had."

"What sample?" says Mrs. Scully.

"What are you trying to say?" says Bill Scully, Jr.

Scully looks up from the lab report. "According to this," she says, nearly unable to speak, "I am Emily's mother."

to be continued...

back story:

Necessity was the real mother of this moving and revelatory episode. During the second week of October, David Duchovny was scheduled to be away from Vancouver promoting his movie *Playing God.* Accordingly, a preseason decision was made to postpone shooting "The Post-Modern Prometheus," which featured Duchovny heavily and was scheduled to air fifth in the order, and film a Scully-only episode instead.

But how best to explain Mulder's absence *and* explore the character of his complicated but often-buttoned up partner?

"As happened a lot of times this season, we were thrown a curve ball," says "Christmas Carol" co-writer (with Frank Spotnitz and Vince Gilligan) and *X-Files* co-producer John Shiban. "And in figuring out how to deal with it we actually took the show to an interesting place that we might not have visited otherwise."

The writers' initial inspiration came from the calendar. Episode 5X05 was scheduled to air in the midst of the holiday season. "We'd been talking about doing a Christmas show together," says Shiban, and one day we were kicking around ideas and we realized we'd all seen—and loved—the 1951 British movie version of Dickens's *A Christmas Carol* that starred Alastair Sim. We all thought: 'This is a classic story of self-examination and rebirth, etc.' And we decided to put Scully into a situation like that, somehow."

After one frustrating dead end attempting to closely parallel Dickens's classic story, the trio decided that instead of encountering ghosts, Scully would be "visited" by earlier versions of her family members and herself, and would be taken on an emotional journey by her descendant, as well.

"We loved the idea of having pieces of her past tied to the decision-making process in the present," says Shiban. "Just as Scrooge had to decide, as he looks at what he's won so far in his life. Has he made the right decisions? Has he been greedy? Has he avoided helping his loved ones when he could have? And can he undo that? Can he change?"

Shiban adds, "In Scully's case the choices are a bit different especially since she's just come through cancer. 'Was it the right thing to do to quit medicine and become an FBI agent? What is most important to me? My career? My relationships? And what does it mean that I might have a child, because even though my cancer is apparently cured, I really don't know how long I'm going to live?'"

Shiban was pleased with the episode. So was Gillian Anderson. The series's star, who "liked the final product," nevertheless believes that she never quite nailed the complex relationship between Scully and her almost-daughter.

"I felt in the end that I was a little low energy, a little too melancholy," she says. "It was hard to find the right attitude for Scully in dealing with a child that's apparently hers; to find the right flavor of relationship to her and this disease she's going through, all mixed up with the aspect of the paranormal. Another trouble was that she had no history with this child so I couldn't play the kind of attachment I would feel if my own daughter, Piper, were going through the same thing."

In contrast with 5X07, the second part of this two-episode sequence, production went relatively—if deceptively (see page 97)—smoothly.

According to props master Ken Hawryliw, his biggest challenge was finding late–eighties era Christmas wrapping paper. "It seems like the mundane stuff is always the hardest to get," he says.

He adds, "Since the actors would be unwrapping the packages on camera, we needed plenty of it. It turns out that over the course of ten years, Christmas wrapping paper has changed. And very few stores keep the old stuff around, so I had my buyer, Gail Irvine, running all over to various places to get all the rolls that we needed."

According to Vancouver casting director Corinne Mayrs, her biggest problem—solved with an impressive burst of inspiration—was finding an actress to play Dana Scully circa 1976. "We'd managed to find matches for everybody else," says Mayrs, "but we couldn't agree on a match for the young teenage Dana. Then, during a casting session, Bob Goodwin leaned over to me and said, 'Doesn't Gillian have a sister? A younger sister?'"

Indeed she does.

"It was incredible!" says fourteen-year-old Zoë Anderson, speaking from the home she shares with her parents in Michigan. "It happened out of the blue. My mom told me when I came home from school. She said, 'Guess what? Gillian just called, and they said they need you for a part.' I started screaming! I really like drama and plays and stuff. I've always wanted to do this."

A veteran of several amateur theatrical productions ("In the sixth grade I was in *A Christmas Carol*, can you believe it?") and a local opera workshop, the eighth-grader memorized her lines one day after dance class and spent a week in Vancouver with her sister and mother. "The plays back home were fun, but doing this was really fun," she says.

The hardest part, she reports, was learning exactly how to stand in each shot. "Every shot was different. Either I was leaning too far into the Christmas tree, or looking the wrong way. But the director, Peter Markle, really helped me. He was great."

And the next hardest part? Perhaps telling a nosy interviewer, months later, that the braces she wore on her teeth onscreen were not issued to her by the wardrobe or special effects department.

"I *wish!*" says the young actress, with feeling.

This is director Peter Markle's first *X-File*. He has also directed several feature films including *Bat 21* and *Youngblood*, numerous TV movies, and episodes of *Millennium* ("Maranatha" 1x21) and *Homicide*.

the post-modern

Deep in the American heartland, Mulder and Scully encounter—then attempt to unravel—the twisted schemes of a modern-day Victor Frankenstein.

EPISODE: 5X06
FIRST AIRED: November 30, 1997
EDITOR: Lynne Willingham
WRITTEN BY: Chris Carter
DIRECTED BY: Chris Carter

GUEST STARS:
John O'Hurley
(Dr. Pollidori)
Miriam Smith
(Elizabeth Pollidori)
Lloyd Berry (Old Man)
Chris Owens (Mutato)
Pattie Tierce (Shaineh)
Stewart Gale (Izzy)
Chris Giacoletti (Booger)
Vitaliy Kravchenko (J. J.)
Xantha Radley (Waitress)
Jean-Yves Hammel
(Goat Boy)
Jonathan Palis
(Postal Worker)
Dana Grahame
(Newspaper Reporter)
C. Ernst Harth (Huge Man)
Andrew Laurenson
(Nerdy Student)
Tracey Bell (Cher)
Jerry Springer (Himself)

PRINCIPAL SETTINGS:
Rural Indiana and
Memphis, Tennessee

prometheus

he cover of a skillfully hand-drawn comic book depicting "The Great Mutato," a grotesque cartoon monster menacing a small town. A hand flips open the cover, revealing its black-and-white interior. An explanatory bubble reads "SOMEWHERE IN THE LAND A MONSTER LURKED . . ."

A small-town Indiana neighborhood in late afternoon; three rather large teenage boys are cold-cranking a vintage Nash Metropolitan. Two of them peer under the hood; one being Izzy Berkowitz.

"You're flooding it, Booger!" says Izzy.

The third kid sits behind the wheel and grinds the starter. The engine finally roars to life in an explosion of white smoke. Izzy's mom, Shaineh Berkowitz, rushes out onto her front porch.

"For God's sake, Izzy!" she says. "You gotta be kiddin'."

The boys drop the hood and pile into the tiny car.

"What?" says Izzy, innocently.

"Don't 'what' me, Izzy," says his mom, sternly, "or you ain't goin' to no comic book convention."

"I'm eighteen," whines Izzy. "I can go anywhere I want."

"Yeah," says Shaineh, "but where you gonna live when you come back?"

"*Mom!*" protests her son, "we gotta get goin'!"

Shaineh shakes her head, relenting. "You drive careful, Booger. He's the only son I've got."

"Okay, Mrs. B.," says Booger. He puts the Nash into gear and *putt-putts* down the street.

Late that night a blast of moonlight illuminates a photo of a smiling Izzy, holding a blue ribbon next to a very large pig. In the darkened Berkowitz residence sits Shaineh, staring slack-jawed at her TV set. On the small screen Jerry Springer is interviewing a young woman holding a very hairy baby. A caption reads DELORES: GAVE BIRTH TO A WOLF BOY.

"I can't believe this!" says Shaineh, transfixed.

She doesn't notice that a sheet of canvas is being draped over the window just behind her. Something unseen lights a burner of her stove; a skillet containing an odd-looking patty is placed upon it. The heat of the flame triggers a chemical reaction, releasing a cloud of dense white smoke. The smoke seeps into the rest of the house, and the faint strains of an old pop standard—Cher's cover of "The Sun Ain't Gonna Shine Anymore"—begin to be heard. A dark, hulking figure leaves the kitchen.

Shaineh becomes alarmed. She mutes the sound on her television.

"Hello? Who's there?" she says.

The large figure pushes through the smoke toward Shaineh, who, increasingly fearful, starts to cough. The door to her room opens slowly, and a man with a horribly disfigured face appears. The music is blasting full volume now. Shaineh gasps in horror.

Seen from the outside, her house is completely enveloped by a large striped canvas tent.

In a rented car, Mulder drives with Scully through an absolutely flat—and monochromatic—agricultural landscape. In a voice just as flat—and with barely concealed skepticism—Scully reads from a letter she's holding. This is the letter she reads:

Dear Special Agent Mulder, I'm writing to you for help. Several years ago I had an experience I could not explain. I was lying in my bed when I felt a presence in the room. Though I was awake, I felt that something had taken control over my body. I don't remember much else, but I woke up three days later pregnant with my son, Izzy.

Scully turns to her partner and gives him a look. Just a look. She continues:

That was eighteen years ago, but now it happened again. I was in bed and could swear I heard Cher singing. The one who was married to Sonny.

Another look.

Then the room got all smoky and I saw some kind of monster. He had a really gross face with big lumps all over his head. Then I got all groggy and conked out for three days. Guess what happened when I woke up? I got your name off the TV. Some lady on The Jerry Springer Show who had a were-wolf baby said you came to her house. Well, I got her story beat by a mile, so maybe you'll want to come see me, too.

Sincerely, Shaineh Berkowitz.

Scully throws another glance at Mulder, but her fellow agent looks eagerly at the road ahead.

"Scully," he asks, "do you think it's too soon to get my own 1–900 number?"

In the Berkowitz house Shaineh Berkowitz pours Mulder and Scully generous soft drinks from a 64-ounce plastic bottle. "So," she says, "did you actually see that werewolf baby? Or was that just a story?"

Mulder explains good-naturedly that the baby in question suffered from *hypertrichosis lanuginosa*—a rare hereditary condition.

"Uh-*huh!*" says Mrs. Berkowitz. "But it was all hairy and stuff?"

Scully impatiently asks Shaineh about her own son. The woman proudly points to the picture of Izzy and the prize pig.

"And Izzy," asks Scully, "was the product of your union with some kind of intruder?"

"I don't know about no union," says Mrs. Berkowitz, "but I sure woke up in a condition."

"Did you report it to the police?" asks Scully.

"Sure I did," she replies.

"Was there an investigation?"

"Not really. Nobody here ever locks their doors. And it took me a month or two to figure it out. I mean, that I was pregnant."

"And now you're pregnant again?"

"Uh-huh," says Mrs. Berkowitz. "But as I told Agent Mulder on the phone, that's what takes the cake."

Mulder says, "Mrs. Berkowitz had a tubal ligation two years ago," he says.

Mrs. Berkowitz nods happily. "You can't plant a seed in a barren field," she says.

"You said you were gone three days, but nobody missed you," says Scully pointedly.

"Do you drink, Mrs. Berkowitz?"

"No," Shaineh replies. "But I'm not so sure my intruders—as you call 'em—didn't have a few."

To back up her claim of an unnatural visitation, she points out three pieces of evidence: the skillet, contaminated by substances unknown; a suspicious ring on her sideboard table; and a mysteriously emptied jumbo-sized jar of peanut butter.

They proceed into Izzy's pigsty of a bedroom. Scully pokes through the rubble, leaving Mulder alone with Mrs. Berkowitz.

She says, "You know what this thing is, don't you, Agent Mulder?"

"Why do you say that?" he replies.

"'Cause you're all quiet and stuff. And you know something you're not sayin'. About alien abductions. They said on *Jerry Springer* you're like an expert!"

Mulder smiles. "I don't think this has anything to do with alien abductions," he says. "To be honest, I don't even know if I believe there's such a thing anymore."

"Aw, c'mon!" scoffs Mrs. Berkowitz. Then, suddenly puzzled: *"Really?"*

Now Scully gets their attention; she seems to have an important clue in her hands.

"Mrs. Berkowitz," she says. "You gave a description of the intruder. You said that he had a gross face and lumps on his head?"

"And two mouths!" says Mrs. Berkowitz. "I don't know if I mentioned that."

"Funny," replies Scully. "It sounds just like this."

Scully holds up a comic book so that both Mulder and Mrs. Berkowitz can see it. It is the same work of art that was displayed at the beginning of the episode.

"Oh, *that*," says Mrs. Berkowitz. "That's the Great Mutato. It's a comic book character my kid Izzy created."

Mulder leans down to give the Great Mutato a closer inspection. At that moment a screen door slams and the creator himself enters.

"What's goin' on?" says Izzy Berkowitz.

His mother says, "These are Agents Mulder and Scully from the FBI."

"The Federal Bureau of Investigation?" asks Izzy.

But his question goes unanswered. Instead, Scully wonders out loud why the suspect in his mother's case looks exactly like the monster in the comic book.

"Because I've seen him, too," says Izzy, matter-of-factly.

"You've seen the Great Mutato?" says Scully, skeptically.

"Yeah," says Izzy, with a shrug. "A lot of people have."

Later that night Izzy—accompanied by Mulder, Scully, and the two buddies last seen wedged into the Nash Metropolitan—places a small object wrapped in wax paper on a tree stump in a forest clearing. He moves off to his observation post. Mulder and Scully trail behind him.

"Peanut butter sandwiches?" asks Scully, pained.

Replies her partner, "You think baloney would be more effective?"

Scully winces. "Why are you humoring them, Mulder?" she says.

"I'm not humoring them, Scully," says Mulder. "This is a very serious crime."

"So is perjury," says Scully. "So is calling out FBI agents under false pretenses."

"For what?" asks Mulder.

"Isn't it obvious?" says Scully.

"What we're seeing is an example of a culture for whom daytime talk shows and tabloid headlines have a become a reality against which they measure their lives. A culture so obsessed by the media and the chance for self-dramatization that they'll do anything in order to gain a spotlight."

Walking slightly ahead of the agents, Izzy fiddles with a small tape recorder and places it in his jacket pocket. Neither Mulder or Scully notice this.

Mulder resumes the debate.

"I'm alarmed," he says to his partner, "that you'd reduce these people to a cultural stereotype. Not everyone's dream is to get on *Jerry Springer*."

Scully replies, "Psychologists often speak of the denial of an unthinkable evil, or a misplacement of shared fears. Anxieties taking the form of a hideous creature for whom the most horrific human attributes can be ascribed. What we

can't possibly imagine ourselves capable of we can blame on the ogre, the hunchback, the lowly half-breed."

As Scully speaks, Izzy breaks away from his buddies and moves to within earshot of the agents. He's playing it cool, but both Mulder and Scully notice him.

Scully continues, "Common sense alone says these legends, these unverified rumors are ridiculous."

"But nonetheless unverifiable," says Mulder, quickly. "And therefore true in the sense that they're believed to be true."

Scully says, exasperated, "Is there anything you don't believe in, Mulder?"

Mulder doesn't reply. He just cocks his head and listens.

"Shhhh," he says, distractedly.

A kind of beastly, melodic moaning begins. It is far away and faint, but nonetheless attention-getting. Izzy stands up straight and steps forward.

"It's the Great Mutato!" he says.

A dark figure emerges from the woods, reaches down, and—using a horribly gnarled hand—picks up the peanut butter sandwich. The group hesitates, then sets out on a run toward it, with Mulder leading the way.

Noticing that he's been spotted, the dark figure retreats into the woods. Scully breaks off her pursuit at the tree stump. She lifts up the sandwich and examines it; it has two distinct bite marks, neatly carved out of adjacent sides.

Mulder doesn't stop. He chases the dark figure through the foggy woods. He finally comes to a halt, a panting Scully pulling up behind him.

"Where did it go?" she asks.

"I don't know," says Mulder. "I lost it."

A moment later, though, he points excitedly toward a nearby slope.

"There! Up there!" he says.

There is a flash of lightning. On the ridge stands the dark figure, looming above them. Scully pulls a flashlight from her jacket, clicks it on, and points it toward the monster.

"Turn that damn thing off!" says her target.

It is a grizzled old man, accompanied by a large pig on a leash. "You're on my property!" he shouts.

Mulder says, "We're with the FBI!"

The old man nods toward Izzy and his friends. "They're not," he says, angrily.

Scully, replies, loudly, that they were chasing what they told us was a monster.

"A monster!?" shouts the old man. "What'd I tell you boys!? There ain't no monster!" He adds, angrily, "*I'll* show you the monster you're lookin' for!"

On the front page of the University of Indiana newspaper, above a photograph of a scientist named Dr. Francis Pollidori, a headline reads PROFESSOR CREATES OWN MONSTERS.

Pollidori himself, wearing a white lab coat, sits at a lab table. He is staring angrily at the FBI agents.

"Who sent you here?" he demands.

"Your father," says Mulder.

"My father is a simpleton farmer," says Pollidori. "He understands nothing of my scientific achievements."

"What achievements are those?" says Scully.

Pollidori looks at her with contempt. "What makes you think you'd understand them any better?"

"Well," says Scully, evenly, "I'm a scientist, for one."

The man's contempt swells exponentially at her remark. "*Well!*" he says, rising and beginning an unguided tour of his well-equipped laboratory, "then you probably know that once in a generation—perhaps once in a lifetime—a truth is uncovered which thrusts mankind into a shocking new consciousness, turning accepted notions of our very existence on their head.

"Consider relativity, the double helix, and now the homeotic hox gene, for which I will no doubt have my place among the Columbuses of science as a visionary leader of men."

A nerdy post-doctoral student appears, holding a covered petri dish containing a colony of fruit flies.

"What do you want me to do with these, Dr. Pollidori?" he says, uncovering the dish. Immediately, all the insects fly away.

"Never mind," says the student, despondently.

Mulder resumes his questioning. "What's the homeotic hox gene?" he asks.

Pollidori replies, "*She's* a scientist. Ask her."

Scully says, controlling her temper, "I believe that it has something to do with growth and development."

Pollidori looks away, irritated mightily. "If you two will excuse me, I really don't have time for this. I have to travel tonight to the University of Ingolstadt to deliver an international address."

Scully levels him with her gaze. "Sir," she says, "unless you want your scientific achievements to end up as a footnote on *The Jerry Springer Show*, I suggest you make the time."

Pollidori considers this for a moment. "*The Jerry Springer Show?*" he says, perhaps a bit too eagerly.

In another part of his lab Pollidori stands in front of a large television. On the screen, a fly pupae is morphing, changing shape, in a time-lapse display of growth. Lightning flashes through a nearby window.

"Witness," says Pollidori, "the morphogenesis of *drosophila*—the fruit fly."

He views his handiwork with smug pleasure.

"What you are watching," says the scientist, "has been going on for millennia, since the Cambrian period some five hundred and eighty million short years ago, when *drosophila* was born. Notice the elegant symmetry with which the pupae grows into a series of beautiful segments."

He walks to a chalkboard and illustrates this with a simple diagram.

"What we have found—what *I* have found—is that these segments represent a linear model for our friend, the fly. Each gene is responsible for the development of its corresponding segment: the legs, the mouth, the body, posterior and anterior. Which, in my genius, I can alter into a creation of my own."

Pollidori points to the monitor, on which now displays a grotesque blowup of a fruit fly's head.

"Behold! *Proboscopedia!*" he says.

Mulder moves closer to the screen and stares at it, amazed.

"This fly has legs—" he says.

"—growing out of its mouth," says Scully.

Mulder is disturbed. "Why would you do that?" he asks.

"Because," says Pollidori, "I can."

Mulder looks to Scully, then back to Pollidori. "Could that be done in humans?" he asks.

"That would go against every scientific convention," says the scientist, obviously not too distressed by the prospect.

"But could it be done?" demands Mulder.

"Theoretically," replies Pollidori, evenly, framed by twin flashes of lightning at his back.

A few minutes later the scientist, briefcase in hand, exits the lab and walks to his waiting luxury car. The two agents look down at him from a high window.

"Goodnight, Dr. Frankenstein," says Mulder.

Scully crosses her arms, frowns, and tells him that, despite what he's just seen, "designer mutations" are virtually impossible in humans.

"That's not what I just heard," says her partner.

"Mulder," says Scully, impatiently, "even if they could, no scientist would even dare perform these kinds of experiments on a human."

"Then why do them at all?" asks Mulder.

"To unlock the mysteries of genetics," says Scully. "To understand how, even though we share the same genes, we develop arms instead of wings. We become humans, instead of flies— or monsters."

Mulder says, "But given the power, who could resist the temptation to create life in his own image?"

Scully says, "We already have that ability, Mulder. It's called procreation." She adds, "And, first thing tomorrow

morning, I'm going to verify the pregnancy of Shaineh Berkowitz."

Later that night, at Pollidori's rural mansion, his small, nervous-looking wife Elizabeth packs her husband's bag for his trip. The scientist, changing clothes in his bathroom— and in a fog of self-absorption—pokes his head out to listen to her.

"When are you comin' home again?" asks Elizabeth, nervously.

"Huh?" says Pollidori.

"When are you comin' home again?" says Elizabeth.

"What?" says Pollidori, impatiently.

"We were goin' to have that talk," says Elizabeth.

"Soon. Soon," says Pollidori, dismissively. "We'll have our 'talk' very soon."

"That's what you always say," says Elizabeth, distressed.

Pollidori says, "Elizabeth, you know how I feel about children. They're mewling little monsters."

"But I want children," says his wife, her voice breaking.

Pollidori turns toward her angrily. "What happened to our dream?" he demands. "About getting out of this place! About getting away from this hick town!"

"I think that's your dream," says Elizabeth, quietly.

Lightning again flashes behind him. Pollidori grabs his wife by the shoulders. "Listen, what do you want?" he says. "A baby? Or a Nobel Prize?"

He gives her a perfunctory kiss on the forehead, grabs his suitcase, and leaves. Elizabeth stands sad and alone for a moment, walks to the window to watch him drive away, then throws herself, crying, on her bed. A sheet of canvas falls over the window behind her.

The next morning Mulder enters J. J.'s, a local "country diner," to an enthusiastic—if inexplicable—reception.

The rather eccentric-looking patrons smile broadly at him as he passes; not entirely impervious to their goodwill, he smiles tentatively back.

Just outside, Scully plucks a local newspaper from a rack. The headline reads FBI HUNTS HOMETOWN MONSTER! AGENT ADMITS STORIES "BELIEVED TO BE TRUE."

Inside the diner, next to Mulder at the counter, sits a twitchy-looking woman in horn rims. An odd-looking waitress scurries toward them, then plunks several dishes in front of the agent.

"Hot plates! Hot, hot, hot!" she says. "Biscuits, fritters, grits, flapjacks! Eggs boiled, scrambled, poached, and fried! We got some monster grapefruits on the way, bigger'n your head, almost!"

Mulder stares at her, befuddled. "I'd just like some coffee, thanks," he says.

The waitress nods happily. "On the house! Compliments of J. J.!"

Mulder glances at the kitchen to see a bearlike, bearded cook smiling back at him. "That's with *two* J's," grins J. J.

Mulder swivels back and catches his seatmate surreptitiously scribbling notes on her scratch pad. Discovered, she stands up, nervously, and leaves. The agent is still digesting all this when the waitress leans into his face.

"Is it true," she burbles, "that Jerry Springer's comin' to town?"

As if in answer, the front door of the diner opens. All eyes turn to Scully as she makes a beeline for Mulder.

"We've been had," she whispers, slapping the newspaper down in front of him. "I'll save you the trouble of reading the article. It's got everything you and I talked about last night. Word for word."

Later that morning an angry Shaineh Berkowitz stands, hands on hips, in her living room. Her huge son pokes his head, timidly, out of his bedroom door.

"IZZY BERKOWITZ! GET YOUR BUTT FRONT AND CENTER!"

"What'd I do?" whines Izzy.

"All I can say," says Mrs. Berkowitz, "is that I hope the answer to that question is *nothin!*"

Scully addresses the lad and tells him that they have reason to believe he's recorded the agents' conversation last night and given it to a newspaper reporter. His assumed motive: to promote the comic book monster he's created.

Mulder says, "Do you own a tape recorder, Izzy?"

"Uh . . ." says the lad.

"CHRISTMAS, 1993!" shouts Shaineh.

Izzy sheepishly emerges from the bedroom, tape recorder in hand. His mother snatches it away. On the tape is a snatch of conversation from the night before. Shaineh reaches up and knocks the baseball cap off Izzy's head.

"That's for starters!" she says.

Mulder rewinds the tape further, hits the PLAY button, and something different comes out. It is a fuzzy recording of Cher's "The Sun Ain't Gonna Shine Anymore."

A light bulb goes off over Shaineh's head. "Hey!" she cries. "Hey, that's it! That's the song that was playin' when I got knocked up!"

The tape plays on. Over the sound of the Cher song, comes a crude vocal accompaniment. Someone with a tin ear and speech impediment is singing along with the record.

"Who the hell is that?" says Scully.

Mulder says, "That's the same voice we heard out in the woods last night."

"That's him!" says Izzy, happily. "That's the Great Mutato!"

Inside the Pollidori house—which is filled with the same gaseous white smoke as we've seen inside the Berkowitz home—the dark creature is belting out the same Cher standard, dancing happily through the house and then disappearing up the stairs.

The agents exit via the front door of the Berkowitz home, Mulder holding Izzy's tape cassette. He tells Scully that he's going to send it to FBI Headquarters to

have the special audio experts filter out and separate the voices. Then, he adds, he's going to confront Dr. Pollidori with the evidence.

"Mulder," says Scully, "this is just a dopey hoax."

Mulder says, "Something recorded its voice on this, Scully."

"And you think Dr. Pollidori has something to do with it?"

Replies her partner, "When Victor Frankenstein asks himself, 'Whence did the principle of life proceed?' and then, as the gratifying summit of his toils creates a hideous phantasm of a man, he prefigures the post-modern Prometheus: the genetic engineer, whose power to reanimate matter—genes into life, us—is only as limited as his imagination."

Scully says, "Mulder, I'm alarmed that you would reduce this man to a literary stereotype. A mad scientist."

"Who else," says Mulder, "would go to such trouble to impregnate Shaineh Berkowitz?"

In their car later that day Mulder drives while Scully scans Shaineh Berkowitz's medical records.

"I have to admit, Mulder," she says, "everything looks in order. Mrs. Berkowitz had a tubal ligation in 1993. Two months ago she had two pregnancy tests, both with positive results."

Mulder stomps on the brakes, bringing the car to a halt in the middle of the road.

"What are you doing?" says Scully.

Mulder throws the car in reverse, swivels his head to look through the rear window, and begins driving in reverse.

"Mrs. Berkowitz said in her letter," he says, "that when she saw her intruder her room had begun to fill with a gaseous white cloud. And that when she woke up three days later nobody knew that she'd been gone."

"Yeah? So?" says Scully.

Mulder halts the car in front of the Pollidori house, which is covered with a striped canvas tent. Muffled music—the song "Gypsies, Tramps and Thieves," to be exact—is emanating from inside. The agents exit the car and, going their separate ways, search for an entrance to the tent. Mulder finds a flap. Gun drawn, he walks into the smoky interior. He searches

the living room, then walks upstairs.

A few minutes later Scully enters the upstairs bedroom. Coughing, she spots Elizabeth Pollidori lying unconscious in her bed. But there is something else present and it is kneeling next to the bed, its head out of view.

Scully's gun also comes out. "Come on! Get up! Move!" she says.

The kneeling figure stirs and rises. It is Mulder, retching loudly.

Scully stumbles over to help her partner up, but she is soon gagging and on the floor herself. They both lose consciousness. A dark figure stands over the agents. It is tall, with two strange protuberances attached to its face. It is the old man, Dr. Pollidori's father. He is wearing a gas mask.

"I told you," he says. "There ain't no monster."

Sometime later the agents come to. "What are you doing in my house?" demands a furious Dr. Pollidori, standing over them.

The house is filled with uniformed police. Elizabeth Pollidori is seated in a kitchen chair, a blanket pulled around her. Mulder and Scully, dazed and disheveled, sit at a table nearby. Scully holds the local newspaper. A headline reads FBI AGENTS' WHEREABOUTS UNKNOWN. Its subhead reads AFTER HEARTY BREAKFAST IN J. J.'S DINER, LAWMEN DISAPPEAR.

"He had this awful face with those hideous tumors," says Elizabeth. "And not one mouth, but two!"

"Oh, my God," says Dr. Pollidori.

Holding his head in his hands, a still groggy Mulder manages to speak. "Dr. Pollidori," he says. "Is there something you'd like to tell us?"

Pollidori advances on him angrily. "Are you accusing me," he says, "of knowing something I'm not telling?"

"I'm accusing," says Mulder, "that your wife may have been impregnated."

"Impregnated? By whom?" says Pollidori.

Mulder staggers to his feet, knocking

some loose items off the kitchen stove. "Oh, I think you know!" he says.

Now it's Scully's turn. "With all due respect, sir," she says, "I think this is all part of a hoax. A shameless publicity stunt."

"Scully!" says Mulder. He holds up a frying pan. "The other victims, they had their frying pans . . . violated."

There is a white residue on the bottom of the pan. He wipes his finger across it, then hands it to Scully, who hands it to Pollidori.

"Do you know what that is?" demands Mulder.

"No. I don't," says Pollidori.

Mulder notices something else. He reaches into the kitchen trash and pulls out an empty jumbo-sized container of peanut butter.

"I think," says Mulder, "we've found our smoking gun."

In a dark basement room, someone is watching the 1985 movie *Mask*, on an ancient round-cornered television screen. Eric Stoltz, as the boy with a serious facial deformity, hugs his mother, played by Cher.

The old man, Pollidori's father, walks down to the basement. He approaches a dark figure sitting in front of the TV, then sets a plate carrying a peanut butter sandwich down on a small table.

"Brought you your favorite," says the old man, with much kindness. "You finish your movie. But don't stay up too late. Okay, son?"

A deformed hand reaches out to take the sandwich. The creature has a grotesque face and two mouths, joined in a deformity. Its eyes are watery as it watches the movie.

"Do you love me?" asks the deformed boy, on screen.

"Oh, what's not to love, baby?" says Cher, hugging her make-believe son even tighter.

A few moments later the old man is in the kitchen. He thumbs through an album containing pictures of himself and the disfigured creature we've just seen. The door opens and Dr. Pollidori stands in the arch-

way, staring with restrained anger.

"Tell me you didn't," he says.

The old man says nothing.

"You wouldn't. *Why!?*"

The old man turns to look at his photos.

"Because I can," he says, calmly.

Pollidori rushes the old man, grabbing him by the throat and knocking him backward. They fall heavily to the floor, the scientist squeezing his father's neck even tighter.

The next morning Mulder enters J. J.'s Country Diner and gets a decidedly different reception. The patrons scowl at him and turn their backs; someone sticks out his foot to trip him as he walks down the aisle. A wad of oatmeal smacks him on the back of his neck. J. J., plainly visible through the kitchen window, spits into a plate of food and hands it to the waitress. The strange waitress plunks it on the counter in front of Mulder.

"What's this?" says Mulder.

"Compliments of J. J.," she says. "Coffee?"

She reaches over and spills hot coffee directly onto Mulder's lap. The agent jumps up from his stool, in shock.

"Whoa!" he says. "That's not a place you want to burn a guy."

Mulder glances at a copy of the local newspaper. The headline reads FBI AGENTS SAY MONSTER A HOAX. The subhead reads SHAMELESS PLAY FOR PUBLICITY.

Mulder reacts to this for a second, until something new captures his attention. People are running past the diner's front window, at first just a few, then the numbers increase. The patrons, in the diner get up to join the migration, as does Mulder. In front of the town post office a burly postal worker is haranguing an angry mob.

"You want to see your monster?!" yells the postman.

"Yeah!" yells the crowd.

"You REALLY want to see your monster?!"

"YEAH!"

The postal worker steps back into the post office and pulls out a heavyset individual wearing a rubber Mutato mask. The crowd reacts in shock, then in indignation. The postman pulls off the mask.

"See?" he says.

"It's Izzy Berkowitz!" yells someone.

As the crowd yells for Izzy's head—his real head—Shaineh Berkowitz pushes herself to the front.

"You let him go!" she says, angrily.

The postal worker says, "I intercepted a package—"

"How would you like your face to intercept my fist, coconut head!?" says Shaineh.

The crowd jeers her.

"THAT IS MY SON YOU'RE TALKIN' ABOUT!" she yells.

On the fringe of the crowd, Mulder is watching this with awed wonder. He is joined by Scully.

"You may have been right, Scully," says Mulder.

"What?" says Scully. "That these people can be reduced to cultural stereotypes?"

"No. That they unmasked the monster," he replies.

Scully says, "I may have found something that says otherwise." The residue on the frying pan, she adds, is an agricultural product, used to anesthetize herds of animals.

"Used by whom?" asks Mulder.

"Farmers. Who have to register with the FDA to even have it in their possession."

"Is someone registered locally?" asks Mulder.

"Um-hum," says Scully, nodding.

In the old man's kitchen Dr. Pollidori's father lies dead. The kitchen door opens, and a dark figure shuffles in. He kneels down and, sobbing, shakes the lifeless body gently. There is no response. The creature lovingly carries the corpse into a barn and, as the animals inside watch curiously, places him lovingly on the ground. Crying and keening he digs a shallow grave in the deepest recesses of the building. A large sow penned nearby grunts sympathetically.

Sometime later the FBI agents' car pulls to a stop in front of the old man's house; Mulder and Scully enter the barn. Mulder finds a box containing white cakes, the same kind used to produce the gaseous cloud. He kneels down and examines the crudely covered grave site.

"We may be too late. I think we are," he says, sadly.

There is a creaking of wood in the hayloft above them. Both react to the sound by standing fast and drawing their guns. They shout for whoever is up there to drop their weapon and come out slowly.

"Please don't. Don't kill me," says a woman's voice.

It is the nervous young woman who had been taking notes next to Mulder in the diner. She is still holding her notepad.

"Who are you?" asks Mulder, holstering his gun.

"I'm with the newspaper," says the woman.

"What's your business here?" demands Mulder.

The newspaper woman says, "The old man was murdered."

Scully asks, "By whom?"

In the old man's house all three look through the scrapbook holding the pictures of the young Mutato. There are similar, framed photographs on the wall.

"It's alive!" says Mulder, with just a touch of triumph.

The newspaper woman says, "I've seen it. In the barn. Burying the old man."

Mulder and Scully stare at her for a moment until their attention is diverted by a sound outside. Through the front door they see an angry mob, carrying lanterns, flashlights, and flaming torches. It's a lynching party, heading toward the old man's barn. At the head of the procession is Dr. Pollidori.

Mulder and Scully leave the farmhouse and interpose themselves between the mob and the house. The newspaper woman cowers behind them.

"Whatever you have in mind," says Mulder, forcefully, "I'm going to have to ask you to stop right there."

Pollidori shouts, "We have come for the murderer!"

Scully says, "What makes you think he's here?"

"I've seen him with my own eyes," says Pollidori. "He is not a man—he is a monster! The fiend must be found and then we'll let justice take its course!"

Pollidori's pronouncement rouses the

mob to new heights of fury. The marchers push past Mulder and Scully and search the barn—the animals inside whinnying, cackling, and grunting in fright. The newspaper woman, notebook in hand, scurries after them.

The FBI agents watch all this helplessly. Until:

"Mulder," says Scully, coming to a sudden realization. "There's only one way Pollidori could have seen that monster—if he was out here himself."

Behind Scully a storm cellar door creaks. She turns around just in time to see a grotesque face, as frightened as it is frightening, ducking down again and out of sight. The agents enter the dark cellar, flashlights and guns drawn, announcing themselves as federal agents.

"Scully, look at this," says Mulder.

He's found a small shrine to Cher, including album covers, movie stills, and autographed photos.

There is a sudden movement in the room behind them and the agents react, shining their flashlight beams into a dark corner. From under a pile of striped canvas slowly rises the Great Mutato. His features are frightening, but his eyes are as sympathetic as those of an injured animal.

"Oh my God!" gasps Scully, involuntarily. The agents lower their weapons.

"You're going to have to come out of there," says Mulder, gently.

"We're not going to hurt you," says Scully. Then, to Mulder: "Do you think he understands?"

"I hope not," says Mulder. "We have to get him out of here, Scully. They're going to kill him."

Above ground, the mob has accidentally set the barn on fire. Flames leap out from the hayloft, silhouetting the panicked animals—and people—caught inside. While they scramble for their lives, the newspaper woman frantically takes notes. The fire burns out of control. Mulder, Scully, and Mutato poke their heads through the cellar door to watch. The

newspaper woman notices them.

"There it is!!!" she cries.

The trio retreats back into the cellar, the mob in hot pursuit. The rioters fling open the doors and punch through the small basement windows. Mutato flees back into his corner, disappearing. First down the stairs, at the head of the mob, is Pollidori. Next to him stands Shaineh Berkowitz.

"Let him go!" says the scientist.

"Where is he?!" demands Shaineh.

"You let him go or we'll burn him out!"

"Where is he? Show the world your horrid, lumpy face!"

The mob cries for blood. Mulder and Scully stand fast. Behind them, Mutato rises up, continuing his innocent, fearful stare. The mob lapses into stunned silence. Until:

"That's him!" says Elizabeth Pollidori, cowering.

"Uck!" says Shaineh.

Pollidori, too, regains his tongue. "That repulsive physiognomy," he hisses, "is the vilest perversion of science."

Mulder turns to him angrily. "Created by who?" he says accusingly.

"A pale student of my most hallowed arts," says Pollidori. "Whose life was taken by that which he gave life. By his own horrible creation. By that monstrosity that you see before you!"

"Who's he talkin' about?" says Shaineh.

Pollidori says, spitting out the words, "My father!"

The crowd gasps. The terrified Great Mutato, who is being comforted by Scully, raises his head.

"No," he gasps, in a meek, hoarse voice.

"He can talk!" says Shaineh.

"Your ears deceive you!" says Pollidori. "It's a trick! Get him!!"

But nobody moves. With a frown and an upraised forefinger, a stern-faced Mulder silences the crowd. The Great

Mutato slumps, sitting down on the small table we've seen before. He gathers his courage, and speaks.

"I'm sorry," he says. "My voice is damaged by the gaseous chemicals. But I would like to explain myself. Despite my appearance, which you see is quite horrible to the human senses, I have never acted to harm another soul."

"These are fiendish lies!" says Pollidori.

"Quiet," says Mulder, admonishing him.

Mutato continues, "Twenty-five years ago my father, having only one son—a spiteful, hateful man of science, incapable of the deeper sentiments—came to realize that his son had been conducting secret experiments. Of which I was the most unfortunate product.

"A simple man, he rescued me and loved me in spite of my deformities. But as time passed I grew restless for friends of my own. Because I couldn't go to school or play sports or even show my face outside this farm, my father set out to learn his son's science so that before he died he might create for me a mate.

"Alas, my father was a simple man, his heart close to the soil he worked, the animals he tended."

At this point Scully and Mulder look around them. With new eyes, they notice that a pecking, cackling chicken shares certain characteristics with the newspaper woman; the horse with one of Izzy's pals; a braying billy goat with another.

Mutato continues, "The experiments he attempted were too advanced, the science too complex for his understanding, the result of his experiments unsatisfactory."

Shaineh speaks up, confused and troubled. "I still—you mean Izzy?" she says. "But who's the father?"

In another corner of the barn the big sow snorts especially loud.

Mutato adds, "Suffice it to say, the experiments failed. And my father is dead."

He looks at Pollidori. His brother. "I am alone and miserable, but one as deformed and horrible as myself would not deny herself to me. If this being you can create, then I will take blame as a murderer."

All eyes are on the scientist. His mouth twists into a spiteful grimace. "I don't know how to recreate you," he says. "You were a *mistake*."

The monster turns to Shaineh, and bows his head.

"What we did was wrong," he says. "But in our trespasses we gave you a loving son. And in your homes I went places I'd never dreamed of. With your books and your records and your home media centers I learned of your world. And of a mother's love I'll never know.

"Cher loved that boy so much," he says, and falls silent.

All around him are moved. Some of the members of the lynch mob are crying. Izzy Berkowitz is the first to speak.

"Hey!" he says, finally. "He's no monster!"

Mutato turns to Mulder. "Arrest me then, as you will," he says.

Instead, Mulder turns to the now-cringing Dr. Pollidori. A few minutes later, policemen in a police car—with siren on and lights flashing—takes the disgraced scientist away.

A little while later Mulder sits at the old man's desk, thumbing through the photo album. Scully approaches and tells him that it's time they go home.

"This is all wrong, Scully," he says. "This is not how the story is supposed to end."

"What do you mean?" says Scully.

"Dr. Frankenstein pays for his evil ambitions, yes," he replies. "But the monster is supposed to escape, to look for his bride."

Scully looks at him sadly. "There's not going to be any bride, Mulder," she says. "Not in this story."

Mulder shakes his head impatiently. "Where is the writer?" he says. "Let me speak to the writer!"

As dawn breaks over the flatlands, a caravan of cars—including Mulder and Scully's sedan and Izzy's Nash Metropolitan—head down a country road. Music begins to play in the background. It is Cher's cover version of "Walking in Memphis."

> Put on my blue suede shoes and
>   I boarded the plane,
> Touched down in the land of the Delta blues
>   in the middle of the pouring rain.
> W.C. Handy, won't you look down over me?
> Yeah, I got a first class ticket, but I'm as blue

as a girl could be.
When I'm walking in Memphis,
I was walking with my feet ten feet off of Beale.
Walking in Memphis,
Do I really feel the way I feel?"

As the music plays, Mulder, Scully, and Mutato ride on—Mulder driving, Scully riding shotgun, and Mutato, sitting behind them, tapping his hands and blue suede shoes to the music. They enter a Memphis night club, and a woman who—from the back at least—looks very much like Cher is singing. She sings:

Saw the ghost of Elvis, on Union Avenue,
Followed him up to the gates of Graceland,
watched him walk right through.
Now security did not see him, they just
   hovered around the tomb,
There's a pretty little thing, waiting for the King,
down in the Jungle Room.

The Great Mutato is in the audience, sitting beside Mulder and Scully and having the time of his life. He is pumping his arms into the air with excitement. Cher looks down and sings out to her number one fan:

When I'm walking in Memphis!
I was walking with my feet ten feet off of Beale!
Walking in Memphis,
Do I really feel the way I feel?

Mulder high-fives the Great Mutato. On *The Jerry Springer Show*, the host is interviewing Elizabeth Pollidori and Shaineh Berkowitz, each cradling a baby Mutato.

"Tell me something," asks Jerry. "Is it hard to love these babies?"

"What's not to love?" says Shaineh, blissfully.

Everybody in the TV studio audience leaps to his or her feet and bursts into applause.

Back in the nightclub, Cher walks down off the stage and, still singing, pulls the Great Mutato back up with her. Mulder stands, smiles, holds out his hand, and leads Scully onto the dance floor.

The last page of a skillfully hand-drawn comic book is of two FBI agents in each other's arms, gazing upward at their new friend and smiling radiantly.

back story:

A vision within a vision. The most idiosyncratic *X-File* of this, or perhaps any other, season. A work that, in a collaborative and homogenized medium, represents the undiluted creativity of just one man.

In short, a stunningly ambitious exercise in rule-breaking.

"I've always wanted to do a Frankenstein story," says Chris Carter, who has fond memories of watching Hollywood's classic black-and-white horror films as a boy, "and I wanted to tell a story as moving to me as the Frankenstein story had always been."

His problem: "For the longest time," says Carter, "I couldn't figure out how to do it. What I wanted to do went against the strictures of *X-Files* storytelling, because the basic story is so unbelievable. Even Mary Shelley knew it was unbelievable when she wrote the original novel."

His solution: to consciously blur the connection between the *X-Files* world and the real one, therefore heightening the fantasy element while still emphasizing the episode's romantic and apocalyptic themes.

One cornerstone of this approach was an atypical—one might even say surreal—casting process. As was widely reported at the time "Prometheus" aired, for that episode the *X-Files*'s creator dropped his series-long ban on hiring recognizable names and faces. The role of Shaineh Berkowitz was originally written for, and offered to, the famous comedienne and sitcom star Roseanne. She turned it down, however. The role of Cher was written for Cher herself, whom Carter knew through his sister, a major *X-Files* fan. The singer-actress also declined—promising to take on a different *X-Files* guest role in the future—but agreed happily to let her own recordings be used in 5X06's musical sequences.

For the role of Dr. Pollidori, the producers chose John O'Hurley, an actor instantly recognizable for his warped rendition of mail order apparel mogul J. Peterman on U.S. television's highest-rated series *Seinfeld*. From somewhere underneath his elaborate prosthetic makeup, the Great Mutato was played by Chris Owens—an up-and-coming actor (see p.184) who had already appeared twice on *The X-Files* as "The Young Cigarette-Smoking Man," and who would figure prominently in the near-future as another recurring character altogether.

The "actor" who played Izzy Berkowitz was actually Stewart Gale, a young guy whom Chris Carter spotted on the street on the way to his gym last summer. Izzy's two buddies, Goat Boy and Booger, were played by Jean-Yves Hammel and Chris Giacoletti; "a busboy where I get coffee in the morning" and "the snake handler on the *X-Files* movie last summer."

Backstage artists found themselves pushed in equally unexpected directions. The use of black-and-white film necessitated extensive test shots by the camera, makeup, costume, and art departments. "We had to make sure everything we built 'read' properly on the gray scale," says art director Greg Loewen.

"We got a request from Chris that we make certain people look like different animals," says hairstylist Anji Bemben. "We had to make a woman look like a chicken, one guy look like a goat, another guy look like a pig. I said 'Great! Here's where I get to be really creative.'"

Bemben and her assistant, Forest Sala, did some on-the-spot research by having *X-Files* animal wrangler Debbie Coe bring a live chicken to their trailer. "The chicken was mostly black, with very even white feathers—a kind of checkerboard," recalls Bemben with a smile. "So, since the actress who played the news-paper reporter and chicken lady had short black hair, we added white hair extensions. It looked like a funky alternative hairstyle—until you realized she also looked like a chicken."

The Great Mutato's makeup, designed and constructed by special effects makeup supervisor Toby Lindala, consisted of five separate pieces; was powered by nine servo-motors, cost $40,000; and took from five to seven hours to apply to actor Chris Owens's face each morning.

Fully costumed, Owens also wore special gloves, contact lenses, and dentures—and earned Lindala's sincere admiration for actually talking coherently, and in character, from underneath several pounds of latex.

Lindala's own trial by makeup came when he had to turn twin infants into Baby Mutatos for the episode-closing *Jerry Springer Show* sequence. "The little babies kept tearing their hair off, we kept gluing it back on," says Lindala, with a smile and a resigned shrug. "I guess we finally wore one of them out. He fell asleep, we put it on him very carefully, and we kind of tiptoed around until Kim Manners whispered, 'Okay, roll cameras.'"

Construction supervisor Rob Maier counts as one of his proudest Season Five accomplishments the complete renovation of a local barn and the building of a totally new facade, sufficiently isolated and insulated from the original structure, for special effects supervisor David Gauthier to set on fire, spectacularly, without harming anything else.

Picture car coordinator Nigel Habgood had no trouble convincing the president of the Vancouver Nash Club to lend him his 1961 Metropolitan, but he later faced an unexpected problem. In the episode's first scene, when Izzy and his two buddies got in all at once, the little car sagged; its door frame warped; and its two doors wouldn't close. The problem was solved by loading one big boy;, closing the door on his side; then shoehorning his two friends through the other side and jamming their other door into place.

Set decorator Shirley Inget, with the help of approximately 1,000 wall-mounted postcards, turned an ordinary diner in the fishing village of Steveston into J. J.'s eclectic country eatery. Decorating the Pollidoris' gothic mansion, she adds, was "outrageously fun."

Composer Mark Snow considers his score for "The Post-Modern Prometheus" his best work for the season, and the main theme—"a very dark, macabre, insidious sort of nasty waltz, with you know, sort of like a calliope sound"—his most memorable bit of music.

Gillian Anderson, too, sees "Prometheus" as one of her series highlights. "Oh, God, that was so much fun!" she says. "It was just so wonderful to be working with Chris while he was trying to do something different, to take risks. I have to tell you, I didn't always understand what he was doing while were shooting it, but when it was all together it turned out wonderfully."

Others agreed with her. When Emmy nominations were announced last summer, "The Post-Modern Prometheus" earned seven of them: for Outstanding Writing, Outstanding Directing, Outstanding Art Direction, Outstanding Cinematography, Outstanding Single-Picture Editing, Outstanding Makeup, and Outstanding Music Composition.

A highlight of the cast and crew's fifth season "gag reel" was an unused ad lib by David Duchovny.

After the waitress at J. J.'s Country Diner dumps coffee in his lap, he complains,"Why'd you go and do that for? Now my crotch is going to be up all night!"

Chris Owens recalls many pleasant on-set conversations with Duchovny—all while he was wearing his elaborate Great Mutato makeup. "Toward the end of the episode," says Owens, "I asked David if he'd like to meet me for a drink sometime. He said, 'Sure! What do you look like?

emily

Scully's biological
daughter is dying.
Mulder uncovers
the little girl's role
in the alien conspiracy—
while Scully fights
to save her only child.

EPISODE: 5X07
FIRST AIRED: December 14, 1997
EDITOR: Casey O Rohrs
WRITTEN BY: Vince Gilligan &
John Shiban & Frank Spotnitz
DIRECTED BY: Kim Manners

GUEST STARS:
Sheila Larken (Mrs. Scully)
Pat Skipper (Bill Scully, Jr.)
Karri Turner (Tara Scully)
Lauren Diewold (Emily Sim)
Patricia Dahlquist (Susan Chambliss)
Gerard Plunkett (Dr. Calderon)
Tom Braidwood (Frohike)
John Pyper-Ferguson (Detective Kresge)
David Abbott (Judge Maibaum)
Bob Morrisey (Dr. Vinet)
Sheila Patterson (Anna Fugazzi)
Eric Breker (Dark-Suited Man #1)
Stephen Mendel (Dark-Suited Man #2)
Mia Ingimundsen (Nurse)
Tanya Huse (Medical Technician)
Donny Lucas (Hyperbaric Technician)

PRINCIPAL SETTINGS:
San Diego and
Chula Vista, California

A desert sandstorm: impenetrable, opaque. Through the blinding gusts walks a barefoot female figure. It is Dana Scully, wearing a flowing black dress. We are privy to her thoughts. They are:

It begins where it ends.

In nothingness. A nightmare born from deepest fears, coming to me unguarded. Whispered images unlocked from time and distance.

A soul unbound, touched by others but never held. On a course uncharted by some unseen hand.

The journey ahead promising no more than my past reflected back upon me.

Scully falls to her knees and reaches for something in the sand before her. It is a cross on a gold chain. She picks it up. And continues:

Until at last I reach the end. Facing the truth I can no longer deny. Alone, as ever.

Scully stares at the cross, a sense of profound loss in her eyes. Slowly, the color drains from her face and hair, transforming her into sand. She begins to blow away, dissolving into the storm around her.

The action continues from 5X05 ("Christmas Carol"). Fox Mulder arrives at the San Diego Children's Center and is directed to the Special Needs Ward. Scully is already there; she is playing quietly with Emily Sim, helping her fill in the pictures in a coloring book. She smiles in greeting to her partner, then turns to the little girl.

"Emily," says Scully, "I'd like you to meet a friend of mine. His name is Mulder. Remember I told you about him?"

"Hi," says Mulder, gently.

Emily does not reply.

"Hey, Emily," says the FBI agent. "What are you coloring?"

"A potato," she says.

Mulder nods sagely. "Have you ever seen Mr. Potato Head?" he asks.

Emily nods sagely, too. Mulder puffs his cheek into a Mr. Potato Head face and they both share a laugh. Mulder notices Scully's gold cross (from 5X05) around Emily's neck. Scully catches his concerned glance.

"I'll be right back, okay?" says Scully to the little girl. The two agents stand and move to a quiet corner nearby.

"Something's wrong, isn't it?" says Scully.

Mulder's expression confirms that there is. "I found Emily's surrogate mother," he says. "I had Frohike hack into the California Social Services adoption database. Her mother of record was one Anna Fugazzi."

"Fugazzi?" says Scully.

Says Mulder, "As in the slang term for fake."

Mulder adds that the entire birth record is false. "There are no true records," he explains. "Emily didn't come into the world through any system that keeps them."

"Well, how *did* she come into this world?" asks Scully.

"Have you asked yourself that?" replies Mulder, accusingly.

"Well, she was born to someone," Scully says, somewhat defensively. "She had to belong to someone."

"*Someone,*" says Mulder, "who's proven that they'll do anything to protect her. Or their interest in her."

Scully turns away. "I can protect her, too."

"And who's going to protect you?" says Mulder. "Emily's adoptive parents are both dead. By no accident."

"I know," says Scully, her voice trembling. "I've considered that. But I've also considered that there's only one right thing to do."

Mulder says, "Why didn't you call me sooner?"

Scully says, "Because I couldn't believe it. And I need you now to be a witness in my behalf at this hearing,"

"And I should have declined," says Mulder, flatly. "If I never want to see you hurt or harmed in any way."

Scully looks at him, her expression unreadable.

"Then why are you here?"

"Because I know something that I haven't said. Something that they'll use against you to jeopardize your custody of Emily.

"No matter how much you love this little girl," he adds, "She was a miracle who was never meant to be."

In a corridor of the San Diego Hall of Justice, Mulder sits, eating sunflower seeds, and waits. Bill Scully, Tara Scully, and Mrs. Scully leave a hearing room. Bill Scully approaches Mulder. There is a palpable tension between them.

"They're ready for you," says Bill, Jr.

Inside the hearing room are Scully and Judge Richard Maibum. Mulder, blank-faced, sits across the desk from him.

"Agent Mulder, help me out here," says Maibum. "Does FBI stand for 'Federal Bureau of Imagination'? Am I to understand that your partner, along with a dozen other women, was abducted by employees of our federal government?"

Mulder replies, "She was missing for four weeks, which is documented in our files."

The judge consults his file. "And you found evidence that during this time she was subject to a series of experiments where you say they extracted her ova?"

"Yes. All of them."

Scully's reaction to this is a shell-shocked stare.

"Can this be done?" asks the judge.

"I believe it can, and was," says Mulder. "And that Emily Sim was conceived as a result of those experiments."

"And that can be done?"

"I don't know how else to explain it. A medical exam of Ms. Scully would show she hasn't given birth."

The judge looks up from his file and eyes Mulder warily.

"You know," he says, "under normal circumstances this petition would be fairly simple. But I'm having a hard time wrapping my brain around this Michael Crichton bit."

He asks, "Can you give me an explanation? Why anyone would kidnap Ms. Scully, then put her child up for adoption?"

"No," says Mulder. "But the fact remains that Ms. Scully is the mother of this child."

That night in Bill Scully, Jr.'s house—decorated for Christmas as in 5X05—Mulder sits alone on the couch in the living room. Scully joins him.

"It takes two of us just to get my sister-in-law into bed," she says.

"When's she due?" asks Mulder.

"Two weeks ago," says Scully.

There is a long, sad silence between them. Scully speaks first.

"Why didn't you tell me, Mulder?" she says.

Mulder says, softly, "I never expected this. I thought I was protecting you."

Scully's expression, a mask of anguish, is unchanged.

"Why would they do this to me?" she says.

Mulder shakes his head. "I only know that genetic experiments were being done. That children were being created."

"Children being created for who?"

"For who, for what, I don't know."

Bill Scully's phone rings. Scully stands up, walks over, and picks up the receiver.

"Hello?" she says.

There is no response.

"Hello? Is anybody there?"

Mulder realizes what is happening. He reaches quickly for his cell phone, dials, and requests a trace on Scully's call. For a few more moments Scully holds the silent receiver in her hand.

"Thank you," says Mulder. He motions for his partner to hang up.

"County Children's Center," he says.

At the Children's Center someone is pounding on a locked rear entrance. A matron rushes to the door, peers through a glass panel, and lets in Mulder and Scully.

"Has anyone been here in the last half hour?" Mulder asks her, urgently.

"No. What's going on?" says the suddenly frightened woman.

The agents brush past her, rush through the center, and enter a darkened dormitory room. Scully walks quickly to Emily's bed. Relief washes over her; the child is sleeping and apparently safe. She switches on the beside lamp: Emily's hair is matted and her face is damp with perspiration. Scully places a hand on the little girl's forehead.

"She's burning up," she whispers. "Call 911."

The matron rushes to a phone. Mulder bends down and lifts the sleeping child. Cradling her, he's taken only a step or two when his hand brushes against something behind her head.

"Scully. Her neck," he says, alarmed.

He brushes aside Emily's hair. Scully leans in for a closer look.

"Oh, my God," she says.

On the back of Emily's neck is a thick, fibrous cyst the size of a nickel. The strange growth has a sickly greenish tinge.

At a local hospital Emily is treated in an examination room. Scully stands outside, looking in. She is joined by Mulder, who tells her that the social worker has been unable to contact Emily's regular doctor. An ER physician named William Vinet emerges to tell Scully that the little girl is running a fever of 102 and that it was good she got to the hospital when she did.

"Do you know what's causing this?" asks Scully.

"Some kind of infection," says Vinet. "Probably related to the cyst on her neck."

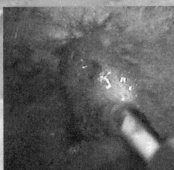

"Do you know what that is?" asks Mulder.

"No," Says Vinet. "I'm having it biopsied. I'll get it off to the lab right away. Now, are you the parents?"

There is a tense silence. Mulder and Scully exchange glances.

"I'm her mother," says Scully.

Vinet accepts this without question and queries Scully about Emily's medical history. She tells him what she knows: that the girl suffers from an autoimmune disorder called hemolytic anemia, and that she'd been undergoing experimental treatment.

"Who's her doctor?" asks Vinet.

"His name is Calderon," says Scully.

Vinet shakes his head. He doesn't know the name.

Inside the examination room a female ER doctor rolls Emily gently onto her side. She swabs the cyst with a local anesthetic, picks up a biopsy needle, and prepares to take a sample of tissue. Mulder looks through the window at this with obvious concern. Something dawns on him and he starts to pound on the glass.

"Wait! Stop! Move away from her! MOVE AWAY FROM HER!" he shouts.

The doctor, turns, looks at him curiously, and turns back to her work. Emily closes her eyes, bracing for the sting. The needle penetrates the cyst and with a hiss, a green, bubbling liquid emerges.

The ER doctor gasps. Vinet moves to enter the exam room, but Mulder restrains him. Inside, the ER doctor reacts violently to the gas, clasping her face in her hands and recoiling backward. She falls heavily to the floor.

Emily sits up on the examining table and watches her, seemingly unaffected.

Sometime later Emily lies asleep in her bed, sedated, in a quarantine room. Mulder and Scully peer in at her, worry and strain on their faces. Mulder tells his partner that the ER doctor is semiconscious.

"How did you know?" asks Scully, sadly.

Mulder forces himself to face her. "If Emily is someone's creation," he says, "it occurred to me that she might share the same body chemistry we'd seen before. So I had them put the ER doctor in a cooling bath, like you did when I was exposed to this (in "End Game," 2X07)."

"So what now?" asks Scully. "I mean, she's still just a little girl."

Mulder shakes his head helplessly.

Scully says, anguished, "You say that I can't protect her. But I can't let this be her life. Just a few days ago she was fine."

"She was also being treated," says Mulder.

Dr. Vinet interrupts. "I need some advice," he says, puzzled. "This Dr. Calderon you say is Emily's physician— he's refusing to transfer Emily's medical records."

"He can't do that!" says Scully. "He's endangering her life."

Vinet says, warily, "He said Emily was in his care, and if you're responsible for stopping that, *you're* the one endangering her."

"It's an ethical violation!" says Scully.

Vinet replies, "He says she was part of a double-blind medical trial. And that he's spoken to you about it."

Vinet pauses, then adds, "He also says you have no authority over this child."

Scully says, "Well, authority or not, I'm not leaving her side."

The corners of Vinet's mouth turn down with hopelessness. "It's beyond me, I'm afraid," he says.

"Yeah," says Mulder. "But it's not beyond Dr. Calderon."

At the headquarters of Transgen Pharmaceuticals in Chula Vista, Dr. Ernest Calderon sits behind a stark, minimalist glass desk.

"I'd like to say right up front," he says, his cultured voice dripping concern, "that I know Emily Sim personally, as your partner probably told you. And my God! I've never met a sweeter, more courageous little girl."

Mulder, who is sitting across from Calderon, nods pensively.

Calderon adds, "My hope is that these custody issues can be resolved so she can resume treatment here. But I'm afraid I simply can't release any information about her as relates to our company's experimental trials."

Mulder considers this for a second or two. "What can I do to convince you?" he says, mildly.

Calderon laughs a sympathetic little laugh. "Well, it's really not about convincing me," he says. "I mean, this is something that, well, we simply cannot do. It's purely a business reality. It has to do with Transgen's exposure to litigation and, of course, our need to protect research which, frankly, represents a significant dollar investment."

Mulder nods slowly and evenly. "So. I'm wasting your time," he says. "This is not worth the life of a three-year-old girl."

Calderon appears sincerely hurt. "No, no," he says. "I wouldn't frame it like that. That's not it at all."

He rises from his chair, and says that he's truly sorry, but there's really nothing he can do. "However," he adds, "I do wish you the very best."

He walks around the desk and holds out his hand to Mulder.

"Okay, then," says Mulder, rising and taking Calderon's hand in his.

With his other arm the agent grabs Calderon's neck and slams his face onto the glass table, then grabs his collar and yanks his body upright again. He slaps him insultingly—once, then twice—across his face.

"How you feeling now?" he says with a sneer.

He throws Calderon to the floor and gives him a kick or two on the backside for good measure.

"Oh! Oh! HELP!" simpers Calderon.

"You smiling little *liar!*" says Mulder. He hauls Calderon upright again, grabs him by the lapels, and pins him against a bookcase. "Why don't you tell me what your company is really in the business of? Huh? Abducting women and stealing their unborn children! Medical rapists, all you are. And now you're going to let that little girl die? She's just a lab rat to you!"

Mulder pulls out his automatic and sticks it in the quivering physician's face. "Why don't you tell me who's life is worth saving—yours or hers? I WANT EVERYTHING THAT WILL HELP THAT LITTLE GIRL!!"

Calderon is too terrified to speak. The door to his office opens and a security guard appears. Mulder appears unimpressed. He tosses Calderon to the floor, holsters his gun, and walks out.

"I'll be back," he says, grimly.

A few minutes later Calderon, badly shaken, leaves the Transgen building, enters his Land Rover, and drives away. Seated in his own car, Mulder watches him leave. He starts his engine.

In a quarantine room at the hospital, Emily lies listlessly in bed, staring at cartoons on a TV monitor. Scully, wearing an anti-contamination gown, watches her through an observation window. She fastens a surgical mask, and enters.

"Sweetie," says Scully, gently. "In a minute a nurse is going to take you to do some tests."

"Mommy said no more tests," says Emily.

Scully says, "We just want you to get better. That's what these test are about."

In another part of the hospital Emily, strapped into a cocoon of blankets, is slid into the tomb-like imaging chamber of a magnetic resonance imaging machine. The huge diagnostic machine starts up, letting loose a staccato burst of machine gun–like sounds.

Calderon pulls out of traffic and

stops the Land Rover at the curb. He walks quickly to an old-style, many-gabled building. One of the dark-suited men we've seen in 5X05 peers at him through the blinds of a second-story window. Calderon enters the room.

"He came to see me. He knows I'm involved," says Calderon.

The dark-suited man turns back to the window and sees Mulder getting out of his car. "Now you've brought him to see us," he says.

The second dark-suited man now stands impassively behind Calderon. Calderon glances around and registers this with some fear.

He turns back to the first man. "What do you want me to tell him?" he asks.

"Nothing" is his reply.

The second man unsheathes an alien stiletto and plunges it into the back of Calderon's neck. As the doctor falls, his wound oozes bubbling green liquid. Both dark-suited men morph into identical copies of Calderon.

Mulder walks up the porch steps of the old building. He's about to open the front door when he notices something inside. He quickly ducks behind a wall, hiding as a man he recognizes as Calderon quickly exits, unlocks the Land Rover, and pulls into traffic. Mulder watches him depart, then heads quickly toward his own car.

At the hospital Scully, Dr. Vinet, and the social worker Susan Chambliss look at an MRI image of Emily's brain. Even to a layman, the picture seems frightening: strange, wispy tendrils wind from the spine and into the brain itself. When Scully speaks, her voice is fearful and trembling.

"I hope you know what this is," she says to Vinet.

The doctor shrugs helplessly. "A neoplastic mass," he says. "A tumorous infection. The cyst in the back of Emily's neck seems to be the point of origin. And from her blood test last night and her SED rate this morning, it also seems to be growing rapidly."

"Is it cancer?" asks Chambliss.

"No," says Vinet. "Cancer grows out of control. These are anaerobic channels following the path of the central ner-

vous system. They have the effect of killing the surrounding tissue, depriving it of the oxygen it needs to survive."

He adds, "Its point of origin is proximal to the brain and the central nervous system. It couldn't be in a worse place."

At this moment the dark-suited man/Dr. Calderon strides quickly through the hospital corridor. He passes the room in which Scully, Vinet and Chambliss are conferring.

"Can you put her on antivirals?" asks Scully.

Vinet shrugs again, stymied. "I've got her on a tevophed drip to keep her blood pressure up, and she's getting steroids intravenously to bring down inflammation. We could attempt radiation therapy."

His suggestion only increases Scully's despair. "No, you can't do that," she whispers. "Her immune system is too weak."

Chambliss looks first at Scully, then at Vinet, then says, "Has anyone spoken to Dr. Calderon about this?"

In the quarantine room some time later "Dr. Calderon," holding a large syringe filled with greenish liquid, stands over a sleeping Emily. He taps the syringe, dispersing the air bubbles, and lowers it to Emily's arm, injecting her.

Scully enters the hospital corridor just in time to see the disguised alien sweep by. If he recognizes Scully, he makes no sign of it.

"Dr. Calderon?" she says, puzzled.

Scully looks into Emily's room and sees the little girl lying face down on her bed. Her IV has been pulled from her arm and her bedside monitor is beeping an alarm. Scully races back into the corridor and hurries after Calderon. She spots his retreating figure and draws her gun.

"Halt!" she yells. "Dr. Calderon! FBI! Stop that man!"

A beefy hospital orderly hears her frantic cries and grabs the fleeing man. Scully runs to the spot, spins the immo-bilized man around, and sees a stranger's face.

In the Transgen parking lot later that night the other Calderon look-alike parks the Land Rover and quickly enters the building. Mulder, parked across the street, answers his ringing cell phone. Scully, calling from the hospital, asks where he is. Mulder tells her that he is following Dr. Calderon.

"What do you mean you've been following him?" says Scully. "I just saw him. There's been a scare here."

She describes the recent incident; says that they've concluded that Emily has been injected with something by Calderon; and tells him that they're running a tox screen on her blood.

Mulder is confused, but only for a second. "Whatever he injected her with," he says, "I don't think he meant to harm her."

"What are you talking about, Mulder?"

"I think Dr. Calderon went there to try to treat her."

"Mulder, that doesn't make sense. Why would he endanger her before only to protect her now."

"That's a bluff," says Mulder. "I don't think they want her dead either, Scully, but for different reasons."

He promises to meet up with his partner later, and hangs up.

Scully turns to see a grim-faced Detective Kresge, who says he's posted two cops outside Emily's room.

"That may not be necessary," says Scully.

Kresge is confused. "But what if this guy Calderon is thinking of coming back?" he says.

Scully replies that there seems to be some indication that he came here to help the girl.

Kresge says, "I don't understand. You said on the phone that he was somehow connected to the death of Emily's parents."

"Because Emily's mother wanted to stop the tests," explains Scully. "Just like I did. And I guess that's why he came here. Because as much as they will do anything to remove what gets in their way, it seems that they need Emily to continue the tests."

Later that night Mulder cautiously pushes open the unlocked front door of the many-gabled house—the same one he's seen Calderon enter earlier. He makes his way through a darkened, old-fashioned hallway; voices and TV sounds filter toward him. He reaches an open room at its far end. On a doorway nearby is a handwritten nameplate: A. FUGAZZI. Mulder knocks and enters.

"Hello," says an old woman, sitting in a wheelchair.

"Anna Fugazzi?" says Mulder.

"Yes," says the woman. "Are you the new doctor?"

"No, I'm not," says Mulder. "Is that your real name?"

"Yes, for the last seventy-one years. Were you looking for me?"

"Not until now," says Mulder.

At the hospital meanwhile two of Emily's MRI films—one noticeably worse than the other—are laid out on a light table. "I don't understand," says Scully. "Just an hour ago you said she was getting better."

"That's right," says Dr. Vinet. "Her fever's down. Her vital signs are back to normal. But these latest MRIs have told me that this growth continues to spread."

He adds, "In her arms, I'm now seeing what looks like a necrotizing of the tissue."

Scully whispers, "It's killing her."

Vinet nods. "Whatever it is, it may already have been present in some amount. Basically, it's shut down her body while it continues to grow. We should be grateful that she's not in any pain."

Vinet exits, and for a moment or two Scully is alone with her pain. Then Susan Chambliss enters, carrying a manila file folder. Scully braces for the worst.

The social worker says, "I presented all this information to the court. And I have to tell you that there is great concern that you are making decisions for this child. They seem to be having no small effect on her health."

Scully replies, defiant, "I am a medical doctor. And the decisions that I make are reasonable and right."

Chambliss shakes her head and tells Scully that, according to her reports, Dr. Calderon's treatment has stopped Emily's decline.

"That's not true!" insists Scully. "The injection that Dr. Calderon gave her is actually making her worse."

"Miss Scully," says Chambliss, not unkindly, "I'm going to say something to you, and I don't want you to take this the wrong way. But I don't think that you are capable right now of responding with any clinical ability."

Scully flares into anger. "Do you think I don't want what's best for this child?" she says. "Do you think that I'm not trying to save her life?"

Chambliss replies, "I'm saying that I'm getting wildly differing reports. I have a job to do. I'm not the final authority here, but you don't have the authority either over this child or her future."

Scully's anger turns into defiance. "You can get a court order," she tells the social worker. "You can try to enforce it. But I suggest that if it's your job to do what's best for this little girl, that you do everything in your power to tell the authorities that if they take Emily out of this hospital, they're going to hasten her illness."

She turns to leave. "And I will make it known," she adds, "that all of you are responsible."

Chambliss is moved by Scully's passion. "What do you want me to tell them that you're doing for her?" she asks.

"I haven't figured that out yet," says Scully, her anger replaced by anguished uncertainty.

At the office of the Lone Gunmen later that night, Melvin Frohike—wearing a telephone headset, and badly in need of a shave—sits hunched over his computer keyboard. He types in a rapid-fire series of commands, scans the screen, and reads:

"Christina Sherman. Delivered a healthy baby girl September 25, 1994."

At the other end of the line is Mulder, in the common room of the old age home, scanning a printout of residents' names.

"Gretchen Miller," reads Mulder.

Frohike enters a few more keystrokes. "Delivered a baby boy March 18, 1996," he says.

"Evelyn Burmeister," says Mulder.

"Evelyn Burmeister," says Frohike. "Delivered a baby boy June 21, 1994."

"That makes eight for eight," says the agent.

"Are you at Adoption Services, Mulder?" asks Frohike.

"No, I'm at the maternity ward."

"Any fetching young mothers in there?"

"Yeah," says Mulder. "I think you might have a shot here, Frohike.

"You know anything about pharmaceuticals?"

"Medicinal or recreational?" asks Frohike.

Mulder tells him that all the women on his list have two prescribed medications in common: abbreviated "PMZ 200" and "Durtab." Frohike replies that they are brand names for estrogen and progesterone—female hormones that would not be given to pregnant women. Mulder looks up to see Anna Fugazzi in her wheelchair, wheeling herself his way.

"You would these," he says to Frohike, hanging up.

Mulder turns to the old woman. "Anna?" he says. "There's a doctor that comes to visit you. A Dr. Calderon?"

"Yes," says Anna, slowly and almost childishly. "Do you know where he is?"

"No, actually, I'm looking for him."

"He was supposed to be here. I was going to start my beauty sleep."

"Your beauty sleep," says Mulder. "What is that?"

Anna smiles brightly. "He said it's taken years off my appearance!" she says.

At the hospital Emily, obviously terrified, is slid into a hyperbaric oxygen chamber. A technician clangs shuts the door of the tubelike vessel behind her. A gowned and masked Scully is standing next to the chamber and watching the little girl through an observation port. She presses a button on the intercom microphone.

"Are you okay in there, Emily?" she says, her voice echoing metallically. Emily nods.

"We're just going to put some extra air in there. So you let me know if your ears start to hurt."

Scully nods to the technician. He turns a valve and oxygen begins to enter the chamber. Emily grimaces.

"You okay, sweetie?" says Scully.

Emily, silent tears flowing, shakes her head.

"Turn it off," says Scully to the technician. She peers inside the chamber. Something snakelike is beginning to stir underneath the skin of Emily's arm.

"Turn it off! NOW!" she shouts.

The technician scans his console frantically. "I'm doing it, ma'am," he says, nervously.

Scully turns to Emily. "It's okay, sweetie, settle down," she says. "We're going to get you out of there as fast as we can."

At the old age home Mulder enters a back room through a frosted-glass door. A half dozen or so elderly women lie sleeping, face up, on hospital gurneys. They are hooked up to meticulously labeled intravenous bags containing PMZ 200 and Durtab, as prescribed by Dr. Calderon. Mulder reaches down and examines the wrist tag on one of the women. It bears the name "Charmaine Villard."

Mulder turns his attention to a refrigerated cabinet in the far corner. He opens it; inside is a medical transport case containing two securely packed glass cylinders. Inside an attached plastic envelope is a printed form similar in size and shape to a Fedex airbill. Mulder reads it: amidst a thicket of impenetrable acronyms and numerals are the names "Villard, Charmaine," and "Scully, DK."

Mulder returns to the refrigerator and pulls out one of the glass cylinders.

It contains a greenish liquid. Suspended within it is what looks like a human fetus, attached by umbilical cord to a floating placenta. The embryo, clearly alive, kicks convulsively.

Mulder recoils at the sight. He reaches into the cabinet and pulls out a small cardboard box. Inside are ampoules of the same greenish fluid "Dr. Calderon" injected into Emily.

Mulder hears a noise. Quickly pocketing an ampoule, he goes to the window and spots the alien disguised as Calderon entering the building. He grabs several more ampoules, exits the room, and starts to walk briskly down the corridor. Out of nowhere, a hand holding an automatic pistol appears.

"Flinch and you're dead! Hands where I can see them!" says Detective Kresge. He is standing behind Mulder, his pistol pointed at the back of the agent's head.

Mulder, an ampoule in one of his raised hands, freezes.

"What have you got there?" asks Kresge.

Mulder is silent.

"Give it to me slowly," says Kresge, taking the ampoule. "Now, up against the wall! Spread your legs!"

Mulder breaks his silence. "Who are you?" he says.

Kresge identifies himself.

"Detective Kresge," says Mulder with forced calm, "I'm Special Agent Mulder, with the FBI."

A door opens at the far end of the corridor and the disguised alien steps inside. "Take that gun off me," says Mulder, "and put it on that man!"

Kresge hesitates for a moment, then trains his weapon on the alien, who is walking implacably toward them.

"Stop right there!" says Kresge.

But the alien doesn't stop.

"Run! Get out of here!" yells Mulder to Kresge.

Instead, Kresge cocks his gun and prepares to fire. He drops the ampoule on the floor, and Mulder kicks it down the corridor, away from the advancing alien.

"Don't use your gun!" says Mulder, beginning to back away. "GET OUT OF HERE!"

Kresge, confused, hesitates. The alien keeps coming at him.

"I said stop *right there*," he says grimly.

Mulder scrambles off down the corridor, scooping up the ampoule on his way. The alien reaches Kresge, grabs him by the gun arm, and flings him like a rag doll to the floor. Then the alien heads toward Mulder, who seems frozen at the sight.

Kresge staggers to his knees and picks up his gun. Mulder watches this with alarm.

"Don't fire, Kresge!" he shouts.

Kresge lets loose two well-aimed shots. They hit their mark, and the alien staggers slightly. Green fluid begins to bubble from his torso. There is a faint hissing noise. Mulder flees through the door.

Inside the corridor, Kresge is getting to his feet when the escaping gas hits him. He grabs his eyes, moans in pain and shock, and sinks slowly to the floor.

Mulder runs down the steps of the old age home and pulls out his cell phone, dialing 911.

"I'm an FBI agent," he says urgently. "I have an emergency situation. I need an ambulance and I need backup."

Inside the house the alien kneels over the prostrate Kresge and eyes him expressionlessly. Then he slowly morphs into the image of the detective.

Outside, on the sidewalk,

Mulder is still talking to the police dispatcher.

"Mulder! I've got him inside!" says "Kresge," exiting the building.

"Do you have your weapon?" asks Mulder.

"He's in there on the floor. I've got him handcuffed," is the reply.

Mulder says, "I got backup coming. And they need the location."

The alien says, "I've got it handled. Just watch this guy."

He walks briskly to Calderon's Land Rover, unlocks it, and gets in. Mulder watches him drive away. At that moment he realizes how he has been tricked—and much more.

In the hospital Scully stands vigil outside the quarantine room. Mulder enters the observation area behind her. Emily lies motionless on her bed.

"She's gone into a coma," says Scully, softly.

Mulder turns away, beyond words.

"It's okay, Mulder," says Scully. "It's what's meant to be."

Mulder says, "If you could treat her—"

Scully says, "I wouldn't. I wouldn't do it to her."

"Are you sure?" whispers Mulder.

"Whoever brought this child into this world," says Scully, "didn't intend to love her."

Mulder looks deep into his partner's eyes. "I think she was born to serve an agenda," he says.

"I have a chance to stop that," says Scully. She adds, "You were right, Mulder. This child was not meant to be."

Mulder sighs, deeply moved. "I'll stay with you," he says.

"I think I'd like to be alone," says Scully.

Her partner nods and turns away, pocketing the ampoule of the greenish serum before he leaves. Scully enters Emily's room and bends down, gently placing her head beside her little girl's.

In a funeral chapel a few days later a black-clad

Scully sits in a pew, deep in thought. Her mother approaches and lays a hand on her shoulder.

"Are you ready?" says Mrs. Scully.

Her daughter looks up. "I think I'll get a ride back with Mulder," she says.

Mother and daughter hug, and Scully is embraced by her brother. Standing next to him is Tara Scully and their newborn son. Scully bends down and gently kisses him on the forehead.

"Bye-bye, Matthew," says Scully.

And then she is alone.

At the front of the chapel lies a child-sized white coffin. Scully stands before it. From the rear of the room a man—Mulder—approaches. He places a bouquet of flowers on the casket.

"Who are these men," says Scully, "who would create a life whose only hope was to die?"

"I don't know," says Mulder. "But that you found her, and you had a chance to love her, maybe she was meant for that, too."

Scully thinks for a second. "She found me," she says.

"So you could save her," says Mulder, gently.

Scully nods.

"How is Detective Kresge?"

Mulder tells him that he is out of the ICU and doing better.

"And the men who did this to him?"

Mulder says that they'd already cleaned out the nursing home, and that there is now no evidence that anyone else at Transgen knew anything about Calderon's work.

Scully gazes at the casket. "There is evidence of what they did," she says.

Mulder removes the bouquet from the casket and turns away. Scully slowly lifts the lid. Inside are several small sandbags, approximately the weight of a small child, also the gold crucifix that Dana Scully once gave Emily.

Scully lifts the tiny cross, letting it hang loosely from her fingertips, and stares at it, a sense of profound loss in her eyes.

back story:

It was a heartbreaking dilemma—and every filmmaker's worst nightmare.

Prior to the start of filming "Christmas Carol" (5X05), the role of Emily Sim was given to a bright, attractive, and very photogenic four-year-old girl whose name, for reasons that will soon be obvious, will not be given here.

"She didn't have much dialogue in the first part of the two-parter, and she was perfectly fine in it," says Vancouver-based executive producer Robert Goodwin. "It was only when we started filming 'Emily' that the difficulty started."

In several important scenes in 5X07 Emily lies in a hospital bed or inside an intimidating-looking piece of medical apparatus. Quite understand-ably—but utterly disastrously—the little girl became so terrified by her surroundings that she would begin to cry and simply could not be com-forted. Shooting ground to a halt. Gillian Anderson had formed a good rapport with the girl (who had spent off-screen time during 5X05 playing with the star's young daughter, Piper); but even her hugs and reassurances could not get filming restarted.

And the clock was ticking. "So I had to make a decision," says Goodwin. Although the little girl's parents assured him that their daughter would soon pull herself together, he realized he had no choice but to recast the role immediately. Shortly afterward a somewhat older child actress—Lauren Diewold, who had previously appeared in an episode of *Millenium*—was chosen to take over the part.

Everybody was pleased with little Lauren's performance (as they were, in general with the episode), but now there was another problem, a big one. In order to match "Emily" with "Christmas Carol," the producers had to somehow insert their new guest star into the earlier episode as well.

Gillian Anderson's shooting schedule, already stretched beyond the limit, could not be changed to allow her to reshoot her "Christmas Carol" scenes with Emily. Instead, precious second-unit time was scrounged to allow Lauren to film her scenes with Anderson's double; the scenes of Scully and her new daughter were then pieced together in the editing room.

But that was the easiest part. In one or two scenes Emily is in the background behind Scully and, since establishing her presence is vital to the plot, the only solution was to use film of Anderson with the first Emily. Luckily, in the original shots Emily's face is turned away from the camera, so in postproduction, visual effects supervisor Laurie Kallsen-George was able to painstakingly color the first girl's blond hair to match Lauren Diewold's considerably darker locks.

At another point in the re-editing process it was noticed that Lauren—whose "Christmas Carol" wardrobe, of course, had to match the first girl's exactly—had in one scene been mistakenly dressed in the wrong costume. In a feat that she had never before attempted, Kallsen-George spent many computer-hours "changing" Emily's clothing electronically.

That adventure cost $15,000 and a few more gray hairs in a month that produced more than its share. "Frankly, I didn't think we were going to make it that time," recalls one production staffer, wide-eyed.

In February 1998, several episodes away from "Emily," Bob Goodwin was still somewhat shaken by the incident. "I had to fire a sweet little girl," he said to a visitor. "Could that be the worst thing I've ever done in this business?"

Though aired on consecutive weeks, "Christmas Carol"/"Emily" was the first *X-Files* two-parter filmed out of sequence.

Ⓧ

Scully's gold crucifix was crafted to props master Ken Hawryliw's specifications by a local North Vancouver jeweler. According to Hawryliw, his Hollywood counterparts on the *X-Files* feature film scoured Southern California—unsuccessfully— for an off-the-shelf equivalent. Ultimately, the movie ended up using a slightly different crucifix than the television show.

Ⓧ

The filming of 5X07 included a bizarre *X-Files*-real world interaction. The ninety-year old building rented to be the aliens' old age home was scheduled to be converted into an upscale condominium complex—much to the chagrin of some of the working-class residents of its east Vancouver neighborhood. A few days before shooting was scheduled to begin, the building was occupied by squatters; after the police evicted them, the site was picketed by anti-redevelopment protesters. Locations manager Todd Pittson, fearing that activists would like nothing more than to call attention to their cause by disrupting a hit American TV series, ordered his prep crew to keep a low profile and remove all *X-Files* insignia from their clothing. In the end, thirty-odd demonstrators were indeed gathered when the film crew arrived: but police and extra security personnel kept them harmlessly across the street.

Ⓧ

John Pyper-Ferguson, who plays Detective Kresge, played the convict named Paul in "F. Emasculata" (2X22).

kitsunegari

The serial killer known as
"The Pusher"—a man with
the inexplicable ability to impose
his own will on others—escapes
from a maximum security prison.
He immediately pursues the man
who captured him: Mulder.

EPISODE:
5X08
FIRST AIRED:
January 4, 1998
EDITOR:
Heather MacDougall
WRITTEN BY:
Vince Gilligan & Tim Minear
DIRECTED BY:
Daniel Sackheim

GUEST STARS:
Mitch Pileggi (AD Walter Skinner)
Diana Scarwid (Linda Bowman)
Robert Wisden (Robert Modell)
Colleen Winton (Physical Therapist)
Scott Oughterson (Older Orderly)
Ty Olsson (Younger Orderly)
Kurt Evans (Todd)
Donna Yamamoto (Asian-American Agent)
Michelle Hart (Trace Agent)
Steven Jones (Field Agent)
Stuart O'Connell (First Falls Church Cop)
Richard Leacock (Second Falls Church Cop)
Clare Lipinskie (ICU Nurse)
Gail Anderson (ER Doctor)
Michael Dobson (U.S. Marshal)
John Dadey (Second U.S. Marshal)
Jill Krop (Reporter)
Mark Holden (Cop)

PRINCIPAL SETTINGS:
 Lorton, Occoquan, and
Falls Church, Virginia

In the hospital ward of Lorton Penitentiary, a physical therapist works intently with a pajama-clad prisoner. The man appears to be a stroke victim or to suffer from a debilitating disease; painfully and slowly, he pushes a blue plastic wheel across the gray-tiled floor.

"Keep going. Keep going," says the therapist, a middle-aged woman. "That's the way. Don't stop now. Come on, keep pushing! No pain, no gain!"

Standing nearby and watching this are two burly prison orderlies—one in his twenties, the other in his late forties. The patient and his therapist struggle to creep forward another nine or ten feet.

"Hit it," says the older orderly, grimly. They roll a wheelchair toward the spot where the disabled man is standing. With the therapist's help, they lower him gently to a seated position.

"Nice and easy," says the therapist, soothingly. She adds, "You're really coming along, Bobby. I'm very pleased with your improvement."

"Back off!" says the older orderly.

He turns to his colleague. "Keep your fingers on your pepper spray, just like I told you," he says, manacling the patient to the arms of the chair. The therapist looks down disapprovingly and asks him if the cuffs are really necessary.

"Yes, ma'am," says the orderly. "I'd say it is."

The two big men wheel their charge down a long prison corridor. "So," says the younger man, "what's this guy's story?"

"Cop killer" is his reply. "Regular-people killer. General all-around waste of skin."

"So, what are you scared of?" says the younger man. "Guy's a freakin' vegetable. What's he gonna do? Run over you with his big plastic wheel?"

The veteran stops and turns to the rookie. "I tell you what," he says. "You want to last more than a week, you don't

ever underestimate this man. Never trust him. Never let your guard down around him. Never. *Capice?*"

"*Comprendo,*" replies the other man, apparently sobered.

The trio reaches the end of the hall, where they are buzzed through a locked door and into a higher-security area. The prisoner's face is at last visible. He is prematurely gray, and has a long scar running from his temple to his hairline. He is expressionless. He is Robert Patrick Modell, a.k.a. "The Pusher," last seen in 3X17. A barred door clangs shut behind him.

Later that night the younger orderly, alone on guard duty, pours himself a cup of coffee. Bored, he peers down the long line of cell doors. A red call light is flashing in front of the one marked MODELL, ROBERT P. He leaves his guard booth, peers in through a small window, and sees Modell sleeping soundly. Unsheathing his pepper spray, he opens the cell door, walks cautiously over to Modell, and checks that the man is securely manacled to his bed.

"What's up, Modell?" says the orderly.

Modell is whispering something, but it is too low to be deciphered. The orderly holsters his pepper spray and cautiously leans down toward the prisoner's face.

The next morning sunlight streams through the prison skylight. The older orderly arrives at work and notices the guard post unmanned.

"Hey, Chuck?" he says.

He notices that Modell's cell door is open. He runs down to the corridor and looks inside. Modell's bed is empty. The younger orderly is huddled in the opposite corner, staring into space. He thumps his head against the wall behind him.

"What the hell happened, Chuck?" asks the older man, urgently. "Where's Modell?"

The younger man looks at him, eyes unfocused. "He had to go," he says.

Later that morning Mulder and Scully arrive at the prison cafeteria, where Assistant Director Skinner is briefing several dozen prison officials, U.S. Marshals, and FBI field agents. Skinner announces that the FBI is taking control of the operation to recover Modell.

He says, "The orderly is being questioned, but judging by his mental state, he's not going to be much help to us. So, there's very little we know for sure at this point."

He adds, "What we do know is that the last confirmed bed check was 2:04 A.M. As of 6:14 A.M., the subject was reported escaped. Since then, there have been no reported sightings or contact."

A marshal asks Skinner how Modell

managed to get out of the prison.

"Every indication," says Skinner, "is that he simply walked out the front door."

He introduces Mulder and Scully, the agents who apprehended the subject the first time around. Mulder takes over the briefing. He tells the lawmen that the escaped convict is Robert Patrick Modell.

"He's a serial killer responsible for at least seventeen murders. Specifically, he targets law enforcement. In 1996 he caused the death of an FBI agent and a Loudoun County Sheriff's deputy. It's all a game to him. He was looking for, in his words, 'a worthy adversary.'"

Now Scully speaks up. "To win," she says, "makes him feel important. He likes to think of himself as a *ronin*, a warrior without a master, adhering to the *Budo*, the Japanese Way of War.

"In truth," she adds, "he's a highly intelligent sociopath who has no fear of dying. In keeping with his game archetype, he likes to leave clues. This is why we expect to be contacted by him—hopefully sooner rather than later."

Mulder says, "Modell refers to himself as 'Pusher.' Technically speaking, all of his victims' wounds were self-inflicted. This man has a unique ability to force his will on others, to push his victims into harming or killing themselves."

A lawman looks at him in disbelief. "Say what?" he says.

"Okay, listen," says Mulder. "Here's all you need to know: Do not trust this man. Do not talk to him. Do not engage him in conversation. Even if he is unarmed, approach him only with extreme caution and then only with adequate backup."

"So, what's adequate backup?" asks a marshal.

"Adequate backup," replies Mulder, "means every cop you can lay your hands on."

The briefing breaks up. Scully pulls out a medical file; Mulder asks her about Modell's physical condition; she tells him it was extremely weakened.

"Mulder, I'm amazed he's even alive," she adds. "The condition we last saw him in, comatose, a bullet in his head—"

"How did he recover?" says Mulder.

Scully reads the file, shrugs, and says that six months ago Modell simply woke up.

"What about that brain tumor?" asks her partner. "Wasn't that supposed to be killing him?"

Scully replies, "It still is."

Mulder asks her who on the prison staff they can talk to about Modell's true condition. Scully suggest the physical therapist, then adds, "If Modell is planning to take up where he left off, where does that leave you? You were his prime target. Should you even be heading this investigation?"

"As opposed to what?" says Mulder. "What's your point?"

"That it's exactly what he wants," says Scully. "That once again, you're playing his game."

At a strip mall in suburban Occoquan, the only clerk at a small sporting goods store watches a TV news report on Modell's escape. The front door opens, and he recognizes his new "customer" immediately.

"Hi," says Robert Patrick Modell, with a wide smirk.

The employee slowly reaches down for a baseball bat stashed under the checkout counter. Modell notices, but is unimpressed.

"You're not scared of snakes?" says the killer. "Looks like a timber rattler."

Confused, the employee looks at his own hand. His eyes widen in terror; he sees a writhing, hissing snake.

"Don't let it bite you," says Modell, smoothly. "Don't drop it. You drop it, he'll get ya."

Modell peers at the terrified man's name tag. "Todd?" he says. "Do you think I can get some service now?"

"Yeah," whispers Todd.

"Go into the back," says Modell. "And put the snake down."

As the clerk retreats, the escaped convict walks around the counter and ransacks a display of protein treats called "CarboBars." (from the makers of "CarboBoost," as seen in 3X17). He tears one open and wolfs it down greedily.

On the TV monitor the report on his escape is continuing. The news footage is jerky, but Mulder and Scully—shown amid the other lawmen on the case—can plainly be seen.

In the physical therapy room the therapist pages through reams of X rays and bullet-wound diagrams.

"He couldn't have been faking it completely, that's all I can say," she says. "The gunshot wound did a hell of a lot of damage."

The woman looks up at her questioner—Mulder. "You're the officer that shot him," she says flatly.

Mulder does not respond.

Scully, holding her own file, has been standing nearby through this. "It says here Modell had a visitor yester-

day afternoon," she says.

"Who?" asks Mulder.

The therapist tells them that Modell was visited by a member of "The Little Sisters of Charity"—an order of nuns whose mission it is to minister to prisoners. Also, that no other friends or family members, if he even had any, ever showed up.

She adds, "He never gave me any grief. He worked hard at getting better. I talked to him sometimes."

"About what?" says Mulder.

"Small talk," she replies. "Nothing important. He'd ask how I was."

"He's a very considerate man," says Mulder, sarcastically.

The therapist bristles. "I don't doubt for a second," she says, "that Robert Modell belongs in prison. But I never had any problem with him personally."

The door to the therapy room clangs open and an FBI man bursts in.

"Agents, it's Modell!" he shouts.

Mulder and Scully depart at a dead run. A few moments later Mulder arrives at the cafeteria, where Skinner, standing in front of a wall phone with its HOLD button blinking, is waiting.

"He's asking for you," says the AD, rapidly. "We're running a trace right now. We just need thirty seconds."

Mulder nods, glances briefly at Scully's expression of concern, and picks up the phone.

"Yeah," says the agent.

"Two words. It's . . . ALIVE!" laughs Modell.

Mulder replies, "I don't feel like playing your game right now, Modell."

"Touchy! Look, Mulder, there's something I need you to hear."

"Tell it to me in person, Modell."

"No. Seriously, listen to me."

"No! You listen to me! Either you come back on your own, or I drag your sorry ass back on the bumper of my car!"

Scully gets her partner's attention.

"Time—four seconds," she says quietly but urgently. "Don't let him rope you in!"

Modell keeps talking. "When did you turn into Clint Eastwood?" he says. "Stop talkin' like a tough guy, and pay attention. I know you're tracing this call, I don't care. I have something I need for you to hear. Mulder, are you going to—"

"Mulder!" insists Scully. "Hang up the phone!"

Mulder calmly cuts Modell off and places the receiver on the hook. All turn to a trace agent monitoring the call.

"We got it," she says.

Shortly afterward the entire armed task force surrounds the sporting goods store in Occoquan. Gun drawn, Mulder enters, and finds it apparently deserted. He spots a half-eaten CarboBar on the checkout counter. Scully reports that Modell is not in the store.

"How far could he get?" says Skinner.

Mulder looks through the store's front window and spots a lone figure wearing prison pajamas, across the street.

"Outside!" he shouts.

Mulder sprints across the avenue—narrowly dodging some passing cars—and runs down the slowly shambling figure. He spins the man around. It is Todd, the sporting goods clerk, dressed in Modell's clothing, eyes unfocused.

Skinner pulls up beside him. "Where is he? Where's Modell?" he demands.

"He had to go," says Todd, in a trance-like voice.

Mulder turns away, frustrated and angered.

At an undisclosed location, Modell—dressed in a brand-new sweat suit from the sporting goods store—stares down at a small framed photograph of an attractive woman. A can of bright blue paint lies spilled on the white-carpeted floor. Modell exits, a door clicking behind him.

Seated in a recliner in the center of the room is a dead man painted blue, head to toe. Not a spot of pink skin shows through the drying enamel.

Shortly afterward, the same apartment—its walls splattered with blue-painted Japanese ideograms—is crawling with lawmen, Mulder and Scully among them.

"I'm gonna take a wild stab here," says Mulder, surveying the scene, "and guess that this, here, is a clue."

Scully inserts a gloved finger into the corpse's mouth. Blue paint pours out of it, trickling over the dead man's chin.

"It appears as if he died ingesting paint," she says. "I imagine he did all this, and drank what was left."

Mulder turns to see Skinner entering the crime scene accompanied by a Japanese-American FBI agent.

"See what you can make of this," he says to the agent. He turns his attention to Scully.

"Modell?" says Skinner.

"Cerulean blue," she says, nodding toward the empty paint can.

Skinner says, "What the hell's the point of all this?"

"Maybe his choice of victim," says Scully, with a shrug. "This is Nathan Bowman, with the Loudoun County Attorney's office. He's the prosecutor who tried Modell in 1996."

"So you think it's simple revenge?" says Skinner.

The question has no obvious answer. They turn to face the Japanese-American agent.

"Sir, it's not a manifesto," she says. "It's just the same single ideogram, over and over. The hand it's in is pretty sloppy, but I think it's supposed to be *kitsunegari*—'foxhunt.'"

"Fox Mulder," says Scully.

Mulder turns away.

"That's sort of on the nose, don't you think?" he says, just a bit too casually.

Mulder studies the blue-painted wall and a single blue thumbprint on the frame of the woman's portrait. "Was Bowman married?" he asks.

Scully scrapes some blue paint off the corpse's right hand, revealing a gold ring.

"Yep," she says.

Skinner turns to Mulder, and asks, "What are you thinking?"

Mulder walks to a table phone, spots the name LINDA scrawled on its speed-dial list, and hits the button next to it. Over the speakerphone a female voice answers.

"NovaMax Realty," she says.

"Hi, Linda?" says Mulder.

"I'm sorry," says the receptionist. "Mrs. Bowman has left the office to meet a client. May I take a message?"

Mulder says, "Do you know the name of the client that Mrs. Bowman went to see?"

"It's, uh . . . Mulder. Mr. Fox Mulder."

"Do you know where Mrs. Bowman went to meet Fox Mulder? The location?"

"I know it's a commercial property in Falls Church," says the receptionist. "Can you hold on, please?"

"Yeah," says Mulder.

Skinner reaches for his cell phone, punches in a number, then speaks quickly and urgently. "Give me the Falls Church PD," he says.

In front of a nondescript warehouse in a quiet industrial district, a NovaMax FOR SALE sign lists Linda Bowman as the sales contact. A police cruiser slows to a stop at the warehouse entrance, and two Falls Church cops—one white, one black—emerge. They notice that the front door has been jimmied, and call for backup.

"Exercise extreme caution, Six" she replies. "Backup is on route."

The officers enter with guns drawn, their flashlight beams stabbing into the dusty gloom, and climb up an open stairwell.

"Hello, officers! I'm over here!" says a distant voice—Modell's. "Keep on comin'. That's right!

"No, not that way. Not that way, either. But you're getting warmer! Buddy, whaddaya want me to do? Draw you a map?"

The white cop, gun outstretched, rounds a corner, and faces Modell, who is aiming a gun back at him.

"PUT IT DOWN!" shouts the cop. "PUT THE GUN DOWN! PUT IT DOWN NOW ON THE FLOOR!"

The standoff lasts for another second. Then Modell lowers the pistol, places it on the ground, and slowly, arms outstretched, lies down on his stomach.

The white cop reaches for his walkie-talkie. "Morty, I got him!" he says. "Get up here!"

Outside the warehouse a convoy of police cars screeches to a halt. Mulder, Scully, and Skinner run inside with the rest of the task force. "Federal agents!" yells Skinner. "Officer, where are you?"

The white cop yells back with his location. When the agents arrive, they see him holding his gun on his prisoner—his partner.

"I got him!" says the white cop, triumphantly.

"He's gone crazy! Get him away from me!" shouts the black cop, spread-eagled on the floor.

Skinner surveys the scene as the cop is gently disarmed. "He was here," says the AD grimly. "He did come for the woman."

"Why Bowman's wife?" asks Scully. "What would he want with her?"

A gray sedan pulls up in front of the warehouse. Inside is a woman, the woman in Nathan Bowman's framed photograph. She surveys the surrounding chaos, puzzled and somewhat worried.

"Linda Bowman? Fox Mulder," says the first man who reaches her.

"Hi," says the woman, nervously. "You're my twelve-fifteen?"

A few minutes later Linda Bowman, in obvious shock, is sitting in a makeshift office describing how an unknown person

phoned her secretary to make the bogus appointment with Mulder.

"Why would someone do this to Nathan?" she asks plaintively.

"Mrs. Bowman," asks Scully, "Did your husband ever discuss his work as a prosecutor with you?"

"Sometimes," answers the woman.

"Did he ever mention the name 'Robert Patrick Modell'?"

Linda Bowman replies immediately. "Pusher?" she says.

She tells Mulder, Scully, and Skinner that the Pusher prosecution was her husband's biggest case. She responds in shock and horror when told that Modell has escaped from prison, was probably the person who made the real estate appointment, and is the prime suspect in her husband's murder.

"You're safe with us, Mrs. Bowman," says Skinner. He leads her away toward protective custody. Scully prepares to leave, but her partner hangs back, deep in thought.

Mulder says, "Why didn't Modell just kill those two cops? What was to stop him?"

"Well, hopefully," replies Scully, "he was incapable."

"As in too tired?" says Mulder.

"Well, we've seen that before in him," says Scully.

"Maybe," says Mulder. "I don't know. Something's just not making sense."

Mulder walks over to a nearby cop and borrows his radio.

From a high window across the street from the warehouse, Modell gnaws on a CarboBar and looks down on Mulder, walking purposely toward him, and then to a security motorcade, supervised by Skinner, taking Linda Bowman to safety. He turns behind him to face a Latino janitor, who seems somehow unaware of his presence. Modell takes a swig of coffee and replaces the top on the janitor's thermos.

"Gracias, amigo," says the mass murderer.

On the street below Mulder passes through the front door to Modell's office building. He spots an empty CarboBar wrapper on the floor, draws his gun, and walks—senses on red alert—up a staircase connecting the second floor to the lobby. He enters an empty second floor office suite and faces Modell, who stands facing him, hands in his pockets.

"What took you so long?" sneers Modell.

Mulder grabs his walkie-talkie. "Scully, I got him. Come quick," he says.

"Hold on a second, Mulder," says Modell. "Hold on! We need to talk."

Mulder ignores him. He looks around, pinpoints his exact location, and relays it to Scully.

Modell says, insistently, "Mulder, listen to me. There's something I need you to hear."

"Shut up, Modell!" shouts Mulder. "SHUT UP, OR I WILL SHOOT YOU, YOU SON OF A BITCH! I WILL SHOOT YOU! SHUT UP!"

Modell is unfazed. "You're going to listen to me," he says, hypnotically. "You're going to listen to me. You're going to listen to me."

"I will shoot you!" says Mulder, his gun hand wavering slightly.

"Listen, Mulder!" whispers Modell.

A few moments later Scully and a squad of lawmen run toward the entrance of the office building. They are met by Mulder, exiting, his gun hanging limply by his side. Glassy-eyed, He plods right past Scully, who has to turn around and jog after him.

"Mulder. Mulder! What happened? Where's Modell?" says Scully.

"He had to go," says the agent, in a dull monotone. Scully stops and stares at her partner, dismayed.

A few minutes later Scully relays the news to Skinner that Modell has vanished without a trace. She also tells him, without much conviction in her voice, that Mulder is unharmed. She pockets her cell phone and walks over to her partner. Mulder is staring at the ground, dismayed.

"How are you feeling?" says Scully.

Mulder says, "Well, aside from the utter and grinding humiliation that comes from knowing I let our suspect go, pretty good."

"It could have happened to anyone, Mulder."

"No, actually, it couldn't have," he replies. "I didn't find Modell, he sought me out. He wanted me to hear his message."

"Which was what?"

"'Don't play the game,'" says Mulder.

Scully wonders at this, not understanding.

"Whose game? His?" she says.

"I don't think so," says Mulder. "I don't think he's even playing a game."

"What are you talking about?" says Scully, incredulously. "Of course he is. You said yourself he was going to pick up where he left off."

"Then why didn't he kill the cops?" says Mulder. "Or the prison guard. Or, hell, while we're at it, why didn't he kill me? Why didn't he make me eat a bullet out of my own gun? He could have."

Scully says, "He killed Nathan Bowman."

Mulder replies, "Yeah, he was definitely there. But that doesn't prove that he did it."

Scully is shaken by this. She looks at Mulder with more than a tinge of concern and suspicion. "Mulder, this man's affected you," she says. "He's influenced your thinking."

Mulder shakes his head in disgust. "It's not like that," he says.

Scully says, "A man is made to drink a gallon of cerulean blue paint? *Kitsunegari*—foxhunt? You're saying now that's not Modell?"

"Modell is involved," says Mulder. "He's related to it somehow, but not the way you think."

Scully says, "That's your opinion?"

"Yeah," says Mulder, "That's my opinion."

"How can we be sure it's your own?" says Scully.

Mulder nods quickly, tacitly acknowledging her fears, and looks her squarely in the eye. "What do we still agree on here? That Modell was pursuing Linda Bowman?"

Scully says nothing.

"I want to know why," says Mulder.

At an FBI safe house—more like a fenced security compound—in Annandale, Virginia, Skinner, Mulder, and Scully continue to question a distraught Linda Bowman.

Bowman says, "Nathan was very proud of having prosecuted the case. He said this man Modell was extremely clever and dangerous. And that he was a menace to

society. Nathan mentioned that an FBI agent ultimately shot Modell."

She turns to Mulder. "Was that you?" she says.

Mulder nods grimly. "Yes," he says.

Bowman adds, "He said you crippled him, put him in a wheelchair. Nathan said it was too bad you didn't just kill him. That it would have saved the taxpayers the cost of a trial."

Scully says, "Your husband talked with you a lot about it."

"Well, as I said," says Bowman, "he was proud. I guess he felt that it was his brush with greatness."

"Is it possible," asks Scully, "that he could have mentioned you to Robert Modell?"

"No, no. I sincerely doubt it," says Bowman. "You see, Nathan and I, we were only married two months."

"How long did you know him?" asks Mulder, mildly surprised.

Bowman laughs gently. "Well, it was two months and two days. Well, why wait when it's true love? You never know how long you have."

"No, you don't," says Mulder, shooting a glance toward his puzzled partner.

Bowman adds, "It's not like Nathan was impulsive or flighty. I don't want to paint him like that."

Mulder says, to himself, "He was true blue."

The interview concludes and the three FBI agents confer in a hallway.

"She killed Nathan Bowman," says Mulder, flatly.

"*What?*" says Scully.

"Modell was there," adds Mulder. "But for some other reason. She killed her husband."

"Wait a minute! Just hear me out," says Mulder. "Her husband's 'brush with greatness'? She doesn't want to 'paint' him as being impulsive? Who the hell talks like that?"

"You tell me," says Scully.

Mulder says, "She was waving it under our noses! She was playing with us. Modell told me—he warned me—not to play the game. I think it was her game that he was talking about."

"Modell told you," says Skinner, skeptically.

Mulder says, "Has she asked how her husband was murdered? Has she shown any interest in the details? An escaped serial killer is supposedly stalking her. Does she seem particularly fearful to you?"

"The woman's in shock, Agent Mulder," says Skinner, teeth gritted. "She's not herself. And I might add, neither are you."

Mulder turns to his partner "You heard her in there, Scully," he says.

"Mulder, no," she says. "I'm sorry. You said it yourself. You said don't listen to Modell. Don't trust him. But you've done both."

"But what if," he says, "she can do what Modell does?"

Scully is silent. Skinner comes to a painful decision.

"I think you should go home," the AD tells Mulder. "You're suspended until such time I'm confident your judgment is sound."

Skinner asks for Mulder's weapon.

Mulder retorts, "Who are you afraid I'm going to point it at?"

Scully says, with much sadness, "Mulder, I think you should do what he says."

Mulder hands the pistol over. At the same moment Linda Bowman emerges from her room, peers at the agents, and asks for a glass of water.

Skinner tells her that he'll send someone to fetch it. Mulder stares at the woman for a moment, then turns on his heel and walks rapidly away.

"Agent Mulder?" says Skinner.

"Go fetch her some water," he replies, without looking back.

A short while later Mulder is at

Lorton Penitentiary, reinterviewing Modell's physical therapist. The woman protests she doesn't know Modell very well. Mulder asks her if anything he ever said to her struck her as unusual.

The therapist says, "I guess one time, someone else said something about him that struck me as unusual."

She adds, "It was one of the nuns who visits from Little Sisters of Charity. She once referred to him as a 'conquered warrior.' I thought that was kind of weird."

Mulder asks, "Was this the same nun who visited him before he escaped?"

The therapist nods. "Yeah, the same one who always visits."

"How many times has she visited him?"

The therapist shrugs. "Maybe three, four."

Mulder pulls out a photograph of Mrs. Bowman in her bright orange real estate blazer. "Is that the woman? Is that the nun?" he says.

At that moment the therapist's phone rings. She excuses herself, telling Mulder that she has to find her eyeglasses. She walks to her desk and picks up the cordless phone. Impatiently, Mulder reaches down and hands her her eyeglass case. It is empty.

While hunting for her glasses, the therapist carries on a cryptic phone conversation. "Uh-huh," she says. "Uh-huh. Okay. Oh, yeah, he's here."

She walks over to a large wall-mounted fuse box and opens it. At that moment Mulder realizes what is going on.

"NO!" he shouts, leaping toward her.

The therapist places her open palm on the bare copper fuse mountings. A spray of electrical sparks shoot out, and the woman goes rigid. Mulder grabs a wooden mop handle and pries her body from the high voltage. He yells for help, then begins giving her artificial respiration. The telephone receiver, partly melted, lies a few feet from the victim's outstretched arm.

At the FBI safe house later that day a U.S. Marshal guards the front gate. A Falls Church police cruiser pulls up, and the shotgun-toting guard opens the sliding fence. In the driver's seat is a uniformed cop. In the back seat, inside the wire mesh cage, is Modell.

The surprised marshal bends down to speak to the cop. "Hey! You got him!" he says.

The uniformed cop nods nonchalantly toward Modell. The rear window glides open. "Go home," says Modell, calmly.

"What?" asks the marshal, glassy-eyed.

Modell says, "Go home."

Inside the safe house the door to Linda Bowman's room opens. Modell, clearly ailing, enters and locks the door behind him. Bowman stares at him, too shocked to speak.

In the parking lot of a suburban shopping mall Scully, leading a group of marshals and FBI agents, exits a Chevy Suburban. Her cell phone chirps, and she answers it.

"Hey, Scully, it's me. I'm at the prison," says Mulder.

Scully says, "Mulder, you were told to lay off."

"It's a little too late for that now," replies Mulder. He stands in the physical therapy room, watching a corpse being rolled away on a gurney.

"Modell's therapist just electrocuted herself right in front of me. She was on the phone when she did it."

"Okay, it was Modell."

"It was Linda Bowman," says Mulder.

"Mulder!"

"The therapist would have identified her," says Mulder, impatiently. "Verified to me she visited Modell in prison."

"Would have? You don't know that!"

"Listen, Scully," says Mulder, angry now. "Just trace the call and cut off any access that woman has to a phone. I'm headed back there right now."

Scully tells Mulder she isn't at the safe house, but at the Chain Bridge Mall, investigating a suicide. Mulder becomes alarmed.

Mulder says, "Why isn't anyone picking up at the safe house switchboard?"

"Back in the truck," says Scully to her colleagues.

At the safe house Skinner, hears the phone ring unanswered and realizes that the facility has been deserted. He draws his gun and kicks open the locked door to Linda Bowman's room. Inside is Mrs. Bowman standing next to Robert Patrick

Modell.

"On the floor, Modell!" shouts Skinner.

"Hey, it's Mel Cooley," says the serial killer, sarcastically.

"On your face! I said NOW!" shouts Skinner.

Modell turns back toward Bowman, then says calmly, "I have a gun."

He spins around to face Skinner. In his outstretched arm is a large-caliber revolver. Skinner fires, hitting Modell in the breastbone and sending him tumbling to the floor. Bowman gasps; when Skinner looks down, his adversary's gun hand is empty.

Shortly afterward, in the now-bustling safe house, a squad of paramedics wheel Modell—seriously wounded—down the hallway. Skinner is badly shaken; Scully, her expression troubled, approaches him.

"Did he try to speak to you?" she asks.

"He said we got our man," says Skinner, uncertainly.

Mulder runs into the corridor, passing the paramedics and Modell, then joins up with Skinner and Scully. "What happened?" he asks.

"You were told to go home, Agent Mulder," says Skinner.

"What happened?"

"He had a gun," says Skinner, quietly. "I saw it clearly."

"He pointed a gun at you?" asks Mulder.

Scully says, solemnly, "We haven't found a gun yet."

Mulder starts to figure things out. "He *said* to you he had a gun."

Skinner, angered by what his subordinate is implying, says, "Yes. And he did."

The AD heads off to rejoin the search for Modell's weapon. Mulder, left with Scully, speaks to her quietly but urgently.

"Modell was unarmed," he says. "He purposely drew Skinner's fire."

"For what possible reason?" asks

Scully.

"To protect someone," says Mulder.

"Linda Bowman?" asks Scully.

"To take the fall for her," says Mulder, flatly.

Scully responds with sarcasm. "That's one hell of a plan, Mulder," she says. "The serial killer makes us believe he's guilty, in turn diverting suspicion away from the real estate lady? Well, he had me going."

Mulder shakes his head impatiently and asks where Bowman has gone. Reluctantly, Scully tells him that—the danger from Modell gone—she's been allowed to go home.

"It is over," says Scully.

"No, it's not," says Mulder, turning to leave.

"Where are you going?" asks his partner, exasperated.

"If Modell makes it through surgery," he says, "I want to be the first person that he talks to."

"Mulder, talking to him has already done you enough harm."

"Okay, look, do me a favor, Scully," says Mulder. "You give me a call when you think I've come to my senses. All right?"

At Annandale Community Medical Center a nearly comatose Modell lies hooked up to life support and strapped to his bed. Mulder gazes down at him until a nurse arrives and announces that she needs to change her patient's bandages.

"Call me if he wakes up, please," says Mulder.

"Yes, sir," says the nurse, who is now Linda Bowman, a paper tag labeled NURSE pinned to her blouse. She turns and slowly enters the hospital room.

"Bobby," she says, softly. "Why did you do it?"

Modell opens his eyes, but says nothing.

Bowman says, "I didn't ask you to come after me."

She lays her hand on Modell's breastbone.

"Don't," moans Modell. "Don't make a mistake."

"I'm not," says Bowman. "After what they've done, you

think I'd let them get away with this? I'm going to finish what you started."

"No," whispers Modell. "Stop now. Stop!"

Bowman shakes her head. "Bobby," she says. "Bobby, you're not in any pain. You feel wonderful. You've never felt better. Your heart is slowing. It's tired. It's too worn out to keep beating. Let it rest."

The bedside heart monitor begins beeping an alarm. Bowman reaches over and turns it off. She caresses Modell's forehead, then lays her head down on his chest.

"It slows," she says. "It slows. It stops."

The heart monitor traces an erratic beat, then flat-lines.

Several minutes later a team of ICU medics works unsuccessfully to revive Modell. Mulder arrives just as the doctor who heads the team declares him dead. Mulder glances at Modell's nightstand. The card that was once pinned to Bowman's blouse lies there. Mulder flips it over. On the back is written "214 Channel Avenue"—the address of Bowman's commercial property.

Later that night Mulder enters the warehouse, flashlight in hand.

"Mulder?" says a faint voice. It is Scully's.

The unarmed agent runs toward the sound. He rounds a corner and spots his partner, standing in the center of a large room.

"Scully, what are you doing here?" he says.

"You were right about her, Mulder," says Scully, sadly.

She raises her gun hand and aims her weapon at Mulder. "She's making me do this," she says, thumbing back the hammer of her pistol.

"Scully, where is she?" asks Mulder.

"She's here," says Scully, desperation filling her voice. "Mulder, make her stop. I can't help myself."

Mulder shouts out into the darkness. "LINDA BOWMAN!" he yells.

"Mulder, make her stop!"

"SHOW YOURSELF!" shouts Mulder.
"Mulder!"

Scully swings the pistol away from Mulder and slowly—shockingly—points it at her own temple.

"NO!" yells Mulder, lunging desperately toward her.

Scully fires. She falls to the ground, unconscious. Gasping with shock, Mulder kneels over her and searches in vain for a pulse.

A woman's footsteps click closer. It is Linda Bowman, dressed in black, a pistol hanging in her right hand. Mulder grabs Scully's gun and aims it at her.

"I'm gonna kill you!" he says, ice cold with anger.

Bowman aims her own gun at Mulder. "Don't listen to her, Mulder," says Bowman.

"What?"

"It's me," says Bowman. "You were right about her. Linda Bowman is pushing you."

"What the hell are you talking about?"

"I'm Scully. Linda's right behind you. She's telling you I'm her."

Mulder looks over his shoulder. Scully is lying in a pool of dark red blood.

"You killed her!" says Mulder.

"Mulder, I'm Scully," says Bowman, evenly. "I'm not dead. She wants you to shoot me. She knows you'll never forgive yourself."

"SHUT UP!" shouts Mulder, his gun hand shaking.

"Listen to me!" says Bowman. "Your mother is Teena! Your sister is Samantha—"

"SHUT UP!"

"Modell warned you," says Bowman, quietly. "Don't play her game."

Eyes wide with fright and confusion, Mulder wavers slightly. Bowman jerks her gun a hair left and fires. A blurry figure standing just behind Mulder falls to the ground. Mulder turns and sees this, then faces forward, to see Scully walking toward him. At his feet is a woman—the real Linda Bowman—sprawled on the ground and quickly losing consciousness.

"You think you can hold me," mutters the dying woman.

Mulder stands numb, overwhelmed. Scully dials her cell phone and calls for an ambulance.

In Skinner's office at FBI headquarters the assistant director examines an MRI scan of Linda Bowman's brain clearly showing the bullet lodged inside, as well as a few other anomalies.

"She has an advanced temporal lobe tumor," says Scully. "Just like Modell. It seems to run in the family."

"She and Modell are related?" asks Skinner.

"Fraternal twins," says Scully.

Skinner sighs. "He meant to protect his sister."

Scully explains that the two—separated when they were two weeks old—only learned of their existence six months previously.

"Her 'foxhunt,'" adds Scully. "I'm guessing that she wanted revenge for what she feels we did to her brother."

Skinner asks Mulder if he has anything more to add. Mulder shakes his head.

"That about covers it," says the agent.

He and his partner rise to leave, but Skinner asks Mulder to stay behind. Mulder turns and faces the AD, bracing himself.

"I just wanted to say," says Skinner, emphatically, "that you did a good job."

"How's that?" asks Mulder, more skeptical than surprised.

Skinner says, "Nobody could have

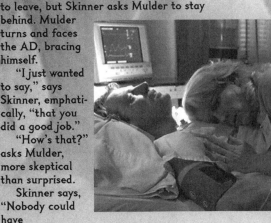

figured this out but you. You knew it was Linda Bowman, and not Modell. You were way ahead of me."

Mulder considers this, still troubled. "I almost killed my partner," he says.

"Mulder, despite that, you prevailed," says Skinner. "You won her game."

Mulder thinks about for this for a long second. He smiles, sadly.

"Then why," he says finally, "do I feel like I lost?"

back story:

On most hit television series, the decision to bring back a memorable villain from a previous season would be a virtual no-brainer. This, however, is *The X-Files*.

"It was a long and complicated process," says story editor Tim Minear, a first-year staffer who had previously worked on *Lois & Clark*, *High Tide*, and *Robin's Hoods*.

Since the beginning of his stint on show, Minear had been carefully nurturing a story line about a hardened prisoner—an atheist—who hears the voice of God. God commands him to kill an evil force at large in the world; the man is then mysteriously transported outside the prison walls. Hundreds of lawmen seek to recapture or kill the man; all except Mulder, who suspects that the prisoner is a genuinely changed man; that his mission is a vital one; and that something horrible will happen if he's not allowed to continue.

"So I pitched it," says Minear. "And I was going to do it, eventually, until we found ourselves at a point in the year where we needed a script really fast. At that point it was Frank Spotnitz's suggestion then that the guy should actually be Modell, from 'Pusher.'"

He adds, "And then we realized that there had to

be some other aspect of his character that could be illuminated to make this worth doing. So that's when we came up with the idea of bringing in his sister, another pusher, and making his mission his effort to save her."

Minear filed away his "Word of God" story line, then teamed with supervising producer Vince Gilligan—whose name also appears on the script—to complete the first draft of "Kitsunegari." After a surprisingly smooth revision process, Chris Carter approved the final version. Luckily, actor Robert Wisden (who guest-starred last season on *Millennium*) was available to reprise his role from 3X17. Diana Scarwid was cast as his murderous sister; she is a well-regarded actress perhaps best known—somewhat unfairly—for playing Joan Crawford's daughter Christina in the camp classic *Mommie Dearest*.

Much of the excitement in Vancouver that week concerned the conversion of a hospital storage facility—scouted by location manager Louisa Gradnitzer—into the Lorton Penitentiary cafeteria. On the plus side: the old room was large enough, undivided, and had an appropriately high ceiling. On the minus side: formerly a pump house, the structure was now completely filled with junk. Before it could be "dressed" and filmed the storage room had to be completely emptied and several massive concrete pump housings slowly and expensively jackhammered into smithereens.

"But afterward, it really worked great," says construction coordinator Rob Maier, wryly. "In fact, the hospital was really glad that we spent all that money to open up the space for them."

To play the part of the late Nathan Bowman, special effects makeup guru Toby Lindala painted one of his in-house dummies the right shade of cerulean blue. To give the dying Robert Modell the correct tinge of sickliness, makeup artist Laverne Basham added a healthy dollop of yellow to his face powder.

Two Japanese translators—one in Vancouver, one in Los Angeles—labored (sometimes disagreeing with each other, er, vigorously) to come up with the correct pictogram for "foxhunt," a term not directly translatable into Japanese. To clarify the episode's complicated denouement, a shadow of the falling Linda Bowman— which Mulder glimpses just before Scully-as-Bowman shoots the female Pusher—was inserted into that scene in post-production.

"I loved the concept of 'Kitsunegari,' just as I liked 'Pusher,'" says Gillian Anderson. "The whole idea of somebody imposing their will on others really intrigues me."

Indeed, as a mid-season stand-alone episode, the result seemed to satisfy most viewers, as well as most insiders.

ⓧ

This was director Daniel Sackheim's first *X-Files* episode since "The Host" (2X02). He was one of the producers of the *X-Files* feature film.

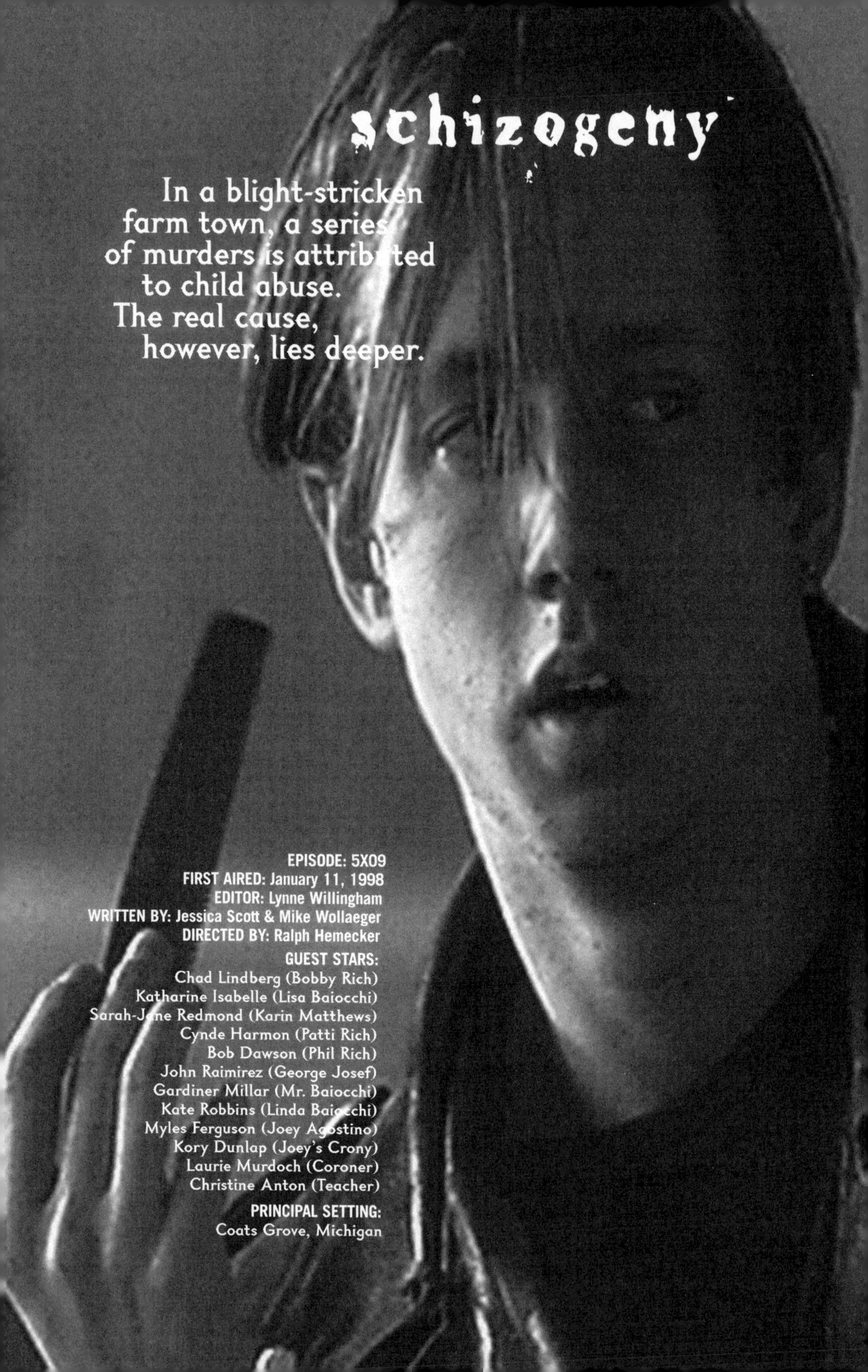

schizogeny

In a blight-stricken
farm town, a series
of murders is attributed
to child abuse.
The real cause,
however, lies deeper.

EPISODE: 5X09
FIRST AIRED: January 11, 1998
EDITOR: Lynne Willingham
WRITTEN BY: Jessica Scott & Mike Wollaeger
DIRECTED BY: Ralph Hemecker

GUEST STARS:
Chad Lindberg (Bobby Rich)
Katharine Isabelle (Lisa Baiocchi)
Sarah-Jane Redmond (Karin Matthews)
Cynde Harmon (Patti Rich)
Bob Dawson (Phil Rich)
John Raimirez (George Josef)
Gardiner Millar (Mr. Baiocchi)
Kate Robbins (Linda Baiocchi)
Myles Ferguson (Joey Agostino)
Kory Dunlap (Joey's Crony)
Laurie Murdoch (Coroner)
Christine Anton (Teacher)

PRINCIPAL SETTING:
Coats Grove, Michigan

In a dark, debris-strewn bedroom, a long-haired, zombielike teenager plays a violent video game on his Playstation. Heavy metal rock music pours through his headphones.

He is on the second floor of a rural house that is surrounded by trees and shrouded in darkness. A blue pickup truck—its door bearing the words RICH ORCHARDS—pulls into the driveway. Phil Rich, a powerfully built man in his forties exits. He sees a shovel protruding from a mound of dirt on the front lawn, and stalks through the front door.

"Bobby!" he yells, and heads for the stairway.

His wife, a worried-looking blond woman, intercepts him.

"Phil—" she says.

"I've had it with that kid, Patti," says Rich.

"I've already talked to him," she says.

"Yeah. Like he ever listens."

Rich brushes past his wife and heads up to Bobby's bedroom. The kid is oblivious to his entrance; Rich angrily yanks the headphones off his head.

"Get up!" says Rich.

"What are ya doin'!?" says Bobby, with perfect slacker accent and phrasing.

"You think this is why I wake up and go to work every day?" says Rich. "So you can sit around on your ass?"

"What'd I do?" says Bobby, sullenly.

"What'd you do?" says Rich. "You never do anything—that's the problem. What kind of a loser are you gonna turn out to be?"

Rich picks up Bobby's shoes and throws them at him, then marches the teenager out the front door and onto the lawn. "You don't leave my tools out in the rain!" he says. "Tools are for work. They cost money."

"All right," says Bobby. "I'll put it away."

"After you finish," says Rich. "Pick it up!"

Bobby stares at him vacantly, not moving toward the shovel. Rich plucks it out of the dirt himself, and flings it to him.

"I'm not gonna let your mother watch you grow up to be a jerk," he says.

"Fine," says Bobby, sarcastically. "I'll put it away, *Phil.*"

His stepfather seethes. "No way," he says. "You'll finish the job."

Bobby stays silent for a

second or two, takes a couple of deep breaths, then snaps, "GET AWAY FROM ME!" He brandishes the shovel at his tormentor like a weapon. "GET AWAY FROM ME NOW!!"

The standoff lasts for a few scary seconds. Surprised at this display of defiance, Phil takes a couple of tentative steps back. His courage suddenly deserting him, Bobby drops the shovel and takes off, running headlong into the muddy orchard that surrounds the house.

He gets about a ten-second head start on his stepfather, who pursues him through an archway of bare-branched trees, shouting his name. As bolts of lightning flash around him, Bobby sprints into a fog-filled grove, stops to catch his breath, and spots a hulking figure of a man, not very far away, staring at him.

The mysterious stranger shrugs and moves away.

Phil Rich continues chasing Bobby until he catches his foot on a thick, protruding root, and falls heavily to the ground. He looks up to see his stepson, exhausted, standing in front of him. The boy has hate in his eyes.

Bobby's mother runs outside to find her son. She arrives at the grove just in time to see Bobby and Phil grappling desperately on the ground. In fact, something is pulling the older man down into the mud. After a few seconds—despite his struggles—he is almost completely submerged. A river of black mud flows from his nose and mouth. Bobby watches from above, his expression unreadable, as his stepfather disappears from sight.

At the Coat's Grove coroner's office Scully plops a last dollop of brown mud onto a medical scale. "Twelve pounds, nine ounces," she says.

"All that came out of his stomach?" asks Mulder, incredulously.

"Most of it," says Scully, with a sigh. "The small amount in his lungs is what killed him."

Mulder says, "Is it possible that he took the term 'mud pie' literally?"

Somehow preventing herself from smiling at this witticism, Scully looks up from her work. "I'm sure if Mr. Rich were alive he would find some humor in that," she says.

"According to his police report, Mr.

Rich was a man who could tell a joke. He grew up here, worked the same fields for twenty years, well liked around town.

"Funny," she adds, "that he should turn up murdered."

To a somewhat abashed Mulder, Scully announces her finding: Rich was probably murdered by his sixteen-year-old stepson, who in his anger held his head forcibly under the muddy surface just a little too long.

"Well, according to the police report," says Mulder, "the coroner had to hire a backhoe to remove the body, which was buried completely in a standing vertical position."

Scully replies that there were some indications that Bobby had already dug the hole, which a rainstorm had turned into a muddy trap.

"Some rainstorm," says Mulder.

"They say it rained four hundred inches a day," says Scully, impatiently.

"Now, that sounds like an exaggeration, don't you think?" says Mulder.

Scully says, "Would you like me to show you how he may have done it?"

Mulder says, "How a six foot four, two-hundred-and-fifty-pound man was buried alive in less than five minutes by a sixteen-year-old kid whose classmates lovingly refer to him as 'Dorkweed'?"

Exasperated, Scully grasps the dead man's wrist, displaying bright red ligature marks. "He may have had an accomplice," she concedes.

Later that day Mulder stands in Bobby Rich's bedroom, taking in the sights. His gaze falls on an interesting poster; it shows a defiant figure standing on top of a giant mound of landfill.

"*Ich bin ein Auslander*," reads Mulder. "'I am an outsider.'"

Mulder smiles, and adds, "You know, when Kennedy told the Germans '*Ich bin ein Berliner*,' he was actually saying, 'I am a cocktail sausage?'"

From a far corner of the bedroom Bobby stares blankly back at Mulder. "Who's Kennedy?" he says.

The agent stares at Bobby for a moment, not certain that he's kidding.

"I'm not here to accuse you of anything, Bobby," he says, finally.

"What are you here for, then?" asks the boy.

"I want to hear your story."

Bobby lowers his gaze, then looks back up. "I wanted to help," he says, his voice flat and emotionless. "I couldn't."

Mulder tells him that the police suspect he's lying.

"So?" says Bobby, sullenly. "What the hell can I do about it? They just want me to confess. So they have someone to blame."

"Right," says Mulder. "But you're not making it very easy for them to believe otherwise. You understand that?"

"Well, what can I say?" says Bobby. "Everyone knows I hated him."

In the living room downstairs Scully is seated across from Bobby's mother, listening sympathetically.

Patti Rich says, "Well, they were really close when Bobby was little—always kiddin' around and stuff. But Bobby got into that teenage stage, and he don't want to listen to nobody."

"And it came to a head last night?" says Scully.

Patti's expression is unreadable. "Phil was late coming home," she says. "He'd been stressed out because of the blight and stuff."

"How do you mean?" says Scully.

"The hazelnut trees all got a disease," she says. "And then Bobby don't help things out with his attitude and stuff."

"Did Phil instigate what happened?"

"It's hard to tell what starts these things," says Patti, her voice lowering to a whisper. "Phil can be stern. Just like his own father was to him. But I never saw him raise a hand."

In the upstairs bedroom Bobby appears to have loosened up just a bit. "When I saw him lying in the mud," he tells Mulder, "I mean, I half expected him to pull me in. Like he had planned it or something."

"Did he ever hurt you?" asks Mulder.

"Phil? He used to get off, shoving me around. Yeah."

"Did you ever shove him back?"

Bobby laughs scornfully. "He's twice as big as me!" he says.

Mulder replies that some people thought he might have dug the hole or attacked his stepfather when he fell in the hole.

"Well, that's their problem, isn't it?" replies Bobby.

Mulder frowns, and asks him if he remembers what was going through his head at the time.

"I guess," says Bobby, "that he had it coming."

In the living room at that moment Patti Rich is describing her son's actions at the death scene. "He was kneeling over Phil," she says, "struggling real hard, and stuff."

Scully asks her if Bobby was definitely trying to help her husband.

"It seemed that way to me," she says.

Sternly, Scully tells her that there is a strong chance that Bobby will soon be charged with his stepfather's murder. Mrs. Rich seems strangely unmoved by this.

"I don't see how," she says, puzzled.

"But if they do," says Scully, leaning forward, "and there's evidence of abuse that you're not coming forward with, it could hurt his chances."

Mrs. Rich shakes her head, her expression unchanged.

"I know everything happens for a reason," she says. "But there still don't seem no reason for this."

In the hazelnut grove outside the Rich house Mulder rubs his finger against one of the bare tree branches. A thin, reddish sap stains his fingers.

"They're all dying," says Scully, joining him. "According to Bobby's mother, that's the big reason her husband blew up. His hazelnut orchard was hit with a blight."

"So he pounds the kid?" says Mulder.

"And the kid pounds back," says Scully.

Mulder is skeptical. In response, Scully confirms that Mrs. Rich never admitted to her that there was any child abuse in her family, but adds that she's probably just decided to wipe the slate clean and move on.

"The kid," says Mulder, "says that his stepfather teed off on him regularly."

"Is that his excuse?" says Scully.

"No, that's his explanation," says Mulder. "He says he's innocent."

Scully says, "What do you think?"

"I think," says Mulder, "that he's a hard kid to love."

The agents walk slowly through the orchard to the spot where Phil Rich was killed. They stare down into the huge hole; Mulder expresses his doubts that the facts and physical evidence can be reconciled.

"Even if Bobby didn't dig this hole," says Scully, "the disease could've killed root systems, creating weakened soil."

Mulder gingerly lowers himself down the side of the excavation. "So how did the victim swallow twelve pounds of the stuff?"

"Well," says Scully, "when you fight for air a vacuum is created. And maybe once he sucked down a mouthful of mud it turned his esophagus into a siphon. With his head pushed down, it filled all his passages like a gas can."

Mulder, kneeling at the bottom of the hole, looks up at Scully with a raised eyebrow we've seen before.

"Well, you asked me for answers," says Scully, huffily. "These are the best ones I've got."

Mulder smiles. "Did you ask if anybody else might be involved?" he asks.

Scully counters that Patti Rich told her that Bobby had trouble making friends and that he'd been in therapy for his anger since 1995.

"That could be me," admits Mulder, almost cheerfully.

As Mulder continues examining the fatal soil, Scully looks up and sees a familiar hulking figure of a man, a large ax in his right hand, standing stock-still in the distance.

"What is it?" says Mulder, catching his partner's expression.

"Someone's watching us," says Scully. "Sir! Hello!"

Scully walks toward the axeman. Mulder struggles to climb out of the hole, but his foot is momentarily trapped under a loop of protruding root. By the time Mulder has reached ground level, the man has walked slowly out of sight behind the arch of hazelnut trees.

"Who was it?" says Mulder.

"I don't know," says Scully. "He's gone."

At the local high school a bell rings and the students filter out into the hallway. A teenage girl—dark-haired and pretty but unhealthily thin—walks nervously toward her locker. Her name is Lisa Baiocchi. There are dark circles under her eyes. She passes Bobby Rich, who is wearing a black motorcycle jacket. It hangs loosely on his slight frame.

"Lisa!" says Bobby, quickly joining her at her locker.

"What are you doing here?" says Lisa, looking a little frightened.

Bobby says, "I called you last night. I mean, why didn't you call me back?"

"They're saying you killed him, Bobby," she says.

Lisa opens her locker door in his face. Not put off by this, Bobby steps quickly around it and looks intensely at the pallid girl. "I finally stood up to him," he says, with as much passion as he's shown yet.

Frightened by this, Lisa says nothing. Her locker door slams shut with a bang.

"Hey, psycho!" says a huskier male high school kid. "Think fast!"

The bully slams Bobby against the wall of lockers.

"Just get away from me, okay?" mumbles Bobby.

The bully grabs his prey by the lapels of his jacket, and lifts. "Or what? What're you gonna do? Huh?"

Bobby looks his tormentor in the eye. "Maybe I'll kill you too, huh?" he says.

His threat hits home. Unable to cover his fright, the bully backs off and stands next to a taller crony.

"Psycho killer!" he shouts, before melting into a crowd of gawking students.

Bobby gathers up his books. "See," he says to Lisa. "All you have to do is stand up."

Lisa ducks her head shyly and moves quickly away.

"I'll see you later, then," says Bobby, calling after her.

At a small cottage at the edge of town, Mulder and Scully knock on the front door and identify themselves. They're invited inside by Karin Matthews—an attractive, surprisingly stylish woman in her early thirties—who is Bobby Rich's therapist. She seats herself in her home office and faces the agents solemnly.

"I first worked with Bobby," she says, "after an incident at school. He's had difficulty developing relationships, and this difficulty has caused him to act out."

"In what way?" says Scully.

"By putting on certain airs," says Matthews. "Affecting an attitude that has drawn the wrong kind of attention to himself. I've seen him come in here pretty beaten up."

"Physical violence?" asks Mulder.

"More than just kid stuff," says Matthews.

Mulder asks her if Bobby's stepfather was ever involved. The therapist demurs, citing the privileged nature of her conversations with her client. Scully tells her that if she knows that Bobby committed a crime, she's under a legal obligation to tell the agents. Matthews is not intimidated.

"Bobby once spilled a glass of milk at dinner," she says coolly, with just the faintest hint of bitterness. "For the next two weeks he was forced to eat in the cellar. No table, no chair, no light. Sometimes he was left down there until the following morning.

"You see," she adds, "there are all sorts of crimes. Not just the ones you might find reason to investigate."

Mulder looks down at Matthews's shoes. They are fine suede, with just a slight bit of mud stuck to the sole near the heel.

He says, calmly, "So you're saying that Bobby would have good reason to kill his father."

"I'm saying," says Matthews, "there are some crimes where there are only victims."

Mulder nods brusquely. "You're free not to answer, Ms. Matthews," he says. "Or you're free to make these vague allu-sions. But your evasiveness is only going to land this kid in jail for a long, long time."

"I'm not sure I understand," says the therapist.

Mulder says, "You make it sound like a justification. Like Bobby did it. And I don't think he did."

Matthews stares into Mulder's eyes, but says nothing.

That night Lisa Baiocchi walks down a dark street. Two headlights loom behind her, and Phil Rich's pickup truck—its radio booming heavy metal—pulls to a stop alongside. At the wheel is Bobby Rich.

"Hey! What're you doin'?" asks Bobby.

"Going home," says the girl.

"Well, I waited for you," says Bobby. "I thought we were, uh, gonna talk soon."

Lisa says, "You scared me today, Bobby."

"Why?" says Bobby. "Was it because I stood up for myself? Or, um, because I didn't let them beat me up, like usual?"

"I gotta go," says the girl.

"You gotta *stand up*, Lisa! You gotta tell your dad you're not gonna put up with this crap!

"There's a way to make it go away," he adds. "Forever."

Lisa backs away from him and walks the rest of the short distance home. Her father is looking at her throughout the front window of their house as Lisa comes up the front walk. Bobby's truck is also visible. When his daughter walks through the front door, he is tight-lipped with anger.

"What the hell business you got with him?" he says.

"Nothing," protests Lisa. "He's just a friend."

She walks upstairs to her room and slumps onto her bed, despondent. Her father barges in after her.

"I don't want you seeing that kid," he says, angrily. "I don't want him coming around here. You hear me?"

Lisa finally fights back.

"Stop it, okay?" she says.

"I'm doing what's right for you—" says her father.

"JUST SHUT UP!" shouts Lisa.

She leaves the bedroom, slamming the door behind her. Stunned momentarily by her outburst, Mr. Baiocchi looks out the window and sees Bobby's car, which is starting up. The instant this sound reaches him the window explodes, spraying glass in all directions. Something grabs Lisa's father around the neck and yanks him toward the broken window's frame.

Scared by the noise, Lisa re-enters the room. She walks to the window and looks down in horror. Her father lies sprawled, lifeless, on the ground.

The next day Mulder stands beneath the broken window. There are shards of glass on the ground; Mulder bends down and pieces together several fragments. They form a yellow "Happy Face" sticker; he looks up as Scully approaches.

Scully says, "The victim's name was Eugene Baiocchi. Forties. He was a foreman for one of the local growers. A single parent."

Mulder asks, "Did you get a look at the body?"

"It had already been removed," says Scully.

She adds that it was obvious, however, what killed him: the police believe that somebody had pushed him out the window.

"'Pushed out'?" says Mulder, skeptically.

Scully adds that Lisa, who made the 911 call, told the police that she and her father had had a fight.

"About what?" asks Mulder.

"Bobby," says Scully.

In Karin Matthews's home office that morning the therapist speaks soothingly to Lisa Baiocchi, who is sitting in heart-breaking agony across the room from her. Matthews counsels the girl to answer Mulder and Scully's questions but to stop if any of their questions become too uncomfortable. As she says this, Mulder and Scully walk through the unlocked front door.

"Can I have a moment with Lisa?" asks Scully.

Matthews agrees reluctantly and walks with Mulder onto the front porch.

Mulder asks, "Is Lisa another of your clients?"

"Yes," says Matthews, curtly. "For four years."

"What were you treating her for?"

"An eating disorder."

"Have you asked her what happened?" asks Mulder.

Matthews looks at the agent with barely disguised disdain. "Isn't that your job?" she says.

Mulder says that he suspects she had a fight with her father over Bobby Rich.

"Well, it doesn't surprise me," says Matthews. "Lisa's father was very disapproving of her generally. Which stemmed to a lot of her problems."

"Had you counseled her father?" asks Mulder.

"No," says Matthews. "My approach is with the victim solely. To allow them to empower themselves."

"In what way?"

"By breaking the cycle of abuse. By owning it. By confronting it, and by standing up against it."

"It seems to be working," says Mulder, laconically.

Anger flashes briefly in Matthews's eyes. She turns away and glances at Lisa through the front window.

"When I told Lisa her aunt was coming to pick her up tomorrow, she started to cry," she says.

"It wasn't out of sorrow."

Later that day Scully enters Lisa's bedroom. Mulder is already there, inspecting the debris around the broken window.

"Three guesses," says Scully, "who followed Lisa home last night. And was sitting outside in his father's truck just minutes before this happened."

Mulder turns and looks at Scully. "Does she think Bobby did it?" he asks.

"She thinks he's quite capable," says Scully.

Mulder says, "I think we're all quite capable."

Scully adds, "She says he also threatened to kill a boy at school."

Mulder chuckles dryly, then motions Scully over to the window. "If Lisa's father was pushed out the window," he says, "then all the glass would be on the outside. Look, there's glass all around here on the inside. And the pane on the mullions? Cracked on the outside, not on the inside."

"I don't understand," says Scully.

"Well," says Mulder, "it seems to me that some facts have been assumed. It looks like to me that Lisa's father was pulled out the window, not pushed."

Scully protests. "There's nowhere to stand," she says, peering out the window. "And even if he did use a ladder, there'd be no leverage especially for a scrawny sixteen-year-old kid."

Mulder says, to his nonplused colleague, "That's my point exactly."

At the high school later that morning Bobby Rich sits at the back of his science class. Scully, accompanied by two local police officers, enters the classroom and identifies herself. Scully turns to Bobby and asks him to come with them.

"What for?" says the teenager, disdainfully.

"To answer some questions," says Scully.

"About what?" he replies.

Scully says, "I don't want to embarrass you in front of your class."

Bobby glances around at his classmates, who eye him with a mixture of disdain and fright. "Well, I ain't embarrassed," he says, with a sarcastic smile.

He stands up, returns the other students' glances, and shambles to the front of the room.

At the local morgue a harried coroner pulls Eugene Baiocchi's body—his face and neck covered with dozens of small cuts—out of the refrigerator.

"I'm fairly certain," says the official, "that this man died of a broken neck."

"Yeah," says Mulder, "but there was a substantial amount of blood loss, wasn't there?"

The coroner protests that all of his cuts missed the arteries and he has X rays of a break between the fourth and fifth vertebrae.

"Were you able to determine if the neck injury was caused by the fall?" says Mulder.

"Well, what else what it have been?" replies the coroner.

Mulder bends down and looks at the dead man's neck. There's something under the skin beneath the jaw—a sliver of wood just barely visible.

"Do you see this?" says Mulder to the coroner.

In an empty classroom at the high school Scully checks Bobby's arms for cuts. His pale flesh seems to be unbroken.

"Are you satisfied?" says Bobby.

"No," murmurs Scully, moving on to examine the boy's jacket.

Mulder enters, and pulls a plastic evidence Baggie out of his pocket.

"What is that?" says Bobby, slack-jawed.

"It's evidence," says Mulder, pointing to the word EVIDENCE on the bag.

"Of what?" says Bobby, nervously.

Mulder just stares at Bobby, turns his back on him, and talks privately with Scully.

"Are you just trying to scare him?" says Scully.

"Nah," says Mulder, "I think he's scared enough as it is."

"Of what?"

Mulder points to the wood sliver, lying in the bottom of the Baggie. Scully, confused, turns and stares at the tiny object.

That evening Karin Matthews opens the front door of her house. She lets in Lisa Baiocchi, who is carrying a small suitcase.

"I'll help getting the rest of your things packed," says the therapist, "but I think it's best that you go to your aunt's as soon as possible."

"When did she say she was coming?" asks Lisa, fighting back tears.

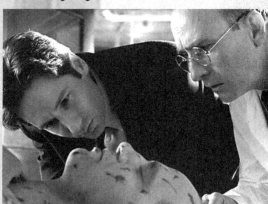

"First thing in the morning," says Matthews, gently. "Feel it—it's okay."

Later that night Lisa lies in bed, wide awake. From the next room come the faint sounds of a couple arguing: Karin Matthews, and an unidentifiable man.

"You never learn!" says the male voice, scornfully.

"I'm sorry," says Karin, frightened. "Please, don't yell."

"What'll you ever amount to?" says the man.

"Stop it. Stop it!" says Karin.

"Where are you going?"

"Up to my room."

"You're ruining my life! You hear me! I wish you'd never been born."

The voices stop. Lisa gets out of bed and tiptoes to her door. She opens it a crack to see Karin Matthews, walking down the hallway and entering an unmarked door.

At the darkened and deserted Baiocchi house, Mulder and Scully enter the side yard.

"What are we looking for?" says Scully, a bit apprehensively.

"That splinter you're holding," answers Mulder, "came out of Mr. Baiocchi's neck. But it didn't come from the broken window."

"Where did it come from?" asks Scully.

"It's green wood," says Mulder, "fresh from a living tree."

They've come to a large tree that faces Lisa's window. It has a thin rope hanging down from one of the lower branches. Mulder grabs the rope and begins pulling himself up. He struggles just a bit.

"Excuse me," he says. "It's been a few years."

Scully watches Mulder's ascent. "You think Bobby climbed this tree to pull Lisa's father out of that window?"

"That begs the question, doesn't it?" answers Mulder, by now on a branch roughly level with the broken window.

He adds, "Hey, Scully! Is this demonstration of boyish agility turning you on at all?"

Scully, gazing skyward at her partner, says nothing. She's senses a presence behind her and when she turns comes face to face with the hulking, bearded axeman. He's dressed in dirty clothes and holding his huge ax loosely by his side.

"Who are you?" asks Scully, a startled quaver in her voice.

"I take care of the trees," says the axeman, whose name is Ramirez, in an unidentifiable accent.

Mulder calls down to his partner—who keeps her gaze focused on Ramirez.

"You were watching us the other day in the orchard," she says.

Ramirez advances slowly toward Scully. "The trees are dying," he says.

"Scully!" shouts Mulder.

"Maybe you should come down here, Mulder," says Scully.

She hands Ramirez the evidence Baggie containing the wood sliver. Ramirez opens it, looks inside, and points to the tree Mulder is still descending rapidly.

"Like this tree," he says, shrugging.

Mulder drops to the ground beside Scully. Now they both face the bizarre giant.

Scully says, "You said these trees are dying. But this splinter is live wood."

Without warning, Ramirez lifts his ax and, as the agents back away reflexively, takes a mighty swing at the tree trunk. Thick red fluid flows out of the ax mark as if he'd wounded a human being.

Ramirez says, "Twenty years ago, this happens."

"What causes this?" asks Mulder.

"A very bad man," says Ramirez, sadly.

At Karin Matthew's house, Lisa, dressed in pajama bottoms and a T-shirt, moves cautiously through the kitchen. She notices muddy footprints leading to the cellar door. She tries the doorknob and finds it unlocked. Walking quietly down to the basement, she steps onto the muddy floor.

Her gaze falls to the far wall and to two men's shoes, connected to a pair of limp legs. She gasps then whirls around when she hears the kitchen light click on behind her. The cellar door is wide open.

"You little snoop!" says a male voice we've heard before. *"She's just like you! Where is she?"*

Then the kitchen light snaps off and the cellar door slams shut—leaving Lisa to face this new terror in darkness.

The next morning Mulder and Scully knock on Karin Matthews's front door and tell her that they'd like to ask her a few questions.

"About what?" asks Matthews, surprised.

"Your father's death," says Mulder. "We need to clarify a few details."

Matthews protests that her father died twenty years ago.

"Yeah, under rather curious circumstances," says Mulder. "His body was pulled from the mud of an orchard."

A moment of pain, or anger, lights Karin Matthews's eyes. She does not invite the agents inside.

"I-I'm sorry," she says haltingly. "I-I was just a young girl. I don't know why you want to talk to me."

Mulder says, "Well, we just thought it was strange that you didn't bother to mention it."

Matthews says, "Well, I don't see that it matters."

Mulder counters, "We spoke to someone who thinks it does."

He adds, "Someone who worked for your father. According to the orchard man, your father's death brought about the end of a blight affecting the trees."

Karin Matthews stares at her questioner with a mixture of fear, anger, and contempt. "Look," she says, "my father was a powerful man. And powerful men are prone to inspire this kind of fantasy. Don't tell me that you've been taken in by it, too."

Mulder stares back at his suspect, unconvinced. Scully asks if Lisa is still staying with her.

Matthews says, "No, she's not. She's gone to her aunt's. Look, I'm sorry I can't help." The woman closes her door in the agents' faces.

Locked in the cellar, Lisa stands on a chair, reaches up, pounds on the thick glass window, and yells for help. She watches Mulder and Scully, unable to hear her, get in their car and drive away. She slumps down, despairing—and hears her therapist's voice, whispering to her urgently from behind the cellar door.

"Lisa!" says Matthews.

The teenager runs quickly up the cellar stairs. "Karin!" she cries.

Matthews whispers, "Lisa, you've got to be quiet! Quiet as a mouse! Or he's going to hear you down there!"

"Karin! I'm scared!" says Lisa, crying. "Let me out. Please!"

"I will. But not until it's safe."

Lisa cries out again, begging to be released, and pounds frantically on the door. But there is no answer. The girl slumps down and curls into a ball.

Late that afternoon the agents are in the middle of the town cemetery. While Scully stands guard nervously, Mulder digs feverishly into a grave site. The headstone reads CHARLES MATTHEWS, 1930–1979.

Scully says, "Mulder, whatever you're hoping to find here, without a court order it won't be admissible."

"I'm not expecting it to be," says her partner.

He reaches the wooden coffin, pries open the heavy lid, and looks down into a nearly solid mass of twisted, gnarled roots. Scully is startled—and very confused—by this sight.

"Mulder? Where's the body?" she says, tremulously.

Shortly afterward an aging Volvo station wagon pulls up in front of Karin Matthews's house. A heavyset woman in her early fifties exits, walks to the front door, and knocks.

"Yes?" says Karin Matthews, sounding impatient and somewhat harried.

"I'm Linda Baiocchi," says the woman. "Lisa's aunt. Are you Karin?"

"Yes," says Matthews, curtly.

"Is Lisa here?"

"No. She went—she's gone to the bus station," says Matthews.

"She has?" says Lisa's aunt, surprised.

"But it was all arranged—"

"Well, I don't know what to tell you," says the therapist, already retreating behind her door. "I'm sorry. There must have been a misunderstanding."

Linda Baiocchi stands in front of the closed door a second, confused, then begins to walk slowly back to her car. She's stopped short by some faint cries coming from the cellar window. It is Lisa, crying hysterically. She has somehow managed to break through the window pane.

"Aunt Linda! I'm down here!" she cries.

Her aunt kneels down and peers down through the cellar window. "What are you doing down there?" she says.

"Just get me out of here!" says Lisa.

The older woman tells her niece not to worry and that she's going to get the police. At that moment a thick branch from a tree behind her swings down, piercing her upper body and impaling her against the broken window. Lisa gasps at the dead body of her aunt and screams. Her cries echo emptily through the dark cellar.

After nightfall Mulder and Scully leave the graveyard and head for their car. A still-confused Scully asks Mulder what happened to the body of Karin Matthews's father.

"I don't think this was an act of grave robbing, Scully," says Mulder.

"No," says Scully. "That's what we were doing."

"It was more like an act of nature."

He adds, "The orchard man said the blight that plagues this town was caused by a man. Implying a connection."

Scully says, "I'm a little afraid to ask what kind of connection."

"Between the people of this valley and their livelihood: the trees," says Mulder. "Look at the victims, Scully."

"Bobby's father, Lisa's father," says Scully.

"Karin's father, twenty years ago," adds Mulder.

He explains that all the victims were people whose lives were tied to the trees, and so were their deaths. Eugene Baiocchi was killed by a wood sliver, and Phil Rich was pulled downward by a root—the same root system that pulled Karin's father from the grave.

Scully protests that there's another connection between the deaths. "These were abused children" she says.

"Who couldn't defend themselves," counters Mulder.

"What? So nature did it for them?"

"Something did it for them," says Mulder. "Or someone controlling nature. Karin said she was counseling Bobby and Lisa in order to empower them. I think we ought to talk to them."

Scully tells him that she called Lisa at her aunt's house twenty minutes ago. There was no answer.

"Then maybe we should talk to Bobby," says Mulder.

"Mulder, we've already questioned him twice," says Scully.

"Maybe we haven't asked him the right questions," says Mulder.

At Bobby Rich's house shortly afterward the teenager and Mulder sit face-to-face. "I don't know what you're talking about," says Bobby, trying to turn away.

"Yes, you do," says Mulder, maintaining eye contact. "Maybe you hated your stepfather, but you didn't kill him. You don't have it in you."

"That's good," says Bobby, sarcastically. "That's really good. Can I go now?"

Mulder reaches out and grabs his arm.

"No," he says. "You can't go until you tell me the truth. For the first time in your life people are taking you seriously. And I think they should take you seriously. You're a serious kid."

No reply. "Not an outsider any more, huh?" says Mulder.

Bobby musters up a last measure of insolence. "Yeah, I'm thinkin' about running for ASB president," he says. "So why don't you just give it up?"

"Why don't *you* give it up?" replies Mulder. "Why don't you tell me what happened that night?"

Bobby's body language betrays a discomfort he can't hide. The FBI agent leans forward. As Mulder speaks, the teenager flashes back to the scene of his stepfather's death. As the scene replays in his mind, it becomes obvious that he was a spectator—not a murderer.

"You took the shovel to him," says Mulder, "but you couldn't do it. So you ran—you ran to the orchard. But not because you'd dug a hole or laid a trap. Because you were afraid.

"Not of Phil. Phil never hit you or hurt you in that way. In fact, you wanted to help Phil. You wanted to save him. You didn't want Phil to die, did you?"

Bobby says nothing, but his tears give away his true feelings.

"What were you afraid of, Bobby?" asks Mulder.

"I couldn't do it," he replies.

"You couldn't do what?"

"I couldn't stand up to him! But she made me!"

"She who?"

"K-Karin," says Bobby, now breaking down completely. "Karin. She made me—"

Mulder says, "Karin made you what?"

Now Bobby's memories hit full force. In his mind's eye he is back in Karin's office, shouting with a frightening ferocity, "YOU'RE A LOSER! YOU UNDERSTAND ME? I WISH YOU HAD NEVER BEEN BORN! YOU'RE RUINING MY LIFE!"

Bobby says, "She made me say those things," says Bobby. "She had me pretend that I was . . . him. That I was—"

"Who made you believe that you were a victim," says Mulder. "But you weren't, were you?"

"She says I had the power to make it all go away," says the sobbing boy. "I didn't mean for him to die."

In the cellar of the Matthews house Lisa Baiocchi sobs, still frightened and shivering. The voice of the man we'd heard previously seeps through the locked door.

"You think you can hide down there?" he says. "You think that you're safe?"

A locking bolt is thrown and the door swings open.

"You'll wish you were dead!" sneers the owner of the voice. It is Karin Matthews, looming frighteningly at the top of the stairs.

At 9:43 P.M. that evening Mulder and Scully arrive outside the darkened—and seemingly deserted—Matthews house.

They notice Linda Baiocchi's abandoned car and walk quickly to the front door. It is unlocked and partially opened.

They move cautiously inside, flashlights shining, and spot the muddy footprints. Mulder unbolts the cellar door and they walk part way down the stairs. They see Lisa's aunt, then the rotted, bug-eaten corpse—what's left of the long-dead body that so terrified Lisa.

"What the hell is going on here?" says Scully.

Mulder says, "I think we're looking at Karin Matthews's father."

"But how did he get here?"

Mulder says, "The same way Bobby's father got pulled down in that mud."

"Mulder, I—" says Scully.

"This has to do with Karin," says Mulder, abruptly. "With her own father's abuse. It was never Bobby that was locked in the cellar, it was Karin. Karin caused all this."

"You say Karin's the killer?"

"I think she's the killer *and* the victim."

The agents are startled by a scream—Lisa's. The cellar door slams shut, but Mulder kicks it open. They run into the kitchen, where the girl is slumped against the wall.

"Lisa, where's Karin?" asks Mulder.

The teenager is too distraught to speak. Scully comforts her while Mulder hurries out to the front porch and sees Matthews entering her compact car. He gets into his own sedan and gives chase until a branch from a large roadside tree swings down, crashing through his windshield. Mulder flings himself to the floor. The thick limb skewers the driver's seat, where the agent had been just a split second earlier. He staggers, dazed and bleeding, out of the car.

Karin Matthews pounds on the front door of the Rich house, where Bobby Rich is sitting huddled on the stairway. Patti Rich goes to the entryway and faces her.

"I need to see Bobby!" says the therapist, obviously over the edge.

"I'm sorry," says Patti, alarmed at her appearance, "Bobby's not here."

"He's in danger!" pleads Matthews.

"Get away from here, please," says Bobby's mother. "He's not here."

"Bobby! BOBBY!" screams Matthews.

She pushes past Patti and runs to the stairs. Fleeing her, Bobby runs out the back door and into the orchard. Winded and lost in the fog, he turns to see Karin—her face twisted into a mask of hate—slowly approaching him.

"Stay away from me!" he shouts. "I'm warning you!"

For a moment Karin casts her eyes downward, and it appears as if Bobby has intimidated her. Then Bobby is jerked downward, one leg, then the other, disappearing into the black mud.

"*You're pathetic,*" says Karin, in her father's voice.

Mulder arrives at the Rich house and runs into the orchard. He arrives in time to see Bobby, flailing helplessly, disappearing into the mud with Karin—as Mr. Matthews—standing over him.

"*You little piece of garbage!*" says Mr. Matthews.

Mulder kneels down and takes Bobby's arm. "Karin! Stop!" he shouts.

"*You stay away from him!*" shouts Matthews.

"Karin! Stand up to him!" shouts Mulder.

"*Karin deserves what she gets,*" smirks Matthews.

Mulder fights a losing battle to keep Bobby from being pulled under. A loop of root emerges from the ground and begins to pull him down.

"Make him stop, Karin!" he shouts. "Tell him what you should have told him twenty years ago! You're not going to take it any more!"

"*Karin's dead,*" says Matthews, calmly.

Mulder and Bobby are now almost completely submerged. Karin/Matthews stands in the heavy fog, unflinching. From behind appears a hulking figure—Ramirez. For a second Mulder's face registers the horror of what is going to happen.

Ramirez raises his ax, then swings, decapitating Karin Matthews with a single fluid motion.

"It's done now," says the woodsman, afterward. "No more."

He drops his ax beside the headless body and walks slowly away. Karin's head is slowly swallowed by the mud, and Mulder and Bobby begin to free themselves.

Afterward, the town of Coats Grove slowly returns to normal, and Mulder, in his final report, attempts to put the entire affair into perspective. He writes:

Coats Grove authorities conducted a detailed examination of the soil and root composition in the Rich family orchard, but could not explain what pulled Karin Matthews's body into the Michigan mud. Nor could the authorities determine how the body of Karin's father was pulled from its grave into her root cellar three years earlier. While the forensic data is inconclusive, I believe the explanation lies in hospital records dating back to Karin's childhood which suggest she herself was a victim of abuse.

Rage, unconfronted, takes its own path. I believe it was Karin's unconfronted rage that forced her to face her buried father. This same rage made her imagine 'victims' in the children around her, trying to instill in them a strength she never found in herself.

What happened to Karin Matthews in the orchard that night was a release. Release for a victim who—unable to face up to her past—was finally consumed by it.

back story:

Teen angst, dysfunctional stepfathers, and murderous foliage are all familiar elements of the horror/mystery genre. But even if 5X09 wasn't the most memorable or highest-rated episode of the fifth season, it's certainly in the running for Best Use of Backstage Gadgets and Gizmos.

"That *was* an interesting one," says *X-Files* special effects coordinator David Gauthier. "Everybody in that orchard was always getting pulled down into the mud so the big discussion was whether we wanted to do all that on a set or on location. We finally came up a kind of cooperative deal where we would do portions of it outside, then do the gags on set, where we could manage and control them. So we had to develop a mud hole that would be people-friendly and would do the things I wanted it do."

For the open-air filming, locations manager Todd Pittson hunted down one of the few existing nut orchards in the Vancouver area; a hobby farm ("The guy who owns it is a doctor," says Pittson) in the small town of Fort Langley. In another stroke of initiative/pure luck, greensman Frank Haddad located *another* hazelnut farmer who, at that very moment, was cutting down many of his overage trees for replacement.

Using Haddad's fireplace-bound wood as scenery, construction supervisor Rob Maier's crew built an exact replica of the fatal orchard on a wooden platform six feet above the floor of a rented sound stage.

Gauthier adds, "Then we built a couple of big tanks to place below the 'green set,' as we called it, and filled them with a mixture of peat moss, mud, and water. We heated the mud so the actors would be comfortable. In one scene we used a hydraulic elevator so that we could stand the actors up on the mud and then draw them down into it. In another one, we placed air-powered ramps on the elevator itself and fastened the young actor's boots to them. That way we could suck in one of his legs and then the other."

The trickiest part of the whole process, says Gauthier, was staging the shot of Karin Matthews's headless body sinking completely into the ooze. "For that sequence," he says, "we had to completely immerse a stunt girl in the mud. And it took a little bit of doing because we had to feed her oxygen so that she could breath while she slowly went under.

"We took the time during rehearsals to ease her in slowly, because in that situation it's not just getting oxygen that's crucial. It's the physical weight of the mud on a person's body. We had to make sure she had enough protection so that she could expand her chest and breathe."

Breathing was not a problem for David Duchovny or the other mud-soaked actors who, as several tongue-in-cheek observers pointed out, were getting the kind of warm mud treatment that pilgrims to hot spring spas pay dearly to undergo.

The killer root that entwines Mulder's leg was a product of Toby Lindala's department, as were the transmogrified remains of Karin Matthews's father, which hangs proudly on the wall of his effects shop at this very moment. Makeup artist Laverne Basham spent much of her week applying fake blood to, and gluing slivers of candy-flavored "glass" on, the guest actors who played Karin Matthews's victims.

The massive tree limb that attacks Mulder's windshield was actually from a massive tree that had uprooted itself over on a nearby plot of public land. With government permission, the deadwood

Bobby Rich's *Ich bin ein Auslander* poster was a collaboration between art director Gary Allen and Vancouver photographer David Gray, who went to the city dump in nearby Richmond and photographed a cooperative young actor standing atop a huge mound of garbage. Director Ralph Hemecker was unsatisfied with the result, reports Allen, to heighten the dramatic impact he requested that the artists airbrush away several garbage-pushing bulldozers, remove hundreds of garbage-foraging seagulls from background, and give the garbage-mountaineering kid a digital haircut.

L.A.-based actor Chad Lindberg, who played Bobby Rich, is familiar to *ER* fans as the cystic fibrosis sufferer who fought to die with dignity during the 1996–97 season. In "Schizogeny," so convincing and authentic was his portrayal of a mumbly, disaffected teen that it was feared during editing that viewers may not understand what he was talking about. As a precaution, the actor was called back into the studio to "loop," or rerecord, his dialogue.

"Schizogeny" itself was conceived by first-year staff writers Jessica Scott and Mike Wollaeger (who had previously worked in non-writing jobs on *The X-Files*), and underwent an even lengthier gestation process than usual.

"It went through many, many incarnations and versions," says co–executive producer Frank Spotnitz. "You know, it was tough."

Composer Mark Snow notes that he's proud of his score for 5X09, which compliments what he calls "a dark tale with a wonderful aura about it." And his choice for much of the episode's musical underpinnings?

"Woodwinds," says the musician, smiling.

Ⓧ

In the version that made it past the Fox standards and practices department, Mulder discloses that Bobby Rich's high school nickname is "Dorkweed." In the original script Bobby's nickname was "Dickweed."

Ⓧ

Actress Katharine Isabelle (Lisa Baiocchi) is the daughter of *X-Files* production designer Graeme Murray. This was her first role on the show, after several tries.

Ⓧ

Actress Kate Robbins (Linda Baiocchi) previously appeared in "D.P.O" (3X03) as the mother of lightning-centric murderer Darin Peter Oswald

Ⓧ

What, exactly, does "schizogeny" mean? "It means that every season around that time we do a show with a lot of S's and Z's in it," cracks producer Paul Rabwin. ("Schizogeny" is in fact a scientific term for asexual reproduction—fission—frequently

chinga

With the help of an eerie playmate,
an autistic child is able to express her
innermost feelings—and terrorize
an entire New England village

EPISODE: 5X10
FIRST AIRED: February 8, 1998
EDITOR: Casey O Rohrs
WRITTEN BY: Stephen King & Chris Carter
DIRECTED BY: Kim Manners
GUEST STARS:
Susannah Hoffman (Melissa Turner)
Jenny-Lynn Hutcheson (Polly Turner)
Larry Musser (Jack Bonsaint)
William MacDonald (Buddy Riggs)
Carolyn Tweedle (Jane Froelich)
Harrison Coe (Dave the Butcher)
Dean Wray (Rich Turner)
Henry Beckman (Old Man)
Gordon Tipple (Assistant Manager)
Ian Robison (Ranger)
Tracy Lively (Supermarket Clerk)
Elizabeth McCarthy (Shopper)
Sean Benbow (Customer)

PRINCIPAL SETTINGS:
Ammas Beach and
Schoodic Lake, Maine;
Washington, D.C.

In the passenger seat of an aging blue sedan sits an oddly expressionless little girl. Her name is Polly. In the child's lap is a small doll—the kind that has hard plastic skin, curly synthetic hair, and blue eyes that open with a click. Its name is Chinga. An attractive but nervous-looking young woman—Polly's mother, Melissa Turner—opens the passenger door, kneels down to her daughter's eye level, and speaks.

"We're just going in for a few things. We won't be long. Okay, Polly?" she says.

Polly doesn't say anything. She merely watches her mother with cold eyes.

"Mommy needs some *groceries*, okay?" adds Melissa.

Again, no answer. Melissa unbuckles Polly from the car, and loads her—still carrying her doll—into the child-carrier seat of a shopping cart. She pushes the cart toward the entrance of small supermarket, passing a frowning, crone-ish woman—her name is Jane Froelich—on the way inside.

Inside, a lone female shopper eyes Melissa and Polly disapprovingly. They pass the meat and seafood counter, where a white-coated butcher makes hesitant eye contact with Melissa. She hurries past, somewhat uneasy about this rendezvous. Her daughter most definitely notices, however, and decides to say her first words.

"I don't *like* this store, Mommy," she says.

"We're only going to be a minute," replies Melissa, soothingly.

But Polly will have none of it. "I want to go home!" insists the little girl.

A second or two later Chinga's plastic eyelids snap open. As if someone has pulled a string attached to its back, a recorded child's voice pours forth from its head.

"*Let's have fun!*" says Chinga, tinnily. Melissa pushes the cart even faster.

They reach the end of the frozen foods aisle; inside the refrigerated cabinet, face pressed against the glass, is the butcher

we'd seen a moment earlier. His form is weirdly flattened; a large knife is protruding from his right eye; and he is mouthing the words "Help, Melissa!"

Melissa flees to the next aisle. "We're going home, Polly," she says, adding, "Please! Don't do this to Mommy!"

She lifts Polly—and Chinga—out of the shopping cart. The sound of breaking glass attracts her attention. Standing in the aisle is the disapproving shopper, slapping herself violently in the face. Melissa glances quickly at Polly, then back at the shopper, who is now ripping at the flesh around her eyes.

Melissa flees through the store, past groups of other shoppers now inexplicably mutilating themselves. She runs through the front entrance and back toward her car, leaving chaos and carnage in her wake.

Out of a back room runs the butcher. He, too, is beginning to claw at his eyes. But he manages to control himself long enough to reach a telephone and punch in 911.

"Stan! It's Dave down at the Supr Savr," he says. "Send whoever you got on duty—"

He trails off, his attention diverted by a reflection in the metal door across from him. It is a large, distorted image of Polly's Chinga doll. The butcher hears the doll's voice, echoing metallically in his ears.

"*I want to play!*" says Chinga.

Dave pulls a large knife out of his belt, whirls, and sees nothing. As if with a will of its own, his knife hand begins curling back toward him. In a few moments the knife blade is pointed directly toward his forehead. He struggles against it, to no avail, and lets loose a blood-curdling scream.

In the small seacoast town of Ammas Beach, Maine, a blue Mustang convertible stops at the local self-serve gas station. At the wheel is Scully, wearing a white T-shirt that reads MAINE, THE WAY LIFE SHOULD BE.

As she sticks the gas nozzle into the filler tube she hears a faint rhythmic chirping noise. She reaches into the car, grabs her keys, unlocks the trunk, pulls out a small suitcase, and retrieves her cell phone.

"Scully!" she says, a bit exasperated.

"Hey, Scully. It's me," says Mulder, from their basement FBI office.

Scully says, "Mulder, I thought we had an agreement. We were both going to take the weekend off."

"Right, right. I know," says Mulder. "But I just received some information about a case. Classic X-Files. *Classic.* I wanna share it with you."

Scully answers slowly and distinctly, as if to a child.

"Mulder, I'm on vacation," she says. "The weather is clear. I'm looking forward to hitting the road and breathing in some of this fine New England air."

"You didn't rent a convertible, didja?" asks Mulder.

"Why?"

Mulder says, "Are you aware of the statistics of decapitation?"

"Mulder, I'm hanging up," says Scully. "I'm turning off my cell phone. I'm back in the office on Monday."

Her partner says, "You shouldn't talk and drive at the same time, either. Are you aware of the statistics—hello?"

Scully hangs up on him mid-wisecrack. She stows the cell phone and drives out toward the open road. Her path is blocked by an aging sedan—Melissa Turner's—backing out of a parking slot in front of her. Melissa shifts into Drive and—with Polly and Chinga sitting alongside her—screeches out of the parking lot. Scully watches her go, then glances casually toward the entrance of the Supr Savr. She sees an old man, his face bloodied, staggering out onto the sidewalk. Scully shifts into Park, exits her car,

and walks quickly in his direction.

"Sir? What happened?" she says.

The old man says, stoically, "I think we need a doctor."

Alarmed, Scully hurries past him and enters the supermarket. Clerks and customers stand as if awakening from a daze. Some have blood on their hands. Others have scratched the area around their eyes raw.

"Who are you?" asks an assistant manager.

"I'm—my name is Scully. I'm an FBI agent. What happened to you?"

"I don't know," says the man. "But Dave the Butcher? I think he's dead."

The assistant manager—who is also mutilated and partially blinded—waves her toward the meat department with a bloody hand. Scully walks past the meat counter and into the back room. Dave is lying face up on the floor, dead. The knife is wedged deeply into his eye socket.

Back in Washington, Mulder is seated at his desk, eating sunflower seeds and screening a videotape. Low, inscrutable moans are emanating from his television. His phone rings and, transfixed by what he's watching, he lifts the receiver absentmindedly to his ear.

"Mulder, it's me," says Scully.

"I thought you were on vacation, Scully," says Mulder. "I thought you said you didn't want to be disturbed. You wanted to get out of your head for a few days."

"I don't," says Scully, "I mean—I do."

The sounds of moaning and groaning grow louder.

"What are you watching, Mulder?" asks Scully.

"It's *The World's Deadliest Swarms,*" says Mulder.

He shows a smidgen of embarrassment, then hits the MUTE button on his remote. "Um, you said you were gonna be unreachable. What's going on?"

BYERS: "I'm here because I wanted to learn **the truth—** I assumed the same went for you."

SCULLY:
"I'm not saying that monsters don't exist. Whether depicted in cartoon, fairy tale, myth or legend— they often represent something quite serious and real."

MULDER:
"The we-only- make-monsters- of-ourselves argument…"

THE WELL-MANICURED MAN:

"It's not a game,
for godsake!"

THE CIGARETTE-SMOKING MAN:

"Sure it is.
It's all a game.
You just take their pieces
one by one.
Until the board is clear."

SCULLY:
"Why didn't you tell me?"

MULDER: "I never expected this.
I thought I was protecting you."

SCULLY: "Why would they
do this to me? And how?"

MULDER: "I know only that genetic
experiments were being done.
Children were being created."

MULDER:
"What I've seen...I saw because
I wanted to believe.
If we look too hard
maybe we become mad.
But if we continue
to look we become liberated.
And we come awake
as if from a dream..."

Scully turns to look through the balcony window of the Supr Savr manager's office. Below, teams of paramedics are tending to the wounded.

"I'm at a market here," she says. "I'm just trying to give the local PD a hand here."

"A hand on what?" asks Mulder.

"Well, I'm not quite sure how to describe it, Mulder," she says. "I didn't witness it myself, but there seems to be some sort of outbreak of people acting in a violent, involuntary way."

"Toward who?" says Mulder, his interest piqued enough that he snaps off his TV.

"Toward themselves," says Scully, now peering over the shoulder of two uniformed cops—one young, one middle-aged—reviewing surveillance video of the incident.

"Themselves?" says Mulder.

"Yeah. One man is dead," says Scully.

"Dead? How?"

"Self-inflicted, it appears."

"Huh!" says Mulder. "It sounds to me like that's witchcraft, or maybe some sorcery you're lookin' for there."

"No," says Scully. "I don't think it's witchcraft, Mulder, or sorcery."

Hearing her say this, the older cop peers, rather surprised, at Scully.

Scully adds, "I've had a look around, and I've seen nothing that warrants that kind of suspicion."

"Hell, maybe you don't know what you're looking for," says Mulder.

Scully says, "Like evidence of conjury or the black arts? Or shamanism, divination, Wicca, or any kind of pagan or neo-pagan practice? Charms, cards, familiars, bloodstones, or hex signs, or any kind of the ritual tableau associated with the occult—Santeria, Voudoun, Macumba or any high or low magic—"

"Scully?" says Mulder, interrupting.

"Yes?" says Scully.

"Marry me!"

Scully says, "I was hoping for something a little more helpful."

"Well, you know," says Mulder, "short of looking for a lady wearing a pointy hat riding a broomstick, I think you've got it covered."

"Thanks anyway," says Scully, sarcastically.

She hangs up the phone abruptly and turns to the surveillance video, which is now showing Melissa carrying Polly out of the supermarket.

"Who's that woman right there?" she asks.

"Melissa Turner," says the younger cop, whose name is Officer Buddy Riggs.

"She's the only one I've seen who looks unaffected," says Scully.

"What's your point?" asks Riggs, glancing nervously at the older officer.

"You might want to talk to her," says Scully, a little puzzled by his uneasiness. Nevertheless, she leaves the manager's office and walks briskly toward the entrance. She almost makes it, too, before the older cop—whose name is Captain Jack Bonsaint—catches up with her.

"Ms. Scully!" says Bonsaint. "You staying in town?"

"Yes," says Scully, warily. "I'm on vacation. Why?"

"Well," says Bonsaint, "what you said back there about Melissa Turner kinda put a spin on this whole business here today."

"How's that?"

"Well, Melissa's caused some stir. People here say she's a witch."

Scully says, "That's not the first time for that accusation in these parts."

"Ah, yup," says Bonsaint, grinning.

"Well, to be honest with you, Captain Bonsaint," says Scully, "I'm not much of a believer in witchcraft."

"Well, y'know, I'm not either," says Bonsaint. "I used to believe it was just 'cause Melissa was pretty. And single. Threatening, y'know?"

"But now you're not convinced?" says Scully.

"Well, y'know," continues the policeman, "I appreciate the trouble you went to and I sure do hope that there's a reasonable explanation, like you said. Just this one thing is gonna persuade folks to your thinkin'."

"What one thing is that?" says Scully.

"Who she's been carryin' on with," says Bonsaint.

"Who she's been carryin' on with?"

"Ah, yup," says Bonsaint. "With Dave. The butcher."

Back in the manager's office Buddy Riggs dials an outside phone number.

"Hey! It's Buddy," he says.

Melissa Turner is on the other end. She stands in Polly's room; Polly sits nearby with Chinga. The kid's song "The Hokey Pokey" is playing on a toylike 45 rpm record player.

"Oh, hi," says Melissa, nervously.

"You okay, Melissa?" asks Buddy.

"I'm fine. Why do you ask?"

"Who's that, Mommy?" asks Polly, as chillingly as ever.

Melissa doesn't answer her. Instead, she listens to Riggs, who has closed the manager's office door for privacy.

"I know you were here, Melissa, down at the Supr Savr," he says.

"I don't know what you're talking about, Buddy," quavers Melissa.

"Hang up, Mommy," says Polly.

Melissa again ignores her daughter, ducking away and taking her cordless phone downstairs.

Buddy says, "There's some talk that you're involved in what happened here today."

Melissa says, still walking, "I'm not involved in anything!"

"I know that," whispers Buddy. "Would you listen to me! I'm not saying that you are."

"What are you saying, Buddy?" asks Melissa—by this time at her front door. Polly, however, is still calling for her.

"That I want to help you," says Buddy. "But you gotta keep it a secret or we're both gonna be answering questions. Now, I've got something to tell you. Something bad."

"What is it, Buddy?"

"Dave's dead," says the policeman. "I gotta see you right away. You need a friend more than ever."

Up in the bedroom, where "The Hokey Pokey" is still playing loudly, Chinga's eyes are open wide. *"Let's have fun!"* says the doll.

Melissa, standing on the front lawn, hears this. "You can't come here, Buddy," she says. "I can't explain it to you now."

Buddy insists, "I'm coming over there. You shouldn't be alone."

Melissa, terrified, says nothing. Behind her is a large white sheet hanging from a clothesline. On it is the shadow of a big Chinga doll, rippling lightly in the breeze.

Shortly afterward Bonsaint and Scully knock on Melissa Turner's front door. There is no reply. Scully looks in through a window and sees that the back door is wide open. In the backyard the hanging sheets are still wet.

In Polly's bedroom upstairs the windows are nailed shut from the inside.

"What the devil's this for?" says Bonsaint.

"Looks like she was afraid of something," says Scully.

"Whatever it is," says Bonsaint, "she's run off in a hurry."

Scully asks the captain how well he knows Melissa.

"Lissy Turner? About as local as you can get," says Bonsaint. "Born and raised here. Married a fisherman. Widowed last year after a boating accident.

"Don't know if the little girl, Polly, ever really understood. Toys in the attic."

"The daughter's autistic?" asks Scully.

"That's what they say. There was the incident last year over at the day care center. Proprietor slapped Polly across the face."

"Slapped her? What for?"

"Well, she said Polly threw a tantrum so fierce there was nothing else she could do. Next thing she knows she's on the ground. Little girl knocked her silly."

"The little girl did?" says Scully, skeptically.

"Well, that's her story," says Bonsaint. "But Polly never touched her, as far as I could figure. Oh, it was a real drama, though. Lady who ran the school lost her license. People calling the kid all manner of names. Saying Melissa's a witch. Polly never went back to school a day since.

Scully looks her colleague in the eye. "This affair, the mother was having," she says, "with the butcher?"

"Dave?" says Bonsaint. He adds quickly, "Oh, I might have given you the wrong impression. That wasn't really an affair. Although Dave did make quite a fool of himself. And his wife."

"So," says Scully. "It was unrequited."

"You could say that," says Bonsaint.

"To the extent that she'd have to nail the windows shut?"

"Oh, no," says Bonsaint. "He wasn't that big a fool." He adds, "You know, maybe she wasn't afraid of something getting *in*. Maybe she's afraid of something getting out."

"Like what?" asks Scully, puzzled.

Bonsaint shakes his head, then shrugs in an exaggerated way. "Just a thought," he says, casually.

At the local Dairy Queen, Buddy Riggs beams as he sets a large ice cream sundae, with a large cherry on top, in front of Polly Turner. The little girl begins spooning it down without even the hint of a smile. Buddy walks over to the next table, and sits across from Melissa.

"Why don't you leave town?" he asks earnestly.

"I've got nowhere to go, Buddy," says Melissa, near tears. "I live on a shoestring as it is."

Buddy leans forward. "Listen to me. I've got some money put away," he says.

"Buddy, I can't!" protests Melissa.

Buddy swallows hard and decides quickly, before he loses his nerve, to speak his piece. "I've had my eye on you, Melissa, for more years than I care to remember. You know. I missed my chance the first time around. I've been waiting in the wings.

"Now—I'm sorry about things. Truly, I am. But you need somebody who can provide."

By now, Melissa is crying. "Don't, Buddy, please!"

"Don't because you don't want to?" asks Buddy. "Or just because you're too proud?"

"You don't understand!" she says.

She glances anxiously over at her daughter. Polly has parked Chinga on her chair, picked up her sundae, and taken it over to the service counter.

Buddy says, "What don't I understand?"

"What happened in the Supr Savr," replies Melissa. "What happened to Dave. I couldn't stop it."

"What do you mean?"

"I've seen . . . things," she says.

Polly has placed her sundae on the counter.

"I want more cherries," she says, catching the attention of a young female clerk.

"What's that, sweetie?" asks the clerk

"I want MORE cherries!"

Melissa leans closer to Buddy, nearly whispering, "I saw Dave dead. Before he was dead! I saw him in frozen foods, all cut and bloody. And it's not the first time!"

Buddy is stunned speechless.

"My husband," continues Melissa. "I saw him, in a window. Dead—before it happened. You know—with a hook?"

The DQ clerk turns and smiles at Polly. "You're gonna have to ask your mom for some money, hon. I just can't give them away!"

The clerk turns her back, walks to the frozen custard dispenser—its glass-covered innards whipping the liquid ice cream to perfection—and starts making an elaborate sundae for a drive-up customer. Polly stares coldly at the clerk's long blond ponytail—and Chinga's eyes pop open.

"Let's have fun!" says the blue-eyed doll.

Polly turns to her mother. "Mommy! I want more cherries!"

Her daughter's bad mood finally registers. "We gotta go now, Polly," says Melissa, rising quickly to grab Chinga.

The DQ clerk continues working on the sundae. Buddy stands, reaches into his pocket, and pulls out a key.

"Take this, Melissa," he says fervently. "It's a place we use for hunting. Up near Schoodic Lake. Or else there's gonna be trouble," adds Buddy. "More than you need."

"Mommy!" says Polly. "Mommy! Mommy!"

Distracted, Melissa can't concentrate on Polly. Buddy presses the key into Melissa's hand just as the clerk lets out an anguished cry.

The girl's ponytail is caught in the frozen custard dispenser. With each revolution of the machinery, her head is yanked closer to the whipping blades. Buddy leaps over the counter and fumbles desperately for the on/off switch as the pale scalp of the painfully sobbing girl starts to drip bright-red blood.

At another location in town Jane Froelich—the middle-aged ex–day care operator—scowls out through a window at Scully and Bonsaint. She reluctantly agrees to talk to them while they remain, standing uneasily, on her front porch.

"You talk to *her*?" asks Froelich.

"Who?" asks Scully.

"Oh, please!" says the spinster.

"Melissa Turner. That whore's a witch sure as sure as I'm standin' here. She's descended from the Hawthornes in Salem and the Englishes, too.

"She comes from cursed lineage! And now she's passin' it on the whelp. God save that little girl if somebody don't do somethin'! Lord know I tried!"

Bonsaint shuffles his feet. "Jane, if we could just come in for a few minutes and talk—"

Froelich says, "I found out last year how much good talking to you does, Jack Bonsaint! I explained everything, and the city closed me down anyway."

Spitting out the words, she adds, "Our great-great-grandfathers knew how to treat witches. They would have driven the demon out of that little girl and given that slattern of a mother what she's got coming."

Miss Froelich closes the door in Bonsaint's and Scully's faces.

"New England hospitality," sighs Scully. "Heard about it my whole life. Finally got a chance to experience it for myself."

They walk slowly back to Bonsaint's police car, Jane Froelich eyeing them venomously through her curtains.

Scully says, "This family tree of Melissa Turner's—"

"Ah, yup."

"—it's all talk. Isn't it?"

"Oh, I never really asked," says Bonsaint, breezily. "Why?"

"Well," says Scully. "I think you need to bring her in. To straighten this out."

"Under what pretext?"

"That she might know something."

"About what?"

"About what I'm sure," says Scully, somewhat unconvincingly, "is a perfectly reasonable explanation for all this."

Bonsaint says, nodding solemnly, "Ah, yup."

Scully turns and ducks sheepishly into the police car. "Well, I wish I could help you out," she says. "I'm just—you know, I'm on vacation."

That night Melissa Turner's car—with Polly and Chinga in the passenger seat— drives down a dark country road and stops at the Schoodic Lake ranger station. A ranger leaves the small building and bends down toward the driver's window, a look of concern on his face.

"Where you headed this time of night?" asks the ranger.

Melissa smiles nervously and tells them they were invited to a friend's place at the lake.

"Uh-huh," says the ranger, disapprovingly. "You got gear? Food and water?"

"We'll be all right," says Melissa.

The ranger glances at Polly, who appears to be sleeping peacefully. "I just want to be sure of that, ma'am," he says. "Winter's in full force up there. Power's iffy. It's just you and the little one?"

"Right for now," says Melissa.

Polly opens her eyes. "I want to go home, Mommy!" she says.

Melissa turns to her. "We're going to go *camping*, Polly," she explains, nearly managing to make her voice sound cheery.

"I WANT my bed! I WANT my records!"

Chinga's eyes pop open.

"*Let's have fun!*" says the doll, to Melissa's alarm.

Disapprovingly, the ranger begins to

take down her license number. Melissa turns and stares, as if hypnotized, at the placid face of Chinga, until something catches her eye—it is the image of Jane Froehlich, splayed horribly across the glass of the car's rear window. Her throat has been cut, and blood flows down the front of her nightclothes.

"Help me!" croaks the mortally wounded woman.

Melissa gasps, and slams the car into reverse. As the astonished ranger jumps out of the way, she squeals into a fishtailing U-turn and heads, tires smoking, back to town.

In a darkened residential hallway "The Hokey Pokey" is echoing faintly. A light snaps on and Jane Froelich, in bathrobe and slippers, shuffles into view.

"Hello?" she says. There's no answer.

She walks down the hallway into the annex that contains her shuttered day care center. "The Hokey Pokey" is much louder now. She clicks the wall-mounted light switch. Nothing happens.

"Who's there? Is anyone there?" she says.

Again, no response.

She crosses the carpeted room, stepping over a scattering of 45 r.p.m records, and lifts the tone arm from a record spinning on a phonograph turntable.

"I want to play!" says a familiar voice behind her.

Miss Froelich whirls, dropping the tone arm back onto the record. She picks up a broken record and thrusts its jagged edge, like a knife blade, in front of her. The phonograph needle sticks and the same phrase—"That's what it's all about"—plays over and over.

"I'm not afraid of you!" Jane Froelich cries, her hand shaking with fright.

As if with a will of its own, her hand begins curling back toward her. In a few moments the jagged edge is pointed toward her throat. She struggles against it, just as Dave the Butcher did. The phonograph needle jumps back into the groove and "The Hokey Pokey" spins merrily to its conclusion.

The next morning, in a motel room nearby, Dana Scully relaxes, her eyes closed, in a luxurious bubble bath. A soothing piano concerto plays on her boom box; a room service feast lies on a serving cart; the telephone at her bedside purrs gently. Scully deftly hooks the bathroom doorknob with her big toe, slamming it shut against the pesky outside world.

Some time later Scully emerges from her bathroom, drying her hair with a thick towel. Her telephone message light blinks steadily. She steadfastly ignores it. Scully walks to the front window, pulls open the curtains and sees Jack Bonsaint, a sheepish expression on his face, standing, hands on hips, waiting for her.

At Jane Froelich's house a few minutes later its former owner's body is being wheeled out by coroner's aides. Bonsaint tells Scully that the obvious cause of death was suicide. Buddy Riggs, who's been working inside, shows them the bloody record fragment that was the apparent instrument of death.

Scully kneels to inspect the broken 45s scattered on the carpet. Bonsaint's cell phone rings. He answers it, then hands it to Scully.

"Hey, good morning, sunshine!" says a familiar voice.

"Mulder?"

"Yeah," says the agent, talking over a persistent pounding noise on the phone line. "I was a little worried about you. I was wondering if you needed my help up there."

"Needed your help on what?" says Scully.

The pounding increases in both frequency and volume.

Mulder says, "I left a message at your motel. You didn't get it?"

"I was up and out this morning," says Scully. "Mulder?"

"Yeah," says her partner.

"What's that noise? Where are you?"

"I'm at home," he says. "They're doing some construction right out through the—hold on a second."

In fact Mulder, in shorts and a sweatshirt, is dribbling a basketball on his desktop.

"Hey, fellas!" he yells. "Can you just keep it down for a second, maybe?"

He tosses the basketball into a wastepaper basket. "Thank you!" he yells, then picks up the phone again.

Mulder says, "Yeah, hey. I was thinking about this case. Maybe it's not witchcraft after all. Maybe there's a scientific explanation."

"A scientific explanation?" asks Scully, suspiciously.

"Yeah, a medical cause," says Mulder. "Something called 'chorea.'"

"Dancing sickness," says Scully, rolling her eyes.

"Yeah. St. Vitus's dance," says Mulder, walking over to his refrigerator. "It affects groups of people, causing unexplained outbursts of, uh, unexplained jerks and spasms—"

"And hasn't been seen or diagnosed since the Middle Ages," says Scully.

Inside Mulder's refrigerator, sitting in lonely splendor, is a plastic container of orange juice. Mulder reaches down for it, takes a healthy swig, and grimaces—desperately fighting his gag reflex. He checks the expiration date. It reads OCT 97. Mulder spits the mouthful of O.J. back into the container, and thoughtfully replaces it inside the fridge.

He says, "You're obviously not a fan of *American Bandstand*, Scully."

"Mulder?" says Scully.

"Yeah?" says Mulder.

"Thanks for the help."

"Hello?" says Mulder, his line suddenly dead. Scully hands the phone back to Bonsaint.

"I'm sorry for eavesdropping," says the policeman, "but does he maybe have some insight on this?"

"No," says Scully, brusquely.

"I see," says Bonsaint, politely.

At the other end of the room Buddy Riggs pokes through the day care detritus and turns on the phonograph. "The Hokey Pokey" begins to play loudly. Riggs shudders, and reaches down to turn off the music.

Scully turns back to Bonsaint. "You know, Jack?" she says. "Can I call you Jack? I've been thinking that maybe we need to explore other possibilities."

"I'm not sure I understand."

"Well," she says, "maybe we need to keep our minds open to . . . extreme possibilities."

"Okay!" says Bonsaint. "But aren't you on vacation?"

Scully grimaces, nods ruefully, but says nothing.

Outside the Turner house Melissa's car is parked at a weird angle in the driveway. "The Hokey Pokey" is playing, of course, and Polly sleeps with Chinga in her nailed-up bedroom.

Her mother tiptoes toward her, nearly making it when the raucous recording ends. The dolly's eyes snap open and bore into Melissa. She jumps back in fright. The record player's tone arm somehow lifts off its turntable, slides back to the beginning of the record, and lowers itself. "The Hokey Pokey" starts playing all over again.

Melissa flees downstairs to the kitchen, sobbing hysterically. She glances up at the window and sees the image of Buddy Riggs. His face has been beaten into a bloody pulp.

"Help me!" groans the deputy, his voice only barely human.

Later that day Scully and Bonsaint are seated at a wharfside seafood restaurant. A server plunks a huge Maine lobster in front of them.

"Ah!" says Bonsaint, happily.

"Oh, my God!" says Scully, astonished. "That looks like something out of Jules Verne. We're supposed to eat that?"

"Little late for anything else," says Bonsaint, expertly twisting off the creature's meat-filled tail.

"Now," he says, "you said you had some 'other directions' you were thinking about?"

Scully says, "I've been thinking about Melissa Turner. Now, you said her husband died in a boating accident?"

"Ah, yup."

"Well, was there anything strange about that? About the way that it happened?"

Bonsaint looks up from his crustacean dissection. "Well, it was never quite explained to anyone's satisfaction, actually. How the man got a grappling hook pulled clean through his skull."

"Well, was Melissa ever questioned about that?" says Scully.

"Melissa?" replies Bonsaint, puzzled. "No, I don't see how she'd be involved." He looks out the restaurant window. "Boat he died on's right over there," he says. "If you're at all wonderin'."

Scully follows his gaze to a trim wooden fishing vessel. An old man is tossing a bucket of water overboard.

"I saw that man at the market," says Scully, astonished.

At the Turner house Polly holds Chinga and puts "The Hokey Pokey" record on the turntable.

"I WANT popcorn, Mommy!" she says, starting the music again. Melissa tries hard to remain calm. She backs out of the room, turns, and faces an angry Buddy Riggs.

"What are you doing here?" asks the deputy. "How come you're back in town?"

Melissa says, "You gotta get outta here, Buddy!"

Buddy's stern expression doesn't change. "I called the rangers," he says. "They said you tried to kill a man. You almost ran him over. You came back here to kill her, too, didn't you?"

Melissa shakes her head frantically. "I didn't try to kill anybody—"

"Jane Froelich!" says Buddy, accusingly.

"It isn't me, Buddy!"

"Well, we're gonna see about that," he says. "You're coming in with me. And your little brat."

Buddy stops, suddenly distracted, and stares, as if hypnotized, at the doll nestled in Polly's lap. Chinga's eyes open suddenly.

"I want to play!" she says.

At sunset Scully and Bonsaint sit on board the docked fishing boat. The old man's eyes are still scratched and bloody. He looks at the pair and smiles inscrutably.

"What happened?" he says. "You ask that question around here, you get as

many stories as—as fishermen."

Scully says, "You were on board the night he died. What do you think?"

The old man says, "I told my story to the chief."

"People's stories change," says Scully.

"Folks blame the widow," he replies.

"Who do you blame?" asks Scully.

The old man shrugs, sighs, and comes to a difficult decision. "He was wild for her," he says.

"He worked very hard to build that little house for her. When that daughter came you'd need a mop to wipe that smile off his face. We'd set out to sea on the girl's last birthday. He was counting the hours before he'd be home again."

In a brief flashback to the fatal night, Melissa's husband Rich hauls a lobster trap out of the water. He opens it and pulls out a drenched Chinga doll. The old man comes out of the wheelhouse to take a look.

"Hey, look what Davey Jones sent my little Polly," he says happily. "Catch of the day!"

"Ah, yup," says the old man, warily.

"Three days later," concludes the old man, back in the present, "he was dead."

Scully asks him if he knew what killed Turner. The old man pauses a second, and remembers. "The eyes play tricks at night. Water up against the hull. Sometimes you see things."

Back on Rich Turner's last voyage the young fisherman hauls up another lobster trap, but it is empty. He hears an unexpected noise behind him.

"What the hell was that?" he says.

He grabs a grappling hook, leaves the pitch-dark fantail, and cautiously enters the wheelhouse. The old man, who's been napping in a chair, wakes up at his entrance.

"What is it?" he asks, groggily.

Turner turns and exits the wheelhouse. A faint voice, coming from inside a locker, says *I want to play!* The flickering shadow of a Chinga doll dances over the woodwork in the cabin.

The old man stands and, frightened,

quickly leaves the wheelhouse. Rich Turner is hanging from a davit, impaled on the razor sharp grappling hook, which has passed completely through his skull.

In the present again the old man stares hauntingly at his visitors.

"Like I said," he says, "the eyes play tricks."

But Scully is not satisfied.

"But you saw something," she says, fixing him firmly in her gaze. "In that grocery store. That little girl and her dolly."

"The moment I saw them," says the old man, nodding solemnly, "I knew."

Later that night Scully and Bonsaint walk briskly down a town street. Her cell phone rings. It's Mulder, in his darkened office at headquarters.

"Hey! I thought you weren't answering your cell phone," he says.

"So why'd you call?" asks Scully, irritated.

"I had a new thought about this case you're working on," he says. As he speaks he idly twirls the long extension cord on his telephone. "There's a viral infection spread by touch—"

"Mulder," says Scully, interrupting him, "are there any references in occult literature to objects that, uh, have the power to direct human behavior?"

"What types of objects?"

"Um, like a doll, for instance."

"You mean like Chuckie?" says Mulder, gleefully.

"Yeah, kinda like that," concedes Scully.

"Well, yeah," says Mulder, quite excited now, "The talking doll myth is well established in literature. Especially in New England. The fetish, or juju, is believed to pass on magical powers to its possessor. Some of the early witches were condemned for little more than proclaiming that these objects existed. The supposed witch, having premonitory visions and things. Why do you ask?"

"Just curious," says Scully.

Mulder says, "You didn't find a talking doll, did you, Scully?"

"No, no," she replies. "Of course not—"

"I would suggest," interjects Mulder, "that you check the back of the doll for a plastic ring with a string on it. That would be my first—hello?"

Pocketing her cell phone, Scully sighs and turns to Bonsaint. "Let's go talk to Melissa Turner," she says.

In the Turner house Polly rampages through the half-lit hallways.

"WHERE'S MY POPCORN!" screams the little girl.

In the kitchen Melissa is beyond hysteria. She stands in front of the stove, shaking a Jiffy Pop container convulsively over a flaming burner. Buddy Riggs, his bloody nightstick in his outstretched hand, lies dead on the floor a few feet away.

Later that night Polly and Chinga lie asleep in their bed. Melissa hurries to a hallway closet and pulls out a hammer and a box of nails. Furiously, she nails shut all the windows and the front and rear doors.

Polly, with Chinga, appears suddenly behind her. "Mommy! I can't sleep," says the girl.

"You go back to bed, Polly," says Melissa, smiling gamely through her fright. "It's way past your bedtime."

"No more pounding!" says Polly.

"Back to bed, sweetheart!" she says, then gasps as Chinga's eyes snap open.

"*Let's have fun!*" says the doll.

Melissa turns to her left and sees an image of herself on a near window. She has a bloody hole in her forehead, because the hammer is buried in it claw first. Her bloody hands are pressed beseechingly against the outside of the window pane.

"Help me!" she moans.

The real Melissa fights her instinct to panic.

"It's going to be all right, sweetie. Everything's going to be all right," she quavers, escorting her daughter up the stairway. "Just go back to bed."

At that moment the police car, with Scully and Bonsaint inside, pulls up in front of the house. Bonsaint is alarmed to notice Buddy Riggs's cruiser parked outside.

Inside, Melissa puts the hammer back into the closet, fastens it with a latch and locks it with a padlock. In the kitchen she deliberately knocks over a kerosene heater; its flammable liquid pours onto Buddy's body. She grabs a large box of wooden matches and, hands shaking, tries to light one.

Bonsaint steps up onto the front porch and pounds on the door to no avail. Scully peers in the front window, but sees no one. Ignoring Bonsaint's cries, Melissa keeps trying to light a match and when she finally succeeds, Polly and Chinga are right there next to her.

"Mommy?" says Polly, a note of childish fright in her voice.

Chinga's eyes snap open and the small flame is blown out by a puff of air.

"Don't play with matches!" says Chinga.

Melissa whimpers with fright. Desperately, she lights match after match, only to watch them blow out.

"Go back to bed, Polly!" she screams. "GO ON—NOW!"

Outside, Bonsaint pounds louder and faster. Scully moves to another nailed-up window and sees Melissa's attempts to set Buddy Riggs on fire. The FBI agent pounds on the glass to get her attention, then yells to Bonsaint for help. The frantic policeman tries to shoulder his way through, then kick down the front door. Melissa throws the matchbox down and runs to her knife drawer. She pulls it open but before she can reach inside, the drawer slams shut with a violent bang.

"Don't play with knives!" says Chinga.

Scully tells Bonsaint that Melissa has nailed the door shut. "She's trying to kill herself!"

"Mommy! Mommy! No more pounding!" cries Polly, hugging Chinga.

In the hallway the locked closet begins to vibrate and shake. Then the clasp breaks off and the doors fly open.

"Let's play with the hammer!" says Chinga.

Scully and Bonsaint take turns driving their shoulders into the front door. When they finally break through they face a maniacal Melissa Turner, brandishing the hammer at them.

"STAY AWAY FROM ME!" shouts Melissa.

Scully looks directly into the crazed woman's eyes. "Put it down, Melissa!" she says.

Polly and Chinga appear behind her. "I don't like you any more," says the doll.

Melissa swings the hammer, claw first, into her forehead. Scully bends down to Polly and grabs at the Chinga doll, but the little girl won't let go.

"Give me the doll, Polly," says Scully.

Polly shakes her head.

"I want to play!" says Chinga. "I want to play! I want to play!"

Melissa strikes herself with the hammer again and again. Polly is distracted by this for a second; Scully grabs the doll out of her arms, rushes to the kitchen, and throws Chinga into the microwave.

"I want to play! I want to play! I want to play. I want to play. I want to—"

Scully slams the oven door shut and pushes several buttons on its control panel. Through the Plexiglas window the doll arcs, sparks, and finally bursts into flame.

In the hallway, Melissa, sobbing, drops the hammer to the floor. Her daughter stares at her impassively.

In the kitchen, Chinga burns. Scully watches with a mixture of awe, fear, and fascination.

A few days later Fox Mulder is sitting in his FBI office, carefully removing a pencil from an electric sharpener. He admires its sharp, fine point and sets it down next to a dozen or so other sharpened pencils, arrayed in parade-ground precision on his desktop. He smiles, albeit guiltily, when Scully opens the front door and enters.

"Oh, hey, Scully! How ya doin'?" he says. "How ya feelin'? Rested?"

"I feel fine," says Scully evenly, staring at something over Mulder's left shoulder.

Mulder follows her gaze. "What!?" he says.

"That poster," she says finally, "Where'd you get it?"

"Oh, I got it down on M Street. In a head shop. About five years ago."

"Hmmmn." says Scully.

"Why?" says Mulder.

"Well," says Scully, shrugging, "I just wanted to send one to somebody."

"You *do*?"

"Mm-hmmm."

Scully walks absentmindedly to her "area." Mulder takes this chance to—clumsily—open his drawer and sweeps the platoon of sharpened pencils into it.

"Who?" he says.

"Oh, just some guy Jack," says Scully. "M Street?"

"Yeah," says Mulder, quickly. "Hey, does this have something to do with that case you were working on?"

"What case? Uh—yeah! Yes it does."

"You solve it?"

"Me? No," she says. "No, I was on vacation, just getting out of my own head for a few days. What about you?" she adds. "Did you get anything done while I was gone?"

"Oh, God!" says Mulder, leaning back in his office chair, beaming. "I mean, it's amazing what I can accomplish without incessant meddling or questioning into everything I do—"

As he says this, a tiny missile falls from the sky, lands on Mulder's shoulder, and bounces to the floor. Another unidentified object hits Mulder's hands. He drops it. Both Mulder and Scully look up to see approximately fifty sharpened pencils hanging point-first into the ceiling.

"There's got to be an explanation," says Mulder, solemnly.

"Oh, I don't know," says Scully, lowering her gaze. "I think some things are better left unexplained."

back story:

When word leaked out in 1997 that mega-author Stephen King had written an hour's worth of *The X-Files*, many fans expected a horror story of one sort or another. What they got, most agree, was a perfectly presentable mid-season episode, containing, to be sure, several bizarre twists and turns; but no weirder, more convoluted, or problematic than usual.

That's pretty much the view from behind the scenes, too.

"The whole thing started," explains Chris Carter, "back when Stephen met David on *Jeopardy. Celebrity Jeopardy*. He beat David, which is something that we have never let David live down.

"Anyway," adds Carter, "he told David that he loved the show and that he'd love to write an episode. Then one day, Stephen called me out of the blue. He said, 'Hey, Chris, you know, I'd love to do a *Millennium*. Which I thought was a little strange, considering what I'd heard, but he told me that he'd wanted to do an *X-Files* but then decided to do a *Millennium* instead. I said, 'Great!' Then he called back and said, 'I want to do an *X-Files* now. I've got some ideas.'

"So, finally, we took him up on his offer. Or actually, he took us up on his own offer. And every now and then I'd get another phone call from him, from his home in Maine. And then he did the episode."

Actually, says the *X-Files*'s executive producer, what happened was that over the months he and King—whom Carter to this day has never met in person—wrote alternate drafts of 5X10, with Carter turning out the final draft. Hence, their shared writing credit.

"Stephen wasn't used to writing for Mulder and Scully," says Carter, "and the Mulder-and-Scully story in his original draft didn't quite work. The problem was, our stories have to track in a certain way. You can't get ahead of the lead characters. The viewers can't see things that they (Mulder and Scully) don't."

Carter also cut King's episode down to size and shifted the story primarily toward Scully by keeping Mulder at home in Washington, D.C. After that, the problems and subsequent improvisations weren't all that different from any other episode.

"Yeah. 'Chinga' was fun," says Gillian Anderson. "But the way the script originally read to me, initially it seemed to me as if Scully kind of stepped up to the plate and played along with the sheriff's humor in a way. So I ended up playing a lot of my lines a little . . . well, not quite tongue in cheek, but just kind of falling into his rhythm. So in the end I got a call from Chris saying, 'You know, there are people dying here, it's not funny. We have to edit out a lot of stuff.'"

Another problem—creating an evil, enchanted doll different from the other evil, enchanted dolls the viewers had already seen—was attacked by assembling Chinga from parts of several different dolls. On set, says props master Ken Hawryliw, Chinga was a stuntwoman with an oversized doll's head plopped on top; this was topped by "the world's largest wig"—actually several wigs sewed together—constructed under the supervision of hairstylist Anji Bemben.

The Old Man's fishing boat was actually a beautifully pristine hobby fishing boat, used as a pleasure craft by a local resident and " de-prettified" by construction supervisor Rob Maier (who got his start as an apprentice shipbuilder, learning how to build icebreakers) for use in the episode.

A Maine accent is quite similar to a Canadian accent, says Vancouver casting director Coreen Mayrs, so finding Downeasters to populate Ammas Beach was not a problem. The requisite wounds, slashes, and sharp-objects-in-the-eye-sockets were all in a day's work for special effects makeup artist Toby Lindala, who nevertheless appreciated the chance to create these classics for a Stephen King project.

The scenes of Scully gassing up at a self-serve station were filmed at the self-serve gas station just across the street from *The X-Files* production office. The supermarket scenes were filmed across town, but in an actual supermarket, not a fake supermarket created from scratch. This was a first for *The X-Files*, according to art director Greg Loewen.

And, finally, Melissa's Turner's premonitions of "Death Under Glass"—including the sight of Dave the Butcher trapped in his freezer door— were painstakingly created in post-production by visual effects supervisor Laurie Kallsen-George. She then tested them out by showing them to her two sons, age nine and eleven.

"I gauge a lot of the shows by whether my kids can stand them or not," laughs Kallsen-George. "If they can't, I figure it succeeded—and 'Chinga' bothered them a lot."

Ⓧ

The title of this episode, in addition to being the name of Polly's doll, is an extremely vulgar Spanish colloquialism—something King was unaware of when he chose the name.

Ⓧ

The classical music selection playing as Scully drives into town—as well as during a later scene, when she takes her bubble bath— is Hummel's Piano Concert No. 3, Opus 89.

METRO

kill switch

A dying computer genius creates
a murderous cybernetic life form.
Mulder and Scully—aided only by the dead
man's disciple—must somehow purge
this predator from the Internet.

EPISODE: 5X11
FIRST AIRED: February 15, 1998
EDITOR: Heather MacDougall
WRITTEN BY: William Gibson
& Tom Maddox
DIRECTED BY: Rob Bowman

GUEST STARS:
Kristin Lehman (Esther Nairn)
Kate Luyben (Nurse Nancy)
Tom Braidwood (Frohike)
Dean Haglund (Langly)
Bruce Harwood (Byers)
Peter Williams (Jackson)
Patrick Keating (Donald Gelman)
Rob Daprocida (Bunny)
Jerry Shram (Boyce)
Dan Weber (Figgis)
Lindsay Bourne (Burn Unit Surgeon)
Steven Griffith (Paramedic)
Ted Cole (Second Paramedic)
Nick Misura (Counterman)
Darwin Haine (Addict)

PRINCIPAL SETTINGS:
Washington, D.C.;
Fairfax County, Virginia

ate at night, in a back booth
of the Metro Diner, a greasy spoon
in a low-rent section of Washington,
sits a pallid middle-aged man, typing away
at a laptop computer. A mug of coffee sits
on his table, untouched; a grizzled counterman approaches carrying a fresh pot.

"Want that warmed up?" he says.

"No," says the patron, in an unhealthy,
hoarse voice. "But I'll buy another if you
leave me alone."

The counterman shrugs and retreats;
the computer man massages the keys
even faster. His laptop beeps; its screen
reads ACCESS DENIED.

"We'll see about that," croaks the lone
hacker, determinedly.

At a crack house not far away, a
slot in a steel door slides open, revealing
an emaciated drug addict. "Eight ball,"
he says.

He shoves a wad of bills through
the slot and gets a powder-filled Baggie
in return. Inside the house a goateed
drug dealer is counting the night's take;
when his cell phone chirps he snaps it
coolly open.

"Yeah," says the dealer, curtly.

"Hello, Jackson," says a stern,
metallic-sounding male voice.

The dealer frowns, annoyed. "How'd
you get this number?" he says.

DINER

"What do you care?" says the voice. "Your partner, Kenny Slater, he took your money, didn't he? I want to help you, Jackson."

"Help me *what?*"

"Slater's in the Metro Diner. Fourteenth and Arlington."

"He's in Florida by now, man!" says Jackson. "Jamaica or Cuba."

"No. He's here. In the Metro Diner. Fourteenth and Arlington."

Jackson hangs up, walks outside to a waiting Porsche, gets into the passenger side and turns to the crew member sitting behind the wheel.

"It's Kenny," he says, snapping a full clip into his automatic pistol. "The fool's come back."

In another drug den—this one run by white dealers—the same informant has phoned the top man, whose name is Bunny. "The men who took your product Friday night are in the Metro Diner," he says.

Bunny snaps his cell phone shut, and grabs a nine-millimeter pistol from an underling.

"Fourteenth and Arlington," he says.

In an Econoline van driving down a city street, another dealer answers his car phone. He hears "Spanish Jack is in the Metro Diner, Fourteenth and Arlington. I understand you wish to speak to him."

The van smokes its tires, speeds through a red light, and careens past two deputy U.S. marshals, sitting in their unmarked car and sipping coffee. Their car phone rings.

"Boyce," says the marshal in the driver's seat.

"Pico Salazar is in the Metro Diner."

"Salazar?" says Boyce. "Who is this?"

"Fourteenth and Arlington," says the voice.

Boyce shifts the Crown Victoria into gear and speeds away, executing a sliding U-turn at the intersection.

In the Metro Diner the computer man is still typing feverishly. His screen still reads ACCESS DENIED. He frowns and stops for a moment. "'How sharper than a serpent's tooth,'" he says, "'to have a thankless child.'"

He types in a string of commands and gets another message: REQUESTING ACCESS TO MASTER OVERRIDE. He smiles tightly, then turns tensely around. A pair of burly, bearded bikers are pushing through the front door. They glance around menacingly and settle down at a nearby booth.

The computer man, relieved, turns back to his work. Again the front door opens and Bunny walks inside with his associate. They seat themselves at the counter. Jackson and his henchman enter and saunter to a table in the back.

The computer man barely notices this; he is engrossed in the data flooding across his screen. "Ah, you know what's coming," he murmurs. "And there's nothing you can do."

He hits three function keys simultaneously. The screen reads ACCESS GRANTED and the computer begins a kaleidoscopic series of uploads and readouts. The computer man coughs convulsively. The front door opens one more time and the dealers from the Econoline enter and stake out their own territory at the counter.

The computer man pulls an unmarked CD-ROM from his pocket.

"You won't feel a thing," he says.

He places the disc into the computer's CD drive, closes the sliding door, and raising a shaky finger over the ENTER button.

Boyce and his partner burst through the door, carrying shotguns.

"U.S. MARSHALS! ON THE FLOOR! DOWN! DOWN!" they shout.

The computer man spins in his seat to face them.

"NO!" he cries, despairingly.

The drug dealers react to the lawmen, drawing their weapons and firing. The diner explodes into a maelstrom of high-velocity bullets and shotgun pellets. The front windows of the diner explode outward and a few seconds later the street falls silent.

At the diner later that night cops and paramedics swarm around the crime scene. Mulder and Scully confer, kneeling next to a sheet-covered corpse.

"Charles Figgis," says Mulder, reading from a file. "Ten-year veteran of the U.S. Marshals Service. Multiple gunshot wounds. High speed Teflon rounds. His partner Gerald Boyce was DOA at Mercy General. Tried to catch a nine-millimeter slug in his teeth."

Scully says, "Looks like they crashed the wrong party."

Mulder adds that Figgis and Boyce had radioed that they were speeding to the diner to apprehend Pico Salazar.

"Pico Salazar?"

"The Colombian cartel's banking liaison," says Mulder. "Salazar escaped from federal custody three months ago. Boyce and Figgis were on the Offender Transport squad that lost him. They took his escape personally. A phone tip told them that Salazar was going to be here tonight."

"A foreign national with his kind of connections?" says Scully, incredulously. "What would he be doing here—let alone in the country?"

"I don't think he is. Or was," says Mulder, inspecting the bodies of the dead criminals. "But there were a lot of very photogenic gentlemen who were."

Scully peruses her folder. "Mulder, these were street-level coke dealers. Minor wholesalers at most."

"Yeah," says Mulder. "Not the type you'd expect to associate with a cartel boss."

"What would they be doing here?" asks Scully.

"Maybe," says Mulder, "it was for the pie."

Mulder squats, lifting the sheet off yet another DB. Scully eyes her partner, irritated.

"It's two forty-five in the morning," she says. "You mind telling me what we're supposed to be looking for?"

Mulder exposes the sickly face of the computer man.

"Donald Gelman," he says, softly.

"Who?"

"Donald Gelman. Silicon Valley software pioneer. He's been missing since 1979."

"And you recognize him?" says Scully.

Mulder says, "He invented the Internet."

Scully shoots Mulder a skeptical look.

"All right," says Mulder, "he didn't quite invent it. But he's a Silicon Valley folk hero. He was writing Internet software even before there was an Internet."

"Why have I never heard of him?" asks Scully.

Mulder explains, "On the eve of the deal that would have set him up as another Bill Gates, he went hiking in the Sierras. He said he'd think about it. He never came back."

"I still don't see the connection," says Scully.

"Maybe that's the point," says Mulder.

Mulder notices that Gelman's laptop is lying next to the body. He flips it open and finds it still functional; he and Scully leave the crime scene, the computer wrapped in his raincoat and hidden from view.

Scully asks her partner what Gelman was doing in the diner.

"I think obviously someone wanted him dead," he says.

Scully says, "You think this was a hit on him?"

Mulder replies, "Eight unconnected dealers, all at the same place, the same time. All tipped off by phone, looking for somebody. Last call's to the marshals. They arrive. The place explodes. Gelman dies in the crossfire. It's genius."

Scully is unconvinced. "Mulder,

did you take a look at him? Why kill a man who's dying? His body is a bag of bones."

"Well," replies Mulder, getting into Scully's car, "when you talk about Donald Gelman, you want to kill the brain, not the body."

Scully slips into the driver's seat. She turns to see Mulder opening up Gelman's laptop.

"Mulder, that's evidence!" she protests.

"Gee, I hope so," says Mulder, sarcastically.

The agent removes Gelman's unmarked CD-ROM, contemplates it for a second, and slips it into the car's dashboard CD player. The song "Twilight Time," by the Platters, begins to play Every light in Scully's car, inside and outside, pulses in time to the music. The agents glance at each other, puzzled, until Mulder smiles, absolutely delighted.

At the Lone Gunmen's office the following day, an awestruck Frohike, Byers, and Langly pore over every inch of Gelman's computer. Frohike, wearing a weird magnifying glass on his head, begins to dissect the machine's innards.

Byers says, reverently, "Jobs and Wozniak at Apple. Gates and Allen writing BASIC. The Homebrew Computer Club's first meetings—Gelman was there."

"Now," adds Frohike, "they're power brokers and billionaires. Back then they were all just inspired nerds."

All three Gunmen cast significant glances at their patron.

"All except Gelman," says Mulder. Byers nods.

"At twenty-eight, Gelman was a part of the group, but not one of them," he says. "At twenty-eight he was the 'old man.' Some say the brightest of all."

Langly looks up. "He wrote some of the earliest viruses—" he says.

"And found himself under investigation by the NSA," says Mulder.

Scully asks him if that was the reason he disappeared.

"Gelman?" says Byers. "Gelman was a visionary, not a capitalist. A subversive."

Frohike, still dissecting, unveils the computer's souped-up motherboard. "This

is a one-off," he says, nearly dumbstruck. "I've never seen anything like it. *Gelman* built this?"

"That might be," says Mulder, "what got him killed."

The Lone Gunmen react in unison, heads whipping from the laptop to Mulder, then Scully. Apparently, they hadn't been told.

"Heavy casualty," says Langly, solemnly.

"Brother goes down," says Frohike, bowing his head in silent tribute.

Mulder takes Gelman's computer disc from his pocket. "I found this in his CD-ROM drive," he says.

"What is it?" asks Byers.

"'Twilight Time,'" says Scully, deadpan.

A few hours later, as Scully sits and reads *The Lone Gunman*, and "Twilight Time" plays sonorously in the background, Mulder and the Gunmen still struggle with the dead genius's legacy.

"We're up against sixty-four-bit encryption," says Langly, typing grimly. "A password that's a random sequence of twelve symbols. Gelman's got this baby sealed up tight."

Byers returns from running a diagnostic on the disc. "This CD has some kind of enhanced background data," he says. "Lots of code. Maybe a program he designed."

"What for?" says Mulder, puzzled.

Scully folds her newspaper, stands, and ambles over to the workbench. "Anyone think to check his e-mail?" she says.

They all look at her, then trade quick looks with each other. Sheepishly, Langly punches some keys. The computer burps. On the screen a mailbox icon appears. The box opens, disgorging the message YOU HAVE ONE PIECE OF MAIL. More keys are punched. The message reads DAVID MISSING. FEAR THE WORST. THE HUNTED HAS BECOME THE HUNTER. HSWT 780022 3 UNTIL SATURDAY, INVISIGOTH.

"'Invisigoth'?" asks Scully.

"Could be an address," says Byers.

"Seven digits," says Frohike. "An alphanumeric string of four."

"Standard ID," says Mulder, finally. "Shipping container."

At a waterfront freightyard later that

night, Scully drives through rows of giant stacked containers while Mulder shines his flashlight onto their ID numbers.

"There must be a thousand containers here," says Scully, "and in no particular order."

Mulder consults a computer generated map. "Frohike says this place is really proud of its accurate tracking," he says.

"If not in their computer security," says Scully.

"Yeah," says Mulder. "It should be straight ahead. Three rows and to the right."

Headlights off, they pull up slowly to a container marked HAGUE SHIPPING HSWT 780022 3. From somewhere nearby comes the strains of a heavy metal guitar riff.

"Sounds like somebody's home," says Mulder.

He opens a door cut into the huge box and identifies himself. A woman's hand emerges and jams a stun gun against his neck. Mulder cries out, then falls to the ground. His attacker runs past him and flees down the dark row of containers.

"Mulder?" says Scully, her gun drawn.

"I'm all right," he groans. "Get her!"

Scully runs, pursuing the black-clad figure through the maze of corrugated metal. She catches the slim woman from behind, tackles her, and is rewarded with two blasts from her stun gun. The woman gets up and runs again, until Scully rises and aims her pistol at her back.

"FBI! Stop or I'll shoot!" she yells.

Scully fires a warning shot. The woman—she is death's head pale, with pulled-back blonde hair and raccoon-ringed eyes—halts and throws her hands in the air.

"Thank you," says the winded and quite pissed Scully.

She handcuffs the woman and leads her back to the container/living space. Its interior is jammed with electronic devices and only the bare minimum of human accommodations. Mulder's flashlight beam probes the bizarre decor. It settles on a narrow unmade cot.

"Home sweet home," says Mulder, dryly.

Scully hustles the prisoner inside. Mulder asks her if she is "Invisigoth."

"How did you find me?" says the woman, angrily. She is wearing a kind of street fashion version punk leather commando outfit, complete with nose ring.

"Donald Gelman's mailbox. You left a return address," says Mulder.

"You know where Donald is?" says the woman.

Scully says, "Why don't you let us ask the questions—"

"Why don't you bite me?" says the woman.

"—like what you're doing here," Scully adds, simmering, "and what all this stuff is."

Invisigoth smirks arrogantly. "Why would I tell you," she says, "even if you could understand?"

Scully says, "You've just committed a felony assault on a federal agent, followed by resisting arrest."

Invisigoth says, "Arrest for what? Unless you've got a warrant, you two just busted in here and seriously violated a buttload of my constitutional rights."

At the opposite end of the container an electronic alarm beeps stridently. Invisigoth turns away from the agent and stares intently at a computer screen. A flood of data is scrolling rapidly across it.

Mulder says, "We had just cause to come in."

"And now," says Invisigoth, grimly, "we have just cause to get out."

Mulder peers into the monitor. "What is that?" he asks.

"It's a surveillance module," she replies. "It monitors computing processes."

Scully steps behind them, watching what the other two are watching. On the screen flashes the words BRIGHT LIGHTS WARM-UP COMPLETED. TARGET ACQUISITION IN PROGRESS.

"It's locking on," says Invisigoth, eyes widening with fear.

"What is?" asks Scully.

"A DOD satellite. Warbird-grade orbital weapons platform."

A satellite's-eye view of Washington, D.C., now pops onto the screen. Greatly alarmed, Invisigoth rises and turns to the agents.

"We've gotta get out of here!" she says.

Scully blocks her path. "A weapons platform?" she says sarcastically.

Mulder stares at the monitor, slowly comprehending.

"Scully—" he says.

"You don't understand!" says Invisigoth. "That thing has optical systems that can read headlines on a newspaper—"

"Scully—"

"It's targeting us!"

On the monitor the images are becoming more and more detailed as the satellite's camera is zooming in on a specific location.

Scully says, "You want us to believe that the Department of Defense wants to kill you?"

"No!" replies Invisigoth. "It's controlling their satellite!"

"You're out of your mind," says Scully.

Mulder turns away from the monitor. "Scully," he says urgently, "we've got to get out of here."

He hustles the handcuffed woman toward the door. "Mulder!" protests Scully. "This is absurd!"

Outside the container now, Mulder yanks at the door handle of the locked car. "Give me the keys!" he shouts to his incredulous partner.

Annoyed, she nevertheless moves quickly to unlock the car. Inside the container, the monitor is showing an aerial view of the container port. Then a mass of stacked containers.

Scully jumps into the passenger seat, slams the car into reverse, and backs furiously through the massed containers. She executes a smoking bootlegger's U-turn, slams the car into gear, then hits the gas.

Back inside Invisigoth's lair an image of container HSWT 780022 3 fills the computer monitor. A crosshair device appears. Then—nearly too fast for the eye to follow—a bright white beam flashes down from the heavens. The container explodes in a huge orange fireball. Scully stops the car. Its three occupants stare back at a scene of total destruction.

After daybreak the trio drives down a country highway, Mulder beside Scully and their prisoner in the back seat. "No

Message To: gelman@com
Message From: invisigoth@com

DAVID MISSING.
FEAR THE WORST.
THE HUNTED HAS
BECOME THE HUNTER.
HSWT 780022 3 UNTIL
SATURDAY, INVISIGOTH.

more screwing around," says Scully to her prisoner. "We need a name. Your real name."

"Invisigoth," replies the woman, sullenly. "You want my address? It's T-O-A-S-T."

Mulder turns to face her. "When you said 'it' was targeting us back there," he says, "you meant an artificial intelligence. Donald Gelman wanted to create a sentient AI. A program with its own consciousness. He succeeded, didn't he?"

Invisigoth turns away and squirms a bit. "Donald wrote an interlocking sequence of viruses fifteen years ago. It got loose on the net—"

"What do you mean it got loose?" says Mulder.

"He let it loose," she says. "So it could evolve in its natural environment. *Urschleim* in silicon."

"'*Urschleim* in silicon'?" says Scully.

"The primordial slime," says Invisigoth impatiently. "The ooze out of which all life evolved."

She adds, "One man alone achieving the equivalent of Copernicus, Magellan, and Darwin."

Scully asks what her role was in all this. "Were you the bass player?"

"Automata theory, MIT '95," says Invisigoth, contemptuously. "Post-doc at the Santa Fe Institute. Headhunted to Kobayashi my junior year. Then Donald showed up in Tokyo and made me a better offer."

"Better offer to do what?" asks Scully.

"You wouldn't understand," says Invisigoth, curtly.

Furious, Scully cranks the steering wheel, bringing the car to a screeching halt in a rest area. She gets out of the car and—struggling for control—strides angrily away. Mulder follows her.

"You believe this load of crap?" says Scully.

"You saw what happened back there," says Mulder. "You saw that container blow."

"She could have rigged an explosive charge! There are no

weapons platforms! There is no such Department of Defense satellite!"

"What about Star Wars?" says Mulder. "Brilliant Pebbles?"

"*They were never built!* We don't even have that kind of technology! I mean, even if an artificial intelligence was targeting us with an armed satellite, why isn't it doing it right now?"

It's a good question to which someone other than Mulder has the answer.

"Because it doesn't know where we are," says Invisigoth, who, though still cuffed, has wriggled out of the backseat of the rental car.

She adds, "If I so much made a phone call right now, it would nuke us right where we're standing."

"How?" says Scully.

"It recognizes my voice," she replies. "It monitors all communication. I haven't used a phone in over a month."

"Then how," asks Mulder, "did it know to target the container?"

"All I can think is that some idiot got on Donald's computer and tried to contact me over the net. Only Donald knew where I was. And David."

"Who's David?" asks Mulder.

"David Markham. He was hardware. Donald and I were software. We'd been caring for the AI, weaning it."

She adds, "Then Donald warned us that the system started to display more than consciousness; it started to display intention. But before we could stop it, it was gone."

"Gone where?" asks Mulder.

"I don't know," says Invisigoth. "One day David was on the system, and it wouldn't come. It wouldn't come when we called it. We knew it was out there, somewhere out on the global net, and Donald was just getting sicker."

"And you can't find it?" says Mulder.

"Well, it's not a program anymore," she says. "It's wildlife loose on the net. And either we kill it—"

She stops and looks at Mulder, then forces herself to ask the question.

"Where's Donald?" she says.

"Donald Gelman is dead," says Mulder. He tells her what happened in the Metro Diner.

"That's the AI, protecting itself," says Invisigoth, shaken. "It'll find David. Then me. It's only a matter of time."

She adds, soberly, "Donald was writing a concatenation of viruses designed to find and immobilize the rogue system. The filename was 'Kill Switch.' Without that, no one will catch it."

"We have Donald's computer," says Mulder.

"No. He'd never leave it on the hard drive," she says.

"And we have this," says Mulder, holding up the CD-ROM. "'Twilight Time.'"

"That's it," says Invisigoth. "That's the kill switch."

At the Lone Gunmen's office that night the boys are huddled over Gelman's laptop. Mulder and Scully enter with Invisigoth in tow; the Gunmen react as if Pamela Anderson has entered the room.

"Ay yi yi!" says Byers.

"It can't be—it is!" says Frohike.

"Esther Nairn!" says Langly.

He adds, "You programmed the autonomous 'bots for 'Ninjitsu Princess'—the gnarliest piece of entertainment software ever!"

Invisigoth eyes her fan club with contempt. "Are these the brain donors who almost got us incinerated?" she asks the agents.

"Don't let their looks fool you," says Mulder.

Scully says, incredulously, "Your name is *Esther Nairn*?"

Esther doesn't pay Scully the courtesy of a reply. Instead, she walks past the Lone Gunmen to their work bench.

"She is *so hot!*" says Frohike, fairly panting.

Esther is already examining the laptop, her hands still locked behind her. "Are you going to remove these cuffs," she says, "or do I have to do this with my tongue?"

Mulder says, "You don't want to take a vote," says Mulder. He unlocks one handcuff and shackles Esther to the workbench.

"Gimme the kill switch," she says.

Mulder hands her the CD-ROM.

Scully says, dryly, "Aren't you worried it's going to track you, Esther? Hunt you down with another particle beam?"

"Not if someone doesn't make another boneheaded Internet connection," she says.

The Lone Gunmen wriggle uncomfortably. On the laptop's screen appears an elaborate disk map of the CD-ROM.

"The sharp end of the stick," says Esther. "Donald probably tried to feed this sector over the net. But it took too long. So the system was able to take countermeasures."

Scully says, "Why didn't it just zap him, too?"

"Its creator?" says Esther, dismissively. "No. It needed to impress Donald. The particle beam would have been overkill."

"Unlike a dozen crack dealers," says Scully, sardonically.

Esther smiles. "Don't you see?" she says, proudly. "That's its sense of humor."

Mulder considers this for a moment. "Oh, right," he says. "But if you load the kill switch, what's to stop if from laying another funny joke on us?"

Esther tells him that uploading the program onto the Internet will allow it to do just that. "There's only one way now. We have to find its home node and physically feed it the poison apple."

"Physically?" says Mulder.

"Right into its eager little CD drive. It knew it couldn't hide over the net forever. Not until it learned to completely disguise itself. It requires a physical nexus of hardware, so somewhere it's built itself a little safe house. David went looking for it."

"Did he find it?" asks Mulder.

"There's no way to know."

Scully says, "Why don't you just call him?"

Everyone else stops in their tracks and looks at her disapprovingly.

"Oh, yeah, right," scoffs Scully, still a disbeliever. "Death from above."

The other members of the group studiously ignore her. "It would need bandwidth," suggests Langly, tremulously.

"It's a pig for bandwidth," declares Esther.

"It'd need a T3 at least," says Frohike.

"A T3?" says Scully.

"A hard line," says Frohike. "Forty-five megs a second."

Byers explains, "Major research labs and Internet service providers have them."

Langly adds, "But the government keeps those records secret for fear of sabotage."

Esther smirks, then turns to Mulder and Scully. "Gee," she says, "you guys know anyone who works for the government?"

Alongside a deserted road in rural Virginia stands a telephone pole. On the pole hangs a large gray metal switch box. Leading into the box is a thick black cable. The next morning a car pulls up next to the pole. It is Mulder's. The agent gets out, consults a map with the pole's location circled, then climbs the pole to the switch box. A label on the box reads OPTIC FIBER CONNECTION. Mulder's gaze follows the cable, which leads to a decrepit farmhouse about a hundred yards away.

At the Lone Gunmen's office Scully lies asleep on a threadbare couch. She awakens and glances at the workbench where Esther had been shackled. No Esther—the cuffs dangle from the bench, empty. She rises quickly and checks a back room, where Frohike is sleeping soundly. Someone jams a handgun into her right ear. It is the smirking, raccoon-eyed woman.

"*Buenos días, muchacha,*" says Esther.

At the decrepit farmhouse Mulder pulls out his cell phone and dials. "Scully?" he says.

"Yep," says his partner, at the wheel of a car.

"I've found something, down in Fairfax County," he says. "A derelict chicken farm with a T3 connection. Paid for by Elaf Industries, Palo Alto. Of which there's no other record anywhere."

"Dandy," says Scully, sourly.

"Where are you?" asks Mulder, peering through the filthy front window of the farmhouse. "Sounds like you're driving."

"You are correct, sir," Scully replies.

"You have Esther with you?"

"In a manner of speaking."

In fact, Esther sits in the passenger seat, aiming the gun at her captive. "Left up here," she orders, grabbing the cell phone out of Scully's hand.

"Where are you going?" asks Mulder.

"To find David!" says Esther, in a comically menacing voice.

"Where?" says Mulder.

Esther hangs up the phone with a click. Concerned and confused, Mulder follows the T3 cable to a trailer sitting in a field behind the house.

On another country road the Lone Gunmen's JFK-era Lincoln Continental—Scully at the wheel—slows to a stop. The gun-toting Esther exits, jogs a few yards, and stares at an adjacent clearing. The clearing is covered with blackened debris—the remains, perhaps, of what had once been someone's house.

Inside the car Scully—who is handcuffed to the steering wheel—sees all this, too. While Esther stands stunned, she carefully reaches into her captor's coat pocket. She finds her handcuff keys, and before Esther returns to the car she's unlocked the handcuffs, leaving them loosely fastened on her wrist.

Esther gets into the passenger seat, distraught, and places the pistol on top of the dashboard. She starts sobbing, almost hysterically. Scully slips her hand out of the handcuffs and reaches slowly for the pistol. Esther grabs it before she does—and to the agent's shock—points the gun at her. Butt first.

"Go ahead," cries Esther. "Put me out of my misery!"

At the abandoned chicken farm Mulder approaches the trailer. A screaming alarm siren sounds, and Mulder grips his ears in agony. Just as suddenly, the alarm ceases. On a computer or video screen somewhere a thermal image of the agent is registering.

"FBI! I'm a federal agent!" shouts Mulder. The machine is also registering his voice in a blurry digitalized simulacrum.

Mulder walks to the trailer door and pushes the doorbell. His fingerprint is scanned and his FBI ID appears on the screen. There is no other response.

At the blasted rural building, Scully and Esther stroll soberly amid the wreckage. "I lied to you," says Esther, sadly and suddenly vulnerable. "I wasn't working with Donald. I mean, I was, but then he found out about us."

"About you and who?" asks Scully.

"David. About our plans," says Esther.

"What plans did he find out?"

"Uploading," says Esther. "The transfer of memory, of consciousness, to the distributive system maintained by the AI."

She adds, "Imagine being mingled so completely with another. You no longer need your physical self. You are one."

"So you were going to—" says Scully.

"Enter the AI. Give up our inefficient bodies so that our consciousness can live together forever."

For a moment, Scully stands stunned. "But Donald Gelman forbade it," she says, finally.

Esther kneels to pluck a singed photo from the wreckage. It's a picture of she and David Markham, in happier days. "He was afraid of what would happened if other people followed us," she says. "I loved him so much."

Scully stands over her, not unsympathetic.

"Well, maybe he wasn't here when this happened," she says. "Maybe he's somewhere else."

At the chicken farm later that day Mulder shines his flashlight underneath the trailer. He spots a thick cable connection, then discovers a metal trap door fastened with screws. He pulls out a pocket tool and starts to open it. Inside, a crablike metal droid activates itself, and—with a whine of servo-motors—swings into action.

Mulder pushes his head through the trap door. His flashlight beam reveals a dark claustrophobic nightmare: a silicon jungle of cables, wires, and electronic devices racked from floor to ceiling. He stands, with some difficulty, and pushes his way through the cagelike structure. At the far end slumps a man, dead, his slashed and desiccated face concealed by rubberized Virtual Reality goggles. Mulder gently removes the mask. He stares at the hideous sight.

"David Markham," he says, softly.

Mulder recoils slightly. At that moment a device behind him spits out a pair of circular metal restraints. They close instantly around his wrists and the agent is yanked backward, struggling helplessly, into a tower of electronic equipment. The entire array short circuits, sending out a cascade of high-voltage sparks. Mulder screams, convulses, and descends into darkness.

Fox Mulder fights his way back to consciousness inside a speeding ambulance. He is strapped to a gurney; a brace of paramedics hover anxiously over him.

The nearest paramedic speaks.

"Electrical burns. Real bad," he says. "Deep tissue injuries to the upper extremities. We got ourselves a real crispy critter here."

Another says, "Alert the burn unit. Tell 'em to scramble the surgical team."

"What's going on?" murmurs Mulder.

"He's coming up on us," says the second paramedic.

"What's that smell?" asks Mulder, horrified. He rises up weakly and looks at his upraised arms. His wrists are burnt horribly—like pieces of meat that have been left on the barbecue too long.

At the receiving hospital—its interior dingy and out of date, as if caught in a 1940s time warp—Mulder is wheeled quickly down a corridor. A Doctor Kildare-ish surgeon trots alongside the moving gurney.

"Frank charring at contact site, along path of current and at exit point," he recites into a small tape recorder. "Looks like the charge grounded through both arms. We've got a lot of work to do here, people, if we're gonna save them."

Mulder struggles to lift his head off the pillow.

"It's bad?" he says, weakly.

A young, blonde nurse—think a *Three's Company*-era Suzanne Somers— looks down at Mulder sympathetically. "You're in good hands," she says.

"My arms hurt," says Mulder.

"That's a good sign," nods the surgeon.

The surgical team crashes through a double door and into a scary old-fashioned operating room. A nurse adjusts the overhead floodlight. A cart of crude-looking surgical instruments is wheeled up.

Mulder reacts with panic. "I want you to call my doctor," he groans. "You have to call my doctor. Call Dr. Scully. Please? Call Dr. Scully. *Call her!*"

The nurse—whose name is Nurse Nancy—grasps Mulder by the temples and forces his head back onto the pillow. "No. No!" shouts Mulder. "What are you doing?"

A much older surgeon arrives in the operating room and peers down curiously at the struggling man.

"Prep the patient," he says, in a geriatric croak.

The old surgeon selects an evil-looking electric bone saw, activates its whirling blade, and moves it slowly toward Mulder.

"No! NO!" says Mulder, frantically.

Nurse Nancy lifts a syringe, then plunges it deep into Mulder's shoulder blade. His eyelids flicker, open wide, then close involuntarily.

In the Lone Gunmen's car that night Scully drives, Esther riding beside her. "I can't get through to Mulder," says Scully, fruitlessly dialing and redialing her cell phone.

"It's the AI," says Esther. "It's had time to analyze my voice. It knows I was using your phone."

"It can interfere with my phone?"

"Give it enough information," says

Esther, "and it'll sue you for palimony."

Shaken by this, Scully thinks hard. "Wait a minute," she says. "Mulder said that he found the system."

"Well, then maybe we can cut off the T3 and kill its communications capabilities," says Esther.

"You can do that?" says Scully.

Esther says, reaching into the backseat for Donald Gelman's laptop, "There's only one way to find out."

At the hospital Mulder is out of surgery. He lies on a cast iron hospital bed; starched white sheets are pulled up tightly underneath his chin. Nurse Nancy enters and gazes down at him compassionately.

"I feel sick," says Mulder.

"That's the anesthetic, Agent Mulder," says Nurse Nancy. "You were injured, and they had to operate."

"I remember—wires?" says Mulder.

"Yes," says Nurse Nancy. "You were doing something dangerous. Something very, very foolish. The good news was that they were able to save the right one."

"What do you mean?" asks Mulder.

Nurse Nancy's expression turns sorrowful. She reaches down and pulls off the sheet. Mulder's left arm has been amputated. Only a ragged stump remains.

"Oh, my God!" cries Mulder. "What did you do with my arm? What did they do to my arm!?"

"Shhh," says Nurse Nancy, pushing Mulder down on the bed again. "Shhhh. Or they'll come back."

"Come back for what?" asks Mulder, horrified.

"They're evil, Fox," confides Nurse Nancy. "They need something from you."

"What!? What do they want?" cries Mulder, hysterically.

"I don't know," she croons. "But if you don't tell them, I'm afraid they'll take your other arm."

"This is crazy!" says Mulder, struggling to regain control. "You have to help me. You have to get me out of here. Please! Help me! *Please help me!*"

He struggles to sit up. Nurse Nancy clasps Mulder to her bosom, pushes his head back onto the mattress, and presses a snow white pillow onto his face.

"Shhh! Shhhh! They'll hear you," she says, pressing down hard to muffle Mulder's anguished cries.

Scully and Esther drive through the night. They reach a small turntable drawbridge; before they can cross it a wooden barrier gate swings down, halting them. Esther glances down at her computer screen; torrents of raw data are scrolling across it.

"Something's wrong," says Esther, startled. "I didn't do anything! I didn't even get on the net!"

She turns to Scully. "I think it's found us," she says.

Scully looks in her rearview mirror. With a whoosh of air brakes a gasoline tanker stops behind them, effectively hemming them in. The word FLAMMABLE is emblazoned on the truck's front grille.

The laptop beeps. On its screen appears a satellite photo of the drawbridge.

"It's zeroing in," says Esther.

"Esther!" says Scully, horrified.

Both women yank their doors open and bail out. Esther, carrying the laptop, ducks under the barrier and runs onto the bridge. Scully runs in the opposite direction, climbs onto the tanker truck's running board, and pounds on the driver's window.

"Sir! You need to get out of the truck! Move it! It's going to explode!"

She gets no response. At a loss, Scully turns to see Esther in the middle of the bridge, which is slowly revolving to its open position.

"STOP, ESTHER!" she shouts, running

toward the bridge. "GET RID OF IT! IT WANTS THE KILL SWITCH! ESTHER! DUMP IT! *ESTHER!*"

Scully runs past the barrier and leaps onto the revolving bridge. At the other end Esther types in several commands, then flings the computer toward the river. A brilliant white particle beam slants down and vaporizes its target before it reaches the water.

In his hospital room Mulder is sleeping. Or unconscious. A shadow falls over his face: It is Nurse Nancy, accompanied by two other angels of mercy, massaging him awake. Mulder stirs, opens his eyes, and looks around him. "I had a terrible dream," he grins. "And then I had . . . a good dream."

"Those weren't dreams, Fox," says Nurse Nancy. She turns to the other nurses. "I believe that's enough for now," she says.

Starting to pout just a little, Nurse Nancy leans over Mulder's bed. "You poor thing," she says. "But I warned you. Nurse Nancy warned you! You have to tell them, Fox. You have to."

"Tell them what?" says Mulder.

"About the kill switch!"

"Nobody asked me anything!"

Nurse Nancy smiles condescendingly, as if to a child. "You've just *forgotten,* Fox!" she says.

"No!"

"I was there," she coos.

Nurse Nancy cups Mulder's face in her hands, long red nails very near his eyes.

"The doctor asked and he was *very cross* when you refused to answer. But he'll be here in just a few minutes and you can tell him then."

She raises her eyebrows, makes a clownish smile of exasperation.

"Otherwise—WHOOPS!"

She claps her hands and makes a silly face.

"There go your legs!"

She whips the sheet off Mulder, revealing that both arms are now missing. Mulder looks right, then left, then screams in holy terror.

Someone kicks the hospital door open. It is Scully—gun drawn and ready for action. "Mulder! These women are SPIES!" she shouts.

"Scully!" yells Mulder, beseechingly.

One of the nurses gets the drop on Scully and karate-kicks her gun away. But Scully punches her thuddingly in the face, then pivots in a surprising roundhouse move and karate-kicks her. She dispatches the other nurse with a few well-placed punches and puts away Nurse Nancy with two or three more.

Scully exhales, blowing her hair away from her face, and walks over to Mulder's bed. "Mulder," she says urgently, "they want the kill switch virus. What did you tell them?"

"I didn't tell them anything!" says Mulder.

"*I need to know!*"

Scully stares at Mulder expectantly, seemingly oblivious to his disfigurement.

"*Do we have it, Mulder? Do we have the kill switch?*"

Mulder stares back at her for a second.

"Of course we do," he says, evenly, then lifts his legs to kick Scully in the stomach. She is knocked backward against the opposing wall, her expression changing from stern to startled.

Her image begins to break up, then dissolve into individual pixels. From Mulder's point of view the entire room begins to dissolve, and he is back in the killer virus's trailer, hanging from the component stack of David Markham.

His arms and legs are still restrained; a VR mask is clamped firmly to his face.

"Scully," he moans.

"Scully, help! HELP! *HELLLLLP!*"

Later that night Scully and Esther arrive at the abandoned farm and pull up behind Mulder's parked car. They walk cautiously around toward the back.

"Here, kitty, kitty, kitty," says Esther.

As they near the trailer the ear-splitting siren goes off. Scully draws her gun and fires twice, severing the cable

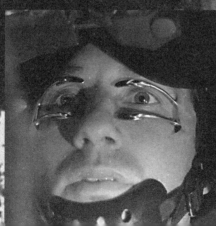

connection and silencing the alarm.

Mulder's voice floats faintly out to her. "Scully," he says.

"Mulder! Mulder, are you all right?" shouts his partner.

Inside the trailer a whirring robot arm—tipped with a whirring rotary blade—cuts a small, neat slit in Mulder's shirtsleeve. Another device plunges a hypodermic needle in his arm. Mulder slumps forward in his restraints. Outside, Scully calls out to her partner. There is no answer. Monitors register her thermal signature.

The trap door opens, and Scully pokes her head through. The little 'droid rolls quickly toward her. Scully ducks down and reaches for her gun, firing two shots directly at the machine. It dies a grisly electromechanical death.

Esther joins her inside the trailer.

"Help me out here," says Scully. "What's its next move? What's it thinking?"

"I don't know," says Esther.

"Who built this?" asks Scully.

"It did," says Esther.

She raises her flashlight beam, then gasps.

"There," she says.

At the far end of the structure hangs a dead man in a VR rig.

"David!" gasps Esther. "Oh God!"

Scully turns away and sees Mulder. Fighting panic, she pulls the VR goggles off his face. He is not moving; his eyes are being held open by metal clamps.

"Mulder, can you hear me? Mulder, talk to me," begs Scully.

Her partner's lips move slightly, but no sound comes out. Scully reacts to a mechanical whine sound behind her, spinning and drawing her gun. It is an empty CD-ROM drive, thrusting itself open as if asking to be fed.

Esther stares at it, still in shock. "It wants the kill switch," she says.

"But we don't have it," says Scully. "You threw it in the water with the computer."

Esther shakes her head, reaches into a pants pocket, and pulls out the disc. She walks quickly to the CD port.

Scully says, "But that's going to kill it, right?"

"Not if it can learn the program and vaccinate itself against it."

A jolt of electricity shoots through Mulder. He spasms painfully, again and again.

"Give it what it wants, Esther!" says Scully.

Mulder spasms again.

"Put it in, Esther!"

Both women look at the nearby computer monitors. Earth satellite photos cascade onto the screens.

"It's targeting us," says Esther, hypnotized.

"Put it in!"

Scully yanks the CD from Esther's hand and slams it into the disc drive. "Twilight Time" begins playing. The message HOLDING appears on the computer screens, and the restraints fly away from Mulder's body. Scully removes the VR rig, talking to him soothingly.

Esther, after a glance back at Mulder and Scully, begins surreptitiously typing on a computer keyboard. The message HOLDING changes to IN PROGRESS. Scully struggles to carry Mulder to safety.

Esther, crying now, continues typing, until Scully—lowering Mulder awkwardly through the trap door—turns back to look at her.

"What are you doing, Esther?" she says.

"Get outta here," says Esther, harshly. "Go!"

The satellite images resume their deadly dance. Scully stops, stares, and ducks out of the trailer, holding Mulder in her arms.

Esther keeps typing. Scully drags Mulder from underneath the trailer, then quickly thrusts her head back up the hatch.

"Esther!?" she calls out urgently.

But Invisigoth is nowhere to be seen. From somewhere, Esther's voice floats through the trailer. "You don't listen, do you?" she says.

"Where are you?" asks Scully.

"Get out of here—now!"

Scully glances at the targeting monitor, then makes a difficult decision quickly. She departs. Back in the trailer, Esther is wearing the full VR rig, a smile of blissful contentment on her lips. Outside, Scully yanks Mulder to his feet and drags him away from the trailer.

"Upload," says Esther, softly.

A microsecond later the monitors fill with intricate abstract images and Esther erupts in a shower of electrical fireworks. Her flesh sizzles, and she spasms into stillness. White smoke emerges wispily from her mouth. The computer images slow, then blank out completely. Mulder and Scully stagger toward the tree line.

A particle beam slashes down from the sky and blows the trailer—and everything in it—to atoms.

The next morning Mulder and Scully walk through the smoking wreckage. "Well," says Scully, sadly, "if Esther wanted to leave her body, she got her wish. At least that part of it."

Mulder kneels down and examines a small satellite dish, last seen on the top of the trailer. "I wonder," he says.

Scully says, "Mulder, she's dead."

"What if she's managed to establish an uplink, Scully?" says Mulder. "A satellite transmission."

"Mulder, are you telling me that Esther may have—that she may not be dead?"

"Artificial life," says Mulder. "It could exist. It could be here among us, evolving."

"Electrons chasing each other through a circuit?" says Scully. "That isn't life, Mulder."

"And what are we," says Mulder, "but impulses, chemical and electrical, through a bag of meat and bones? You're the scientist, Scully. You tell me."

In the Lone Gunmen's office Frohike—completely focused on his work—types commands into a computer. Langly and Byers peer intently over his shoulder, then glance at each other uneasily.

BITE ME says a red block-letter message on the screen.

At a trailer park in North Platte, Nebraska, two teenage boys play catch. Their football flies too far and falls into a chain-link enclosure. Inside the enclosure is a solitary Winnebago, its windows covered from the inside with aluminum reflectors.

A teenage couple watches from a park bench, snickering. "You did it now, Harley!" says the boy.

"They'll getcha if you go in there," says the girlfriend.

The two players walk apprehensively toward the fence. "You get it," says one.

"Uh-uh," says the other.

"Mama says no one lives in there," says the first boy, shrugging.

He scales the fence, picks up the ball, and climbs quickly back over. A tiny camera atop the motor home swivels to follow him. Somewhere, thermal images of the boys appear on a computer screen.

back story:

If you're a serious *X-Files* fans, you may experience a common and seductive fantasy. So familiar are you with the series–and so thrillingly intimate with the fictional relationship between the two lead characters—that it seems just a small step to sitting down at the keyboard and writing your own wonderful episode. *I've got the story right here in my head,* goes your wishful litany. *Now, all I need to do is download it into Chris Carter's.*

And you may, in fact, be absolutely right, *if* you happen to be a Nebula and Hugo Award–winning science fiction novelist. And if you've had considerable experience working on screen adaptations of your own books and short stories. And if you live in Vancouver, British Columbia. And if you fly back and forth between that Canadian city and Los Angeles.

A lot.

"I met Chris on an airplane, I think, about two or three years ago," says William Gibson, the author of *Neuromancer, Count Zero, Mona Lisa Overdrive,* and several other works that established him as the founder and master of the "cyberpunk" school of sci-fi writing. "Then Chris and I kept bumping into each other, either coming down or going up. We seemed to be always on that plane, going one way or another.

"My purpose in introducing myself, as I remember it, was to weasel a set visit for my then–thirteen-year-old daughter, who is of course a big fan. It was during yet another one of those flights, though, that he said to me, 'You can do one of these.' And I said, 'Oh!' But that was a long time ago. It took a long time to get the green light on this one."

To collaborate on what would eventually become "Kill Switch," Gibson—who had written both story and script for the 1995 movie *Johnny Mnemonic*—recruited his friend Tom Maddox, a novelist, essayist, and head of the writing program at Evergreen State College in Olympia, Washington.

The plotline itself was pieced together tailfirst. "It started, as I recall," says Gibson, "with Tom pointing out a completely deserted house not far from his. Its windows were shuttered and it was surrounded by a chain-link fence.

Right in the middle of a normal neighborhood. Very strange! It wasn't too much of a jump for us to turn it into a house trailer filled with a big artificial intelligence."

As his many readers know, Gibson has written for years about the interaction of human and artificial intelligence. The notion of the two "species" merging on the World Wide Web is something that had long been floating around cyber-futurist circles—"The Media Lab at MIT is crawling with 'upload freaks,'" says Gibson—and the character of Esther Nairn is a cross between a cyberpunk and a member of the alienated, extremely sunlight-averse Generation Y subspecies known as the Goth Movement.

All of which was extremely well-received by the show's permanent writing staff, but in no way prevented the rewriting and revision process from becoming long and arduous, even for *The X-Files.* "We kept working, turning out piles of paper," says Tom Maddox. "Months passed. Years. We'd get a call from the show now and then," says Tom Maddox.

Several Vancouver story meetings with Frank Spotnitz and Chris Carter were canceled at the last minute, due to emergencies on other episodes and/or work on the *X-Files* movie. Finally—and, of course, at the last minute and under incredible time pressure—several plot and character development problems were ironed out. "Chris sort of upped the attitude on Esther's character," says Tom Maddox. Gibson says, "We had been reluctant to make her that much of a pain in the ass, which she actually needed to be to actually make her work. Chris made her quite abrasive and punky. I think we had been using her too much as a bid for sympathy."

Carter and Spotnitz also fine-tuned the attitudes and reactions of Mulder and Scully, resulting in the loss of one of Gibson's favorite vignettes. "Because Esther has a nose ring," he recalls, "we had written a little bit at the bottom of one page where Scully sees a piece of hardware lying in the Lone Gunmen's pile of spare parts and kind of wistfully picks it up and models it for herself in the mirror. She holds it up to the side of her nose, sort of like a woman trying on earrings, until someone interrupts her and she guiltily tosses it back into the pile.

"This was deemed to play too fast and lose with the essential nature of Scully," adds the novelist, somewhat sadly. "Which I certainly understand. They're Chris's characters, and he knows what they can and cannot do."

Fewer restrictions, however, were imposed regarding settings, scenery, and pyrotechnics. No less than three major explosions—an *X-Files* record—were set off. The interior of the artificial intelligence trailer proved superbly cybercentric and claustrophobic on film (and so hot, airless, and confining to the human beings working inside it that Gillian Anderson describes it as "the set from hell.") The nasty autonomous robot that attacks Mulder—inspired by the NASA Mars Rover, according to special effects coordinator Dave Gauthier—was battery-powered and radio-controlled and cost $23,000 to build and operate.

To set the scene surrounding Esther Nairn's waterfront lair, picture car coordinator Nigel Habgood rented forty-five intermodal shipping containers, trucked them to a Port of Vancouver container loading facility, and had them meticulously stacked according to the directions laid out by the art department. Filming of the action and dialogue proceeded smoothly; after that, unfortunately, the owners of the dock withdrew their permission to blow up Esther's container on the site. So Habgood trucked his entire container fleet to a huge empty lot in South Burnaby, and, with a crane, hoisted them ponderously into place again in the exact same configuration. "It was like solving a puzzle. Like doing a Rubik's Cube," says Habgood, who'd never done anything even vaguely similar in his life.

To obtain authentic astronaut's-eye photos of Washington, D.C., producer Paul Rabwin contracted with SPOT, the French-owned commercial satellite surveillance company. To create a suitably impressive water geyser when the AI zaps Gelman's laptop from space, Dave Gauthier's crew sank a huge high-pressure air cannon in the Fraser River (next to a venerable turntable bridge that opened and closed ponderously via a minuscule three horsepower motor) and fired it off on cue. Due to strong currents and tides, however, the effect was unsatisfactory. It was considerably augmented in post-production by visual effects coordinator Laurie Kallsen-George.

It was computer whiz Kallsen-George, in fact, who inadvertently set in motion the most startling special effect of all. Asked to create the sputtering computer-image breakdown when Mulder karate-kicks his "partner" and breaks out of Nurse Nancy's virtual-reality hospital, she commissioned a freelance computer artist to create a 3-D cybernetic image of Dana Scully.

"I had in mind a kind of wire-frame model," says Kallsen-George. "Like a gridwork in computer space, a fairly simple thing. And I thought I'd made myself clear, but when I came back four or five hours later, this very talented young guy had done a 3-D model of Scully *naked*."

The schedule was tight, she adds, but not that tight. Despite her admiration for the work, she ordered his effort confined to her hard drive.

ⓧ

In "Kill Switch," computer pioneer Donald Gelman is described as "writing Internet software before there was an Internet." In his novel Neuromancer, William Gibson coined the phrase "cyberspace"—in 1984.

ⓧ

This was not the first fake double amputation in *X-Files* history. Special effects makeup artist Toby Lindala created the same effect (on Sergeant Leonard "Rappo" Trimble) in "The Walk" (3X07).

ⓧ

Editor Heather MacDougall won an Emmy award for her work on "Kill Switch."

bad blood

Mulder sticks his neck out— and then some—to capture a small-town serial killer.

EPISODE: 5X12
FIRST AIRED: February 22, 1998
EDITOR: Lynne Willingham
WRITTEN BY: Vince Gilligan
DIRECTED BY: Cliff Bole
GUEST STARS:
Mitch Pileggi (AD Walter
Skinner)
Luke Wilson (Sheriff Hartwell)
Patrick Renna (Ronnie
Strickland)
Forbes Angus (Funeral Director)
Marion Killinger (Detective)
David Major (Vampire)
PRINCIPAL SETTINGS:
Cheney and Dallas, Texas;
Washington, D.C.

A full moon hangs over a flat, scraggly field. A teenage boy runs frantically across it, stumbling and falling and crying out in terror.

"Help!" he yells. "Somebody help me! He's going to kill me!"

He is being ruthlessly chased by a man in a long, dark coat. The boy runs into the piney woods, but his pursuer—who carries a sharp wooden stake—is much faster. The young man trips and falls, and the man is on top of him like a flash.

There is a brief struggle—in fact, a fight to the death. The pursuer lifts the stake high with both hands, and buries it into the teenager's chest. He picks up a nearby rock and uses it to bang the fatal spike home.

Dana Scully, panting with exhaustion, runs up to the death scene, kneels down next to the dead boy, and turns, appalled, to his assailant—Fox Mulder.

"Look at that!" says Mulder, pointing to two sharp incisors—vampire fangs—among the dead kid's upper front teeth. "Huh? *Huh?!*"

Scully reaches down gingerly, presses gently, and removes a pair of fake plastic costume fangs. She lifts up this curious dental appliance, holds it up for Mulder's inspection, and watches the sweat-soaked FBI agent commence a minor nervous breakdown.

"Aww, sh—" says Mulder, despairingly—the final syllable obscured by a lucky burst of theme music.

At FBI headquarters a day later a plainly stressed-to-the-max Mulder is at his desk doing paperwork. Scully enters, and sits down across from him. She hasn't had a very good night, either.

"Mulder—" she says.

"Don't! Don't even *start* with me," says Mulder.

He balls up the sheet of paper he'd been working on and tosses it toward his trash can. It bounces off it and falls to the floor, nestling there against ten or so other near-misses. Mulder calmly rises, walks over to the receptacle, and proceeds to kick the crap out of it. Catharsis over, he sighs and turns to his partner.

"I know what I saw," says Mulder.

Scully folds her arms and looks downward, glumly. "Skinner wants our report in one hour," she says. "What are you going to tell him?"

"What do you mean, what am I going to tell him?" says Mulder. "I'm going to tell him exactly what I saw." He bristles at his partner's skeptical glance. "What are *you* going to tell him?"

"I'll tell them exactly what *I* saw," says Scully, bristling right back at him.

"Now, how is that different?" demands Mulder.

Scully's expression is unchanged.

"Look, Scully," he says. "I'm the one who may wind up going to prison here. I've gotta know if you're going to back me up, or what?"

Now it's Scully's turn to bristle. "First of all," she says, "If the family of Ronnie Strickland does indeed decide to sue the FBI for, I think the figure is four hundred and forty-six million dollars, then you and I both will most certainly be codefendants.

"And, second of all—I don't even have a second of all, Mulder. Four hundred and forty-six million dollars! I'm in this one as deep as you are—and I'm not even the one who overreacted! I didn't do the—" She mimes poking someone with a wooden stake. "—with the thing!"

"I did *not* overreact," says Mulder. "Ronnie Strickland was vampire!"

"Where's your proof?"

"You're my proof!" says Mulder. "You were there!"

Scully sighs and shrugs.

"Okay, now you're scaring me," says Mulder. "I want to hear exactly what you're going to tell Skinner."

"Oh!" says Scully, accusingly. "You want our story straight?"

"No, no. I didn't say that," says Mulder. "I just want to hear it the way you saw it."

Scully says, huffily, "I don't feel comfortable with that."

"Prison, Scully," says Mulder. "Your cell mate's nickname is gonna be 'Large Marge'? She's gonna read a lot of Gertrude Stein?"

Scully holds her face in her hands. "All right," she says, weakly.

"All right, start at the beginning," says Mulder.

"The *very* beginning?" says Scully, appalled.

Mulder raises an admonitory, don't-mess-with-me finger.

"Fine," says Scully.

Her flashback begins with a brief burst of narration:

Yesterday morning, when I arrived at work, you were characteristically, uh, exuberant.

At the X-Files office the previous morning Mulder flings an airline ticket folder down on his desk.

"Hope ya brought yer cowboy boots!" Mulder says, insensitively and boorishly, as indeed he will remain throughout Scully's entire account of the incident.

"You want us to go to Dallas?" asks Scully, calmly and maturely (ditto).

"*Yee-ha!* Actually, a town called Cheney about fifty miles south of there, population three hundred and sixty-one. By all accounts, rustic and charming. But of late, ground zero for a series of myste-

rious, nocturnal exsanguinations."

"Exsanguinations?" asks Scully.

In reply Mulder clicks on his slide projector, displaying in living color a spavined creature lying dead on the ground.

"How's that grab ya?" he boasts.

"It's a—"

"Dead cow!" crows Mulder. "Exactly. Or more specifically, a dead nine hundred–pound Holstein—its body completely drained of blood! As was this one. This one. This one. This one and so on. Six, all in all, approximately one a week, over the past six weeks."

"Is there any sign of—" asks Scully.

"Two small puncture wounds on the neck?"

"That's not what I was going to ask," says Scully, patiently.

"Too bad! We got 'em. Check 'em out!"

Mulder advances the slide show to present a gruesome close-up of a cow's throat. Scully considers this patiently, not thrown in the least.

"Well, these may be syringe marks," she says, "they're placement meant to emulate fangs. Such ritualistic bloodletting points toward cultists of some sort, in which case . . ."

Scully trails off, glancing at Mulder, who's having a really hard time not snickering. "What?" she says.

"*Yeah*, that's probably it: satanic cultists." says Mulder, unable to contain his scorn. "*Come on*, Scully!"

Scully says, "You're not going to tell me that this is that Mexican goatsucker?"

"*El Chupacabra?* No, they got four fangs, not two. *And* they suck goats. Hence, the name."

"So, instead, this would be—?"

"Classic vampirism," says Mulder, dramatically.

"Of a bunch of cows," says Scully, skeptically.

"And one human. Last night a vacationer from New Jersey. C'mon, we've gotta go."

Scully replies, a tad angered, "Why the hell didn't you tell me that from the beginning?"

"Lock the door on the way out," says Mulder, already out of the office.

Scully's narration continues:

The town of Cheney is too small to maintain a morgue facility. As such, we made our way to the Peaceful Slumbers Funeral Home in order to examine the body of one Mr. Dwight Funt, recently deceased.

It was there that we were met by a representative of the local law enforcement. Sheriff—

"Lucius Hartwell," says a handsome young Texan wearing among other things a silver star, cowboy boots, and a long black duster. He doffs his cowboy hat, and smiles.

"You the FBI agents?" he says.

Scully smiles back at the lawman. "Yes, I'm—"

"Agents Mulder and Scully," says Mulder, breaking in annoyingly. "What do you say we go take a look at your victim?"

"Yeah, by all means," says Hartwell, gazing at Scully soulfully. "After you."

"C'mon, Scully, get those little legs moving," says Mulder, "C'mon!"

In the embalming room of the funeral parlor lies the corpse of a sixtyish man covered by a blanket.

"Nice threads!" says Mulder.

Scully yanks on a pair of latex gloves. "No exam has been done?" she asks.

"No, ma'am," says Hartwell. "He's just like the way we found him in the motel room. Once I heard you folks were interested, I figured we'd best leave him to the experts."

Mulder nods, pulls down the victim's shirt collar, and points out the twin puncture wounds. "Your satanic cultists," he tells Scully sarcastically, "have some sharp little teeth."

"What satanic cultists?" asks Hartwell.

Mulder smirks, then does those obnoxious finger symbols that represent quotation marks and heavy duty irony. "Go ahead," he says, "tell him your, uh, 'theory.'"

With admirable dignity and forbearance, Scully turns to Hartwell.

"My theory," she says, "has evolved. Basically, I think we are looking for someone who's seen one too many Bela Lugosi movies. He believes he is a vampire, therefore—"

"Therefore they act like one! Yeah," muses Hartwell, admiringly. "That makes a whole lot of sense."

He turns to Mulder. "I think she's right!"

Mulder doesn't particularly want to hear this. "What about the fang marks?" he says.

"Well," says Scully confidently, "someone so obsessed might well file down their incisors. I think that a moulage casting should help us make an identification."

Mulder turns away in disgust. Hartwell's admiration for Scully palpably increases.

"Moulage casting," marvels the sheriff. "It's a good idea! Now, isn't there some sort of a disease that makes a person think they're a vampire?"

He moves closer to Scully, gazing deeply into her eyes.

"Well," says Scully, flattered, "there is a psychological fixation called hematodipsia which causes the sufferer to gain erotic satisfaction from consuming human blood."

"Erotic," says Hartwell, grinning flirtatiously. *"Yeah."*

Scully, obviously enjoying this, continues, "There are also genetic afflictions which cause a heightened sensitivity to light, to garlic. Porphyria, xeroderma pigmentosis."

Hartwell nods, his perfect teeth gleaming whitely. "You really know your stuff, Dana," he says.

Back at FBI headquarters—and in the middle of their postmortem—Mulder sits at his desk and stares at his partner incredulously.

"'Dana'"? Mulder scoffs. "He never even *knew* your first name."

Scully says, primly, "You gonna interrupt me, or what?"

Mulder shuts up. Scully continues.

"Anyway," she says. "That's when you had your first . . . breakthrough. Whatever."

Back at the funeral parlor—in Scully's flashback—Hartwell nods again. "You really know your stuff," he says, worshipfully.

Mulder interrupts. "Sheriff," he says, "you say that this man is exactly as you found him?"

"Yes, sir," says Hartwell, "to the letter."

Mulder walks purposefully over to Dwight Funt's white Thom McCann boaters. "Have you noticed," in his best PBS *Mystery* manner, *"that this man's shoes are untied?"*

Both shoelaces are indeed untied. "Yeah, they sure are," says Hartwell.

"Mulder, what's your point?" says Scully.

Mulder thinks deep thoughts. "This means . . . something," he mutters. "Sheriff, do you have an old cemetery in town, off the beaten path, the creepier the better?"

"Uh, yeah," says Sheriff Hartwell.

Mulder snaps his fingers. "Take me there!" he says, already heading for the door.

"Mulder—" says Scully.

"Scully," says Mulder, "we're gonna need a complete autopsy on this man. The sooner the better."

"Whoa, whoa, whoa. Whoa!" says Scully. "What am I even looking for?"

Mulder squeezes her shoulders encouragingly and gazes deeply into her eyes.

"I don't know," he says dramatically.

With that, Mulder pivots and exits the room, calling for the sheriff to follow him. Hartwell looks at Scully, not sure what's up. She shrugs apologetically.

"He does that," she says, helpfully.

Hartwell smiles at her wistfully, and leaves. Left behind, Scully sighs and leans on the embalming table. It's just her and dead Mr. Funt.

Shortly afterward Scully is gowned and gloved and ready to cut open the body.

She picks up a large scalpel and a small tape recorder. "Four fifty-four P.M.," she says, wearily. "Begin autopsy on white male, age sixty, who is arguably having a worse time in Texas than I am—though not by much.

"I'll begin with the Y-incision. Yee-ha."

A few moments later, her mood still on the blue side, she plops Dwight Funt's former heart onto a hanging scale.

"Heart weighs three hundred and seventy grams. Tissue appears healthy."

Next, a squishier, less well-defined body part.

"Left lung weighs three hundred and forty-five grams. Tissue appears healthy."

Last, a truly horrifying lump of dead meat so large it slops over the sides of Scully's weighing device.

"Large intestine, eight hundred and ninety grams. Yada yada yada."

Then:

"Stomach contents show last meal, close to the time of death, consisting of . . . pizza. Topped with pepperoni, green peppers, mushrooms—"

She stops and thinks about this for a second. It's been a long time since lunch.

"That sounds really good," she says.

Scully continues her narration:

Having completed the autopsy, I checked into the Davey Crockett Motor Court.

From back in his office, presumably, Mulder interrupts Scully's monologue. He says:

The name of it was actually the Sam Houston Motor Lodge.

That night at the Sam Houston Motor Lodge—an old-fashioned bungalow-type hostelry—a weary Scully flops down on her bed. She shoves fifty cents into an ancient "Magic Fingers" device, falls backward onto the bedspread, and stares up at the ceiling, vibrating.

Mulder kicks open the motel room door. He stands, exhausted, in the door-

way. His suit and face covered with gobs of dried mud.

"C-c-chloral hydrate," says Scully, still vibrating.

"What?" says Mulder.

"What the hell happened to you?" says Scully, sitting up.

"Nothing," says her partner, plopping down into a thrift-shop style armchair. "Chloral hydrate?"

"Yeah," says Scully. "That thing you didn't know that you were looking for. Chloral hydrate—more commonly know as knockout d-drops. I-I found it in abundance w-when I sent the tox screen in on our m-murder victim. But seriously, Mulder," she adds, "what happened to you?"

"Nothing," says Mulder. "Who slipped him the Mickey?"

Scully raises her fingers in quotation marks, mimicking Mulder. "My 'theory'?" she says. "Your 'vampire.' He found it necessary to dope poor Mr. Funt to the gills before he was able to extract his blood. Probably did it to the cows, too."

Mulder shakes his head, puzzled. "What kind of vampire would do that?"

"E-exactly," says Scully, triumphantly.

Mulder exhales wearily. "We got another dead tourist," he says. "You gotta do another autopsy."

"Tonight? I just put money in the Magic Fingers!"

Mulder says, "I won't let it go to waste."

He plops down noisily on the bed and spread-eagles alongside her. Scully leaps to her feet with alacrity.

"He-he-he-he-he-he-he-he-ha-ha-ha-ha-!" giggles Mulder, grinning idiotically.

Scully prepares to leave. "This one's my room," she says, genuinely offended. "Don't get mud everywhere."

"Yeah, yeah, yeah, yeah," he says, shaking like a badly tuned Plymouth Valiant. "Okay! Hee hee!"

Scully exits. As she leaves, she sees a pizza delivery car pull up.

"Excuse me, ma'am," says the delivery boy, "did you order a pizza?"

"Yeah," says Scully, glumly. "The guy in there'll pay for it."

She leaves. The pizza guy ducks into his car and pulls out his insulated pizza bag. It is the teenager Mulder staked in the opening scene.

Back in the embalming room Scully faces a new dead tourist and begins work anew. She narrates:

Forgoing both dinner and sleep, I was soon at the funeral home examining one Mr. Paul Lombardo, from Naples, Florida.

Nearly out on her feet, Scully clicks on her tape recorder and begins a severely truncated version of her prior autopsy.

"Heart," she says.

"Lung."

"Large intestine."

She rinses her hands and staggers to the recorder. "As with the previous victim," she says, "it appears that the subject was most likely incapacitated with chloral hydrate, and then exsanguinated."

Her cell phone rings. She goes to answer it, still talking.

"The drug was either injected or ingested—I'm not sure which. Scully?"

Through the phone she hears heavy breathing.

"Hello? Hello?"

She hangs up, then staggers back to the corpse. "Where was I? Stomach contents. Stomach contents include—" She wields her scalpel wearily. "—pizza."

Her eyes focus, and a sudden shadow of fear crosses her face. She now realizes what this all could mean.

"The chloral hydrate is in the pizza," she says. "The pizza guy! Mulder!"

Gun in hand, she kicks open the motel room door in time to see the half-eaten pizza fall off the vibrating bed.

"Mulder!" she cries.

A pair of stockinged feet stick up from behind the bed. From behind it a frightening figure springs into view. It's the pizza guy and when he opens his mouth and hisses, two large, sharp fangs are prominently displayed.

Scully takes a step back and fires. The pizza guy streaks by her, and although

though she flings herself heroically to the ground and fires several more times, he's out the door and gone almost instantly.

Back in his FBI office the next day, Mulder looks bored.

"That's it?" he says.

Scully stiffens indignantly. "Well, luckily I had gotten there in time. I mean, although you were drugged, you were more or less unharmed."

Back to her flashback: At the motel room Scully kneels down anxiously over the prostrate Mulder and slaps his cheeks gently. "Mulder, are you okay?"

Mulder says, "Who's the black private dick who's the sex machine with all the chicks? SHAFT! Can you dig it? They say this cat Shaft is a bad mother—shut your mouth!"

And right back out of her flashback: "I did *not!*" says Mulder, rising indignantly from his desk.

Scully's expression indicates otherwise. "Long story short," she says. "Though my first four shots obviously missed Ronnie Strickland, with my fifth I was able to shoot out a tire on his car, forcing him to escape on foot.

"I left you behind and entered the woods in pursuit. I assumed that you were incapacitated. Then I heard screaming. When I arrived in the clearing I found you had caught up with him first, and had . . . overreacted. And that his vampire teeth were false."

"*That's* what you're going to tell Skinner?" asks Mulder.

"Well," says Scully, "I'm going to argue that we caught a killer—an utterly non-supernatural killer, but a killer nonetheless. And that your zeal to catch up with him was augmented by the chloral hydrate you were given."

Mulder eyes Scully disgustedly and points an accusatory finger.

"You are afraid to tell the truth," he says.

"Excuse me?"

"That's not the way it happened at all! I mean, what are you afraid of? That if you tell it the way it really happened, that you'll look like an idiot? Like me?"

Scully stands and stares at him for a long moment.

"Mulder," she says, finally, "Why don't you tell me the way you think it happened?" She smiles sarcastically. "Starting at the beginning."

Mulder turns away indignantly. "You're damn right," he mutters.

"Yesterday morning began like any morning," he says. "You arrived at the office—characteristically less than exuberant." Thus begins Mulder's alternate flashback:

"I hope you brought your cowboy boots," says Mulder politely, placing an airline ticket folder on his desk.

"Why are we going to *Dallas?*" says Scully, whining with bitchy negativism—a tone she will steadfastly maintain throughout Mulder's entire recap.

"Actually," chuckles Mulder, "it's a little town just south of there called Cheney, Texas. They've had some incidents down there recently that I think are pretty unusual."

"Like *what?*" demands Scully.

"Well," says Mulder, "I've brought some slides with which to better illustrate. Here we go!"

Mulder flashes the first dead cow on the screen.

"It's a *dead cow,*" complains Scully.

"Uh, it's actually six dead cows," explains Mulder. "And here's the really interesting thing—"

"Why am I looking at *six* dead cows?"

"Um, well," says Mulder, "because of the manner in which they died. All six were mysteriously exsanguinated."

"*And?*" demands Scully.

"And two little puncture marks on the neck," says Mulder. "Look! I've got a slide of that one."

Scully watches, frowning impatiently, until Mulder reaches the slide of the bovine puncture wounds. Scully shrugs. Mulder continues manfully.

"And one dead human victim, too," he says. "Last night, a vacationer from New Jersey. His body completely drained of blood, and two little puncture wounds on his neck."

Scully remains stubbornly unimpressed.

"Okay, look, Scully," says Mulder. "I don't want to jump to any hasty conclusions, but on the strength of the evidence that we have here I think what we may be looking at is a series of vampire, or vampirelike attacks."

"On what do you base *that*?" says Scully.

"On, uh, well—on the corpses drained of blood and the fang marks on the neck. But as always," he adds, "I'm very eager to hear your opinion."

Scully snorts. "Well, it's obviously not a vampire," she says.

"Well, why not?" says Mulder.

"Because they don't exist?" scoffs Scully.

Mulder nods thoughtfully. "Well, that's one opinion, and I respect that. Nonetheless, I'm thinking that a murder has been committed here and we can go down there and bring a killer to justice in whatever form, mortal or immortal, it may take."

Scully grudgingly acquiesces to this. She has another thought.

"It's not that Mexican goat sucker either," she says.

Mulder smiles painfully. His narration of the incident begins:

Upon arriving at the funeral home I made an interesting observation. One which you apparently didn't hear.

"That's a whole lot of caskets," says Mulder.

"Largest in-stock selection in the state!" says a funeral director, hitherto unseen, proudly.

"Well, why would a town of only three hundred and sixty-one need that?" asks Mulder.

"Repeat business!" says the funeral director.

He gets no reaction. "Mortician humor," he says, downcast. "Excuse me." Narrates Mulder:

Apparently your mind was somewhere else.

"Hoo boy!" says Scully, watching the local sheriff—still young, still tall—enter the room. She smiles goofily at him. This time, though, Lucius Hartwell has a goofy set of buck teeth.

"Y'all must be the gummint people!" says Lucius Hartwell. "I'm Lucius Hartwell!"

Back at the FBI office Scully looks at Mulder skeptically. "He had big buck teeth?"

"He had a slight overbite," concedes Mulder.

"No, he didn't!"

Mulder smiles smugly.

"And that's significant?" says Scully. "How?"

"I'm just trying to be thorough," he says. "So anyway, then we went to take a look at the body."

Back into Mulder's flashback:

"Here we go!" says Hartwell, whipping the sheet off Dwight Funt's body.

"No exam has been done?" asks Mulder.

"No, sir," says Hartwell. "This is exactly like we found him in his hotel room."

Through this entire exchange Scully has been gazing dreamily at the Texan. "No exam has been done?" she asks.

"Uh, no, ma'am," says Hartwell, smiling back a little uncomfortably. "I figured we'd best leave it to the experts."

Mulder pulls down Funt's shirt collar, exposing the fang marks in his neck.

Hartwell says, "Now, that can't be what it looks like, right?"

Scully makes a silly face and shakes her head.

Mulder says, "It depends on what you think it looks like, Sheriff Hartwell."

He adds, intensely, "Vampires have always been with us, in ancient myths and stories passed down from early man. Every culture has them—from the Babylonian *ekimmu* to the Chinese *kuang-shi,* the Hebrew *motetz dam,* the *mormo* of ancient Rome—"

Scully, watching this with arms folded, smirks and mouths, "Yada yada yada."

"—right down to the more familiar *nosferatu* of Transylvania."

"*Mormo,* uh, yeah," says Hartwell.

"In short, Sheriff, no," says Scully. "This can't be what it looks like." She adds, "I think what we're dealing with here is simply the case of some lunatic who's watched too many Bela Lugosi movies. He *wishes* that he could transfigure himself into a 'creature of the night.'"

The sheriff—who apparently has lost thirty IQ points between Scully's and Mulder's versions—nods, ruminating on this.

"Uh, yeah," he says. "Okay. Uh, what she said? That's what I'm thinkin', and uh, yeah."

Mulder speaks up. "But still," he protests, politely, "that leaves us in something of a quandary. Because there are as many different kinds of vampires as there are cultures that fear them. Some don't even subsist on blood. The Bulgarian *ubour*, for instance, eats only manure."

Scully yawns. "Thank you," she says, sarcastically.

"But to the Serbs," continues Mulder pointedly, "a prime indicator of vampirism was red hair. Some vampires were thought to be eternal. Others were thought to have a life span of forty days. Sunlight kills certain vampires, while others can come and go as they please, day or night."

These words do nothing but irritate Scully. "If you have a point, Mulder," she says, "please feel free to come to it."

Mulder says, "My point is, that we don't know exactly what we're looking for. What kind of vampire—or if you prefer—what kind of vampire this killer wishes himself to be."

Scully's only response is silent scorn. Mulder resumes his study of the dead body. He notices something, then moves to the far end of the table and stares intently at Dwight Funt's white Thom McCann boaters.

"Hey, look at this!" he says. "His shoes are untied!"

Back at the FBI office Scully is baffled. She steels herself and asks, "Why was it so important that his shoes were untied?"

"Getting to it!" says Mulder, happily. He adds, "Now, while you stayed behind to do the autopsy, the sheriff drove me to the town cemetery."

Back to Mulder's flashback:

At a deserted old graveyard, Sheriff Hartwell looks around, puzzled. "Agent Mulder," he drawls, "You mind me askin' why we're out here?"

Mulder walks slowly among the weathered gravestones.

"Well, historically," he says, "cemeteries were thought to be a haven for vampires. As are castles, catacombs, and swamps, but, unfortunately, you don't have any of those."

"We used to have swamps," says Hartwell, "only the EPA made us take to callin' 'em 'wetlands.'"

"Uh, yeah," says

Mulder. "So we're out here looking for signs of vampiric activity."

"Which would be?"

"Broken or shifted tombstones, an absence of birds singing—"

"There you go!" says Hartwell. "'Cause, hey, I ain't heard any birds singin'! Right?"

He pauses and reconsiders. "'A course, it's winter. And we ain't got no birds. Is there anything else?"

"A faint groaning coming from under the earth," says Mulder. "The sound of mandication—of the creature eating his own death shroud."

"Nope," says Hartwell, listening. "No mana—"

"Mandication," says Mulder.

The agent adds, "Now, sheriff, I know my methods may seem a little odd to you, but—"

"Hey!" says Hartwell, wholeheartedly. "You all work for the federal government and that's all I need to know."

Mulder says, "It's just that my gut instinct tells me that the killer will visit this place. That it may well hold some fascination, some siren call, for him."

Hartwell struggles to digest all this. In the meantime, someone driving a red Gremlin honks his horn at him from an adjacent road. It's the pizza delivery guy.

"Howdy, sheriff!" he shouts.

"Hey, Ronnie," says Hartwell. "How's it goin'?"

"Can't complain," says Ronnie.

"Well, all right, then," says Hartwell, as the pizza guy drives away. Mulder, gazing pensively into the distance, does not turn to watch him. "Maybe after nightfall, sheriff," he says solemnly. "But he'll come. He'll come."

"Mulder—shoelaces?" says Scully, back inside the FBI office.

"Huh?" says Mulder.

"On the *corpse*. You were going to tell me what was so meaningful about finding untied shoelaces."

Mulder nods. "I'm getting to it," he says. Back at the graveyard in Mulder's flashback:

That night Mulder walks purposefully among the tombstones, carefully sprinkling sunflower seeds onto the dark earth behind him. He narrates:

So, we staked out the cemetery.

"Sunflower seed?" asks Mulder, getting into the front seat of a police car beside Hartwell.

"No thanks," says Hartwell, uneasily. "You mind me asking you what you were—?"

Mulder nods authoritatively. "Historically, certain types of seeds are thought to fascinate vampires. Chiefly oats and millet, but you gotta make do with what you have. You remember before when I said we didn't know what kind of vampire we were dealing with?"

"Yeah?" says Hartwell, his forehead furrowed in concentration.

"Well, oddly enough," says Mulder, "there seems to be one obscure fact, which—in all the stories told in all the different cultures—is exactly the same. And that's that vampires are *really, really* obsessive-compulsive. Hey! You toss a handful of seeds at one of them," he adds, "and no matter what he's doing, he has to stop, and pick them up. And there's more: If he sees a knotted rope," continues Mulder, "a vampire has to untie it."

"In fact," concludes the agent, "that's why I'm guessing that our victim's shoelaces were untied."

A light bulb shines dimly above Hartwell's head. "Obsessive," he says. "Like *Rain Man!*"

A few moments later the cruiser's radio crackles to life. The police dispatcher, Charlene, tells them that there is "something of a situation" down at the RV park. Roof lights flashing, they pull up to the Rolling Acres RV Camp ("Overnights Welcome"). A small crowd of Chenians are standing mute, watching an old Winnebago motor home, driverless, racing around backward in circles.

"Hey again, sheriff," says Ronnie the pizza guy.

"Hey again, Ronnie," says Sheriff Hartwell.

"I guess you got yourself a runaway, huh?" says Ronnie.

"Well, yeah, Ronnie," says the sheriff. "I guess we do."

The sheriff turns to Mulder.

"What do you think?" he says. "We ought to shoot the tires out?"

Back at the FBI office, Mulder squirms uncomfortably. "Anyway, skipping ahead—"

"Why skip ahead?" asks Scully, arms crossed.

Mulder shrugs sheepishly. Back into his flashback:

Mulder and Hartwell aim and fire after shot at the circling Winnebago, absolutely no effect.

Okay, here's something you may not know: Shooting out the tires of a runaway RV is a lot harder than it looks. I then tried a different approach.

Mulder grabs hold of the Winnebago's front grille. For his pains, he is dragged, yelling and screaming, along the ground behind it for several complete revolutions.

"Whoa, boy! Bird-dog it! Thattaway!" whoops Hartwell, enthusiastically.

Finally, Mulder lets go of the motor home and tumbles, mud-spattered, to a halt. Hartwell helps him to his feet just as the Winnebago runs out of gas and sputters to a stop.

Finally, we prevailed.

Mulder yanks open the Winnebago's door, and a thirtyish man—his throat punctured by two tiny fangs—tumbles out head first.

"That's the same as the others," says Hartwell.

"Right down to the shoes," says Mulder.

The dead man's low-cut hiking boots have had their shoelace untied.

We interviewed everyone present. No one had seen anything. Frustrated, and lacking a solid lead, I just wanted to get cleaned up. I had the sheriff drop me at the motel. Which is where I ran into you.

"What do you *mean,* you want me to do another autopsy?" demands Scully, her voice rising and falling shrewishly to a Magic Fingers beat. "And why do we have to do it right now? I just spent hours on

my feet doing an autopsy—all for you!
I do it all for you, Mulder! You know, I
haven't eaten since six o'clock this morning, and all that was was one half of a
cream cheese bagel. And it wasn't even
real cream cheese; it was lite cream
cheese! Now you want me to run off and
do another autopsy!"

In the motel room doorway, a weary
Mulder stares blankly into space. Finally,
Scully notices his disheveled condition.

"What the hell happened to you?" she
says with a scowl.

Finally, she left.

"Don't you touch that bed!" shouts
Scully, slamming the door behind her.

Alone at last, Mulder pulls off his
shoes, coat and shirt and goes into the
bathroom to wash up. Someone knocks on
the door, and enters. It is Ronnie the
pizza guy, holding his insulated pizza bag
and looking uncomfortable.

"Uh, hey again," says Ronnie. "The
lady outside, she said that you'd pay for
this."

"She ordered a pizza from you?" asks,
Mulder, in his underwear. "How much?"

"Twelve ninety-eight." says Ronnie.

Mulder hands him thirteen bucks.
Ronnie's eyes light up.

"Okay then," he says. "Enjoy."

Ronnie leaves. Mulder opens the box
and sniffs happily. Sprawled atop the
vibrating bed, he scarfs down a slice of
vibrating pizza.

*So I ate your dinner. And that's when
I saw it.*

Lying atop the covers, watching TV,
Mulder reaches over to place another
fifty cents in the Magic Fingers. He
glances at his shoes, which lie neatly
arranged on the floor, their shoelaces
untied. Which is not the way Mulder left
them.

But by then it was too late.

Still vibrating, Mulder blinks, already
feeling the effects of the chloral hydrate.
He reaches across the bed to his cell
phone and grabs it just before he tumbles
to the floor. He thumbs the speed dial,
and Scully answers.

"Scully!" she says.

Mulder moves his lips to talk, but
can't.

"Hello? Hello?" says Scully.

Mulder moans unintelligibly.

"Creep!" says Scully, hanging up.

Ronnie reenters the room. He opens
his mouth wide, big fangs extended. His
eyes glow bright green.

Mulder fights to remain conscious. He
reaches up and fumbles along the top
of the dresser. With his last ounce of
concentration, he feels around for his
pistol. His fingers touch it, then move on.
He grabs his bag of sunflower seeds and
tosses a salvo of them at Ronnie's feet.

"Oh, man!" says Ronnie, disgustedly.
"Why'd you have to do *that* for?"

Compelled by his unshakable obsession, the vampire kneels down to pick up
the loose seeds one by one.

"You are in *big trouble*," he tells
Mulder.

Mulder can't fight the anesthetic any
longer. He keels over onto the floor
beside the bed.

*Then I was out cold. I don't know for
how long, but when I finally came to—*

Ronnie looms over Mulder, his mouth
wide open and his fangs fully extended.
The door flies open, and Scully, gun in
hand, enters.

"Mulder!" she shouts.

Ronnie springs to his feet. Scully
shoots him twice in the chest. He growls,
then leaps clear across the room to the
opposite end.

Back in the FBI office Scully squints at
her partner skeptically. "You're saying
that I actually hit him two times?"

"Square in the chest," says Mulder.
"No effect."

"And then he sort of flew at me like a
flying squirrel?"

"Well," says Mulder, frowning, "I
don't think I'd use the term 'flying squirrel' when I talk to Skinner. But, yeah,
that's what happened."

Back into the flashback: Someone is
smashing the armchair in the motel room
to bits.

*You checked on me, then left to pursue
Ronnie Strickland into the woods. Once I
recovered, I knew what I had to do.*

Mulder breaks off a chair leg, then
contemplates it. It will be a more than
serviceable stake.

A full moon hangs over a flat, scraggly
field. A teenage boy runs frantically
across it, stumbling and falling and crying
out in terror.

"Help!" he yells. "Somebody help me! He's going to kill me!"

He is being ruthlessly chased by a man in a long, dark coat. Mulder continues: *I caught sight of him, chased him over hill and dale, and in the end—*

Mulder lifts the stake high with both hands, and buries it deep in the teenager's chest. Ronnie, the ex-pizza guy, howls.

Back at the office Scully looks at Mulder with a mixture of disbelief and pity.

"Mulder, it's not just me," she says. "Nobody in their right mind will ever believe that story."

Mulder says, "They'll have to once they examine Ronnie Strickland's body."

At the Dallas–Fort Worth Regional Pathology Lab that morning a blasé coroner enters the forensic morgue, approaches a sheet-covered body, and starts to dictate his case notes.

"Case number 0026198," he says. "Ronald LaVelle Strickland."

The coroner pulls off the sheet, revealing a naked Ronnie. The armchair leg is still embedded in his chest.

"Probable cause of death—that's a tough one," he says.

He grabs the stake with two latex-gloved hands and pulls; walks the bloody object over to a nearby table; and begins to rummage around among his instruments.

Behind him, Ronnie sits up abruptly. The coroner senses something behind him, and whirls to face Ronnie, fangless but with eyes glowing. Ronnie hesitates, running his tongue over the spaces where his fake fangs used to be. Then he pounces.

Later that day Mulder and Scully sit nervously in Skinner's outer office. Scully leans over toward Mulder.

"Mulder," she whispers, "please just keep reminding him that you were drugged."

"Would you stop that!" Mulder hisses back.

"Couldn't hurt," whispers Scully.

Skinner pops his head through his office door. Mulder and Scully leap to their feet.

"I was drugged!" declares Mulder.

Skinner blinks, sighs, and addresses both agents. "I want you back in Texas," he says.

He tells them that Ronnie Strickland's body has disappeared from the morgue and, possibly in conjunction with that, a coroner has been attacked.

"His throat was bitten," he says.

"A coroner's dead?" asks Mulder.

"No," says Skinner. "His throat was bitten. It was sort of gnawed on."

Mulder and Scully stand and look at each other, astonished.

"Daylight's burning, agents," admonishes their boss.

That night at the Cheney cemetery Mulder and Scully sweep their flashlight beams over the tombstones.

Scully says, "So we should find Ronnie out here, because . . . ?"

"Because tradition states," says Mulder, "that a vampire needs to sleep in his native soil."

"But, Mulder, he had fake fangs," says Scully.

"Why would a real vampire need fake fangs? I mean, for the sake of argument."

Mulder replies that fangs are "very rarely" mentioned in the folklore, that they're really an invention of Bram Stoker's.

He adds, "I think maybe you were right before when you said that this is just a guy who watches too many Dracula movies. He just happens to be a real vampire."

Scully sighs and looks around her. "So where the hell is he?" she says.

Mulder shrugs. "What about his family?" he asks. "The ones who were going to sue us for four hundred and forty-six million dollars?"

Scully tells him that the litigants are Ronnie's aunt and uncle, who get their mail general delivery at the local post office.

"No home address?" asks Mulder, perking up.

Scully shakes her head and is distracted by the sound of an approaching vehicle. It's Sheriff Hartwell's police cruiser.

"Evening, agents," says the sheriff. "I heard y'all were back in town. Thought I might be of some assistance."

Mulder nods and smiles. "Yeah, actually you can. You can stay behind here with Agent Scully and keep an eye on things while I check something out."

He turns to Scully, and winks. "Don't say I never did nothin' for ya!" he says, in a comic Texas accent.

Scully is startled. "Where are you going?" she says.

Mulder asks, "Where might you be living if your mail came general delivery around here?"

"The RV park?" says Hartwell, slowly.

"You're good," says Mulder, before waving jauntily and disappearing into the foggy darkness.

A few moments later a happy Scully sits with Hartwell in the front seat of the cruiser. The sheriff unscrews his thermos and pours some steaming coffee into a cowboy boot–shaped mug. The agent takes a grateful sip.

"So, what do you think about vampires?" says Hartwell.

"You mean, aside from the fact that I don't believe in them?" says Scully.

"Yeah. Aside from that," drawls Hartwell.

"Well," she says, "they're supposed to be extremely charming. Seductive. I mean, even if they did really exist, who's to say they'd actually be like that. As Agent Mulder says, 'There are many different kinds of vampires.'"

Hartwell nods and frowns. It seems as if he has something important on his mind.

"I really mean to apologize to you about Ronnie," he says. "He makes us all look bad. He's just not who we are anymore."

Over in the passenger seat, Scully is suddenly feeling a little woozy.

Hartwell adds, "I mean, we pay taxes. We're good neighbors. Ol' Ronnie, he can't quite seem to grasp the concept of 'low profile'."

Now Scully is confused and conking out fast. Hartwell lifts her coffee cup, and carefully moves it away from her.

"But though he may be a moron," he says, turning toward her,
"he is one of our
own."

The sheriff's eyes glow green. Scully, losing consciousness, can only stare, slack-jawed, back at him.

Back at the Rolling Acres RV Park, Mulder walks among the rows of trailers and motor homes. Something crunches underfoot. He stops and picks it up. It is a pizza spacer—
a white plastic tripod that keeps the pizza from getting stuck to the top of the box.

The lights are out in the nearest RV. Mulder enters it cautiously, and shines his flashlight on something big and wooden lying on the floor.

"Hello," he says.

He's looking at a brass-handled casket. Mulder lifts the lid. Inside lies Ronnie Strickland, his eyes closed, wearing a Walkman headset from which faint sounds of rock music emerge.

"Sleeping late," muses Mulder, coolly.

Ronnie's glowing green eyes snap open. He growls ferociously, and reaches upward for Mulder. Mulder throws himself down on the lid, slamming it shut. He climbs atop the casket, trying to keep it closed.

"You have the right to remain silent!" says Mulder, riding the coffin lid like a bucking horse. "Anything you say can and will be held against you! *C'mon! Cut it out, Ronnie!*"

Mulder glances through the RV window. Other RV folk—six or seven, all told—are slowly approaching the motor home in zombielike fashion.

"Oh, damn," says Mulder.

He pulls out his handcuffs and snaps them onto the casket's handles, crudely chaining it shut. He looks around frantically for a weapon. He finds a small bag filled with stale pizza breadsticks, grabs it, and steps outside the motor home.

The RVers—their eyes glowing green— keep moving forward. Mulder holds up a pair of crossed breadsticks, trying to keep the vampires at bay. They have no effect. His attackers rush forward, surround the screaming agent, and slowly submerge him in their midst.

The next morning Mulder lies sprawled in the front seat of 1his rental car. A figure wearing a familiar duster and silver star approaches. It is Scully.

"Mulder?" says the agent, waking him.

"Scully, what happened?" groans Mulder.

"I came to in a cemetery. That's all I know."

Mulder—after inadvertently honking the horn with his foot—staggers out of the car, and examines Scully's neck for vampire bites. Nothing. He looks around the RV park. Every one of the transient vehicles is now gone.

"They pulled up stakes," he says, then looks down, kneels, and reties his shoelaces.

Later that day Mulder and Scully sit across from Skinner in his office.

"So that's it?" asks the AD. "They simply disappeared without a trace?"

Mulder, looking uncomfortable, nods. But Skinner looks far from satisfied.

"And that's exactly the way it happened?" he asks. "From start to finish?"

Scully looks at Mulder.

"Well," she says, "I can neither confirm nor deny Agent Mulder's version of events which occurred outside my presence."

"Neither can I confirm nor deny," says Mulder, "Agent Scully's version."

Scully says, "Anyway—I was drugged."

Mulder says, "That is essentially . . . exactly the way it happened."

"Except for the part about the buck teeth."

back story:

Rashomon meets Anne Rice in the comedic highlight of the fifth season.

If the reaction to screened excerpts at the ten *X-Files* Expos earlier this year were any indication, fans enjoyed "Bad Blood" at least as well as they did last year's dark comedy, "Small Potatoes" (4X20).

Once again, writer/supervising producer Vince Gilligan combined pure satire with a keen sense of the pricklier, edgier, semi-undercover aspects of the Mulder-Scully relationship.

"It started out as a total panic situation," recalls Gilligan. "My episode was going to be filmed right after the Christmas break, so I knew I had to have it ready by the time we came back. And I was not real happy about that, because I'd been looking forward to this vacation for a long time. And in fact I'd been working on a different idea for a long time. It wasn't working out, and I was getting more and more nervous and frustrated."

As Gilligan not-so-fondly remembers it, this aborted comedy would have consisted of a typical *X-Files* adventure presented as a typical episode of the NBC series *Unsolved Mysteries*. Robert Stack would have hosted, of course, and for his real-life true-crime simulation Mulder and Scully would have been played by a couple of other actors. (When Gillian Anderson and David Duchovny got wind of this, reports Gilligan, "they definitely liked the sound of a week off.")

"But I just couldn't figure out how to do it," admits the writer. "And now it was a week before Christmas and I said, 'Oh, man, I'm screwed.'" Desperate, Gilligan appealed for help to co–executive producer Frank Spotnitz. "And as we were sitting there banging our heads against the wall," he says, "Frank sud-

denly remembered—of all things—an episode of the old *Dick Van Dyke Show*."

In the half-hour episode, which was titled "The Night the Roof Fell In," Rob and Laura Petrie have a fight, then each tell their neighbor their version of what led up to it. Gilligan says, "I just thought it was a cool way to tell a story. And I wondered if I could do that." He adds, "I also realized that if you're going to tell a story this way, the way you're telling it is the gimmick—not the story you're telling. And because of that, and because you really only have half the time as usual, I thought the best approach would be to tell a very simple paranormal story, one that everybody understood. So I thought 'Vampires—hell, everybody gets that.' And you know, we'd only told one other vampire story before, really."

Newly energized, Gilligan put his *Unsolved* idea out of its misery and finished the script for "Bad Blood" on schedule. The result delighted almost everyone. "Oh, yes!" says Gillian Anderson, happily. "I loved that episode. As far as I'm concerned it's one of our best ones ever. I think it really showed how well David and I can work together, even though it was very complicated to make, and while we were doing it nobody except Vince really knew how it was going to come together."

Adding a little bit to the actors' confusion—but cutting down considerably on labor-intensive camera setups—both the Mulder- and Scully-centric versions of each scene were filmed one after the other, using the exact same sets and camera angles. Anderson credits veteran director Cliff Bole with guiding her to the correct and consistent levels of bitchiness or wounded innocence in each take.

Other behind-the-camera staffers also did their best to bring Gilligan's whimsical visions to life. To find an appropriate location for the Rolling Acres RV Camp, locations manager Louisa Gradnitzer went back to the site of an abandoned sawmill that had previously been used in "Gethsemane" (4X24) and had subsequently burned to the ground, leaving a lovely expanse of gray concrete slab. To stock the Peaceful Slumbers Funeral Home, art director Greg Loewen rented twelve very expensive caskets—"They were works of art. They came with 'grand piano craftsmanship,'" he recalls, smiling—from an astonished local wholesaler.

vampire victims' puncture marks were applied by makeup artist Laverne Basham. "Vince helped me with those," she says. "He bit the back of his hand to show me exactly what he wanted."

As Sheriff Hartwell, the Texas-born Wilson—who starred in Vince Gilligan's 1998 movie *Home Fries* opposite Drew Barrymore, his own real-life girlfriend—inadvertently held up production by sending David Duchovny into hysterics during the scenes they filmed together.

As killer pizza guy Ronnie Strickland, ex–child actor Patrick Renna (*The Sandlot*, *The Big Green*), apparently provided just the right interpretation.

"At first I was a little unsure of the character," recalls Renna. "So before we started I asked if Ronnie was pretending to be a moron. They told me, 'No. He's really just a moron.'"

Ⓧ

"Hartwell" is the middle name of writer Vince Gilligan's girlfriend, Holly Rice.

Ⓧ

For "Bad Blood," composer Mark Snow reached deeply into his classical-music grab bag. Incidental themes included the "Rondo and Capriccio" by Saint-Saens and "The Ride of the Valkyries" by Richard Wagner. Other composers quoted in 5X12: Mozart, Brahms, Stravinsky, and Prokofiev.

Ⓧ

To make their eyes appear to glow in the dark, several of the vampires who swarm Mulder in the RV park have fluorescent materials glued to their eyelids, which accounts for their somewhat vacant expressions—they couldn't see.

Ⓧ

To shoot inside Ronnie Strickland's lair, crewmen cut an entire side wall out of a brand-new motor home. "Afterwards," recalls picture car coordinator Nigel Habgood, "[production manager] Ron French came over and asked me: 'Did we buy that thing, or was it rented?'" Oops.

To get the late Mr. Lombardo's motor home rolling backward in a circle, special effects coordinator David Gauthier rigged up an auxiliary steering station in the back of the vehicle. The RV's stunt driver, out of camera range, looked out the back window while controlling the front wheels. He steered backward, as if he was driving a fork lift. In the scenes in which Mulder is dragged behind the motor home, David Duchovny stretched out on a small hidden "creeper" rig.

Luke Wilson and the other lead vampires were equipped with removable "funny fangs" by special effects makeup coordinator Toby Lindala. "The retainers I had to wear as a kid never fit as well," says Wilson, admiringly.

For the shots of the various corpses, the

patient X

As a disillusioned
Mulder denies all evidence
of extraterrestrial visitors,
Scully—along with thousands
of other abductees—
is drawn toward
a final confrontation.

EPISODE: 5X13
FIRST AIRED: March 1, 1998
EDITOR: Casey O Rohrs
WRITTEN BY: Chris Carter & Frank Spotnitz
DIRECTED BY: Kim Manners
GUEST STARS:
Nicholas Lea (Alex Krycek)
Laurie Holden (Marita Covarrubias)
Veronica Cartwright (Cassandra Spender)
Chris Owens (Special Agent Jeffrey Spender)
Alex Shostak, Jr. (Dmitri)
Andrew Star (Dmitri's friend)
Jim Jansen (Dr. Heitz Werber)
Max Wyman (Dr. Per Lagerqvist)
Barbara Dyke (Dr. Dominique Alepin)
Ron Halder (Dr. Floyd Fazio)
Bruno Verdoni (UN Officer)
Raoul Ganeen (Gulag Guard)
Anatol Rezmeritsa (Gulag Commandant)
Oleg Feoktistov (Gulag Doctor)
John Neville (The Well-Manicured Man)
Don S. Williams (First Elder)
John Moore (Second Elder)
Willy Ross (Quiet Willy)
Brian Thompson (The Bounty Hunter)
Allan Franz (Man in VW Van)
Kurt Max Bunte (Ranger)

PRINCIPAL SETTINGS:
Kazakhstan;
Cambridge, Massachusetts;
Tunguska, Siberia, Russia;
Vladivostok;
Washington, D.C.;
New York City;
Skyland Mountain, Virginia;
Ruskin Dam, Pennsylvania

The vast canopy of the night sky—crowded with stars and planets, galaxies and nebulae—is spread out before us. The heavenly bodies begin to move toward us as if we were traveling among them. We hear the voice of Fox Mulder. He says:

Before the exploration of space, of the moon and planets, man held that the heavens were the home and province of powerful gods, who controlled not just the vast firmament but the earthly fate of man himself.

And that the pantheon of warring deities was the cause and reason for the human condition. For the past and the future, and for which great monuments would be created, in earth as in heaven.

Specific star formations begin to resolve themselves, brightening and forming the constellations, and changing into illustrations of the various gods they represent. Mulder adds:

But in time, man replaced these gods with new gods, and new religions, that provided no more certain or greater answers than those worshipped by his Greek or Roman or Egyptian ancestors.

The illustrations fade away, then disappear, as one star grows brighter than the rest and begins to float away from the others.

And while we've chosen now our monolithic and benevolent gods, and found our certainties in science—believers all—we wait for a sign, a revelation; our eyes turned skyward, ready to accept the truly incredible; to find our destiny written in the stars.

But how do we best look to see? With new eyes, or old?

The bright star plummets down, passing behind a jagged granite mountaintop. It is watched by two teenage boys, standing in a forest clearing in the former Soviet province of Kazakhstan. They speak to each other in Russian.

"They're here!" says the first boy.

"Do you think the others have seen them?" says the other.

His friend says, "Let's go tell them!"

They run off into the forest, then abruptly halt.

"Do you smell that?" asks the first boy.

"Fire!" says the second.

They start running again, more fearfully this time, and the air fills with smoke, which becomes heavier and thicker as they go. They emerge into a second clearing, this one an inferno of blazing automobiles.

"Mama! Papa!" screams the first boy.

There is no answer. A man emerges from the dense smoke. He is completely engulfed in fire. Arms waving frantically, he runs straight for the boys. The boys run for their lives, splitting up. A strange figure blocks the first boy's path. This man is hideously scarred—his eyes, mouth, and nose crudely cauterized shut.

A few yards away, the second boy hears his friend scream in agony. He stands paralyzed with fear.

The next morning a convoy of United Nations troops enters the burnt-out clearing. Accompanying them is Marita Covarrubias, last seen in 4X21 ("Zero Sum"). She surveys the scene with deep concern and foreboding.

The troops douse the still-smoldering cars with fire extinguishers; in some of the vehicles sit horribly incinerated corpses. The first teenage boy is crouched in the nearby bushes, watching the UN troops intently. A pair of jackboots appear behind him. He scrambles to his feet and turns around to face the scowling visage of Alex Krycek, last seen in 4X10 ("Terma").

Krycek speaks in Russian.

"What is your name?" he says, patting the boy on the shoulder with his prosthetic arm.

"Dmitri," says the frightened boy.

"You saw what happened here?"

"Da," says Dmitri.

Krycek switches to English.

"Too bad for you," he says.

In the clearing Covarrubias and a UN officer stand over a hideously burnt corpse. It is Dmitri's friend.

"It's like the flesh is cooked," says the officer. "All the way through."

Covarrubias stares down and says nothing.

"You there!" says a Russian-speaking voice behind her. "Under what authority are you corrupting this crime scene?"

It is Krycek. He is leading a small unit of rifle-carrying Russian soldiers

Covarrubias turns, pulls out her UN identification, and responds in the same aggressive manner. "Under the United Nations charter," she says in Russian. "Chapter seven, articles thirty-nine and forty-two."

Krycek smirks, and responds in English. "Your authority isn't recognized here. Only your lies."

Covarrubias says, also in English, "These are UN peacekeepers. This is a mission of mercy."

"This is a mission of fear!" replies Krycek. "Yours and the men you work for."

Covarrubias says, "I don't know what you're talking about."

Krycek says, "You go back and you tell them what you've seen here, what you've found."

Covarrubias stands fast. She tells Krycek angrily that she is a special representative to the Secretary General of the United Nations. Krycek treats this declaration with scorn.

"I know who you are, and I know who you work for," he says. "And you go back and tell them—"

"Tell them what?" says Covarrubias. "What happened here?"

Krycek says, "Tell them that it's all going to hell."

Covarrubias blanches, but says nothing. Brusquely, Krycek commands the Russian troops to seize Dmitri.

Covarrubias asks, "Does the boy know?"

Krycek says nothing, and turns to leave.

"*Did he see?*" the UN operative demands.

Krycek turns back, spits at Covarrubias's feet, and eyes her with a mixture of contempt and anger.

"Tell them to kiss my American ass," he says.

In a large lecture hall at the Massachusetts Institute near Boston, a videotaped interview of an attractive middle-aged woman in a wheelchair is projected on a large screen. The interviewee is smiling and serene. She says, "During my last several abductions I have experi-

enced no fear whatsoever. And it was the absence of fear that allowed me to communicate with them, and them with me. They told me that I was an apostle, here to spread the word of a dawning of a new age of supernatural enlightenment."

The lights come up in the lecture hall to loud applause. The woman's image remains frozen on the screen; on a dais at the front of the hall sit seven panelists. The first one to speak is the moderator, a white-haired bearded man named Dr. Per Lagerqvist.

Lagerqvist says, "Sensibly, it's not a question of truth versus fiction, but of truths which are incomprehensible. Because we have no physics, no real language for explaining Patient X's story, much less the existence of extraterrestrials. Nothing to prepare us for the ontological shock, which is bound to follow the—"

A bookish woman—the nameplate in front of her reads DOMINIQUE ALEPIN—interrupts him. "We talk about the need for evidence, for proof, as if it would serve some purpose, make some difference," says Alepin, who is seated next to an uncomfortable, and apparently disapproving, Fox Mulder.

She adds, "What we should be seeking is exactly what this woman is describing: Not if they are, but why—and what their business is."

Impatiently, a gray-suited man named Dr. Floyd Fazio cuts her off.

"In my conversations with her," says Fazio, "she believes this business, the abductions and the experiments, are due to their plans for us. And that we are not simply breeding cows for them, as some have suggested, but subjects. Much like we think of our relationships with God.

"And that there are sites—what she calls lighthouses—around which there will be great activity."

Now it's Mulder's turn to break in.

"All this conjecture," he says, "the 'ontological shock' that you speak of, for which we are so ill-equipped is, in my opinion, not only false, but dangerous."

He gestures toward the video screen.

"This woman presents no good or credible testimony beyond the feel-good message she promotes."

Fazio eyes him skeptically. "You think she's lying?" he says.

"No," says Mulder. "I don't think she's lying. I think that if you prepare people well enough to believe a lie, they will believe it as if it were true."

He adds, "And if you tell them a really big lie, like there are aliens from outer space, much more than a small one, they will believe it. And if you suggest to them that these aliens are doing bad things to them, the power of this will be to make certain people believe that certain psychopathologies and neuroses that they're suffering from can now be attributed to that."

Lagerqvist eyes him incredulously, "Agent Mulder, she has physical ailments," he says.

Dominique Alepin demands, "Are you discounting *any* belief in the existence of extraterrestrials?"

Mulder says, "I just question mindless belief."

Fazio says, accusingly, "But you've cited evidence. You've made claims yourself!"

"What I've seen," says Mulder, wearily, "I've seen because I wanted to believe. I—"

He faces out toward the audience, his expression troubled.

"If you look hard," he says, "you can go mad. But if you continue to look you become liberated. And you come awake, as if from a dream, and realizing that the lies are there simply to protect what they're advertising: a government which knows that its greatest strength is not in defense, but in attack."

The audience responds to Mulder's opinions with a faint buzz of dissatisfaction. Mulder notices this, but presses on.

"It's strongly held by believers in UFO phenomena," Mulder adds, forcefully, "that there is military complicity or involvement in abductions. But what if there is no complicity?"

He faces down his fellow panelists.

"What if," he says, "there is simply the military seeking to develop an arsenal of weapons against which there is no defense—biological warfare—which justifies in their eyes making an ass out of the nation with stories of little green men. A conspiracy, wrapped in a plot, inside a government agenda."

A short time later the discussion is over. Looking tired and discouraged, Mulder grabs his briefcase and steps down from the stage and toward the exit. Only a few people remain seated in the audience, including a man the agent recognizes instantly.

"Dr. Werber?" says Mulder.

"It's been some time," replies Heitz Werber—the man who performed regression hypnosis on Mulder in the pilot episode.

Mulder says, "Almost five years."

Werber replies, "I came down expecting to hear how your work has progressed. I'm surprised, to say the least."

Mulder averts his eyes. "So much has changed," he says.

Werber says, "You seem to have abandoned something you believed so completely, in spite of what I know about from our work together. And the memories I helped you recover about the experience with your sister."

Mulder says, "I've come to distrust a lot of things. I've come to distrust those memories."

"I'm sorry," says Werber.

"For what?" asks Mulder.

Werber says, "I've taken a lot of criticism for my work with alien abductees, and in the field itself. The regression hypnosis work I did with you—"

Mulder interrupts him.

"Look, I'm not questioning your methods, Dr. Werber," he says. "I'm questioning myself—and how I was tricked. How I was led to believe through an elaborate staging of events that my sister had been abducted.

Werber shakes his head. "A man with faith can indulge in the luxury of skepticism," he says.

Mulder says, quickly, "I don't think you understand. There's just too much evidence that it's all been a lie. The conspiracy is not to hide the existence of extraterrestrials. It's to make people believe in it so completely that they question nothing."

Werber says, with a touch of sarcasm mixed with disappointment, "So you and I have just been advocates of insanity all along? Is this the extreme possibility you believe in now?"

"Is Patient X any more credible?" asks Mulder.

"I hope so," says Werber. "I'm her doctor. I think you should meet her. I think you might change your mind."

In a Siberian gulag (last seen in 4X10, "Terma") a doctor and a prison guard push a rolling cart through a dark, dank cell block. They stop outside the entrance to a small cell. Inside is Krycek, breathing heavily. On his hands and knees is Dmitri, who has obviously just been beaten.

Krycek says, speaking Russian to the doctor, "The boy has told me what I need to know. You may now begin."

"But he is only a boy," says the doctor. "We do our experiments only on the criminal."

"Do you argue with me?" asks Krycek, menacingly.

The doctor says, "I have orders—"

"And now you have new orders," says Krycek, staring at him with murder in his eyes.

The doctor enters the cell. Krycek walks over to the prison guard and presses a roll of bills against his chest.

"You were never here," he says coldly. The guard takes the money and leaves. Krycek watches him go, then reaches down and pockets a vial of amber liquid from the rolling cart.

Inside the cell the doctor kneels next to Dmitri and gazes sympathetically at his bruised and bleeding face.

Dmitri looks back at him, suspiciously, though his one good eye.

"Are you going to kill me?" asks Dmitri.

"No," says the doctor.

"Why not?" asks the boy.

The doctor says, sadly, "We are doing a test."

In a psychiatric hospital in the United States Dr. Werber leads Mulder into a sun-dappled room. Inside sits a woman in a wheelchair—the same one who addressed, via videotape, the panel discussion at the Massachusetts Institute.

"Cassandra?" says Werber.

"Hello," says the woman, turning around.

She wheels herself over to the two men.

"Fox Mulder," she says, smiling happily. "I'm so glad to finally meet you. You are a hero of mine."

"I am?" says Mulder, uncomfortably.

Cassandra tells the agent that she first read about him three years ago, when he helped Duane Barry, who'd escaped from the hospital in "Duane Barry" (2X05) and claimed he was being summoned by aliens.

"And you," she adds, "were the only one who believed him."

Mulder says, "You may not like me as much as you like that story."

"That story saved my life!" replies Cassandra, with a chuckle.

"I have been a multiple abductee for over thirty years," she adds. "I had been afraid to seek help. Nobody would ever believe me, really, until I read about you. That's how I came to meet Dr. Werber."

"Cassandra—" says Mulder, pained.

"He told me that you," continues Cassandra, "had been through hypnotic regression yourself. That's how you had learned your sister had been abducted."

"Cassandra—" interrupts Mulder.

"Yes?"

"Are you here voluntarily?"

"Yes," Cassandra replies. "Under doctor's supervision."

Mulder glances at Werber, and looks back at the patient. "Whatever you're afraid of," he says, evenly, "I suggest you

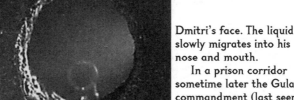

check yourself out of here as soon as you can. Start living your life."

Cassandra is taken aback. "Now is not a real good time," she says, nervously.

Werber steps forward. "Cassandra is experiencing the sensation that she is about to be called," he says.

Cassandra says, urgently, "Now is a time of war and stress among the alien nations. The different races are in upheaval. And I will be summoned to a place just like Duane Barry!"

His patience wearing thin, Mulder tells Cassandra that Duane Barry is dead. "He died in a room after I'd been interrogating him. After he received a visit from some men from our government."

Cassandra says, "Oh, I'm sure the government is involved. They don't want us to know about it all."

"Cassandra—"

Mulder turns away, troubled.

He says, "There was a time when I would have believed what you were saying. Without a doubt."

"There is no *doubt*, Mr. Mulder," says Cassandra. "I know what I've experienced. I have been through the terror and the tests more times than I can count. I've had an unborn fetus taken from me. But they're not here for the reasons you might think. They're here to deliver a message. Except something has gone wrong. There are other forces at work. They're going to be calling me. I can feel it. And you of all people need to know about this. Because you're the one who can do something."

Mulder stares at Cassandra, not unsympathetically.

"I'm not," he says, finally, then looks at Werber, and leaves.

In another part of the Siberian gulag Dmitri lies pinned under a lattice of wire mesh last seen in "Tunguska" (4X09). The doctor watches him through a small, wire mesh–covered window. The window slides shut. In the ceiling, a small metal door slides open. After one more moment of sheer terror, droplets of black oil—last seen in "Terma" (4X10)—fall down onto

Dmitri's face. The liquid slowly migrates into his nose and mouth.

In a prison corridor sometime later the Gulag commandment (last seen in "Tunguska") walks briskly, the corrupt guard alongside him.

"Why was I not informed of this?" he demands angrily, in Russian.

"Krycek was giving orders," says the guard.

He tells the commandment how the boy was captured and that all the others at the site were burned alive.

"What did the boy say about this?" asks the commandant.

"I don't know," says the guard. "Only Krycek knows."

The two men enter the chamber where Dmitri was exposed to the alien oil. The boy is long gone, but the doctor who performed the test is hanging by his neck from the ceiling, dead.

The *Uroff-Koltoff Star of Russia*—a rusting, nondescript freighter—steams out of the port of Vladivostock and into the open ocean. Below deck Krycek enters a small compartment near the engine room. He speaks to someone lying at his feet.

"I've brought you water," he says in Russian. "Can you hear me? If you can hear me, I need you to nod your head."

Dmitri—his eyes, mouth, and nose sutured crudely shut—moves his head slightly. Krycek reaches down and mops his forehead with a wet rag.

"We're gonna take good care of you," he murmurs in English.

In Washington, D.C., Dana Scully, deep in thought, walks down a corridor of the FBI Building. She is intercepted by a young agent, who introduces himself as Jeffrey Spender.

"Is there something I can help you with, Agent Spender?" says Scully.

Spender replies, "I feel kind of funny approaching you like this. I just haven't been able to reach Agent Mulder."

"About what?" says Scully.

Spender takes a deep breath. "About somebody he's been talking to. Somebody who claims to be an alien abductee. Who I'd really prefer he weren't talking to."

Spender pauses. Scully looks at him, a bit irritated.

"Are you going to tell me who this is?" she asks.

Spender says, "This is going to sound weird. It's, um, my mother."

Scully is taken aback. Spender is uncomfortable and embarrassed.

"It's a very long story," he says. "She's . . . an exceptional person, but for reasons that are probably kind of obvious, I'd rather this didn't get out. Appearances being what they are."

Scully asks if Mulder's interest in Mrs. Spender is part of a case.

"No," says Spender.

"Then why is he talking to her?"

"I don't know," says the agent. "She just called me, and she's—she's a very disturbed woman."

He adds, "This is something that caused a lot of pain about twenty years ago. I'm just trying to save myself any extra humiliation. I'd like to build a reputation here, not be given one."

Scully nods. "I think I understand," she says.

At a nondescript office on East 46th Street in New York City, Marita Covarrubias delivers her report to several high-ranking Syndicate members. Quiet Willy, the Syndicate assassin last seen in "Redux II" (5X03) is also present.

Covarrubias says, "Whatever happened in Kazakhstan, there was no one left to give an accurate account."

The Elder asks how many bodies were found. Covarrubias tells him that there were forty-one—all burned beyond recognition by an intense biochemical reaction

none of the UN medics had ever seen.

"Not in the Gulf," she adds, "or any battlefield. The corpses were literally carbonized from the heat."

A few discreet, grim glances are exchanged. Another Elder asks if anyone was testing a new weapon.

"There's no intelligence on that," growls the First Elder.

Covarrubias says, "There's no clear data on the victims or their relationship, but I found at least two of these among the dead."

She holds up a small, clear vial in which two metal computer chips rest. Seeing this, the Well-Manicured Man turns to his colleagues and speaks with quiet authority.

"I think it's fairly certain that all the victims had them," he says. "That what was taking place was a staging. For a group abduction."

The Second Elder says, confused, "What the hell is that?"

The Well-Manicured Man replies, "In the final phases before it begins, there will most likely be assemblies—"

"We're years away from that!" says the Second Elder.

"If we're to believe their timetable," says the First Elder.

"Unless it's already begun," says the Well-Manicured Man.

"We're fifteen years away!" protests the Second Elder.

The conspirators, at an impasse, eye each other. Marita Covarrubias steps forward to offer her opinion.

"I don't think this was planned," she says. "I think something—or someone—set this in motion. An act of war against us and our plans."

She turns toward the Well-Manicured Man. "Krycek was at the burn site. With a unit of Russian soldiers."

The First Elder says, "Krycek did this?"

"He was there," says Covarrubias, "probably acting on the same data we got. But whether he had any direct involvement in what happened, he knows what caused it."

"Knows how?" asks the Well-Manicured Man.

"He captured a boy at the site; a survivor. Someone who saw," says Covarrubias.

The First Elder asks, "What does Krycek want?"

"I don't know," says Covarrubias.

"Well, how do we find out?" asks the Second Elder.

At that moment the telephone on a nearby desk rings. A small red light on the instrument blinks discretely. The Well-Manicured Man glances apprehensively at his colleagues, picks up the receiver, and speaks.

"Yes," he says.

"Well! Look who's answering the Batphone," says a familiar arrogant voice.

"Alex Krycek," says the Well-Manicured Man.

The other Syndicate members snap to attention.

Krycek says, still in the ship's hold, "Those fellas too cheap to offer you a pension plan?"

"Where are you?"

"I'm in town, actually. New York City."

The Well-Manicured Man says, "Just tell us what you want."

Krycek says, "You've been working on a vaccine. Against the black oil."

"Unsuccessfully, you know," says the Well-Manicured Man.

"Yeah, well," says Krycek, "I figured you and your buddies must've been busy while I've been gone."

"Our research continues," says the Well-Manicured Man, huffily.

"I'll take everything you got," says Krycek.

"In exchange for?"

"The boy," says Krycek, who has come to the compartment where Dmitri lies.

"Why is that in our interest?" says the Well-Manicured Man.

"Because without what he knows," says Krycek, "you ain't gonna need any vaccine."

"*What does he know?*" asks the Well-Manicured Man.

Krycek says, "This is my opening offer. The longer you wait, the skinnier this kid gets."

At FBI headquarters Mulder sits at his desk, desultory, doing paperwork. Somebody tosses a newspaper in front of him. There's an article illustrated by a photo-

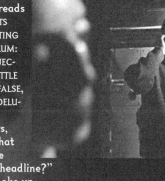

graph of Mulder. Its headline reads MASSACHUSETTS INSTITUTE VISITING LECTURERS FORUM: ALL THIS CONJECTURE ABOUT LITTLE GREEN MEN—FALSE, DANGEROUS, DELUSIONAL.

Scully says, "Shouldn't that be my picture next to that headline?"

Mulder looks up.

"Or is it," says his partner, "that you're just having a little fun?"

Mulder asks, "Do I look like I'm having fun, Scully?"

"You look constipated, actually," she replies.

"Makes sense," says Mulder. "I've had my head up my rear end for the last five years."

Scully sighs and sits across from Mulder. "This wouldn't have anything to do with Cassandra Spender," she says.

"Cassandra Spender," says Mulder, wearily, "is living proof that the truth I've been so boldly seeking for the last five years is the truth of a madman."

"How's that?"

"One more anal-probing, gyro-pyro, levitating-ectoplasm alien anti-matter story, I'm gonna take out my gun and shoot somebody."

Scully smiles wryly. "Well, I guess I'm done here," she says. "You seem to have invalidated your own work. Have a nice life."

Mulder looks at her, not amused. He pushes a file across the desk at Scully.

"How do you know about Cassandra Spender?" he says.

"Her son accosted me in the hall. He's an FBI agent."

"Great," says Mulder, smiling at the irony.

Scully says, "He's of the same opinion as you, by the way. That she's not well."

Mulder leans back in his chair.

"You know," he says, aggravation mixed with regret, "you try to reveal

what's hidden, you try to incite people with the facts, but they'd rather believe some insane nonsense, refusing to believe what our government is capable of."

Scully stares at her partner, her opinion unreadable. "You've come a long way, Mulder," she says evenly.

"Yeah and still nobody believes me."

Scully looks up from the file, troubled.

"What?" says Mulder.

Scully says, "Cassandra Spender was abducted at Skyland Mountain," she says. "That's where I was taken. That's where Duane Barry took me."

Mulder frowns, irritated. "The woman is a nut, Scully," he says.

"And it says here," says Scully, "that she has an implant. At the base of her neck."

"Where the government no doubt removed her brain," says Mulder, getting up abruptly to leave. "Isn't that what her son stopped you to say, Scully?"

"No," says Scully, reading the file intently. "He asked if you would please not talk about this with anyone."

"Wish granted," says Mulder, curtly, before exiting.

That evening, on a country road twenty miles from Skyland Mountain, a long, unbroken line of cars heads toward the Virginia recreation area. At a ranger station a bearded man at the wheel of a Volkswagen van nervously shines his flashlight at a road map. A ranger comes out of his guard shack with a clipboard in hand, regarding the man with suspicion.

"Hi!" says the bearded man, hesitantly. "I'm looking for, uh, I'm looking for—"

"You're looking for what?" asks the ranger.

"A—a mountain," says the man.

"You and everybody else," snorts the ranger.

"How's that?"

"Well, you're a little late to the party," says the ranger, making out a pass. "Six dollars. Hope you find some parking."

The man nods, confused, and pockets the parking pass.

In her hospital room that night Cassandra Spender sits near her window,
pressing her finger to the glass. She lifts her finger slightly, then admires—or at least inspects with great curiosity—the oily fingerprint it leaves. Someone enters the room, quietly, behind her.

"Cassandra?" says a woman's voice. "Ms. Spender?"

Cassandra turns around. "Yes?"

Scully shuts the door.

Cassandra says, "Oh, yes. Do I know you? Of course I do."

"I don't think so," says Scully.

"No, I'm sure of it," says Cassandra, swiveling her wheelchair so as to stare at Scully intently. "Are you a doctor?"

"Uh, yes," says Scully. "But not a practicing one. My name is Dana Scully, and I'd like to ask you some questions."

"Questions about what?"

Scully hesitates briefly. "I think you should know," she says, gently, "I learned about you from your son."

She tells Cassandra that she's an FBI agent, and that Jeffrey Spender has asked her to prevent her story from getting out.

Scully adds, "I guess I'm betraying that by coming here, but I—I'm here for more personal reasons, actually. I took the liberty of reading your medical file."

Cassandra, thrilled by this unexpected intimacy, smiles knowingly. "You're feeling it, too, aren't you?" she says. "Here."

She reaches out to Scully and gently touches the back of her neck. Scully senses their connection and is frightened.

Cassandra says, "You wake up at night, knowing you need to be somewhere, but you don't know where it is. Like you forgot an appointment you didn't know you had."

"That's not why I'm here," says Scully, fighting to maintain her distance. "No," she adds. "I'm here because I—because I wanted to tell you that you should not remove the thing that you have in your neck. Not without possible consequences. I became very ill."

Cassandra smiles. "I'd never dream of removing it. I want to go. Wherever it is. Oh, they have so much to teach us! You being a doctor, you'd want to know—

they're great healers. Maybe that's why you were chosen."

On the road to Skyland Mountain the bearded man in the VW van drives anxiously through the smoky darkness. On both sides of the road cars have been abandoned with their doors open and interior lights illuminated. Out of the gloom comes a frantic, terrified man running directly at his vehicle.

"Oh my God!" says the bearded man, more out of confusion than fear.

The frantic man runs smack into the VW's windshield, bounces off, then slides to the locked passenger door and tries to pull it open.

"Help me!" he pleads.

Behind him appears a man with no face, holding a metallic wand. The faceless man presses his wand into the running man's back, setting him on fire. The burning man writhes in pain and terror as the driver watches helplessly.

At Skyland Mountain the next morning, policemen, rescue personnel, and TV newsmen rush through the smoky fog, assessing the scope of the calamity. Mulder gets out of his car and walks quickly through the scene. He joins up with Scully inside a makeshift morgue. The body count is in the dozens and growing.

"Are there any survivors?" asks Mulder.

"No," says Scully. "Not as of this moment."

Mulder says, "From the smell—"

"They've all been burned," says Scully. "There are plenty more being bagged as we speak."

Mulder asks his partner if there are any preliminary theories. All Scully can say is that it appears that most of the victims came by car. Most of the dead were congregated in a wooded area a short distance off the road.

"Self-immolation?" asks Mulder.

"There's no evidence of that right now," says Scully. "There's no accelerants, no incendiary device."

"And what was their relationship to each other? Were they families?"

"Well, there's no

way to ID their bodies right now," says Scully. "That's going to be a painstaking dental process."

Mulder looks around. He won't meet Scully's eyes.

"Mulder, why are you tiptoeing around the obvious fact, here?" she says. "I mean, this is Skyland Mountain. We're right back here on Skyland Mountain."

Mulder asks, "And you think it's related to your abduction from the same place?"

"Well, you can't deny the connection," says Scully.

"You think this is some kind of abduction scenario?"

"I'm not saying that," she replies.

"Do you have any evidence of that?"

"What do you mean by evidence?"

Mulder says, "That's what I'm asking you."

Scully sighs. "Well, are you going to give me your theory, then?"

"No," says Mulder. "I'm going to give you an explanation."

At the Syndicate office in Manhattan the assembled notables watch a news report of the carnage.

Marita Covarrubias says, grimly, "This is the same scene we saw in Kazakhstan."

The Second Elder says, panic in his voice, "What the hell is going on? This is in our own backyard."

"This is no good!" says the First Elder. "I don't like being in the dark about this."

The Well-Manicured Man appears more annoyed than afraid. "Someone," he says, "is going to great lengths to sabotage our work."

"Who?" asks the Second Elder.

"One way or another," says the Well-Manicured Man, "We'd better find out, before it's determined we're unable to handle this ourselves. We have to put a stop to it before the Colonists intervene."

Without a signal from anyone Quiet Willy—the assassin—rises immediately and leaves the room.

On another monitor—this one in Cassandra Spender's hospital room—a similar news report plays. A list of the deceased victims scrolls down the screen. Cassandra watches tearfully. Behind her, Mulder and Scully open the door, and enter.

"Cassandra? You called us?" says Scully.

Cassandra says, plaintively, "This is not supposed to be happening. I knew these people. They were friends of mine."

"Friends from where?" asks Scully.

"A long time ago," says Cassandra. "This is not supposed to be happening. Not like this."

She turns to Mulder. "You have to do something about it."

Mulder says, "What would you like me to do?"

"You have to stop it."

"Stop who?"

"I don't know."

Scully stares at the fingerprint smudges on Cassandra's window. They look like a row of bullet holes or the stars in the constellation Cassiopeia. A depressed Mulder turns to leave the room, Scully following. They pass Jeffrey Spender on their way out. Cassandra's son, struggling to control his anger, introduces himself to Mulder.

"I'd asked you to leave her alone," says Spender, to his fellow agent.

Scully intervenes. "Your mother called us about the incident in Virginia," she says. "She said she knew some of the dead."

"Of course she did," says Spender. "They were in the same ridiculous cult as she used to be."

"There you have it," says Mulder.

Scully asks, "She was in a cult?"

"A UFO cult," says Spender, distastefully, "who believed they were going to be carried to immortality in some kind of flying motherwheel."

"I'm sorry," says Mulder. "We won't be bothering you or your mother anymore."

Mulder turns away from Spender and walks down the hallway, Scully several paces behind him. They pass a man waiting in the corridor—it is Quiet Willy. He waits until the agents are out of sight before entering Cassandra Spender's room.

On the *Uroff-Koltoff Star of Russia*, now docked in New York Harbor, Krycek keeps the disfigured Dmitri alive—barely—by squeezing a dirty rag and dripping a stream of water onto his face. Krycek leaves the compartment and is startled to see a waiting Marita Covarrubias.

"You think you can pull this off, don't you?" says Covarrubias.

With his good arm Krycek seizes the woman, then kisses her roughly on the lips. Covarrubias returns the kiss; in the midst of their passionate embrace Krycek murmurs his deepest desires.

"They give me what I want," he says, "I'm going to rule the world."

Covarrubias gasps, passionately, "We've got them on their knees, Alex. Let's get out of this hole."

In a darkened bedroom the stars shine through an uncurtained window. Dana Scully awakens with a start, gets out of bed, and—rubbing the back of her neck—stares out into the night sky. She is disturbed by something, affected by some troubling, unknown force.

In the freighter's hold Krycek walks back to the compartment where Dmitri is imprisoned. But the little room is empty and behind him stands the Well-Manicured Man, holding an automatic pistol.

"Well," says the Syndicate leader, angrily. "Where's the boy?"

At the FBI Building the next morning an unhappy-looking Scully enters her office to find Mulder already at work.

"Are you ready for this?" Mulder says. "I've been going over the initial forensics and pathology reports from the incident at Skyland Mountain and, while the event itself is unexplained, I think it's less than a mystery who's involved. At least for me, and certainly for you."

Mulder walks to a light box and clips up a set of X rays.

He says, "Our pathologists here haven't finalized their reports, but I had three victims selected at random. That's how I found these. Small pieces of what looks like metal in the charred cervical tissue. Here, here, and here. Implants.

"I followed up with the families of the three victims, and found that none had any cult associations, but two out of the three belonged to local Mutual UFO Networks. And both of them claimed abduction experiences, and both of them were being treated by mental health practitioners over the last few months."

"For what?" asks Scully.

Mulder hands her another file from her desk. She reads aloud, "'Major Depressive Disorder characterized by periods of sustained anxiety and paranoia.' 'Patient believes he will be contacted or called to an undisclosed place where he will be abducted by aliens.'"

Scully looks up at Mulder. He's made a major leap.

"The implants triggered those responses," he says. "Those people were led to Skyland Mountain."

"By whom?" asks Scully.

"By the same government that put the implant in you. To function as a homing mechanism."

"Mulder, that doesn't make sense," says Scully.

"Why not?" says Mulder.

"A tracking system using military app satellite technology. To monitor test subjects or to stage what people might otherwise believe are alien abductions."

"But they weren't abducted," says Scully. "They were led to their deaths. And for what purpose?"

"I don't know that yet," says Mulder.

The phone rings. Mulder moves to answer it.

"Hell, Mulder," says Scully, hesitantly,

"maybe you shouldn't be so quick to rule out what Cassandra Spender has to say."

Astonished at his partner's change of heart, Mulder stares at her, nods solemnly, then answers the phone.

"Mulder—" he says.

"Agent Mulder. This is Marita Covarrubias. Is this a secure line we're on?"

"Yes."

"You were at Skyland Mountain. Are you aware of a UN report of a similar incident in the former Soviet Union?"

"No."

"I was in Kazakhstan, Agent Mulder. There is a connection. I have someone who knows it. I have him with me now."

In fact, Dmitri sits in a gray sedan parked behind Covarrubias. The Russian boy is tugging at the stitches that have sewn closed his eyes.

"Where are you?" asks Mulder.

"At a pay phone on Skodol Road, just off the I-90. Come here, wait for my call. For directions."

Marita turns to see Dmitri standing outside the phone booth, black oil leaking from his wounds. The boy reaches for the glass door. She gasps, and drops the phone.

"Marita?" says Mulder.

There is no answer—and Scully is gone. She is in the FBI corridor, walking in a trancelike state. She bends to drink from a water fountain, then straightens up, expressionless.

Near a busy highway in the D.C. area Mulder stops his car, gets out, and looks at the booth Marita Covarrubias phoned him from. The receiver dangles off the hook and there is a thin film of oil on the booth. He picks up the phone and dials. His call is answered in Cassandra's hospital room.

"Hello?" says Mulder. "Who's this?"

"This is Special Agent Spender. Who's this?"

"This is Fox Mulder."

"Why are you calling here?"

"I'm actually looking for Agent Scully. I haven't been able to reach her. She said that—"

"She's not here," says Spender, curtly. Behind him stands Dr. Werber.

"Nor is my mother."

Mulder asks, "What are you talking about?"

"She's gone from her room," he replies.

"Gone where?" asks Mulder.

"Look, she's just gone," says Spender, angrily. "Don't you get it? She's got nowhere to go."

That night the stars shine down on Ruskin Dam—a magnificent Depression-era structure with an illuminated spillway. On an attached cantilever bridge a silent crowd mills aimlessly on the roadway. Among them are Cassandra Spender, Quiet Willy, and Dmitri—his eyes no longer sewn shut. And Scully.

"Look!" someone yells.

The pilgrims look up to see a bright light in the pitch-dark sky. The light slowly approaches the bridge, growing brighter still. When it is directly overhead it bursts into dozens of individual lights, mesmerizing the people below even more. The lights pass, as if in formation, overhead.

Slowly, Scully walks slowly toward Cassandra Spender. The wheelchair-bound woman reaches out her hand.

At the other end of the bridge a man bursts into flames, and screams in pain and terror. Behind him are two faceless aliens, metallic wands in their hands. Scully is horrified—and rooted to the spot. A faceless alien approaches her.

To be continued . . .

back story:

Chris Owens heard all the rumors: That he was the replacement for David Duchovny; that he was the threatened replacement for David Duchovny; that he would appear in eight episodes next season; that David Duchovny would appear in eight episodes next season; that his casting was a sure sign that the show would remain in Vancouver; that his casting was a diabolically misleading sign that the show would be leaving in Vancouver.

"People kept telling me to be prepared for big news," smiles the good-natured thirty-six-year-old actor, standing on the *X-Files* set during the filming of the fifth season's final episode. "And I kept asking myself: 'What is it?'"

In truth, the real news is that Owens—a tall, thin man who had labored in semianonymity for nearly half his life—is neither a bargaining chip, an insurance policy, or a plot device. What he is is simply a talented actor on his way up, with a role that had been written especially for him, and inserted into the center of one of the highest-profile television series in the world.

"Believe it or not, I didn't have to audition for the part of Jeffrey Spender," says Owens, incredulously. "Which is a great privilege. The most substantial I've gotten so far."

Owens smiles happily when recounting pleasant conversations with the likes of Duchovny, Gillian Anderson, and Chris Carter. It wasn't too long ago that he was bartending and waiting tables between roles. Many of these roles had titles like "Soldier" and "Young Security Guard." When asked about this period of his life Owens nods, smiles slightly, and says proudly, "I've supported myself since I was eighteen."

Owens was born and raised in Toronto. His father was a radio broadcaster; his mother a jazz

singer; and his stepfather a musician-turned-magician-turned-optician. He studied acting at the University of Toronto and at the prestigious Herbert Berghof Studio in New York City. "I was there for two stints of three and four months apiece," he says. "It was a great learning experience."

Back in Toronto, he had his "career ups and downs", including small roles in the Tom Cruise film *Cocktail*; the cable TV movie *Almost Golden: The Jessica Savitch Story*; and several stretches filled primarily with food-service and other temporary jobs.

In mid–1996 he moved west to Vancouver in search of further opportunity, which found him in the form of "Musings of a Cigarette-Smoking Man" (4X07). He guest-starred in that episode as the Young Cigarette-Smoking Man, messing with the minds of such reimagined notables as Lee Harvey Oswald and James Earl Ray, and giving such a cool, tightly controlled, and sometimes frightening performance that he got almost as much notice as "Musings," one of the most noticeable episodes of the fourth season.

Then came a real fright: After "Musings" wrapped, he applied for several waiter jobs and for the first time in his working life didn't get a single one. "Nobody knew me in the Vancouver restaurant world," says Owens, wryly. "But luckily, after a little while *The X-Files* called me and said they needed me for a flashback," says Owens.

That flashback was as the Young Cigerette-Smoking Man in "Demons" (4X23); a standalone episode written by executive producer R. W. Goodwin. Shortly afterward, he was also cast in an early second-season hour of *Millennium*.

Clearly, he was now part of Chris Carter's extended stock company. Early in *The X-Files's* fifth season, Owens was called in to audition— naked-faced—for the nearly impossible role of the Great Mutato, the grotesquely featured centerpiece of "The Post-Modern Prometheus" (5X06). He won the role and the right to guest star, completely unrecognizable, beneath several layers of elaborate and unwieldy prosthetic makeup. Acing this exhausting assignment earned him a prized back-handed compliment from Carter.

"After 'Prometheus,' we ran into each other at a local bar one evening," says Owens, grinning. "When Chris saw me he shook my hand and said, 'I didn't know they served guys with two faces here.'"

What Owens didn't know was that another admirer—David Duchovny—had taken careful notice of Owens and recommended to Carter that he be brought back on to the show as soon as possible. Thinking much along the same lines, Carter took advantage of Owens's Young Cigarette-Smoking Man heritage to create Jeffrey Spender; a foil to Fox Mulder and a character whose murky and Mulder-like alleged genetic connections to the Cigarette-Smoking Man could be exploited to the fullest.

That's when the rumors started. "I always knew David wasn't leaving," scoffs Owens. He does, however, admit that the announcement that *The X-Files* was moving to Los Angeles came "exactly one hour after I'd figured out it was definitely staying in Vancouver."

A final update: After the big announcement things started moving even faster. Signed for approximately half the episodes of the sixth season, Owens filled out the paperwork for his green card and sublet an apartment in Hollywood. Left behind in Vancouver was his steady girlfriend, law student Tara Parker, but Owens hopes that this state of affairs is strictly temporary.

As this volume goes to press, Owens is studying his Los Angeles street maps; signing photographs for posting at his new dry cleaner; and marveling at the upward curve his career trajectory has been taking lately.

"What a way to get to L.A!" exults Owens. "Never in my wildest dreams did I imagine anything like this happening."

Ⓧ

Veronica Cartwright (*Money Talks, The Right Stuff*), who plays Cassandra Spender, is the older sister of actress Angela Cartwright (*Lost in Space, Make Room for Daddy*).

Ⓧ

For her role in "Patient X" and "The Red and the Black," Cartwright received an Emmy nomination for Outstanding Guest Actress in a Drama Series.

the red and the black

The world turned upside down:
Recovering from a near-death
experience, Scully is convinced
that her memories of alien enounters
are true. For his part Mulder clings
to skepticism and science and uncovers
new, even more dangerous, conspiracies.

EPISODE: 5X14
FIRST AIRED: March 8, 1998
EDITOR: Heather MacDougall
WRITTEN BY: Chris Carter & Frank Spotnitz
DIRECTED BY: Chris Carter
GUEST STARS:

Mitch Pileggi (AD Walter Skinner)
Chris Owens (Special Agent Jeffrey Spender)
Nicholas Lea (Alex Krycek)
Veronica Cartwright (Cassandra Spender)
Laurie Holden (Marita Covarrubias)
William B. Davis (The Cigarette-Smoking Man)
John Neville (The Well-Manicured Man)
Alex Shostak, Jr. (Dmitri)
Don S. Williams (First Elder)
John Moore (Second Elder)
George Murdock (Third Elder)
Willy Ross (Quiet Willy)
Brian Thompson (The Bounty Hunter)
Jim Jansen (Dr. Heitz Werber)
Chapelle Jaffe (Dr. Patou)
Michal Suchanek (Young Jeffrey Spender)
Derek Thomas Versteeg (MP)
Jack Finn (Young Boy)
Jenn Forgie (Nurse)
Klodyne Rodney (Medic)
PRINCIPAL SETTINGS:
Ruskin Dam, Pennsylvania;
Washington, D.C.; New York City;
Wiekamp Air Force Base, West Virginia;
Silver Springs, Maryland

An old-fashioned IBM
Selectric typewriter; someone,
somewhere is writing a very personal
letter. The letter reads:

Dear Son,

*I hope this letter finds you well. I get
reports of you from time to time and
follow your progress with great interest.*

*I know these letters come as a sur-
prise. You must wonder about me after
all that's happened. But time is passing
quickly. I fear you will be put off course
and stray from your destiny.*

*I remind myself of a Navajo story.
Twin war gods come to their father,
seeking magic and weapons to eliminate
the monsters of the world. My hope is the
same for you, and we might reconcile
the differences between us.*

Signing himself "Your Loving
Father," the writer pulls his letter out
of the machine.

On a snowy backcountry road a
young boy wearing snowshoes tramps
steadily uphill. He tramps past a cluster
of mailboxes, turns down a small
adjoining road, and reaches a tiny,
Ted Kaczynski–type cabin. He knocks
on the front door; it opens part way.
A hand extending a red envelope—and
a Canadian $5 bill—emerges.

"Thanks, mister," says the young boy.
"I'll mail it off right away."

The door slams shut. The boy turns
and starts to walk away, but stops to read
the address on the envelope.

"Federal Bureau of Investigation," he
reads, his eyes growing wide with awe.

He glances back at the house and
turns again to leave. Inside the cabin,
someone pulls aside a window curtain
to watch him leave.

At Ruskin Dam in Pennsylvania,
the morning following the alien massacre
and abduction in "Patient X" (5X13) is
filled with death, confusion, and fear.
A red search-and-rescue helicopter hovers
over the bridge, spotting numerous fire-
ravaged corpses—as well as Cassandra
Spender's empty wheelchair and the fire-
blackened body of the Syndicate assassin,
Quiet Willy.

Ambulances, police cars, and fire
trucks arrive at the scene as does
Fox Mulder. He leaves his car and runs
toward the bridge, anxiously scanning

the still-smoking corpses. One of them,
badly disfigured, has a shock of red hair.
He braces himself and leans over for a
closer look.

"Agent Mulder!" shouts Assistant
Director Skinner, from the opposite end
of the span.

Mulder straightens. "Was she here?"
he demands. "Is she here?"

"Yes," says Skinner. "And the medics
are all over her."

"She's alive?"

"Yes," says Skinner. "They're working
on her now. Come on."

Skinner hustles his subordinate into
the makeshift triage tent where Scully lies
on a cot, unconscious. The AD tells
Mulder that his partner was found by the
search-and-rescue pilot, with fifty other
survivors, in a nearby woods. She is suffering from minor burns and a severe and
highly abnormal electrolyte depletion.

"She's in vasogenic shock," says a
nearby medic, brusquely. "And unless you
gents are doctors, you're in the way. This
woman needs to get to a hospital."

The FBI agents move aside as Scully is
lifted onto a litter. They follow anxiously
as she is loaded
onto the rescue
helicopter.

"What hap-
pened here, Agent
Mulder?" shouts
Skinner, over the
engine noise.

Mulder replies,
"The answer just
got loaded onto
that chopper."

They watch as
the helicopter lifts
off and speeds
away. For the first time they notice
Jeffrey Spender, also part of the disaster
team, talking to several rescue workers
nearby. Spender spots Mulder and
Skinner and walks grimly toward the two
men.

"Can I talk to you, please?" he says
to Mulder, pushing past the AD. "Is she
here? Was she found?"

"Who?" says Walter Skinner, over-
hearing.

"My mother," says Spender, walking
away angrily.

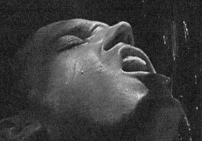

In an undisclosed hospital a female physician, Dr. Patou, tends to a quarantined patient. The Well-Manicured Man, wearing surgical scrubs, stands next to her.

"I'm fairly certain it's not a question of dosage," she says. "We've administered three intramuscular injections over the past twenty hours, since we found her on the roadside."

"And you've seen no effect?" says the Well-Manicured Man.

"No," says Dr. Patou. "It doesn't look good. At all."

On the bed below her lies an unconscious Marita Covarrubias. The Well-Manicured Man dons a surgical mask and lifts her eyelid. Globules of black alien oil swim across her eyeball. He lets Covarrubias's eyelid down, turns anxiously to the doctor, and glances upward at a circle of grim-faced Elders looking down from an observation gallery.

At Memorial Hospital in Washington Dana Scully, in her own hospital bed, lies hooked up to monitors and intravenous lines. A hand reaches down to stroke her hair. She awakens.

"What time is it?" asks Scully, groggily.

"What time is it?" asks Mulder, standing over her with a broad smile of relief. "Time to thank your lucky stars."

Scully asks, "Why are you laughing?"

"I'm not laughing at you," says Mulder, helping his partner into a sitting position. "I'm just very happy to be standing here talking to you, that's all."

Scully looks around her, confused. "Mulder, what am I doing here?"

"You were airlifted here in vasogenic shock," he says.

"From what?"

"You don't remember?" says Mulder.

"Mulder—" says Scully, anxiously.

On a silent wall-mounted television equipped with closed captioning a news report on the deaths at Ruskin Dam is playing. With mounting horror, Scully watches the carnage and the rescue workers transporting body bags from the site.

Mulder asks, "Is any of this coming back to you?"

"I was there?" Mulder nods.

"Doing what?" asks Scully.

Mulder says, "I was hoping you were going to answer that question for me."

A nurse enters the room and insists that Scully be allowed to rest. Mulder nods, and prepares to leave.

"Mulder—" says Scully.

"I'll come back," he says, exiting, and runs into Jeffrey Spender in the hallway.

"They didn't find her," says Spender. "She wasn't among the victims. They only found her wheelchair."

"I'm sorry," says Mulder.

Spender eyes him angrily. "What were you doing with her?" he asks.

"What was I doing with her?" says Mulder. "What makes you think we had anything to do with this?"

Spender is unconvinced. "My mom's a cripple," he says. "She hasn't driven a car in I don't know how long. They found her wheelchair a hundred and thirty miles from the hospital where, I'm now told, Agent Scully was meeting with her privately."

"Look—" says Mulder.

"No! *You* look!" says Spender. "She's my mother. She's not some test subject of yours."

"Your mother will be found," says Mulder, evenly.

Spender replies, his temper barely under control, "All I want is for you to leave it alone. Is that too much to ask?"

At the New York City dock the Russian freighter is still berthed; a weak-looking Krycek is chained into the same compartment in which he'd kept Dmitri. The Well-Manicured Man approaches, carrying a bucket of water.

"You're probably thirsty," says the Well-Manicured Man.

Krycek eyes him sullenly. "Remind me to complain to the captain about the service," he says.

"You may well have that opportunity," says his captor, dryly. "This ship is bound back to Vladivostock tomorrow. I gather there'll be quite an enthusiastic homecoming."

He squeezes a wet dirty rag and drips some water into Krycek's mouth. Krycek sucks at it greedily, then stops, thinks, and spits it out.

"Do you have the boy?" asks Krycek.

"No," growls the Well-Manicured Man. "Ms. Covarrubias took him."

Krycek studies his captor warily.

The Well-Manicured Man adds, "Your alliance with her was as misguided as ours. But it appears she was unaware of the consequences of her deception. You were clever. Infect the boy to insure infection of anyone would try to learn what he knows, who would cheat you."

Krycek smiles fiercely. "Then where's the boy?" he asks.

"Dead. The victim of another mysterious holocaust. Unable now to tell what he knew or saw."

"Then you've got no choice but to deal with me," says Krycek.

The Well-Manicured Man stands. "I'm afraid there's no deal to be made," he says.

Krycek scowls. "I'm the only one who knows what those incidents are. What they mean. I know what that boy saw."

"You've as much as told me what I need to know," says the Well-Manicured Man, evenly.

Krycek says, "You know nothing!"

"If the boy was your trump card," says the Well-Manicured Man, "why infect him unless you could also cure him? With a vaccine. One developed by the Russians. One that works."

The Well-Manicured Man eyes Krycek intently for a long second. "It would mean," he says, slowly, "that resistance to the alien colonists is now possible."

"You're dreaming!" sneers Krycek.

His captor ignores this. "Do you have the vaccine?" he says.

"You need what I know!"

"*Do you have the vaccine?!*"

Krycek stares at him defiantly, but the Well-Manicured Man won't be defied. He kicks over the pail of water and it soaks under Krycek. He turns his back and starts for the metal door.

Krycek calls after him. "Give you the means to save Covarrubias after what she did?" he says.

The Well-Manicured Man turns and faces him.

"Give you the means to save yourself," he says, coolly.

At Wiekamp Air Force Base a projectile slants down from the sky, crash-landing in a dark field and bursting into a bright-orange sheet of flame. At the epicenter of the firestorm is a large, triangular-shaped craft. Sirens wail and emergency vehicles race toward the site. Next to the downed spaceship stands a dark figure—one of the faceless aliens. He bends over an injured or dead comrade, and looks up to face a circle of military policemen, their assault rifles pointed directly at him.

In Scully's hospital room the next day the agent sits up in bed. She looks, uncomprehending, at a series of photographs of the Ruskin Dam disaster.

"I don't know what to say," says Scully. "I mean, I don't have the first clue. There's nothing here—"

Mulder says, "Well, at least you're not alone. None of the other survivors has been able to give a cogent account, either."

Scully stares at one last photograph. "Mulder, I have never been here. I couldn't tell you how to get here, let alone drive it."

Mulder asks, "Do you remember when you last saw Cassandra Spender?"

"She was there, too?"

Mulder nods, obviously concerned. Scully also is very worried about this.

Mulder says, "I ran more X rays. I haven't told anybody yet what I found, though."

"You found more implants?"

Mulder nods again. "That would explain why you were directed to the site. And why you can't remember. It would explain the sensation Cassandra Spender was describing, her abduction fantasies. It would explain Skyland Mountain."

Scully says, "No, but it wouldn't explain why they want to kill me. And it doesn't explain why I survived."

Mulder leans forward. "It all comes down to a question, Scully. One that hasn't been answered or I don't even

think honestly addressed. Who made that chip in your neck?"

Now Mulder is angry. "That chip was found in a military research facility. *Our government made that chip.* Implanted it in your neck as part of a secret military project to develop a biochemical weapon to monitor your immunity or to destroy you like a lab rat if the truth were to be exposed.

"Your cancer, your cure, everything that's been happening to you now—it all points to that chip. The truth I've been searching for? The truth is *in* you."

Scully considers this in silence for a few moments, then finally, in a voice barely audible, speaks.

She says, "Mulder, when I met you five years ago, you told me that your sister had been abducted by aliens. That that event had marked you so deeply that nothing else mattered. I didn't believe you. But I followed you on nothing more than your faith that the truth was out there. Based not on fact, not on science, but on your memories that your sister had been taken from you. Those memories were all that you had."

Mulder says, "I don't trust those memories now."

Scully says, "Well, whether you trust them or not, they've led you here. And me. But I have no memories to either trust nor distrust."

Her voice rises and gains conviction. "And if you ask me now to follow you again, to stand behind you in what you now believe, without knowing what happened to me out there, without those memories, I can't. I won't."

Mulder stands, stares at the window, and turns.

He says, "If I could give you those memories, if I could prove that I was right and what I believed for so long was wrong—"

Scully turns to her partner, deeply troubled.

"Is that what you really want?" she asks.

In the observation gallery above the quarantine room a conclave of Syndicate members looks at a photograph of the faceless alien pilot in military custody. The First Elder comments that the alien's facial scarring appears to be self-mutilation, done as protection.

"Protection against what?" asks another Elder.

"Infection by the black oil," says the First Elder.

He turns to the Well-Manicured Man and explains that the alien was the sole survivor of the West Virginia crash.

The other Elder asks, "What the hell is he?"

"He's an alien rebel," says the Well-Manicured Man, fascinated. He adds, "This is what the boy saw in Russia. The last face the dead saw at Skyland Mountain. And most surely who killed our man at the dam in Pennsylvania. He's a resistance fighter. Against the alien colonists. This is what Alex Krycek knew. That a war had begun."

The First Elder asks, "What good is that knowledge? Without the vaccine against the black oil, no one can survive."

"We have a vaccine," says the Well-Manicured Man. "Developed by the Russians. Stolen by Krycek. Given to me."

He looks down from the observation gallery at Dr. Patou, preparing to give Marita Covarrubias, still unconscious, an injection of the amber-colored fluid Krycek stole in "Patient X" (5X13).

"You see what this means?" says the Well-Manicured Man. "Resistance is possible! We have the weapons and the magic in hand!"

"We don't know the vaccine works," says the First Elder.

"It will!" says the Well-Manicured Man. "And if it doesn't, we have a new alliance to be made."

"Side with the Resistance?" says the First Elder, shocked.

"It's suicide!" protests his fellow Elder. "They'll squash

us as they do them. We must turn the rebel over."

"But first," says the Well-Manicured Man, sharply, "wait until we know the vaccine works."

He stares down his fellow Syndicate members, daring them to defy him, then raps on the table. It is a signal to Dr. Patou. She lifts Covarrubias's eyelid—the black oil still swims across her pupil. The physician picks up a large hypodermic needle, examines it for a moment, then carefully plunges it into her patient's arm.

At Dr. Heitz Werber's office in Silver Springs, Scully sits uncomfortably on a leather couch. Mulder is perched—just as uneasily—at its other end.

"Hi, Dana. Nice to meet you again," says Werber, facing her. "Are you okay with this?"

"I'm okay," she says, unconvincingly.

Werber says, "There's a few things I want to say I didn't touch on over the phone. I'm sure Agent Mulder told you how this works. Have you ever been hypnotized?"

"Uh, once," says Scully. "But I have to be honest with you. I didn't have much luck."

Werber tells her he hopes they can do better today. He explains that he will put her into a hypnagogic trance—a mental state where some of the mind's filtering process is relaxed.

Scully nods. A female assistant starts a tape recorder and lowers Scully to a reclining position.

Werber says, "I'm going to ask you to go back to the place we talked about on the phone. Just close your eyes, and take long, deep breaths. Relaxing all parts of your body. Long, deep breaths. Relaxing your hands, and your feet. Relaxing your jaw, your pelvis. Long, deep breaths. Back to the night place."

Scully relaxes a bit despite herself. "I don't think this is working," she says, and flashes back immediately to the moment on the Ruskin Dam bridge when the first alien spacecraft hovered over her.

"Oh, my God! Oh, my God! Oh, my God!"

She sits bolt upright, still in a trance. Mulder edges closer.

"Where are you, Dana?" asks Werber.

"Are you in the night place?"

"Yes."

Scully is standing next to Quiet Willy. Cassandra Spender, in her wheelchair, is on her other side. The spacecraft lifts upward, then speeds away.

"And then it was gone," murmurs Scully. "Oh! No!"

Mulder reaches over to take her hand.

"Oh! They're back!" says Scully, anguished.

"Who?" says Werber.

"They're on fire! Oh, God!"

She sees the burning man before her once again.

"They set them on fire! I can't—"

"Who? Who's doing this?" asks Werber.

"Their faces! They have no faces! They have no eyes! Oh, God. They're coming at us!"

On the bridge Scully stands rooted to the spot, the faceless alien moving toward her. Quiet Willy pulls out his gun and moves toward the attacker. By now, several more humans are in flames.

"They're surrounding us!" says Scully. "They won't stop! They won't stop! There! There's another one! There's another ship! I see it! They were attacking them!"

The second spacecraft arrives over the bridge and the surviving humans look up, as do the alien rebels. Light beams flash down from the craft, setting more bodies on fire.

"Who were they attacking, Dana?" asks Werber.

"The—the faceless men. My God, I can't—"

"Do you want to stop, Dana?"

"No!"

The second spacecraft slowly descends, hovering closer to the bridge.

"Now it's coming at us! Oh, my God! "

Another light beam—this one bigger and stronger than the others—shines directly down to the bridge.

"No! Cassandra!" shouts Scully.

"Where's Cassandra?" asks Werber.

"They're taking her. They're—oh, my God!"

On the bridge, time slows down. As the others watch, arms upraised, Cassandra is slowly levitated by the light beam, floating upward into the spacecraft

"Dana? Dana, I'm going to stop now," says Werber.

He asks her to open her eyes and to come back. Scully slowly—painfully— emerges from her trance. She looks at Mulder, sitting somberly near her.

"You've been here the whole time?" she asks.

Mulder nods grimly, says nothing, and gets up to leave.

In Skinner's office the next day the AD, looking uncomfortable, holds an audiocassette. Mulder and Scully sit across from him.

"I reviewed the tape of the session, as you requested," he says. "I have to say I wasn't prepared for what I heard on this."

"No, sir," says Scully. "Neither was I."

"Agent Mulder?"

"I'm familiar with the regression process and Dr. Werber's work," he says, evenly. "I've heard hundreds of those types of abduction scenarios."

"But what do you make of this one?" asks Skinner.

Mulder says, "The imagery is startling, but not atypical. Bright lights, weightless- ness, stolen memory, lost time—expressed as a close encounter, an abduction, reli- gious rapture, a kind of dark night of the soul."

"Expressed?" says Skinner.

"Described and then interpreted into a linear narrative," says Mulder. "A gestalt impression of a subjective non-linear expe- rience."

"And your interpretation?"

"That Agent Scully witnessed a very powerful event. Not unlike the one I described on my regression tape. Of the false memory of my sister's abduction."

Skinner nods. "Agent Scully?" he says.

Scully says, "I've listened to the tape several times," she says, hesitantly. "And I don't have a clear recollection of what I hear myself saying. But I also don't see any reason why I'd be saying it."

Skinner turns back to Mulder. "I've got a problem," he says. "And the problem is: I've got to head up the investigation into this incident. I don't have the luxury of interpretation. I have to make a report and that report must state a reason, or cite a fact, or at least make an assumption. As I sit here right now I'm unable to do that. I need to know what happened."

"It was staged," says Mulder, abruptly.

"To?"

"To test a classified military project or to cover it up."

"Then what, I want to know," says Skinner, "happened to Cassandra Spender?"

"Cassandra Spender was taken aboard a military aircraft as part of the staging."

Skinner stares at Mulder, and sighs.

He says, "Over the past five years I've doubted you, only to be persuaded by the power of your belief in extraterrestrial phenomenon. And I'm doubting you now, not because of that belief, but because extraterrestrial phenomenon is frankly the more plausible explanation."

Mulder says, curtly, "Then I suggest you put that in your report."

He stands and leaves as a silent Scully trades a searching glance with Skinner.

At the Syndicate medical facility, Dr. Patou lifts Marita Covarrubias's eyelid, then looks up and shakes her head. Black oil still swims in the unconscious woman's eye.

From the observation gallery the Syndicate members watch this. "The vac- cine has no effect," says the First Elder.

"We must give it time!" insists the Well-Manicured Man.

"We must survive first," says the First Elder. "Survival means collaboration."

The Well-Manicured Man protests, "Turn over the alien rebel, and you turn over any hope of resistance."

The First Elder says, turning away from him, "It's already been done."

In the bowels of the FBI building Scully enters her office and sees Jeffrey Spender, who is staring thoughtfully at Mulder's "I Want To Believe" poster.

"I heard about this office," he says. "It really is in the basement." Spender turns to face Scully. "I'm here about my mother. I spoke with Dr. Werber. He said you'd been to his office."

"Did he say why?"

"No," says Spender. "He didn't have to. I'm assuming, knowing the facts I do, that you're wondering about the possibility of alien abduction. I'm sure you know enough about it. Agent Mulder surely pushed the idea."

"No, actually," says Scully, "Agent Mulder hasn't."

Spender replies that he finds this hard to believe. Annoyed, Scully reminds him that he came to the X-Files office to ask about his mother.

"You went to see her," says Spender. "I'd like to know what you talked about."

"We talked about how she was feeling," says Scully, somewhat evasively. "We talked about . . . a lot of things."

"You talked about abduction? About her experiences?" asks Spender. "Did she talk about me?"

"In what way?" says Scully.

Spender turns away. "I've got something here," he says, "that might explain a lot for you."

He slips a videocassette into Mulder's VCR and clicks it on. On the screen is a young boy sitting on a chair in an office much like Werber's. The boy, his eyes closed, is talking to an off-screen interviewer. He says, "And there's a bright light. There's people standing around—"

"That's me. I'm eleven years old," says Spender. He turns away from the screen, but the boy's monologue continues:

"I'm looking up into the sky where the bright light is, and I'm starting to cry. I'm really, really scared and I want to get back to the car, but I can't find my mom. And then I see her.

"There's something in the sky and it's all flashing lights. And it's so bright it hurts my eyes. And—and then she's going up in the sky, and I'm yelling 'Mommy, Mommy, Mommy!' And then I feel my feet, and they aren't on the ground. I'm floating up—"

Spender reaches over and turns off the video. "Seen enough?"

Scully says, "Is that what you were afraid people were going to find out?"

Spender says, "Yes. But not because it's true. None of this happened."

Scully says, "I don't understand."

"I made it up," says Spender. "Or, I should say, my mom did."

"She told you to say those things?"

"Essentially," says Spender. "She told me that story so many times that I believed it. Absolutely. It became a kind of truth when it was really just a substitute."

"For what?" asks Scully.

"For the fact that my dad had left his family and had driven my mom insane.

Only, I was eleven years old and I didn't know it."

Scully frowns at Spender impatiently. "Why are you here, Agent Spender? Why did you show this to me?"

Spender replies, "Because I think the process is bogus—Dr. Werber and his whole regression of memory. It's b.s. It's like having a dream and pretending it's real."

Scully nods curtly. "I think Dr. Werber would beg to differ," she says.

Spender says, angrily, "He indulged and infantilized my mother. For his own purposes. I think he's dangerous, and I think his methods are unsound. And if you went through it, I'd hope you'd question what came out of it."

Scully bristles. "Well, I appreciate your opinion, Agent Spender," she says. "But I don't have a mother feeding me abduction stories."

"You've got Agent Mulder, don't you?" he replies.

Spender adds, "How many times have you heard the stories he's told? How about the one about his own sister?"

Scully does not reply. Spender hits the eject button and pulls out his tape. "Don't let yourself be used," he says.

At Mulder's apartment that night the agent unlocks the front door and lets himself in. He spots a note—that might have been pushed through the door—lying on the floor of the dark entryway. Mulder bends down to look at it. The note reads, "Things are looking up."

At that moment someone comes up behind Mulder, grabs him by the back of the neck, and slams him headlong into the coffee table. The attacker pulls Mulder's gun from his holster and—standing over the agent triumphantly—jams it into his face.

"You must be losing it, Mulder," sneers Alex Krycek. "I can beat you with one hand."

Mulder replies, "Isn't that how you like to beat yourself?"

Krycek cocks the gun.

"If those are my last words," says Mulder, quickly, "I can do better."

Krycek says, "I'm not here to kill you, Mulder. I'm here to help you."

"Hey, thanks," says Mulder.

Krycek says, "You know, if it wasn't in

my best interest, I'd just as soon squeeze this trigger."

"What's stopping you?"

Krycek leans closer to Mulder, the gun still in his face. "Hear this, Agent Mulder. Listen very carefully, because what I'm telling you is deadly serious. There is a war raging. And unless you pull your head out of the sand, you and I and about five billion other people are going to go the way of the dinosaur. I'm talking planned invasion. The colonization of this planet by an extraterrestrial race."

Mulder laughs in Krycek's face. "I thought you were serious," he says, smiling.

Krycek is serious. "Kazakhstan, Skyland Mountain, the site in Pennsylvania. They're all alien light-houses where the colonization will begin, but where now a battle is being waged. A struggle for heaven and earth. Where there is one law: Fight or die. And one rule: Resist or serve."

"Serve who?" says Mulder, dismissively.

"Not who," whispers Krycek. "What."

Mulder thinks for a moment, then says angrily, "Krycek, you're a murderer, a liar, and a coward. Just because you stick a gun in my chest I'm supposed to believe you're my friend?"

Now it is Krycek's turn to smile. "Get up," he says, his gun still pointed at Mulder, who moves carefully to a sitting position.

Krycek says "I was sent by a man. A man who knows, as I do, that resistance is in our grasp. And in yours."

He adds, "The mass incinerations were strikes by an alien rebellion. To upset plans for occupation. Now, one of these rebels is being held captive and if he dies, so dies the resistance."

Krycek abruptly moves forward and kisses Mulder on the cheek. He uncocks his pistol, lays it at Mulder's feet, and stands. Mulder picks up the gun warily, keeping his eyes on his nemesis.

"Good luck to you, my friend," says Krycek, in Russian.

He turns his back and exits, slamming the door behind him. Deep in thought, Mulder watches him leave.

At the cyclone-fenced boundary of Wiekamp Air Force Base, a familiar figure—that of the Alien Bounty

Hunter—appears. He appraises the barbed-wire tipped boundary, looks around, leaps upward and over, and runs into the fog-filled darkness.

Sometime later Mulder is still in his apartment, slumped disconsolately on his living room couch. There is a knock on the door, and Scully pushes it open.

"Mulder?"

"Yeah."

"What are you doing sitting here in the dark?"

"Thinking."

"Thinking about what?"

"Oh, the usual," says Mulder. "Destiny. Fate. How to throw a curveball. The inextricable relationships in our lives that are neither accidental nor somehow within our control, either."

Scully nods. "I've just taken a long walk," she says. "And I've reconsidered that I may have been wrong about what I believed happened to me."

"I've been doing some reconsidering of my own," says Mulder.

He stands, handing Scully the note Krycek left him on the floor. She reads, "Things are looking up." She turns the paper over. It reads, "Wiekamp Air Force Base."

"What is this?" says Scully.

"Maybe an answer," says Mulder. "To a question you and I were destined to ask."

At Wiekamp Air Force Base later that night a car carrying Mulder and Scully—Mulder at the wheel—pulls up to a guard gate at the fence line. A young military policeman emerges. Mulder flashes his FBI ID.

He says, "We're federal agents requesting permission to enter the base."

The guard says, "Do you have any paperwork to go with that, Agent Muldower?"

"It's Mulder," says the agent, briskly. "I wasn't aware that any special authorization was needed to enter."

The guard looks carefully at Mulder. "Well," he says, "due to the nature of our facility and the hazardous chemicals on site, I can only allow pre-cleared civilian and military personnel on base."

Mulder says, "Are you aware that there's been a leak and contamination in one of the lab facilities, and that the

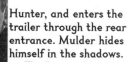

personnel inside are in need of immediate medical attention?"

"No sir, I wasn't."

"Why don't you check on that, son? I'd hate for someone to die because you were uninformed."

The MP gives Mulder a cold, hard look before reentering the guard shack. Mulder sees a military truck coming the opposite way, exiting the base. A sliding fence starts to open to let the truck out.

"Buckle up, Scully," says Mulder.

Scully says, alarmed, "Mulder, he's armed and well within his jurisdiction."

By now the gate is nearly opened, and both Mulder and Scully stare at the truck, a large "china top" tractor-trailer with canvas siding. Scully looks upward through the truck's windshield at the driver.

"I know that man," she says.

"Who?" says Mulder.

"The driver. I know his face."

It is Quiet Willy, dressed in camouflage fatigues. Mulder stares at him, too, then glances at the MP, talking on the phone in the guard shack. The truck exits, passing the agents' car on its left side. After it clears, the MP hangs up his phone and walks out to the agents' car. Mulder is no longer in the driver's seat—he is clinging to the back of the moving tractor-trailer.

"Stop that truck!" yells the guard, who then pulls out his pistol and aims it at Scully, sitting calmly in the passenger seat.

On a desolate rural highway the trailer truck speeds away from the base. Mulder finds a canvas flap and struggles into the dark interior. He shines his flashlight ahead of them and sees a small metal compartment attached behind the tractor cab. He shines his light through a wire-mesh window. Crouched inside is the faceless alien.

The truck pulls to a halt. Quiet Willy sets the hand brake and turns off the engine. He takes off his military beret, morphs into the Alien Bounty Hunter, and enters the trailer through the rear entrance. Mulder hides himself in the shadows.

The Bounty Hunter walks slowly to the window of the metal compartment, peers at the faceless alien, pulls out his stiletto, and releases its blade with a lethal hiss.

The faceless alien cringes. Still in hiding, Mulder pulls out his gun. At that moment a bright light erupts atop the trailer—its hot white energy bursting through every seam and crack. The Bounty Hunter looks up, diverted from his task, and walks toward the rear of the trailer.

At the rear entrance, silhouetted by the intense beam, is a second faceless alien, holding his fire wand. Mulder steps out from hiding and faces him.

"No!" screams Mulder.

Blinded by the bright light, the agent holds his gun in front of him and fires into a sudden and overwhelming darkness.

At the Syndicate medical facility Dr. Patou shines a penlight into Marita Covarrubias's pupil. It is clear of the black oil. The doctor looks up. The Well-Manicured Man, standing alone in the observation gallery, nods down at her.

Inside the china top trailer, a dazed Mulder is accosted and inspected by a squad of MPs. They shine their flashlights in his eyes. He turns away and looks into the metal compartment. It is empty, its door ajar.

The MPs escort him to his car, where Scully awaits. Mulder lowers his head to his hands.

"What happened?" asks Scully, worriedly, taking her partner's hand.

"I don't know," says Mulder, staring deeply into her eyes.

At FBI headquarters sometime later Jeffrey Spender enters Walter Skinner's office. The AD holds a file in his hands.

Skinner says, "I'm sorry. There's been no news about your mother."

Spender nods, and looks down at the folder.

Skinner adds, "I appreciate your wanting to keep this discrete. I'll try and do that. But you should know Agent Mulder has opened an X-File on this case."

Spender nods again, his eyes flashing, but says nothing.

"This hasn't reflected on you, Agent Spender," says Skinner.

"Thank you, sir," says Spender, at the door.

Skinner says, "You'll do fine. It seems you have a patron outside this office who thinks highly of you."

"Who's that?" says Spender.

"I don't know," says Skinner. "Someone working with a high level of influence."

Spender thinks for a moment, frowning, then exits. He walks into the corridor. An FBI clerk approaches him and hands him a red envelope. He looks at it—and at its Canadian return address—and puts it in his breast pocket unopened.

Deep in the snowy woods the young boy we've seen before tramps upward to the front door of a mountain cabin. The door opens and he thrusts forward a red envelope.

"Sorry about that, mister," says the boy.

Attached to the envelope is a bright yellow sticker reading, RETURN TO SENDER/NO FORWARDING SERVICE AVAILABLE. Cancer Man eyes it sadly, then takes another drag on his cigarette.

back story:

You say you blinked a couple of times—or worse, left your Barcalounger for a cold one—at some point during this two-parter? Too bad.

"Patient X" and "The Red and the Black"—quintessential mythological episodes both—marked a mid-season high point in character development, plot complication, and overall demands on the viewer. New characters were introduced; old conspiracies turned on their heads; the lead characters' season-long moods, quests, and obsessions underlined, amplified, challenged, and re-examined. "It was a way of establishing the mythology by providing a threat to it," explains Chris Carter, patiently.

Carter adds that these linked episodes' revelations about Earth's potential alien occupiers were all important clues to the emerging bigger picture and essential plot elements leading to the X-Files movie.

From the other side of the Fourth Wall comes the not-so-shocking news that "Patient X" and "The Red and the Black"—stuffed with special effects, elaborate sets, and difficult locations—were the most challenging and logistically complex projects of the season.

"Well before the Christmas break," says locations manager Louisa Gradnitzer, "Chris came to us about these two episodes and he told us what he wanted was 'a spectacle, something that dominated the landscape.' After several scouting trips to hitherto unfilmed local wonders—including the Squamish Chief, a massive granite mountain near the British Columbia resort town of Whistler—the location chosen was Ruskin Dam, a seventy-year old hydroelectric facility located approximately fifty miles east of downtown Vancouver.

"What's great about Ruskin Dam is that it has this wonderful 'industrial gothic' look—and we'd never done anything there before," adds Gradnitzer. The dam also has a magnificent spillway; a visually striking connecting bridge and powerhouse; safe landing zones for helicopters; good parking; and numerous camera positions in the surrounding hills. The dam could also be rented from the local utility, B.C. Hydro, for a reasonable fee, plus $1,400 each hour that water was diverted from the generators to cascade dramatically into the water below.

The dam's connecting bridge, not exactly in pristine condition, was suitable only for light service traffic. To make it suitable for carrying emergency vehicles, camera crews, equipment, and huddled masses of doomed alien abductees, The X-Files's construction department laid down a complete temporary roadbed, painted much of the existing structure, and installed seven replacement lamp standards—duplicates of the three remaining originals—designed and built by Graeme Murray's art department.

Filming the actual abduction scenes on location was impractical, however, so construction supervisor Rob Maier launched his biggest project of the season: a nearly full-scale replica of the Ruskin Dam bridge, in wood and steel, was built from scratch inside a cavernous A-frame warehouse in the nearby town of Delta. The abduction of Cassandra Spender was accomplished by seating a stuntwoman in Cassandra's wheelchair, winching her upward with an adjacent crane, then painstakingly erasing the stuntwoman's wire harness from the picture during post-production.

The lights of the alien spaceships overhead were actually an elaborate high-intensity lighting rig, custom-built by an outside expert who specializes in rock concert light shows, combined with footage filmed at the actual bridge. This complicated combination was done, via computer, by special effects supervisor Laurie Kallsen-George (who was thoroughly drenched by an unexpected spillway cascade during a scouting trip to Ruskin Dam).

The other maximum-effort set piece was the crashed alien spaceship. At Chris Carter's direction it was built sixty feet in diameter, twice the size of any alien craft previously fabricated for the show. The steel-hulled spaceship was also constructed in the A-frame, then transported to an open area—the same one used last season for the oil well explosion in "Terma" (4X10)—and dragged along the ground to leave a sixty-foot long skidmark. Special effects supervisor Dave Gauthier set off twenty-five closely spaced explosions to simulate the saucer crashing to a halt in flames; he then burned the rest of the wreckage to get a shot that lasted no more than a few seconds.

To portray the victims of the alien rebels, stunt coordinator Tony Morelli suited up for five "full body burns"—a single-episode X-Files record. Picture car coordinator Nigel Habgood was momentarily stumped when asked to find a gaggle of Russian passenger cars for immolation in the opening scene of "Patient X."

Habgood says, "I couldn't get real Russian cars, so I decided to get creative and go seriously European. We burned a couple Saabs, a couple of Ladas, some Fiats, a Peugeot, a Skoda, and a BMW 2002. I'm sorry we couldn't get any Yugos. I would have loved to burn some of them."

Props master Ken Hawryliw created the alien fire wands out of "materials not found on Earth—just in Canada"; and, after consulting a reference work titled Blue Helmets Under Fire, decided to outfit his entire UN peace-keeping force with Netherlands Army uniforms and ordnance.

Special effects makeup supervisor Toby Lindala, moving at warp speed, supervised the creation of the faceless aliens, the facial mutilation of young Dmitri, and the "crispy critters" on the bridge lying partially incinerated at the dam site following the rebel alien attacks.

After experimenting on his brother Robin, Lindala also designed the rig that allowed alien oil to ooze into Dmitri's face. Actually, the oil oozed out until the film was reversed in the final edit.

Lindala says, "Let's see—we broke his nose a little bit, we had his left eye swollen shut, then we had a tube rigged that was set up to come underneath, then just over his ear, underneath his left eye, and down his nostril, and then a separate little denture rig with a balloon bladder in it that we filled with this oil. He could squeeze the bladder with his tongue so that both his nostrils and his mouth oozed this black oil. We had to get him set up in a certain position so that gravity worked in our favor. But in reverse, it looked really neat."

Perhaps the most striking footage in the two-parter, however, was obtained by the small fleet of helicopters that hovered over the dam site almost constantly. On one memorable day, for instance, the civilianized Huey that doubled as the red Search and Rescue chopper was sent up just minutes before sunset to film scenes of devastation on the bridge's roadbed.

At the last possible moment the craft swooped over and below the dam; settled into a hover alongside the active spillway; got the shot, as monitored by director Chris Carter gazing at a ground-based video feed; then landed on the roadway by the entrance.

The pilot kept his engine running, but Carter indicated his approval. The crew applauded, then started to pack up for the journey home.

Ⓧ

The televised list of Skyland Mountain victims viewed by Scully in her hospital room is made up of the names of X-Files staffers. Jack Finn, who plays the Cigarette-Smoking Man's messenger boy, is the son of X-Files producer J. P. Finn. Alex Shostak, Jr., who plays Dmitri, is a seventeen-year-old high school student whose family emigrated to Canada from the Ukraine in 1996. Shostak translated his own lines from English into Russian. In his opinion, Nicholas Lea's (Krycek's) painstakingly learned Russian pronunciation and accent was "not bad." His father, Oleksiy Shostak, had a small role last season in "Terma" (4X10).

travelers

One year before reopening the X-Files,
young Agent Mulder investigates
a bizarre murder. The answers he seeks
lie in the not-so-distant past:
during the Red Scare of the 1950s.

EPISODE: 5X15
FIRST AIRED: March 29, 1998
EDITOR: Lynne Willingham
WRITTEN BY: John Shiban & Frank Spotnitz
DIRECTED BY: Bill Graham
GUEST STARS:

Darren McGavin (Agent Arthur Dales)
Fredric Lane (Young Arthur Dales)
Garret Dillahunt (Edward Skur)
David Moreland (Roy Cohn)
Brian Leckner (Hayes Michel)
Dean Aylesworth (Young Bill Mulder)
Eileen Pedde (Mrs. Skur)
Mitchell Kosterman (Sheriff)
J. Douglas Stewart (Landlord)
Cory Dagg (Bartender)
David Fredericks (Director)
Jane Perry (Dorothy Bahnsen)
Roger Haskett (Coroner)
Eric W. Gilder (Old Edward Skur)
John A. Sampson (First Cop)
David Alan Pearson (Second Cop)
Peter Nicholas (FBI Agent)
Tom Bougers (Neighbor)
Dean Barrett (Roy Cohn's Assistant)
PRINCIPAL SETTINGS:
Caledonia, Wisconsin;
Leesburg, Virginia;
Chevy Chase, Maryland;
Washington, D.C.

It is 1990. In a weed-choked rural clearing sits a dilapidated house, its windows boarded shut. A police cruiser pulls up in front; the sheriff, accompanied by the house's owner, gets out.

"Looks like nobody's home," says the sheriff.

"Oh, he's here," says the sour-looking landlord. "He knows the minute he steps out I'm changing the locks on him."

Somebody is watching the pair through the slats of a plywood-covered window. The sheriff steps toward the house, his jaw set.

"It's an old guy, huh?" he says. "I don't much enjoy evicting old folks."

The landlord says, "This particular one'll change your way of thinking."

Nailed to the front door is an eviction notice addressed to a man named Edward Skur. The sheriff knocks loudly.

"Mr. Skur! It's the sheriff. Will you open up, please?"

No response. The sheriff unholsters his gun, turns to the landlord, and tells him to unlock the door. The landlord pulls out his passkey, opens it, and recoils from the stench.

"God, almighty!" he says. "What the hell's he got in here?"

The sheriff crosses the threshold, and glances into the squalid interior.

"Smells like a whole lot of something went bad," he says. "Mr. Skur! I'm armed! You want to come out now!"

Again, no response. The landlord nods in the direction of Skur's upstairs bedroom. The pair go up a staircase; the hardwood is crawling with cockroaches. The sheriff kicks open the bedroom door and pokes his gun inside. Nothing. The landlord peers inside the bathroom and recoils, retching.

"What is it?" asks the sheriff.

The landlord scurries down the stairs, covering his mouth to keep from throwing up. The sheriff watches him flee, then moves cautiously to the bathroom.

Draped over the edge of the bathtub is what seems like an innocuous object.

"It ain't nothing but a glove," he says. "No reason to—"

He moves in closer and slumps to the floor in horror. The glove is in fact a flattened human hand attached to a flattened human body, which is lying inside

the tub. The naked corpse has collapsed, its flesh just a sack holding loose bones.

"Oh my God," gasps the sheriff.

At that moment he is yanked down violently from behind. The sheriff fires his gun, blasting his attacker down the stairs. He rises and staggers downstairs, too. He sees an old man, unarmed, lying face up on the floor. Thick white mucous bubbles from his mouth. He is struggling to speak. The sheriff bends down to listen.

"Mul-der. Mulder," gasps the dying man.

In Washington, D.C., later that same year a gray sedan pulls up in front of a battered-looking tenement building. Fox Mulder gets out, enters the building, trudges up a dingy stairway, and knocks at an apartment door. A man in his sixties opens the door a few inches. He peers at the agent from behind a security chain.

"Arthur Dales?" says Mulder, tentatively.

"Who's asking?" says the tenant, suspiciously.

Mulder flashes his FBI ID.

"I'm a profiler with the Behavioral Sciences Unit," he says. "You are Arthur Dales, former Special Agent with the Bureau?"

The man says nothing.

Mulder says, "I need to ask you some questions about a man named Edward Skur. You opened a file on him in 1952."

Dales frowns slightly and shakes his head. "I don't recall," he says.

"I brought the case file with me," says Mulder, quickly, before the old man can close the door.

He proffers a yellowed case file. On it is stamped the case number X–525652. Dales frowns at the file, but makes no move to take it. "How long have you been in the Bureau?" he says, crankily. "Do you know what an X-File is?"

"It's, uh, an unsolved case," says Mulder,

"No!" says Dales. "It's a case that's been designated unsolved."

Mulder nods, a bit nervously. He opens the case file. In classic Freedom of Information Act fashion, much of the typescript has been blacked out.

"Mr. Dales," he says. "Most of your report has been censored, as you can see. Now, if somebody's trying to bury this case, I'd like to know why." Mulder adds, "According to your report, Edward Skur disappeared thirty-eight years ago, before you had a chance to arrest him for a series of stranger killings in which the victims' internal organs were removed."

"And now you've found him?" says Dales.

"Yes," says Mulder. "Last week."

Mulder tells him of the bizarre circumstances of Skur's death and of the eviscerated body found in his bathtub. Dales nods.

"Well, if he's dead," he says, pushing his door shut, "there's nothing you need from me."

The younger man blocks the door with his hand.

"Sir, my name is Mulder," he says. "You know that name and so did Edward Skur. How?"

Dales bows his head.

"You ever heard of HUAC, Agent Mulder?" he says. "The House Un-American Activities Committee? No, no, no. That was before your time. You wouldn't know."

Dales looks up into Mulder's eyes. "They hunted Communists in America in the forties and fifties. They found prac- tically nothing. You think they would have found nothing, unless nothing was what they wanted to find? Hmm?"

Mulder stares at Dales. "I'm sorry, sir," he says. "I don't see the connection."

"Maybe you're not supposed to," says Dales, slamming the door in Mulder's face.

Later that day Mulder sits on the couch in his apartment, nibbling on sunflower seeds and watching old news- reel footage on his television set. On the screen is a congressional hearing, circa 1950s. The newsreel announcer intones:

"The nation's chief red hunters, Senator Joseph McCarthy and FBI Director J. Edgar Hoover, join forces! Working through Congress, the senator from Wisconsin and the legendary lawman now to wipe out the Red Menace within our own federal government!

"Roy Cohn, chief counsel at the McCarthy hearings, warns Communist mind control can strike anywhere, at any time!"

Mulder pulls out the old X-file

and peruses it. All of one page has been blacked out, except three names: George Gissing, Edward Skur, and Terrill Oberman.

The announcer continues:

"It is those Americans sympathetic to the Communist cause—the so-called fellow travelers—who pose the greatest threat to our national security. So says the young U.S. Attorney, and he should know. It was Mr. Cohn that brought those atomic spies, the Rosenbergs, to justice.

"It was his staunch defense of the American way of life that first brought Roy Cohn to the attention of Senator McCarthy."

Mulder turns to the next page of the file. Something falls out; it is a yellowed membership card for the Communist Party U.S.A., bearing the name and address of Edward Skur.

Mulder examines the card, then glances back at the screen. Something catches his attention. He puts on his eyeglasses and leans forward.

"With the support of the FBI, Mr. Cohn and Mr. McCarthy vow to work tirelessly to root out the more than seventy suspected Communist spies and the untold number of—"

Mulder stops the tape, then replays the footage several times. Spotting a young man seated behind Cohn and McCarthy in the hearing room, he carefully freeze-frames a clear image of the man's face. He shakes his head, rewinds the tape, then freezes the newsreel at the same spot once again.

"Dad!" he whispers, severely shaken.

The next morning Mulder, a Styrofoam cup in his hand, knocks on Arthur Dales's door. Dales opens it a crack, mightily irritated.

"Good morning, Mr. Dales," says Mulder. "I brought you some coffee."

"Speak!" says Dales, gruffly.

Mulder says, "Edward Skur died saying a name—my name. My father's name."

"Go ask your father," says Dale.

Mulder grimaces. "My father and I don't really speak."

Dales shakes his head. "I told you I can't help you."

He closes the door. But this time Mulder doesn't leave.

"Mr. Dales," says Mulder, through the

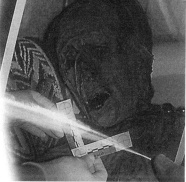

door, "I want the truth. And I will subpoena you to get it if I have to."

Dales opens the door angrily. The two men size each other up. Finally Dales speaks.

"Before his disappearance," he says, "Skur worked for the State Department, just like your old man did. You had to have suspected the connection before you came here yesterday. But you said nothing."

Mulder asks, evenly, "The men that Edward Skur killed thirty-eight years ago. Was my father involved?"

Dales nods, his face unreadable.

"How?" asks Mulder, incredulous.

A few moments later Mulder sits inside the shabby apartment. Dales examines the photo of Skur's hollowed-out victim.

"Skur killed this man the way he did all the others," says Dales. "All the soft tissues—the internal organs, the ligature—all were removed without tearing the skin."

Mulder says, exhaling a cloud of cigarette smoke, "The coroner wasn't able to determine how."

Dales says, "Oh, I can tell you how. What I can't tell you is why."

Mulder tells the older man that in the report he read Skur was suspected of being a Communist.

"Well, that's what they said he was," replies Dales, sadly. "That's what they said they all were. To us, Skur was just another name on a list."

Dales's recollection begins. The year is 1952; the setting Leesburg, Virginia, at the site of a picture-perfect white frame house in front of which flies the American flag. The older man narrates:

Another Communist spy at the State Department. We had no idea who—or what—Edward Skur really was.

Two conservatively dressed young men walk up to the front porch of the frame house. One of them knocks on the

front door; it is opened by a Donna Reed-ish housewife dressed in her Sunday best.

"May I help you?" asks the woman, smiling.

"My name's Arthur Dales, ma'am. I'm with the Federal Bureau of Investigation. This is my partner, Agent Michel. Is your husband in?"

The woman's smile fades. "What do you want with him?" she asks.

She is interrupted by her husband, a man in his mid-thirties, also conservatively dressed and fairly nondescript.

"Supper's getting cold, sweetheart," he says. "I'll take care of this."

Mrs. Skur retreats toward the interior of the house. Young Arthur Dales stares at the man.

"Edward Skur?" he asks.

"Yes?"

Agent Michel rushes inside and pushes Skur face-first into the wall. Then he pulls out his handcuffs.

Dales says, "You're under arrest for contempt of Congress—failure to appear before the committee."

"Hey!" protests Skur, "I'm a family man, for God's sake!"

Michel twists Skur's hands behind his back. "Well, you should have thought of that before you decided to betray your country, Red."

Mrs. Skur calls out to her husband anxiously. She is standing in the foyer with her three young children by her side. As Michel manhandles Skur out the door he hands his partner a small white card.

"Look what I found!" says Michel.

It is the same Communist Party card that Mulder will someday discover.

"You planted that!" protests Skur.

Michel says, "I'll plant one in your keister if you don't watch your mouth, Bolshevik!"

Michel shoves Skur outside. Dales lingers, turning to look at the Skur children. They blink back at him silently.

"I'm sorry, I—" says Dales to Mrs. Skur.

"Get out!" she says angrily.

Dales pockets the membership card, closing the door behind him.

That evening at a Washington watering hole called the Hoot Owl, a rain-soaked Dales enters and heads straight for the bar. He's obviously a regular customer.

"Geez, Louise," says the bartender. "What'd you do—take a swim in the Potomac?"

"I'd probably be dryer if I had," says Dales. "Got something to warm me up?"

The bartender pours out a stiff drink and asks Dales where his partner is. Dales replies that he's processing a prisoner.

"You guys still bustin' Reds?" asks the bartender.

Dales replies, "Until Mr. Hoover tells us different."

"Good for you, Mr. Dales," says the bartender, with feeling.

The telephone at the bar rings. The bartender answers it and hands it to the Dales. It's Michel, his partner, at his desk in the FBI bullpen.

"You trying to reach me?" asks Michel.

"No. Why?"

"I thought maybe you heard about Skur."

"What about him?"

"He's dead," says Michel. "He hung himself in his cell. Guard found him about twenty minutes ago."

Shocked, Dales says nothing.

Michel adds, "Whaddaya figure? Commie Central Command tells these mopes to snuff themselves in the event of capture?"

Dales isn't really listening. "Gotta go," he says, and hangs up on his astonished partner.

The bartender says, "Everything okay?"

"No, nothing a little bourbon won't cure," says Dales.

Later that evening, Dales—who is fairly plastered—sits drinking in his car, parked outside Edward Skur's house. From 1990, Agent Dales narrates:

I don't know what I should say to her. 'I'm sorry about your loss, Mrs. Skur. If there's anything I can do . . . ?' The words sounded hollow. No matter what I said, I was the man who busted her husband. Turned her life upside down. I sat there for over an hour, trying to find my courage in a bottle. And then—and then, I saw someone I shouldn't, I couldn't have seen. Now it was my life being turned upside down.

"Edward Skur!" yells young Dales.

He has seen the "dead" man walking purposefully along the sidewalk outside his house. Dales scrambles out of the car and launches himself in pursuit. Skur sprints around a corner, but Dales catches him in a trash can–filled alley. They grapple furiously. Dales loses his gun and Skur gets on top of his quarry, pinning him to the ground.

Something terrifying happens to Skur's face. His veins bulge and his eyes roll back, showing only the whites. His jaw begins to unhinge; from the black hole of his elongated mouth brown-black tendrils, like the spindly legs of a hermit crab, creep out and hook over his lips, pressing into the flesh. Now Skur's face is inches from Dales's, the tendrils arching over his mouth as if about to expel some creature from inside his body.

"Hey! Who's down there!?" yells a neighbor from a nearby bedroom window.

Skur turns to look. In an instant, Skur appears normal again. He gets up and runs, disappearing from the alley the way he came. Shaken, Dales sits up, unsteadily, and stares after him.

At the pre–J. Edgar Hoover Building FBI headquarters, in the agents' bullpen, on a black-and-white television set, a newsreel report is blaring. The announcer intones solemnly:

"Dateline Washington—The Justice Department vows no mercy for A-bomb spies. Julius and Ethel Rosenberg once again manage to delay their date with the electric chair. Prosecutors say they are confident Judge Kaufman's death sentence will be upheld by the highest court in the land."

Hayes Michels enters and walks purposefully through the room. Old Arthur Dales narrates:

The world still seemed clear to me that morning, despite what I'd seen the night before. I still thought I knew who the bad guys and the good guys were. But that was all about to change.

Michel, carrying a file folder, stops at the desk of Dales, who is talking on the phone. He tells him to hang up, then motions him over to the water cooler.

"What'd the watch commander say?" asks Michel, in a low voice.

Dales says, "They're still going door to door in the neighborhood. No sign of him yet."

Michel nods toward the file folder. "They're not going to find anything, Artie," he says. "Open it up."

Dales opens the folder. Inside are photos of Edward Skur, hanged in his cell.

Michel says, "Maybe you want to change your description of the suspect who assaulted you."

"When were these taken?" asks Dales.

"Last night," says Michel. "Two hours before you say Skur attacked you." The agent adds, tersely, "You'd had a few. You were feeling bad about what happened. It's understandable."

Dales says, "I-I didn't have that much to drink."

Michel says, "Just leave Skur's name out of the report. Nobody else has to know."

Dales replies, "I already filed my report. An hour ago."

Michel nods grimly. Another agent in the bullpen calls out to Dales, telling him he's wanted on the telephone. Dales picks up the receiver, tells his caller he's on the way, and turns to his partner, who's standing over him, concerned.

"It's the Justice Department," says Dales, uneasily. "They want to talk to me."

Shortly afterward Dales walks down an imposing wood-paneled corridor. He stops in front of a frosted-glass door; the lettering on it reads ROY M. COHN, SPECIAL ASSISTANT TO THE ATTORNEY GENERAL, INTERNAL SECURITY SECTION.

A young male assistant leads Dales into Roy Cohn's large office. Cohn tells him to sit down—his assistant remains standing nearby—and perches on the edge of his desk across from him.

"You know who I am?" he says, with just a hint of menace.

"You prosecuted the Rosenbergs," says Dales, somewhat intimidated. "Now you're working with Mr. Hoover and Senator McCarthy."

"Then you know how important my work is," says Cohn, condescendingly. "How vital it is to the future of the country that these rats, these vermin, who dare call themselves Americans be exposed as the traitors they are."

Dales says, nervously, "I don't interest myself in politics, Mr. Cohn."

Cohn exchanges a smirk with his assistant. "Everything is political, Agent Dales," he says. "Like this report you filed this morning."

Cohn picks up the report by one corner, holding it like a piece of trash.

Cohn says, "We've spoken to Mrs. Skur and the neighbors. You seem to be the only person who can identify that man as Edward Skur."

Dales asks, "Do you believe me, then?"

Cohn frowns and leans forward. "We are fighting a powerful enemy in a war of ideology. In any war there are secrets—truths—that must be kept from the public in order to serve the greater good."

"You want me to amend my report?" asks Dales.

Cohn says nothing. He stares into the agent's eyes.

"Take out any reference to Edward Skur?"

Again, silence.

"I don't understand—" says Dales.

"You're not supposed to understand!" says Cohn, lips pursed. "You're supposed to follow orders."

Later that day a plainly chastened—and disillusioned—Arthur Dales sits at

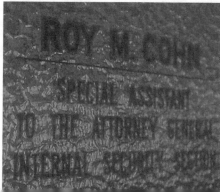

his desk at FBI headquarters. He skips a printed report form into his typewriter. In a blank space under the heading SUSPECT, he slowly and carefully types UNKNOWN.

"Agent Dales?" says a woman's voice.

It is an FBI clerk named Dorothy Bahnsen. "I pulled that file," she says.

"Oh, right. Thank you," says Dales, distractedly.

She gives him the file on Edward Skur. He opens it. All the names but three—George Gissing, Edward Skur, and Terrill Oberman—have been blanked out.

"Dales!" says a man's voice.

It is Hayes Michel, dressed to leave the office, motioning for his partner to join him. Arthur Dales grabs his coat and follows, leaving Edward Skur's file lying open on his desk.

At an upper-middle-class suburban house Dales and Michel pull up the circular driveway in their blue sedan. Old Arthur Dales continues:

I never so much faked an expense report or used a Bureau car to drive home, so lying didn't sit well with me, even if I was under orders. I wanted to leave behind the business of Edward Skur and never hear that name again. But it was too late. By then, Skur had already become a murderer.

Dales and Michel get out of their car and walk cautiously to the front door.

"Homicide call came in from Chevy Chase PD," says Michel. "Advise and assist."

Dales looks around. There are no uniformed cops in sight.

"Then where are they?" he says.

"They must have come and gone," says his partner.

Dales pushes open the unlocked door. Inside, a scratchy German recording of "Lili Marlene," is playing on a phonograph.

Dales says, drawing his gun, "I know this song. They were playing it the day my unit rolled into Berlin."

"Guy must be a Kraut," says Michel.

Dales looks at a framed photograph on the wall. An older man in a lab coat is shaking hands with President Truman in front of a building bearing the sign VETERANS ADMINISTRATION HOSPITAL.

"Yeah," says Dales, "a well-connected Kraut."

Michel snorts. "There you go," he says. "I got six ounces of German shrapnel in my can and this Kraut gets to shake hands with the President."

Dales turns away from the photograph, and sniffs. "You smell that?" he says.

"Yeah, kinda," says Michel. "Hospital smell."

The two agents follow the scent, entering the kitchen and seeing a withered hand on the floor. A flattened corpse is connected to it.

"What the hell happened to him?" says Dales.

Before Michel can answer his partner the rear door to the kitchen bangs open and the agents are confronted by two uniformed cops, their guns drawn.

"Hands in the air!" shouts the first cop.

"Over there! Now!" shouts the second.

The agents raise their hands. "Whoa, fellas, FBI. FBI!" says Dales.

"Credentials in my front coat pocket," says Michel.

The first cop reaches for his badge.

"Hey, easy on the material," says the agent.

After a few scary moments they succeed in reassuring the jittery cops of their identity. They both holster their guns.

The first cop says, "Who called you guys out here?"

"You did, you mope," says Michel. "We got the call from your department."

The second cop says, "We don't know nothin' about that."

"Then what are you doing out here?" asks Michel.

The first cop explains that one of the doctor's nurses called in, saying that he hadn't shown up for surgery that morning.

"Well, something tells me he ain't gonna make it," says Michel.

As this conversation proceeds, Dales spots something on a nearby counter. It is a cardboard coaster from the Hoot Owl bar. Dales turns it over. On the blank side is a handwritten message, "Come alone."

At the Hoot Owl that night Dales enters and looks around. Old Dales narrates:

I was summoned to the bar by a man who'd already been to the doctor's house that morning. It was the man, Agent Mulder, you came here to ask me about.

Dales searches in vain for a familiar face, then notices a curtained booth. He can see a single pair of men's legs inside. He pulls the curtain open, enters, and sits down.

"Skur?" he says.

"No," says a conservatively dressed man in his late twenties. "But I came here to warn you about him."

Dales stares back at the man, distrustful. "Like you warned that doctor you murdered in Chevy Chase?"

"I tried to save that man," replies the stranger, with nervous intensity. "But I was too late."

"Skur killed him?"

The man nods. "He'll kill you, too."

At Hayes Michel's bachelor apartment that night the agent, carrying a bag of groceries, pushes open the door and enters. He sets the bag down on his kitchen counter and pulls out a bottle of beer. He hears a noise behind him and turns around to see his living room window open, its curtain billowing in the breeze. He puts down the beer, walks into his living room, and peers through it.

"Myrtle?" he says.

A loud meow draws his attention to a wing chair, where his large house cat is stretched out. Michel smiles, shakes his head, and slides the window closed.

Back in the Hoot Owl bar Arthur Dales is still talking to the nervous stranger.

He says, "I don't know what you're talking about," he says. "What is this, some kind of Communist plot?"

"Skur's not a Communist," says the man. "He's a patriot. All of these men are patriots."

"What are you talking about? What men?"

The man says, "There were three men. Veterans. Working at the State Department. Skur, Gissing, and Oberman."

Dales nods. "Gissing and Oberman," he says. "I read those names on a censored report."

The man tells Dales that the two men are now dead.

"Murdered?" asks Dales.

"No," says the man. "Dead by their own hand. They couldn't live with what they'd become, what they'd been turned into. Skur was the last."

Dales asks, "Why did they put out that story about him hanging himself?"

The man says, "Because they had to do something to cover up what they'd done to him. They label him a Communist, say he killed himself, then put him up someplace where no one's even going to look for him. But his escape threatens everything."

"Threatens what?" says Dales. "What did they do to him?"

The man looks around, reluctant to answer.

"Look," says Dales, impatiently. "You asked me here."

The man leans forward, fire— and fear—in his eyes. "And I've risked my career and my family by coming here," he says.

"But the crimes these men have committed against innocent people— I can't have it on my conscience anymore. Someone needs to know the truth."

Dales leans forward. "Who are you?" he asks.

"My name is Mulder," he replies. "I work at the State Department."

At Michel's apartment the off-duty agent clicks on his television. For a brief second, before the picture tube warms up, the reflection of a man—Edward Skur— appears on the black screen.

Michel sits down, loosens his tie, and watches a news program featuring an interview with Senator Joseph McCarthy.

"Attaboy, Tailgunner," says Michel. "Give 'em hell."

Myrtle leaps off her chair, overturning the beer bottle. Michel groans, gets up from his chair, and sets it upright. He picks up a church key and opens the bottle—which, thoroughly shaken, spews beer in all directions.

"Damnit! Damnit, Myrtle!" says Michel.

In the booth at the Hoot Owl Dales looks at the man sitting across from him skeptically.

"All right then, Mr. Mulder," he says. "Who is this 'they' you want me to arrest?"

Young Bill Mulder shakes his head bitterly. "You can't arrest these men," he says.

"Why not?"

Bill Mulder hesitates. "It's . . . political," he says.

Dales stares for a second, remembering this phrase. "What are you telling me?" he says. "Are you telling me that Mr. Cohn and Senator McCarthy are involved in this?"

Bill Mulder stares back at him, saying nothing.

Dales asks, "Is Skur after them, too?"

Bill Mulder says, "Skur wants vengeance for what they did to him. He's a killer now. He can only guess at the dimensions of this conspiracy, but he thinks you're part of it. You and your partner."

Dales lets this sink in, then leaves the booth, rushes to the bar, and demands the telephone from the bartender.

"What's the number?" asks the bartender.

"KLondike 5-0133," says Dales.

The bartender dials. The phone rings in Dales's ear, but not in Michel's apartment. The phone wire is pulled out from the wall jack.

"C'mon! C'mon!" says Dales, anxiously.

In Michel's apartment the agent wipes the spilled beer off his shirt front. "I knew I shoulda got a dog," he says.

He removes his gun from his holster and lays it on the table. Someone leaps onto Michel, knocking him over like a rag doll. It is Skur, who pins the stunned agent to the floor. He brings his face close to Michel's as his eyes roll back, showing only the whites. Skur's jaw unhinges, opening impossibly wide. Something is inside, trying to get out.

Michel starts screaming.

Two spindly legs extend from Skur's lips. With crablike jerks, the black body of the creature extends into view. Trailing tendrils of mucous, the disgusting apparition crawls from Skur's mouth into Michel's.

The next morning Michel's desiccated corpse lies on the floor of his apartment, which is swarming with uniformed police. A photographer snaps pictures with a Speed Graphic. A young coroner kneels and examines the body nervously. He glances upward at Dales, who is struggling to control his emotions.

"You sure," says the coroner, shaking his head, "that a man did this?"

Dales nods.

The coroner says, "I suppose, um, he could have force-fed him a corrosive agent of some kind . . . an acid. Except I don't know why it wouldn't have burned through the skin."

Dales says, "Could that account for the smell?"

"Yeah, maybe," says the coroner. "But we won't know for sure 'til we get a toxology report. Hopefully, we can get an answer for you in six to eight weeks. Meanwhile," he adds, "we can at least start on a physical exam of the body such as it is."

Two orderlies begin to load the corpse onto a gurney. At that moment Roy Cohn—trailed by his assistant—swaggers through the apartment door.

"Agent Dales!" says Cohn, with a sarcastic simulation of bonhomie.

Dales cringes. Cohn frowns and points his fingers at the orderlies.

"Hey! Hey!" he says. "Where do you think you're taking that? This man's a veteran. The body goes to Bethesda."

He turns to his assistant. "Howard, take care of it," he says.

Dales interrupts him. "Mr. Cohn, these men are going to the county morgue. An autopsy needs to be performed."

Cohn, irritated, stares at Dales. "C'mere," he says.

Dales stands his ground. Cohn gives up and addresses the head of the police unit. "Give us a minute," he says.

The room clears out. Cohn approaches Dales, all pretense of civility dropped.

"You wanna test me," he says, chillingly. "See how fast I can pull the chain and flush you. You wanna see your name on a list—'Are you now, or have you ever been . . . ?'"

"What are you talking about?" says Dales, angrily. "I'm no Communist."

Cohn says, his face a mask of cunning and ambition, "You are if I say you are."

Cowed, Dales says nothing. Cohn turns to the waiting orderlies. "This is a matter of national security," he says. "Take this body outta here. Get it out."

He turns to Dales. "See?" he sneers. "You're a patriot again." The older Dales continues:

When your partner dies, a piece of you dies with him. I'd been threatened by Mr. Cohn but I couldn't leave it alone. Not while Michel's killer was still out there. Not if I wanted to live with myself.

I knew that Skur had killed Michel out of vengeance for what had been done to him. Your father had told me as much. But your father also said that there were two other men who had the same thing done to them. Men who were already dead. Finding out what happened to them would at least help me understand what Skur had become. Understand how my partner was killed.

Later that day Dales enters the FBI bullpen and slumps down at his desk. He studies the file folder he'd left on his desk with growing interest. A few moments later he tosses the file down in front of Dorothy Bahnsen, the clerk who'd retrieved the file for him earlier.

"What's this?" asks Dales, pointing to a heavily blacked-out document.

Dorothy tells him that it was the deposition that named Gissing, Skur, and Oberman as Communists.

"It's all censored," says Dales.

"By the committee," says Dorothy. "To protect the identity of the witnesses."

Dales turns away. "There was no witness," he says, bitterly. "This whole thing's been manufactured. Edward Skur's no Communist. Neither were these other two men. I want to see their files."

Dorothy shakes her head. "I already checked—they're missing," she says. "But I recognized one of these names. It's in an X-File."

"An X-File?" asks Dales.

Dorothy walks to a nearby file cabinet. "Yes. Unsolved cases. I file them under *X*."

Dales asks, puzzled, "Why don't you file them under *U* for 'unsolved'?"

"That's what I did until I ran out of room," says Dorothy, rummaging through a file drawer. "Plenty of room in the *X*s."

Dales walks over to her, suddenly interested. "Who decides when a case gets an *X*?"

"The Director's office," says Dorothy. "It's kind of a dead end. No one's supposed to see them but they make for interesting reading. Here it is."

She hands Dales a file. He begins flipping through it. Dorothy tells the agent that it's the file of a German emigre, a Dr. Strohman, who was found dead the previous week in his office at the V.A.

"Let me guess," says Dales. "They weren't able to explain how his body had kind of collapsed, right?"

"Yes," says Dorothy, surprised.

He asks if Gissing's name is in the file. She nods, saying that he was a patient found dead at the scene. His death was determined to be a suicide.

"I guess he didn't much care for his treatment," she says.

"They think he killed his doctor and then killed himself?" says Dales, incredulously. "How did Gissing kill this man?"

Dorothy smiles, happy to make everything clear. "That's why it's an X-File," she says. "They don't know."

At the county morgue that night Dales watches as the coroner pulls George Gissing's body out of the freezer. He tells the agent that it's lucky that the body is still here. The V.A. has been trying to have it transferred.

"Why haven't they?" asks Dales.

The coroner says, "Well, this fella was a bigwig in the State Department. His family's been kicking up a stink."

The coroner pulls the sheet of the graying corpse. There is a four-inch scar on the corpse's chest, just below his throat.

"What's this?" asks Dales.

"Looks like he had some surgery," says the coroner. "Judging from the color of the scar, I'd say it was fairly recent."

Dales says, bracing himself, "I want you to cut this man open."

The coroner looks up, startled. "No, I can't do that," he says. "His family'll have my head."

Dales says, "Gissing and a man named Skur were patients of the same doctor. I think whatever was done to this man was done to the man who killed my partner."

He adds, "It may be the only way to explain how he died."

The coroner looks at Dales for a moment, then makes up his mind. A short while later he and Dale stand over the corpse's open chest cavity. They peer inside, puzzled. A white sac of some kind of organic material is nestled within the esophagus.

"What is that?" asks Dales.

"I don't know," says the coroner. "It looks like it's lodged into his esophagus. Wait a minute! Those are sutures. Whatever this is, someone put it there."

The coroner lowers his scalpel to the cocoon, slicing it open. Dales flinches as the black legs of the spider emerge. The rest of the creature begins to climb out from the corpse's chest cavity. The two men step back, horrified.

Later that night Dales knocks on Edward Skur's front door. Mrs. Skur opens it and eyes the agent with cold fury.

"Mrs. Skur, I hope I'm not disturbing you—"

"You have a lot of nerve coming here!" replies the woman.

Dales takes a deep breath. He says, "Your husband—you know he's not dead."

"How dare you!"

"Your husband was discredited in order to cover up a crime, Mrs. Skur. A crime that was committed upon him. Against his will."

Mrs. Skur moves to close the door. "Whatever was done to my husband, you're a part of it."

Dales pushes the door back open.

"According to V.A. records, your husband underwent surgery for war injuries. So did two other men he worked with at the State Department. But the surgeries they received, it wasn't what they thought it was. It had nothing to do with their war injuries."

"Then what was it?" says Mrs. Skur, confused.

Dales says, "It's called xenotransplantation. It's the grafting of another species into the human body. It's a procedure that Nazi doctors experimented with during the war."

He adds, "And I believe they continued their work here, using your husband and these other two men as unwitting test subjects."

Mrs. Skur says nothing. Dales hands her the coaster Bill Mulder left for him.

"I want to expose what was done to your husband, Mrs. Skur," he says. "I can't do that unless I have his help."

Dales turns to leave. For a moment, Mrs. Skur watches him go, then silently closes her door. As Dales walks toward the street a black sedan approaches from down the street, coming to a stop between him and his car. Its rear door opens; Roy Cohn gets out. The prosecutor faces Dales.

"Get in," says Cohn brusquely.

Dales hesitates.

"*Just get in!*"

Dales complies—reluctantly—and climbs into the backseat. Already sitting there is a silent Bill Mulder. The car drives off.

A few moments later Mrs. Skur exits through the back door of her house. Looking around nervously to make sure none of her neighbors are watching, she walks quickly to a fallout shelter in her backyard. Opening a trap door, she climbs down a ladder to its stark interior.

"Ed?" she says.

She pulls a string, illuminating a single bare light bulb. Edward Skur lies huddled in a corner, shivering. His wife hurries over to him.

"Are you all right?" she says.

"I told you not to come down here," he gasps.

"That FBI agent came back," she says.

Skur is too sick, too tortured, to care. He battles to control himself.

"I'm getting worse," he groans.

"He says he wants to help you," pleads Mrs. Skur.

"It's too late to help me," says Skur, turning toward her. "I can't help myself anymore."

He moans, gags, and lunges at his wife. Her screams echo through the quiet suburban night—then stop.

Later that evening Cohn, Dales, and Mulder arrive at FBI headquarters. Cohn leads them inside the director's large office and orders Dales to sit at the end of a long conference table. The director— J. Edgar Hoover—stands with his back turned, looking out the window at Pennsylvania Avenue below.

"Leave us alone," says Hoover.

"Mr. Director—" protests Cohn, nervously.

"Leave us."

Cohn departs reluctantly, taking Bill Mulder with him. Hoover stills stares outside. After a long pause, he begins speaking.

He says, "In 1945, at the time of the first conference to map out the peace after the Second World War, there lived within the Soviet orbit one hundred and eighty million people. Lined up on the antitotalitarian side at the time were one billion, six hundred and twenty million people."

Hoover slowly turns to face Arthur Dales.

"Today, Mr. Dales—just seven years later—there are eight hundred million people under the absolute domination of Soviet Russia: an increase of over four hundred percent. On our side, the figure has shrunk to around five hundred million. In other words, in less than seven years the odds have changed from nine to one in our favor to eight to five against us."

Hoover moves toward Dales.

"The threat of global Communist domination is a reality that can be ignored only at the risk of our own annihilation."

Dales finds his voice. "The men we arrested weren't Communists," he says, tremulously.

Hoover glares at Dales, enraged.

"If we are to defeat the enemy, we must use their tools!" he declaims. "We must go further. We must do those things which even our enemies would be ashamed to do. It is only through strength that we can make our enemies fear us and thereby ensure our own survival!"

Dales is speechless, completely intimidated.

Hoover says, more calmly now, "You have only one chance, Mr. Dales, to save yourself. To demonstrate you have the strength to serve your country."

Dales can only stare back, numb at the raw power of the man.

Later that night Dales rides with Bill Mulder and Roy Cohn's assistant in Cohn's car. They pull up to the Hoot Owl Bar. Dales fastens a small microphone and radio transmitter underneath his shirt.

"Make your meeting with Skur," says Cohn's assistant, tersely. "Let him think you're alone. Put him at ease. We'll be in when the time's right."

Dales turns to the State Department man. "Is this why you came to see me, Mr. Mulder?" he says. "To make me your stalking horse?"

"I follow my orders," says Bill Mulder, gravely.

Cohn's assistant pulls Dales's revolver from his holster.

"I might need that," protests Dale.

Cohn's assistant says, "We want him alive."

Dales enters the closed bar.

"I turned the lights off out front," says the bartender. "Just pull the door shut when you go."

"Thanks for your help," says the agent, slipping the bartender a sheaf of folded bills.

"Anything to help out the Bureau," says the bartender, exiting.

Dales goes to the bar and pours himself a drink.

Edward Skur steps out of the shadows. "Did you come here to kill me?" he says. "Or to save me?"

Dales turns to face Skur. "I'm here to help you. Just like I told your wife."

"My wife is dead!" moans Skur. He adds, "I'm already dead, too. Inside. Because of this thing they put in me.

For what? To turn me into some kind of killing machine? Or just to see what would happen?"

His words are being broadcast—crudely and scratchily—to a bulky radio receiver in Cohn's car. Dales's eyes go to the door.

Skur says, "They're not coming, you know. They wanted me to kill you, or you wouldn't be here. You're part of their test now, too."

Dales says, anxiously, "I don't want to kill you."

"I know," says Skur, sorrowfully and immediately lunges at his prey.

Inside Cohn's car, Bill Mulder starts toward the door at the sound of the struggle until Cohn's assistant puts a hand on his shoulder. Bill Mulder slumps back into his seat.

In the bar Skur has Dales pinned to the floor. His eyes roll back, his jaws unhinge, and the spider crawls out. Dales

manages to unsnap his handcuffs from his belt, snap one end around the foot rail of the bar, and lock the other around Skur's wrist.

In the black sedan the radio receiver falls silent. Bill Mulder and Cohn's assistant rush inside the bar. They see Skur handcuffed to the foot rail and Dales standing out of Skur's reach, staring at them accusingly.

Back in old Arthur Dales apartment—in 1990—Fox Mulder slumps down and shakes his head. He mops his right hand across his forehead; a gold wedding band catches the light.

"I can't believe my father threw in with these men," he says. "He let them dictate his conscience."

Dales grimaces. "Oh, don't fool yourself," he says. "None of us are free to choose. I was ruined for my 'insubordination.' You keep digging through the X-Files," he adds, "and they'll bury you, too."

Mulder asks, "Skur died saying my father's name. Why?"

"I haven't the slightest idea," says Dales.

Mulder stands and pulls on his jacket. "But there was one thing you didn't explain," he says. "How Skur was able to get away. How he was able to live in obscurity for thirty-eight years."

Dales looks up in wonder. "Thirty-eight years!" he says. "My God!"

He pauses, letting the memories wash over him. "Well," he explains. "I kept hearing things through the years, you know—people tell me things. I'd heard that he was dead, that he'd been kept in some secret lab while they finished up the experiment. I'd even thought that maybe some poor innocent bastard—somebody with a conscience—had let him go."

On a stretch of Midwestern farmland, in 1952, Arthur Dales's blue sedan courses down a country road. Young Dales stops the car, gets out, tosses the keys to a handcuffed Edward Skur, and—without looking back—walks slowly back to town.

"But why would anyone do that?" asks young Fox Mulder, in 1990. "Why would anyone let a killer go free?"

Arthur Dales says, "In the hope that by letting him live, the truth of the crimes that were committed against him and the others might someday be exposed."

back story:

A complex and challenging episode even in a series that specializes in them, "Travelers" is in large part a tribute to one man. His name was Howard Dimsdale—a talented screenwriter victimized by the vicious anti-Communist blacklist of the 1950s. Unable to obtain writing assignments after the witch hunts began, he worked for several years in exile in Europe. He also wrote Hollywood movies, secretly, under the pseudonym Arthur Dales.

Dimsdale died in 1991. During the latter part of his life Dimsdale was a respected writing teacher and mentor at the American Film Institute in Los Angeles. Two of his students—and admirers—were *X-Files* co-executive producer Frank Spotnitz and co-producer John Shiban.

"Howard Dimsdale was a wonderful man," says Shiban, "who told incredible stories about that period, which was a part of American history we'd always been interested in." Early in *The X-Files*'s fifth season the two writer/producers decided that the paranoia, treachery, and double-dealing of that dark era would fit nicely into the *X-Files* ethos.

Spotnitz says, "We wondered 'What if the witch-hunt was actually a smoke screen to conceal something else?'" Once into the story, he adds, he and his writing partner realized that (1) FBI Agent Arthur Dales's dilemma when ordered to go against his principles and arrest an innocent man neatly mirrored the pressure on blacklisted individuals to "name names" and save their own skins; and that (2) setting most of the episode in the distant past would open up new opportunities to trace the roots of both Fox Mulder and the X-Files. They'd also solved a tricky scheduling problem. During 5X15's eight-day March production schedule both David Duchovny and Gillian Anderson were needed in Los Angeles for reshoots on the X-Files movie.

Accordingly, a more-thorough-than-usual search was launched to find an actor who could hold on to the viewers in their absence. At virtually the last minute, the part of Young Dales was given to Fredric Lane, an experienced TV and movie actor whose credits include Dallas, Mancuso, FBI, and last year's megahit Men in Black.

The episode's major casting coup, of course, was in convincing seventy-four-year-old Darren McGavin to take the role of Arthur Dales circa 1989. Over the past five years McGavin—whose 1974 drama Kolchak: The Night Stalker was a major creative influence on the teenage Chris Carter—had turned down numerous invitations to guest-star on The X-Files. The question of why, exactly, he accepted this offer produces only smiles and shrugs among the show's casting and production staff—plus the news that McGavin was subsequently signed to reprise his role in several episodes during Season Six.

After this, all that remained was to create a polished, convincing period movie in less time than is considered humanly possible. Costume designer Jenni Gullett and her staff scrambled frantically to rent, borrow, or sew all the vintage '50s clothing they needed; picture car coordinator Nigel Habgood rounded up as many 1952 and 1953 sedans as he could find; and art director Gary Allen perused old articles about the FBI in National Geographic magazine to help him recreate J. Edgar Hoover's headquarters of the time period.

"And then we did the bomb shelter, which was easy," says Allen. "Because when I was growing up in Southern California my father was a contractor and when he built them he took me along to help."

Special effects makeup supervisor Toby Lindala constructed both the fifties-ish monster and the elastic facial appliance that allowed it to crawl out of the tormented Edward Skur's mouth. A Vancouver restaurant called the Meat Market was turned into the Hoot Owl; and in the post-production process a special bleaching process was used to give the final film print a somewhat mellowed, vintage appearance.

The result, say both writers, was a finished product that they feel does justice to both the painful controversies of the 1950s and the contemporary TV series they work for. But alas, not everyone was completely satisfied.

Frank Spotnitz says, "We hired a retired FBI agent to serve as a technical advisor on the script. This was a gentleman who'd been with the Bureau for twenty or thirty years, and he was very offended by our script. He was angry that we would even suggest that J. Edgar Hoover—whom he still calls 'Mr. Hoover'—would be involved in any of the plots, or take any of the positions that he takes in the script. Then he told me that he'd never actually seen our show. 'But if this is the type of story that you're telling,' he told me, 'I can't imagine that it would be very popular.'"

(X)

Red-baiting U.S. Senator Joseph McCarthy, who died of alcoholism in 1957, was nicknamed "Tailgunner Joe" because of his service in the Army Air Corps during World War II.

(X)

J. Edgar Hoover's paranoid rant to Arthur Dales about the Communist menace was taken almost verbatim from a speech by Senator McCarthy.

(X)

David Fredericks, who played J. Edgar Hoover in this episode, played the same role last season in "Musings of A Cigarette Smoking Man" (4X07).

(X)

The controversial and sinister Roy Cohn, who died of AIDS in 1986, was portrayed recently by James Woods in the HBO movie Citizen Cohn and by Ron Leibman in the Pulitzer Prize-winning play Angels In America. David Moreland, who played the role in 5X15, had seen both productions before creating his own version of this real-life figure.

(X)

"Lili Marlene," a song popular with soldiers of both sides in World War II, was sung most notably by actress Marlene Dietrich. However, the version playing in the German doctor's house—carefully selected by a certain X-Files producer—is attributed to a hitherto-unknown female singer. Adroit freeze-framers might just be able to read the name on the record label: "Paula Rabwini."

(X)

Mulder's 1989 apartment is virtually the same as his 1998 apartment—except for the absence of a fish tank and computer.

(X)

Internet lines pulsed frantically on March 29 after observant fans noticed Mulder's wedding ring and cigarette habit in "Travelers." As in "Unusual Suspects" (5X01), these interesting details were added by David Duchovny himself—and will be explained, or maybe not, in later episodes.

(X)

Agent Hayes Michel was named after the fiancé of Mary Astadourian, Chris Carter's executive assistant.

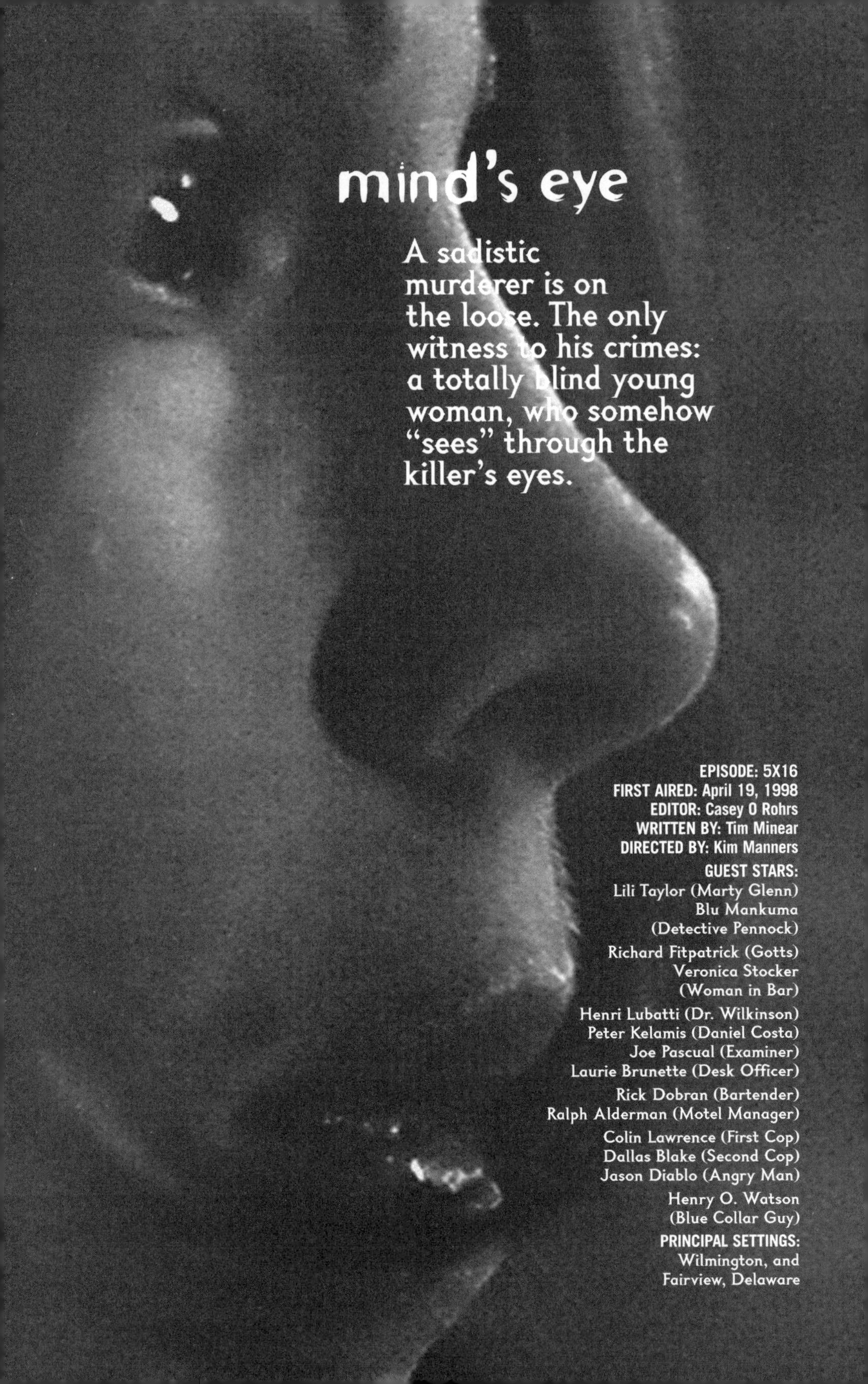

mind's eye

A sadistic murderer is on the loose. The only witness to his crimes: a totally blind young woman, who somehow "sees" through the killer's eyes.

EPISODE: 5X16
FIRST AIRED: April 19, 1998
EDITOR: Casey O Rohrs
WRITTEN BY: Tim Minear
DIRECTED BY: Kim Manners
GUEST STARS:
Lili Taylor (Marty Glenn)
Blu Mankuma
(Detective Pennock)

Richard Fitpatrick (Gotts)
Veronica Stocker
(Woman in Bar)

Henri Lubatti (Dr. Wilkinson)
Peter Kelamis (Daniel Costa)
Joe Pascual (Examiner)
Laurie Brunette (Desk Officer)

Rick Dobran (Bartender)
Ralph Alderman (Motel Manager)

Colin Lawrence (First Cop)
Dallas Blake (Second Cop)
Jason Diablo (Angry Man)

Henry O. Watson
(Blue Collar Guy)

PRINCIPAL SETTINGS:
Wilmington, and
Fairview, Delaware

At a shabby apartment building in Wilmington, Delaware, a young woman enters the front door. She carries her groceries up the stairway to her apartment. Inside, she clicks on the television, pulls a carton of cigarettes out of her grocery bag, and lights a smoke from her stovetop burner. She relaxes in her easy chair in front of the television.

She shudders, gasps, and stands. She is experiencing a vision of a murderous assault, of a young man in a light blue shirt, in a bathroom.

That night a police car pulls up to the Paradise Motel, a no-class establishment next to a nearby highway. Two cops get out. With guns and flashlights drawn, they search a motel room and through a slightly opened bathroom door, spot a dead man, dressed in a light blue shirt, sprawled in a pool of his own blood.

"Geez!" whispers the first cop.

He slowly pushes the bathroom door open. Someone is standing behind the translucent shower curtain in the bathtub.

"Police! Don't move!" says the cop.

He yanks open the curtain. The young woman raises her hands, dropping a bloody sponge. The policeman spins her around and cuffs her. Her hands are covered with blood.

The first cop blinks, startled. "Hey, Keith," he says to his partner, "I think you might want to check this out.

He shines his flashlight directly into his prisoner's eyes. She does not blink, and her pupils are opened wide.

"I think she's blind," says the cop.

At FBI headquarters the next day Scully switches on a slide projector and projects a gruesome close-up of the murdered man.

"The deceased is Paco Ordonez, a.k.a. 'Little Monster,'" she says. "Street dealer, liked to use grade-school kids as couriers. Out on bail for possession with intent. Two-time loser looking at life."

Mulder studies the picture intently.

"I have the same pair of pants," he says, nodding his head in wonder. "Who exterminated him?"

He turns to a Wilmington detective—whose name is Pennock—standing nearby.

"That's a subject of some debate," says the detective.

Scully flashes several more slides, telling them that the killer carved a single C-shaped cut up through the right kidney; fatal blood loss came in less than thirty seconds.

Mulder says, "I'm going to assume the killer knew what he was doing, and the 'C' wasn't one of his initials."

Pennock says, "Your assumptions are correct. Only the killer isn't a he."

Pennock hands Mulder a police file, and Scully projects a booking photo of the woman caught behind the shower curtain.

"Marty Glenn," says Pennock. "Twenty-eight. We found her at the scene doing a Formula 409. Under normal circumstances my department would have her dead to rights. There's just one little snag—"

"She's been blind from birth," says Mulder, reading from the file.

Pennock grimaces. "Now, before your heart goes out to her," he says, "check out her rap sheet."

Mulder reads off a laundry list of crimes: fraud, petty theft, aggravated assault.

"Believe me," says Pennock, "She's a real piece of work."

Scully adds, "Her juvenile records are sealed. But Detective Pennock has it on authority that two of them were drug busts. Possession, and possession with intent."

"So what?" says Mulder. "You think she caught Little Monster trying to snatch the pebble from her hand?"

Pennock says, "Nothing else makes sense."

"Including," says Mulder, "how a blind

girl can get the drop on an ex-con and bleed him out with surgical precision."

Scully explains that Marty Glenn took a $60 cab ride—alone—straight to the motel and asked the driver to direct her to Room 10, then told him to get lost.

"Thirty minutes later," adds Scully, "one dead heroin dealer."

Mulder nods, and turns to Pennock. "All right," he says. "So you really believe she did this. You just don't know how."

Pennock says that he has a theory. "I think," he says, "that she's got some kind of sixth sense that lets her see in the dark. Like a bat, or something. I've got forty-eight hours to convince the DA," he adds. "Or wait until she kills somebody else."

Mulder says, "How soon can I meet her?"

Later that day Marty Glenn sits up on her bunk bed in a Wilmington PD jail cell. Detective Pennock is standing at the door of her cell. Mulder and Scully are standing behind him.

"Oh, it's you," she says.

"See what I mean?" says Pennock.

"It's not magic," says Marty, scornfully. "It's your crappy cologne. Who's that with you?"

"I'm Special Agent Mulder."

"And the lady?"

"I'm Special Agent Scully. We'd like to ask you some questions, Marty."

Marty smiles and turns to Pennock. "You must be having trouble with your case, Detective," she says.

Pennock tries to take her by the elbow, but she jerks loose angrily.

"Fine, suit yourself," says Pennock.

Marty exits the cell, but stops when she reaches Mulder. "What are you staring at?" she says.

Mulder says, "An innocent woman, I hope."

They go to a nearby interrogation room. Marty faces Mulder and Scully, a sarcastic half-smile on her face.

"So," she says, "I'm all ears."

Scully says, "I'm curious why you refused your right to an attorney."

Marty shakes her head. "Unless you're gonna charge me," she says, "I don't plan on needing one."

Scully replies, "You can be charged right now for the fact that you've given

no compelling reason why you were in that motel room. What were you doing there, Marty?"

Marty smirks. "Putting mints on the pillows," she says.

Scully glances at Mulder—who looks like he's enjoying himself—and tells Marty that the cab driver has placed her in Room 10 around the time of the murder.

"Is that a crime?" says Marty.

"If you were involved in any way," says Scully.

"You mean," says Marty, "like an eyewitness?"

Scully fights to keep her patience. "Did you intend to buy drugs from Paco Ordonez?"

Marty takes a drag from her cigarette and says nothing.

Scully asks, "Did you kill him?"

Marty exhales a cloud of cigarette smoke.

"Hey, maybe it was just his time to go," she says. "I mean, other than the stab wound, did you check his cholesterol level, or anything?"

"How did you know there was just one stab wound?" Mulder says.

"Did I say that?" says Marty, realizing her mistake. "I guessed." She adds, recovering, "You know what the problem is? You've got no murder weapon. And I bet that's driving Stinky back there crazy."

Pennock is indeed watching the interview from behind a one-way mirror. Marty raises her voice.

"Isn't it, Stinky?" she says.

She turns to Mulder and Scully. "Why's he hiding?" she says. "It's not like I could see him."

She raises her voice again.

"You know what I did with it, detective?" she shouts. "I fed it to my seeing eye dog!"

Mulder doesn't crack a smile. "I'm curious, Marty," he says.

"Yeah?" says Marty. "About what?"

"If you didn't kill him, why you were at the crime scene cleaning up? And doing such a piss-poor job of it?"

Marty says nothing.

Mulder says, "Why don't we stop playing games here, okay? I mean, you probably don't know a feather duster from a duck's ass, do you? And it's ridiculous. You're a blind woman, for

God's sake! So why don't you just tell us who did kill Paco Ordonez, and Agent Scully and I can go rest up. And you can go home and work on your angry young blind girl comedy routine."

Marty frowns slightly, but again says nothing.

"Or," adds Mulder, "we can just stay here and entertain each other for the next forty-eight hours."

Mulder casually pours himself a glass of water—an act that would be close to impossible for his prisoner. Marty strikes out, knocking away the cup just as Mulder pours.

"Go to hell," says Marty, furious.

A few minutes later Marty sits alone, stewing, in the interrogations room. Mulder and Scully join Pennock behind the mirrored wall.

Pennock says, "See what I mean? Put a knife in her hand—"

"All I see," says Mulder, "is a woman who has adapted to her impairment admirably. She's honed all her other senses around her blindness."

"She's taunting you," says Pennock.

Mulder replies, "I don't know. I think she just wants us to think she's strong, independent. It's important to her."

Pennock says, flatly, "She wants us to know she did it."

Mulder disagrees again.

"Then why won't she help us?" asks Pennock. "It's been my experience that innocent people don't act like that, Agent Mulder."

Mulder shrugs. Scully stares at Marty, who is sitting, fidgeting, in the interrogation room. She says, "She wouldn't explain her presence at the crime scene, and she avoided all discussion of the murder."

Pennock reminds Mulder that she knew that there was only one stab wound.

Mulder nods non-committally.

"Detective, did you snake all the plumbing in the bathroom?" asks Scully.

Pennock replies, testily, "I turned that place upside down and inside out."

Scully says, "Well, if you find the weapon with her fingerprints on it, she's as good as convicted. Short of that, she's going to walk."

Pennock invites Scully to examine the crime scene with him one last time. Scully agrees. Mulder tells them to both go ahead.

"I want to investigate something," he says.

Shortly afterward Marty sits across from Mulder. She is hooked up to a lie detector. The machines operator—the examiner—is also in the room.

"I'm going to ask you a series of questions," says the examiner. "Respond only with a yes or no. Do not judge the content of the questions, simply answer truthfully. Is your full name Martell Francis Glenn?"

"Yeah," says Marty.

"Are you a resident of the state of Delaware—"

"Let's just cut through the bull," says the blind woman. "Or I'm going to decide not to cooperate at all."

The examiner looks at Mulder. Mulder thinks for a second, then makes up his mind.

"All right," he says, "let's get to it."

"I need to establish a baseline—" protests the examiner.

"I'm a resident of the state of Delaware, okay? Let's move on," says Marty, brusquely.

The examiner sighs and checks at the polygraph needles, which are steady. He asks Marty if it's her intention to lie during the course of the examination.

"I'm sure you'll tell me if it is," she says.

The examiner asks, "Did you stab Paco Ordonez, also know as 'Little Monster'?"

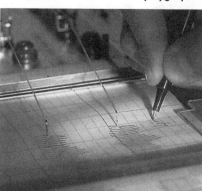

"Nope," says Marty.

The polygraph needle is steady.

"Did you arrange or plan the murder of Paco Ordonez?"

"No."

"Have you ever met Paco Ordonez?"

"No."

"Would you ever have occasion to see Paco Ordonez, or know him in any other way?"

The needle jumps. Mulder and the examiner both notice.

"Strike that," says the examiner, embarrassed. "Would you ever have occasion to interact with Paco Ordonez or know him in another way?"

"No," says Marty.

The needle is steady.

"Were you present during the murder of Paco Ordonez?"

"No."

While the examination is going on Mulder reaches over for a legal pad and pen and scribbles a question. It is "Did you see the murder?"

Marty cocks her head and listens. Mulder holds the pad up to the examiner, who squints at it in confusion.

Marty says to Mulder, "Why don't you just ask it yourself?"

Mulder leans forward. "Did you see the murder?" he says.

Marty says nothing. The needle jumps erratically.

"Did you see the murder?"

"I don't 'see' anything," says Marty, uneasily.

"Yes or no only, please!" says the examiner.

"Then the answer is no!" says Marty, defiantly.

The machine spasms strongly— the biggest needle deflection yet.

In the motel room where Paco Ordonez was killed Scully and Pennock search in vain for a murder weapon. Scully's cell phone rings. It is her partner.

"She's lying," says Mulder.

"About what?" asks Scully.

Mulder replies that Marty knew Ordonez, but that he doesn't think she murdered him; the polygraph answers indicate that.

"Would you like me to remind you," says Scully, "why polygraphs are inadmissible in court?"

"No. She cracked, Scully," says Mulder. "She was lying, I'm sure of it."

"Well, maybe she was, Mulder," says Scully, "but don't make me say the obvious. She didn't see anything—"

"Not with her eyes."

"Well, how else did she see?" says Scully. "Bat vision?"

Mulder replies that he doesn't know. At that moment Scully spots something above the bathroom sink: an old-fashioned disposal slot marked SHAVING BLADES ONLY.

"Well, Mulder," says Scully, "when you figure it out, give me a call."

She hangs up, then presses her finger against the disposal fixture. It moves slightly, as if it had been recently pulled out and poorly reattached. She grabs a tissue and pulls off the wall plate.

"Detective Pennock?" she says.

The policeman ambles over. Scully sticks a latex-gloved hand through the hole in the wall, reaches around, and pulls out one leather glove. It is covered with blood.

Later that day Marty Glenn is back in her holding cell. She has another vision: This time she is in a low-class establishment called the Blarney Stone, near a good-looking young woman sitting at the bar. The woman is angrily fending off the advances of someone—unseen—sitting next to her.

This vision alarms Marty. "Hey, somebody!" she yells. "I need a phone! I get to call a lawyer, somebody! I NEED A PHONE!"

A few minutes later she is seated at a desk in the police station bullpen. A uniformed cop stands over her and pushes a desk phone toward her.

"I got it!" says Marty, impatiently.

Marty dials. The cop hovers nearby.

Marty says, "You know, I'm sure the ACLU is gonna be very interested in how you violated a blind woman's rights by eavesdropping on her private phone call."

The cop gives her an "up yours" arm gesture, then moves away angrily.

"Same to you," says Marty, as the call goes through.

The phone rings at a low-class bar; the bartender picks it up. "Blarney Stone," he says.

He listens. "Let's see—the guy hittin' on the redhead at the end of the bar?

Yeah, we got somebody matching that description."

The bartender walks to the end of the bar and hands the phone to a rough-looking, gray-bearded man—his name is Gotts—who is becoming increasingly obnoxious in his harassment of the red-head.

"It's for you," says the bartender.

Puzzled, Gotts picks up the phone. "Yeah," he grunts.

"Leave her alone," says Marty.

Gotts looks over his shoulder. The red-head has taken this opportunity to make a quick escape.

"Who is this?" he says, angrily.

"You just leave her alone," says Marty. "I'm watching you."

Later that day Marty is back in the interrogation room; Scully and Pennock sit across from her. Marty picks up the evidence bag containing the bloody glove, and feels it.

"Let me guess," she says, finally. "Your killer is O.J. Simpson."

Scully says, evenly, "They were found at the crime scene with blood all over them. We believe they were worn by Paco Ordonez's killer."

Marty nods. "You're good," she says, sarcastically.

"We think they belong to you," says Pennock.

"Well, they don't," says Marty.

"Well," says Pennock, genially, "how about you try one on for us?"

"And put my prints all over them?"

"Your prints are already all over them," says Scully.

Marty says nothing. Mulder watches through the one-way mirror while Pennock places the glove smoothly on the suspect's hand. It fits perfectly.

"Somewhere, Marcia Clark weeps," says Marty. "But you still haven't got a weapon."

Pennock says, "Well, that's just a matter of time."

"But you haven't got time," says Marty, triumphantly.

Scully leaves the interrogation room and joins up with Mulder. "I hope you

saw what happened in there," she says.

Mulder says, "Even if the gloves do fit, you can still acquit."

Scully disagrees. "I think it's arrogance, Mulder. Which is the same reason why she agreed to take the polygraph test. She knows that the prejudices in this case are all in our favor."

"I don't think it's that simple," says Mulder. "Look at this."

He hands Scully the case file.

"She lives in poverty," he says, "but she's never taken advantage of the disability benefits available to her. Never once. It's poison to her; the mere suggestion that she's anything but a whole or complete person is offensive to her.

"It's not arrogance, it's pride."

"So you think that it was pride that made her ditch the bloody gloves?" asks Scully. "Her prints are all over them, Mulder. Why would she do that?"

Mulder shrugs. "I have no idea," he says.

"Okay," says Scully. "So by your reasoning the murderer took off with the murder weapon, but not the gloves, leaving Marty to come in, go straight to the gloves, and hide them in the one place where no one would easily think to find them."

Mulder looks his partner in the eye. "I think," he says, "that's the most accurate scenario available to us right now."

Scully thinks for a second. "Wait a minute," she says. "Maybe it's much simpler than that."

"What?"

"What if," asks Scully, "she's not really blind?" She adds, "She hasn't applied for any of her disability benefits. Maybe that's because she knows she couldn't pass the medical screening?"

"You think she's faking it?" asks Mulder, skeptically.

"No," says Scully. "But possibly it's a conversion disorder. Or a form of blindsight—a split consciousness whereby a person has a certain level of visual ability, but they're not aware they're actually seeing. It's worth checking out."

At the French Street bus terminal a jittery Gotts, carrying a briefcase, is talking on a pay phone. The voice on the other end is that of a drug dealer.

"Yo, man," says the drug dealer. "Moving Little Monster's H ain't gonna be easy. See, a lotta people respected him, you know?"

Gotts says, "You buyin' or not? If you're not buyin', I can go to somebody else."

The dealer laughs softly. "No, you can't," he says. "But I'm feelin' magnani-

mous. Swing by in a couple of hours and maybe we can do some business."

"Good," says Gotts. "But there's something I've gotta look into first. When I'm done, I'll be in touch."

Gotts hangs up, walks over to a rental locker, and slides the briefcase inside.

In the interrogation room an ophthalmologist named Wilkinson has Marty leaning into a diagnostic device called an autorefractor. Her eye, magnified many times, is visible on an attached monitor.

"Eyes wide, try not to move too much," says Wilkinson to Marty. Wilkinson twists the controls to stimulate Marty's eye, but her pupil is wide open and fixed as before.

"Are you aware of any sensation at all?" he asks.

"It's a miracle!" exclaims Marty, facetiously.

Wilkinson excuses himself and walks over to Mulder and Scully.

"I'm not getting anything," he says. "I don't think there's any activity in either the cerebral cortex or the superior colliculus."

Scully asks, "There's no way she could fool the machine?"

"We're talking about wholly involuntary physical responses," says the ophthalmologist. "I wasn't getting any reading."

At that moment Mulder glances at the monitor. Marty's pupil contracts sharply.

"So what is that?" asks the agent.

Marty is having a vision: In the Blarney Stone an unseen man is hitting on a dark-haired woman.

Mulder leans down toward her. "What is it, Marty?" he asks, softly. "What do you see?"

Marty says nothing.

Detective Pennock sticks his head inside and summons the agents into the hall. He introduces them to an assistant district attorney named Daniel Costa.

"So, what did we find?" asks Costa. "I hear the girl can actually see with some limited ability."

"No," says Mulder. "No. According to her examiner, she is completely without sight or any light sensitivity."

"But she is still our best and only suspect," says Scully.

Irritated, Costa turns to Pennock. "I'm not gonna try to indict a blind girl on some lousy prints."

Mulder says, "She doesn't exactly fit the definition of 'blind girl'."

Perplexed, Pennock asks Mulder what he's talking about. Mulder tells him that there is evidence of some kind of neurological activity, activity that caused her pupils to dilate.

"To me," adds Mulder, "It indicates some reaction to stimuli. Some kind of physical response to images in her mind's eye."

Costa shrugs. "How does that make her the killer?" he asks.

Mulder says, "I didn't say it did."

Costa turns to Pennock. "Kick her loose," he says. "I'm not trying her. Not without a murder weapon. Kick her loose."

In the police bullpen shortly afterward Marty Glenn is released from custody. She signs for a manila envelope of personal possessions, then pulls out her wallet and counts the bills inside.

"These better still be twenties," she says to the desk officer, sharply.

"No," replies the cop, sarcastically. "I replaced 'em with fifties since you're so damn sweet."

Marty smiles, snaps open her expandable cane, and taps her way slowly down the corridor. Mulder watches her go, as Scully joins him.

Scully says, "Want to hear the latest? Detective Pennock ran the gloves for blood typing and found two different samples. One type matching Marty Glenn's."

"Well, she was examined," replies Mulder. "There were no cuts and wounds on her."

"Yeah, well, all the same," says Scully, "I'm going to hand-deliver them to the lab in Washington. Expedite a PCR to see if it's a match."

Mulder shakes his head and points to Marty, who is still making her way slowly down the hallway.

"Look at her," he says. "Do you really think she's capable?"

"I'll let you know as soon as I get the test back," says Scully, coolly.

On a busy city street Marty Glenn is making her way back home, tapping the sidewalk ahead of her. She stops suddenly; something is seriously bothering her. It is another vision: The red-haired woman from the night before is being slammed against the outside wall of a building. In fact, what Marty is 'seeing' is actually happening. The woman's assailant is Gotts, who has his hand pressed frighteningly over her mouth.

"Who called me last night?" snarls Gotts. "Who's watching me?"

He removes his hand from the terrified woman's mouth.

"What!? I-I don't know what you're talking about!" she says.

Gotts asks her if she's a cop. The woman desperately denies it. As he begins to attack her Gotts stifles her screams

Marty Glenn flinches, than stiffens.

"I need to get to Spring Street!" she shouts. "Which way is Spring Street? Somebody! Answer me!"

Most of the passersby eye her suspiciously and give her a wide berth. A blue collar guy, though, stops and speaks up.

"Four blocks to the left," he says.

Marty hears him, but her vision is continuing: The red-haired woman is being threatened by a long switchblade knife.

Marty turns left and walks right into a busy street. Traffic screeches to a halt behind the blind woman.

In Marty's mind's eye, the red-haired woman is screaming.

The blue collar guy dashes into the street, grabs Marty by the shoulders, and escorts her onto the sidewalk. A few minutes later they are standing at the edge of the crime scene she has just envisioned.

"Where?" asks Marty, frantically.

"Here," says the workman. "There's an alley here. Right here."

"Okay!" says Marty. "I'm fine! Leave me alone!"

The workman reluctantly retreats.

Marty feels her way down the now-deserted alley, until she comes to a barred window she saw in her vision. She feels her way to a large metal Dumpster nearby, and struggles to lift the lid. She reaches inside and feels the body of the woman Gotts murdered.

Sometime later Marty, in shock, stands before the desk officer who had previously released her.

"Excuse me," says Marty, softly. "Excuse me, somebody."

"Yeah?" says the desk officer, not exactly thrilled to see her.

"I killed them," says Marty. "I killed them both."

She holds up her hands. They are covered with blood.

Later that day Marty sits, disconsolate, in the interrogation room. Mulder enters and sits across from her.

"I read your 'confession'," he says, somberly. "Detective Pennock is typing it up as we speak."

Marty says, "I'll sign it."

"You'll make him a very happy man," says Mulder.

"Can't have everything," says Marty

Mulder stares at her for a moment. "As for me," he says, "I'm a little puzzled by this sudden change of heart."

"Please," says Marty. "Too much charity of heart and I wanna puke."

Mulder turns away. "Why kill them?" he says, puzzled. "Paco Ordonez? Susan Forester?"

Marty says nothing.

"Did you even know that was her name?" asks Mulder. "Susan Forester. She was thirty years old. Native of Wilmington. She waitressed part time. She lived alone with her two cats—"

"Shut up!" says Marty, anguished. "Why are you doing this? I'm giving you people everything you want!"

She places a cigarette in her mouth. Mulder strikes a match and lights it for her. Marty takes a long drag.

Mulder leans forward. "I like you, Marty," he says. "I admire you. And I don't want to see you confess to crimes you didn't commit."

"You just feel sorry for me," says Marty.

"No, I don't," says Mulder. "Not the way you think I do."

Marty says, intensely, "Read the confession. I got it all perfect. Every detail. How could I do that if I'm innocent?"

Mulder looks her in the eye. "I believe you witnessed both murders. You saw them, somehow. But you were way across town when they happened! You were a sixty-dollar cab ride away!"

Marty scoffs, not hiding her surprise very well.

"You're crazy," she says.

"I think you tried to stop them," says Mulder. "You tried to, but you didn't get there in time."

Marty takes her head. "I don't have to talk to you any more," she says.

Mulder grabs her hand. "Marty, whoever is doing this, they're going to kill again. And you can help stop that."

Marty is near tears. "I can't stop anything," she says, softly. She stands up abruptly. "I don't have to talk to you any more. Period. Officer! We're done!"

Mulder stands also. "Who's worth pleading guilty for, Marty?" he says.

"Officer! We're done!"

As the cop arrives to take her away, Mulder leans in closer. "You didn't do it," he says, forcefully. "And I'm not going to let this happen. Do you hear me?"

At the bus station Gotts is talking to the drug dealer on a pay phone.

"Sorry, man, deal's off," says the dealer.

Gotts says, angrily, "What do you mean 'deal's off?' You can't back out!"

"Hey, look here, brother," the dealer replies, "I do what I need to do to stay down when somebody's shining his light on me."

"What are you talkin' about?"

"Somebody's gunnin' for you, man, and I ain't gettin' in the middle of it."

"Who? Who's gunnin' for me?"

"Some old girlfriend of yours. Called last night and told me I should steer clear. Said she was passin' the word."

Gotts says, "Listen to me. She's nobody. She knows nothing. You and me, man, we're still cool. Trust me!"

The dealer says, "Yeah, well, if she don't know anything, how'd she get this number?"

"Listen to me!" Gotts fairly hisses into the phone. "I got nowhere else to take this stuff!"

"That's not my problem," says the dealer, totally unimpressed. "Just don't you call here again."

In the police interrogation room Mulder sits alone, reading a yellowed case file. It is dated January 27, 1970, and contains the information that a murder victim was found lying face down, having sustained a single stab wound to the right kidney.

Pennock enters, wearing a self-satisfied smile.

"Well, I appreciate your help here, such as it was," he tells Mulder, "but I'd say we're doing all right. She just signed her confession."

"Congratulations," says Mulder, unhappily.

Pennock frowns. "I don't feel as good as you might think, you know."

"All you got is a signature," says Mulder. "No lawyer's going to let her go down based on that."

"I'm aware of that," says Pennock, defensively.

"Doesn't it bother you, detective," says Mulder, "that you still have no clear motive?"

Pennock eyes Mulder warily. "Well, she just now gave us that," he says, slowly. "Drugs—just like I thought. She even told us where to find them."

In the bus station shortly afterward a maintenance man uses his pass key to open Gotts's locker. With Mulder watching, Pennock pulls out the drug-filled briefcase.

Pennock says, happily, "I'd say this is going to make a pretty short trial."

Mulder remains stubbornly downbeat. "If you think about it," he says, "it actually proves nothing."

Annoyed, Pennock points at the plastic bags of heroin. "There it is! Just like she said!"

"Just like she *described*," says Mulder.

Pennock stares at Mulder as if he's gone crazy. "You know, the thing I find most surprising about this case is *you*. You are one *skeptical* guy, Agent Mulder."

"Skeptical?"

"Oh, yeah!"

"I've been called a lot of things," says Mulder. "Skeptical, however, is not one of them."

Mulder's cell phone rings. "Skeptical!" he mutters to himself.

The call is from Scully at FBI headquarters. She tells him that she's got the PCR results from the bloody gloves.

"And?" says Mulder.

"Neither one was Marty's," says Scully. "You were right. She didn't do it."

"Yeah," says Mulder. "You know that and I know that, and so does whoever Marty's protecting. But Pennock is salivating right now.

"What we have to do is convince Marty. I've got an idea. I'll get back to you."

Behind Mulder, Pennock has finished tagging the drug briefcase and is heading for the exit. On a nearby bench sits Gotts, numb with rage. Once the policemen leave, he follows them.

Back in the police station Marty sits on her bunk in the holding cell. She frowns slightly at the sound of familiar footsteps.

"What do you want now?" she says, wearily.

A cop unlocks the cell door and Mulder enters. He sits on the bunk bed beside her.

"I know who you're protecting, Marty," he says. "And I think I know why. You're protecting the man who killed your mother."

Marty is stone-faced. She shakes her head.

"I don't know who you're talking about."

"I've got the original police report from 1970," says Mulder, quietly. "Your mother died from a single stab wound to the right kidney, as did Paco Ordonez and Susan Forester. Dead at the hands of an unknown assailant."

Marty is expressionless. "I never knew my mother," she says.

"No," says Mulder. "But for once, you were there when it happened. She was pregnant with you at the time. She died on the operating table as the doctors were trying to save her."

He adds, "You were born—just barely. But the interruption in blood flow you suffered most likely caused your blindness."

Marty blinks away tears. "What does that have to do with anything?"

"I believe that during that time as you lost one sense, you gained another. That somehow, a connection was formed between you and your mother's killer."

"What connection?" asks Marty.

"You see through his eyes," says Mulder. "You always have. You don't want to, you just do. And because of that you feel responsible for his actions, which you're not."

His words obviously hit home. But Marty is silent.

Mulder adds, urgently, "And you're sitting here in prison, for crimes you didn't commit. It isn't going to accomplish anything, Marty."

The cell door is opened. Detective Pennock pushes through. He tells Mulder that Marty is being transferred.

The agent keeps his eyes on the blind woman. "There's absolutely no point to your doing this, Marty," he says. "We're going to find him with or without you."

Marty rises and is led out of her cell. She stops momentarily and turns back to Mulder.

"I'm sorry," she says, gently.

Sometime later Marty—her hands and wrists shackled—is led out of the police station into an attached underground garage. She stops, and gasps—and has a vision of herself. Whoever's eyes she is looking through are looking right at her.

At street level, behind a chain-link fence extending to the garage's ceiling, Gotts looks down directly at Marty Glenn. He knows he's found what he's looking for.

At the Women's Detention Center in Fairview Marty is led from her cell into a visiting room. Behind a Plexiglas partition, Mulder sits across from her.

"What's going on?" asks Marty.

Mulder says, "Detective Pennock is with the warden right now, arranging for your release. The charges are being dropped. You're no longer a suspect in this case."

Marty becomes visibly agitated at this news. "How can they do that?" she says. "I confessed."

"Well, a confession is worthless if it's a lie. And yours was a lie."

Marty shakes her head, dismayed. "What have you been telling them?"

"Just that you're innocent. Which is something they would have found out on their own, anyway. The locker you sent us to? It had prints on it, but they weren't yours."

"I was careful," insists Marty.

"Yeah, but somebody else wasn't so careful. Charles Wesley Gotts. Ex-con. Convicted in 1970 of aggravated assault. Was paroled three weeks ago and he's been missing ever since."

"Never heard of him," says Marty.

"I happen to believe that," says

Mulder. "PCR test confirm that it was his blood on the gloves."

Mulder leans forward, his expression one of deep sadness. "The tests confirmed something else, Marty," he says. "He's your father. That was the connection."

Marty is crying now. She nods.

Pennock appears behind Mulder. "Okay," says the detective. "Everything's set. That is, if everything's taken care of at this end."

"What's he talking about?" asks Marty, softly.

Mulder says, evenly, "Detective Pennock has agreed to not pursue aiding and abetting charges against you if you agree to help us find him. We need your help, Marty. You can end it, now."

Marty nods. "I can end this," she says, softly.

"I'm sure that's what you always wanted," says Mulder.

"I never wanted to spend my life in a place like this," says Marty. "I had no choice."

She turns toward Pennock. "If I help you," she asks, "will you protect me until he's caught?"

Pennock says, solemnly, "I will personally guarantee your safety."

Marty says, with infinite sadness, "Take me home."

Later that day Mulder and Scully join the Wilmington PD surveillance of the Blarney Stone.

"Just in time for the surprise party," says Mulder.

Scully asks Mulder whether Marty told him that Gotts would be here.

"She described the place," replies Mulder. "Right down to the matchbooks."

"What made her decide to cooperate?" asks Scully.

"She wants to stop him," says Mulder.

"All of a sudden?" asks Scully, unconvinced. "If she were so anxious to stop him, why didn't she tell us his name before now?"

Mulder replies that she didn't know his name. They'd never met; he'd been in prison her entire life.

Scully is still skeptical. "Well, yet according to you, she was seeing through his eyes all that time—"

"I don't think she was sure of what she was seeing," says Mulder, impatiently. "It was more like a constant image in her mind. That she'd learned to live with over time. Up until three weeks ago."

"When the murders started?" asks Scully.

Mulder nods. "He was paroled, and everything changed."

"Well, if all this is true," she says, "let's go get him."

Now, however, Mulder seems troubled.

"Everything's changed for her, Scully," he says, glancing across the street at the bar. "I don't think we're going to find him in there."

At Marty Glenn's apartment the blind woman gathers up her clothing. Pennock stands guard.

"Need some help there?" says the detective.

"No," says Marty, brusquely.

"Should have known," he replies, with a frown of resignation.

Marty continues to pack her belongings. Pennock tells her she doesn't have to take so much—she won't be in protective custody very long.

Marty stands stock still. "It's too late for that, anyway," she says.

"Why's that? What are you talking about?" asks Pennock, puzzled.

Marty walks into her kitchen and picks up a large coffeepot.

"He's been keeping tabs on me for about a day," she says. "Now he knows where I live. He's reading the names on the mailboxes right now."

"What?" says Pennock, glancing at the front door.

At that moment Marty rushes toward him and hits him on the back of the head with the coffeepot. Pennock sprawls flat, knocked unconscious. Marty frantically rummages under his coat, coming out with his pistol. She leaves her apartment and walks, listening intently, into the hallway.

In the lobby of the building Gotts scans Marty's name on the mailbox. He walks slowly up the stairway.

At the Blarney Stone Mulder and Scully are quickly exiting via the rear door. Mulder has his cell phone to his ear.

"How did you know he wouldn't be in there?" asks Scully.

"She didn't want us to get him," says Mulder. "She misdirected us on purpose."

"She's still protecting him?"

"No, she's not. She never was."

Mulder clicks off his phone. "Pennock's not picking up," he says.

"What do you mean?" asks Scully.

"It's not him she's been protecting," says her partner, entering their car. "If he goes back to prison, so does she. She's never had a choice until now."

Inside the apartment building Gotts walks through Marty's front door, ready to kill. Her place looks deserted—except for Pennock lying crumpled on the floor. Gotts's eyes narrow at the sight. He clicks open his switchblade. Crouched behind the kitchenette counter, Marty flinches at the sound.

Gotts searches the living room as Marty sees through his eyes. He checks the closet, then the bathroom, and turns, finally, toward the kitchen. He walks to the counter. Marty stands up and points the gun at his face.

"I hate the way you see me," she whispers.

She pulls the trigger. There is an explosion and everything goes black.

Later that day the two FBI agents arrive at Marty's apartment and Scully is the first to spot Gotts's body on the floor. Shortly afterward, the apartment is filled with policemen. A now-conscious Pennock handcuffs Marty's arms behind her back.

"She did this one," says the detective. "Trust me."

Sometime later Mulder walks slowly down a prison corridor. He stops at Marty's cell, stands outside the bars, and sees her sitting on her bunk.

"Not much to look at, is it. At least, that's what they tell me," says Marty. She walks to the cell door and takes Mulder's hand. "You were at the sentencing, Agent Mulder," she says.

"Is it my cologne?" he asks.

"No," she says, smiling. "I just knew you'd be there."

Mulder nods sadly. "Marty, let me speak to the judge on your behalf—"

"No," says Marty, firmly.

Mulder nods again.

He says, "We found where he'd been staying. It's a motel not far from where Paco Ordonez had been murdered."

"And before that, Atlantic City," says Marty. She smiles. "I'd never seen the ocean before. And now, when I close my eyes, and even when I open them, that's all I see."

Mulder gazes at her, understanding. A prison matron appears beside him.

"Well, you're lucky he wasn't a fan of the Ice Capades," he says.

Marty laughs. The matron taps Mulder on the shoulder.

"Lights out!" announces a harsh male voice over the loudspeaker.

Mulder slips his hand gently from hers. Marty turns, smiles sadly, and walks slowly into the shadows.

back story:

A classic stand-alone episode with a relatively straightforward—but suitably creepy—premise, "Mind's Eye" revolves around the concept of "remote viewing." This sub-group of paranormal theory posits that certain individuals possess the ability to observe events—either through the eyes of others or on their own—that occur beyond the range of conventional vision. In the 1970s, the U.S. Central Intelligence Agency underwrote a $20 million research project to determine if remote viewing (a nice ability to have if, say, you're searching for an enemy missile site) actually exists.

Another party with a keen interest in the subject: *X-Files* story editor Tim Minear. "Supposedly," says Minear, with a wry smile, "some remote viewers have 'gone' to Mars."

Minear adds, "It seemed to me that it would be a good topic. But then I thought: It might be a good idea for a short story, but how do you make the whole thing work visually? Then, as it usually happens when you have these unworkable ideas, the best thing is to stop concentrating on it and make the thing about a specific person instead. That's when, for some reason, I hit upon the idea of the remote viewer being blind.

"This intrigued me and I was also intrigued with the idea of doing the story of a blind woman who was not Audrey Hepburn. I wanted to make her a bitch, because the fact is that disability doesn't necessarily ennoble a person. I know I wouldn't be ennobled. In fact, I'd be pissed!"

After several intensive story meetings with Frank Spotnitz, John Shiban, and Vince Gilligan (plus the post-Christmas fizzle of a previously scheduled script) Minear was given the go-ahead for his first solo episode. More good news came during the casting process. "When they sent me off to write it," says Minear, "the guys asked me to think about actors who would be good for Marty. Without hesitation, I said 'Lili Taylor'."

Lili Taylor—a New York–based actress who starred with Julia Roberts in *Mystic Pizza* as well as in *Dogfight, I Shot Andy Warhol,* and many other well-regarded independent films—was thought to be decidedly not interested in taking TV guest star roles. Unbeknownst to the production staff, though, Taylor was a fan of the show (as well as a drama school classmate of Gillian Anderson) and had already contacted L.A. casting director Rick Millikan.

Millikan says, "Two or three weeks before the script came out, her managers called me and said she would love to do an episode. When 'Mind's Eye' was finished we all looked at it and said, 'Perfect.'"

With these main elements in place shooting went fairly smoothly. A brief debate broke out, however, when the time came to design and build Marty's apartment. After art director Greg Loewen pointed out that a blind woman wouldn't actually need or use lamps or ceiling lights, the lighting department countered that although *The X-Files* was a dark show, it wasn't that dark.

"To tell you the truth," says Loewen, "I could see their point."

Ⓧ

Canadian actor Blu Mankuma, who plays Detective Pennock, previously appeared as computer expert Claude Peterson in "Ghost In The Machine" (1X06).

Ⓧ

The staccato, nightmarish quality of Marty Glenn's remote visions were created mainly in post-production by visual effects supervisor Laurie Kallsen-George.

Ⓧ

As documented by his cover profile in *Vanity Fair* magazine, the wisecrack "even if the gloves do fit—you can still acquit" was an on-set improvisation by David Duchovny.

Ⓧ

For her performance as Marty Glenn in "Mind's Eye," Lili Taylor was nominated for an Emmy Award in the category of Best Actress in a Dramatic Series.

Ⓧ

Editor Casey O Rohrs also received an Emmy nomination for his work on 5X16.

all souls

After a handicapped
young woman
is killed in the act
of prayer, Scully is pulled
into the case
and forced to search her
own soul for answers.

EPISODE:
5X17
FIRST AIRED:
April 26, 1998
EDITOR:
Heather MacDougall
TELEPLAY BY:
Frank Spotnitz & John Shiban
STORY BY:
Billy Brown & Dan Angel
DIRECTED BY:
Allen Coulter
GUEST STARS:
Emily Perkins
(Dara/Paula/Roberta
/Fourth Girl)
Jody Racicot
(Father Gregory/
Dark Figure)
Glenn Morshower
(Aaron Starkey)
Arnie Walters
(Father McCue)
Patti Allan
(Mrs. Kernof)
J. P. Finn (Priest)
Eric Keenleyside
(Lance Kernof)
Lauren Diewold (Emily)
Lorraine Landry
(Pathologist Vicki Belon)
Tracy Elofson
(Four-Faced Man)
Todd Harris (Orderly)
Bob Wilde
(George Vincent Dyer)
Tim O'Halloran
(D.C. Sergeant)
PRINCIPAL SETTINGS:
Alexandria and
Mount Lebanon, Virginia;
Washington, D.C.

It is late evening in a solidly middle-class suburb; a gray sedan stops in front of a neat two-story frame house. A man in black gets out, removes a bulky case, walks up to the front door, and knocks.

"Good evening, Father," says a plain, middle-aged woman. Her name is Jane Kernof.

"Is she ready?" asks the man in black.

His name is Father McCue—the Scully family priest last seen in 5X03 ("Redux II").

Mrs. Kernof smiles, and nods.

Father McCue steps over the threshold. He prepares the instruments of baptism: a small cross, a golden bowl, and a vial of holy water. He carefully, reverently, pours the water into the bowl.

"Baptism is the rite of initiation," he says. "This holy water takes away original sin. The sacrament confers the grace of God, bringing the soul into God's family."

As he speaks, Mrs. Kernof's eyes well with emotion. She glances at her husband, Lance Kernof. He is lifting their severely retarded sixteen-year-old daughter, Dara, out of her wheelchair. With some difficulty, he carries her to where Father McCue is standing. The Catholic priest dips his fingers into the holy water, then touches Dara's forehead gently.

He says, "Dara, I baptize you in the name of the Father, and the Son, and the Holy Sprit. Bless you, my child."

Later that night—midnight—a violent thunderstorm sweeps over the Kernof house.

In their bedroom, Mr. and Mrs. Kernof are asleep. Upstairs, Dara Kernof carefully swings her legs over the side of her bed, and stands.

A few moments later something awakens Lance Kernof. He sits up groggily, stands, and shuffles to the bedroom door.

"Dara?" he says.

He walks into his daughter's bedroom. It is empty. Frightened, he rushes to the window. Dara is walking haltingly down the rain-soaked street, barefoot, in her nightgown and bathrobe.

"Oh my God!" says Kernof.

He rushes downstairs. In the middle of the street, Dara is staggering toward a faceless dark figure, who is standing with his arms outstretched.

"Dara!" yells Kernof, running desperately toward his daughter.

As Dara nears the dark figure she falls to her knees, her arms raised upward in supplication.

"Dara!" shouts Kernof.

There is a flash of lightning and the dark figure is gone. Nearly blinded by the flash, Kernof shields his eyes and runs to his daughter's side. She is still in a kneeling position, her palms upraised. She is dead—her eyes gone, as if they've been burnt out. Wisps of smoke rise from the empty sockets.

"Oh no! Dear God!" says Kernof, clasping the dead girl to his chest.

He hugs her tightly, screaming her name out into the night.

At St. John's Church in Alexandria, Virginia, a lone woman enters through the rear of the sanctuary. It is Scully, visibly troubled. She walks up the center aisle, stops, and pulls a photograph from her pocket. It is a snapshot of a little girl: her late daughter Emily, last seen in 5X07.

Scully enters a confessional. The divider slides open, revealing a priest, nearly hidden behind by an ornate screen.

Scully says, "Bless me, Father, for I have sinned. It's been several months since my last confession."

The priest says, softly, "You have a sin to confess?"

In anguish, Scully hesitates. "Father, I'm an FBI agent," she says, finally. "I've taken it as my code and purpose to uphold the law. To save lives."

"And now your work has come into conflict with your faith?"

"In a way," says Scully. "I was here for Easter services last week, and Father McCue approached me for my help."

"Why did he come to you?"

"Because there was a family that he felt needed my help," says Scully. "But it was more than that."

Scully begins to cry. "Father, I had a daughter who died," she says. "A strange and sudden death several months ago."

The priest says, "Father McCue thought that by helping these people you might in some way help yourself. To come to terms with your grief."

"Yes," says Scully.

"But you haven't."

Her eyes streaming tears, Scully nods. "Father, I told you that I had a sin to confess. But the sin of which I'm guilty of, I'm not sure you can offer forgiveness."

"What is the sin?" asks the priest, gently.

"An innocent girl is dead because of me. I could have saved her life, but I let her die."

One week earlier Mr. and Mrs. Kernof leave St. John's after Easter services. Several yards behind them, walking alone, is Scully. As she walks down the front steps, someone calls after her.

"Dana!" says Father McCue. "Do you have a moment? I need to speak with you in private."

A short while later Scully sits across from Father McCue in his office. Light streams down from an ornate

stained-glass window behind him.

"I must say, Dana," says Father McCue, "It's been nice seeing you at Mass again. I'm almost starting to get used to it."

Scully smiles, shyly. "I've been making an effort to go," she says.

Father McCue says, sighing, "I don't mean to take advantage of your attendance. But I've become involved in a difficult situation with a couple who are also members here. Do you know the Kernofs?"

Scully tells him that she's afraid that she doesn't. He tells her that they've recently lost their daughter. Scully admits that she hadn't heard about Dara's strange death.

Father McCue says, "The circumstances of the girl's death were sudden and I'm afraid the police haven't been able to help them much."

"Are you asking for my help?" says Scully.

Father McCue says, "The Kernofs are devout. But their faith is giving them little comfort. I thought with your background, your words might carry a certain weight. Can I tell them you'll be visiting?"

Sometime later Scully sits, somewhat uncomfortably, in the living room of the Kernof house. Mrs. Kernof proudly shows her a picture of Dara in her wheelchair, flanked by her beaming parents.

"That's Dara on her sixteenth birthday," says Mrs. Kernof. "We couldn't have children of our own. I persuaded Lance six years ago to adopt."

She adds, "At first he was reluctant to accept a special needs child. But he became so attached to her and this happens. You make the choice never imaging something like this. Or how vulnerable you are.

"Dara had just been baptized. I

know in my heart she's gone to a better place, but Lance is angry. Angry at God. They say time heals."

Mrs. Kernof falls silent. Scully, who has been withdrawn through all this, forces herself into the present and asks the woman whether the police have any theories concerning the girl's death.

Mrs. Kernof says, "They think she may have been struck by lightning, but no one seems to know for sure. How she even got out of the house onto the street is a mystery."

"What do you mean?" asks Scully.

"Dara suffered from congenital spinal deformities. She's been wheelchair-bound all her life."

"Could someone have taken her from her room?"

Mrs. Kernof shakes her head. "Lance said he saw her walking. And that when he found her she was on her knees, praying."

She adds, "I think that's the hardest part for my husband. He'll never understand how God could forsake the life of an innocent girl. How God in his mercy could let this happen to our Dara."

One week later, Scully continues telling her story in the confessional. "Mrs. Kernof was talking about her husband," she says. "But she might as well have been talking about me."

"You were angry at God?" asks the priest.

Scully says, "I felt drawn to these people, Father. In a very personal way. I was determined to help them understand why the daughter had been taken."

"And did you?"

Scully hesitates, then speaks. "As much as I have my faith, Father," she says, "I am a scientist, trained to weigh evidence. But science only teaches us how. Not why."

Earlier that week Scully is in the Prince William County morgue, talking to the female pathologist in charge of Dara Kernof's case.

"If you want me to stand by my report, I will," says the pathologist. "But I have to say it's not exactly open

and shut on the cause of death."

Scully says, "You think it was lightning?"

"I'm guessing it was lightning," says the pathologist. "The way her eyes were burned suggests the bolt may have gone to ground through the top of her head. Funny thing is," she adds, "there was no other sign of arcing except for the face."

Scully reminds her that Dara was found in a kneeling position.

"Genuflecting," says the pathologist. The doctor turns to face Scully.

"Are you a religious person?" she asks.

"Why do you ask?" replies Scully.

The pathologist says, "I haven't been to church since I was a kid. But I went last Sunday. I'm going to show you something."

The woman rummages through a stack of X rays and photographs. "Her body was rigored," she says, "such that I had to do my examination in the position she was found. I found this almost as disturbing. I've never seen anything like it."

She hands Scully a photo of Dara genuflecting and one of Dara's hand. There is a long, thin scar down the side of it.

Scully says, "It looks as if there was surgery done on her hands."

"She was poly-dactyl," says the pathologist. "Same with her feet. I haven't asked her parents yet—haven't had the heart to—but I assume they had the extra fingers removed."

"What's the connection?" asks Scully.

The pathologist says, "I found no other evidence of any other tissue damage or electrical burns or any other serious trauma. As if God himself struck her down."

Scully shudders slightly. "Dara

Kernof was adopted," she says, evenly. "I don't suppose you requested any information about the birth mother?"

"I can do that if you like," says the pathologist.

"No," says Scully, "that's okay. I have someone I can ask. Someone I'd like to confer with, actually."

At the State Psychiatric Hospital in Mount Lebanon shortly afterward, a black-clad figure parks his battered sedan. A small crucifix hangs—upside down—from the rearview mirror.

The man enters the building. A hulking orderly escorts him down a dark corridor; they reach Room 213. Inside the room, a young woman wearing a hospital gown crawls painfully across the floor. She has six fingers on each hand.

In the corridor, as the man in black watches, the orderly starts to unlock her door.

"Hey, hold it!" shouts another man, running down the corridor toward them. Panting, he slows as he nears the pair outside the door. "Are you Father Gregory?" he asks.

"Yes," says the man, who is in his late thirties and is wearing a clerical collar.

"I'm Aaron Starkey from the Department of Social Services. I am very sorry, but we've had a mix-up."

"What are you talking about?" asks Father Gregory, suspiciously.

"Your adoption petition for Paula Koklos," says Starkey. "It's missing an approval."

The orderly holds up a certificate. "I've got the court order right here," he says.

"No," says Starkey, with a regretful smile. "That's the mix-up. You see, it should never have gone to family court without getting a social worker assigned to the case. And that's me."

"Well, give it to me here, then," says Father Gregory, "and we'll be on our way."

"No, I can't—at least, not yet," says Starkey. "I've just been assigned to Paula. So I'll need time to familiarize myself with her case—"

"Look! I've already been through all this," says Father Gregory, irritated.

"I'm here to take the girl home."

Starkey purses his lips officiously. "I'm sorry, Father, but you have to wait. Until I can get the paperwork in order."

That night Scully sits at the desk in her apartment, carefully examining the photos of Dara Kernof's corpse. Hesitantly, she reaches into a drawer and pulls out the photo of Emily. Her face registers silent anguish.

The phone rings. It is Mulder, huddled in a phone booth in the middle of a rainstorm.

"Hey, Scully, I'm returning your call," he says.

"Hi," says Scully, still distracted by her photo. "Something's come up. I was hoping, uh, you could do me a favor."

"Hey, what's going on?"

"This isn't official FBI business," she says, "so I was hoping that we could keep it outside of work."

Mulder glances nervously over his shoulder. "Yeah, look. I'm kind of tailing a possible suspect right now, so I'm kind of rushed—"

"I need some birth and adoptive records on a Dara Kernof," says Scully.

"Who?"

"Dara Kernof. I can't tell you much more than that, Mulder. Sorry."

"You wanna give me a hint? Anything?"

"Not until you get me those records," says Scully.

"All right. I'll talk to you later," he says.

Mulder hangs up and quickly exits the booth. He hustles toward a small movie theater, where a short line of men in raincoats wait for their tickets. The theater marquee reads A DECADE OF DIRTY DELINQUENTS.

At the State Psychiatric Hospital that night Paula Koklos, still in her room, is huddled in the corner, rocking back and forth. A man in black walks down the corridor toward Room 213. He opens the door and stands, in shadow, before her. An intense halo of light surrounds him. Paula stares at him and holds out her hands in supplication. The room is enveloped in a blinding whiteness.

The next morning Paula—her eyes burnt out—lies dead on the floor. Scully watches as forensic technicians cover her corpse and carry it out. Scully walks over to the girl's bed; a small gold cross hangs upside down on the wall behind it. Scully fingers the inverted symbol, fascinated.

Mulder, wearing casual clothes, enters from the hallway. "Scully? Aren't you the secret squirrel?" he says.

"What do you mean?" asks Scully.

Mulder says, "I got a look at that body they wheeled out of here. You've been holding out on me."

"Mulder, it's not what you think," says Scully, sheepishly. "I-I didn't want to involve you. I got asked to look into this as a favor. For a family."

"Dara Kernof's family?"

Scully nods. She asks Mulder if he's found Dara's records.

"Her birth records," says Mulder, handing Scully a file. "Her adoption records have been sealed."

Scully glances at the file. "I think one of my questions has already been answered," she says. "Dara was a twin."

"No," says Mulder. "Actually, she was a quadruplet. One of four girls."

Mulder notices the crucifix. He asks if it was found hanging that way.

"Yes," says Scully. "As far as I know. Why?"

"It's inverted. Upside down. That's a protest. A sacrilege against the church."

"Put there by whom?" asks Scully.

Mulder gazes coolly at his partner. "It's your case, remember, Scully? You have any suspects?"

"Not at this time," says Scully, curtly.

Mulder eyeballs the room, asking Scully if Paula could have hung the cross upside down. She tells him that it is doubtful: that Paula Koklos was as severely impaired, mentally and physically, as her sister, Dara.

"So they both died the same way?" asks Mulder.

"It appears that their eyes were burned out," says Scully. "Their bodies frozen in a position of prayer."

"Their physical deformities could have accounted for that," says Mulder.

Scully says, reluctantly, "They might."

Mulder pauses, then approaches his partner. "Look, Scully, I know you don't really want my help on this, but can I offer you my professional opinion?"

Scully nods.

"You got a bona fide super-crazy religious wacko on your hands," he says.

"What makes you sure?"

"Well, the mote in the eye; the eyes as windows to the soul; an eye for an eye. He's working from ancient scripture, ancient text. Maybe even the Bible." He adds, "He may even think he's doing God's work."

Before Scully can answer she is interrupted by the entrance of Aaron Starkey, Paula's social worker. He introduces himself; expresses shock at Paula's death; and implores the agents to find the murderer.

Scully says, "Mr. Starkey, do you know if that cross over there belonged to Paula?"

"I don't remember seeing it before," says the caseworker. "I'm sure it didn't."

"Did she have any visitors? Or anybody who might have left it behind?"

"Well, she had no family," says Starkey. "No friends, really." He adds, "I don't know if you knew this, but Paula was about to be adopted."

"By who?" asks Scully, surprised.

Later that day Mulder and Scully pull up to the Church of St. Peter the Sinner: a shabby-looking house of worship located off a semi-rural road. At the entrance is a portable rent-a-sign reading THE DARKNESS IS UPON US. The building itself, filled with wooden folding chairs, seems to be an abandoned commercial structure of some sort.

The agents enter the sanctuary. No one else is present. Mulder walks to a makeshift altar and picks up a ring-bound sheaf of papers—a home-

brew bible with an inverted cross on its cover. Mulder skims through the photocopied pages, intrigued.

"Hey, Scully, look at this," he says. "The Gnostic Gospels. Enoch. The Book of J. Apocrypha—"

Through a crack in a nearby door, someone—breathing with shallow, raspy breaths—is watching Mulder and Scully.

"—I'm surprised there's nothing here from *Jesus Christ, Superstar*."

Scully glances around uneasily. "What kind of church is this?" she asks.

"No telling," says Mulder.

They are interrupted by a male voice, slightly annoyed.

"Can I help you?" says a thirtyish man in clerical garb—Father Gregory—last seen at the State Psychiatric Hospital.

Scully identifies herself and informs him of Paula's death; the cleric is staggered by the news. He tells the agents that he was trying to adopt Paula.

"We hear you were very anxious to do so," says Mulder, completely unmoved.

Father Gregory looks at him sharply. "I hope to God you're not suggesting I had something to do with this?" he says.

"Why adopt her?" asks Mulder.

"Do you think I was interested in harming her?"

"Why adopt her?"

"I-I was trying to protect her," says Father Gregory. "I knew her mother."

Scully asks, "Do you know where she is?"

The priest sets his jaw. "Yes," he says, defensively.

Scully says, "We were looking for her name. It's not listed on the girls' birth records."

"Why would you want it?" asks the priest.

"The other two girls may be in dan-

ger," says Scully. "We're hoping she might be able to help us find them."

Father Gregory is unimpressed. "Their mother died in childbirth," he says brusquely.

Scully glances skeptically at Mulder. He returns the sentiment.

"Can you give us a name?" asks Scully, finally.

Father Gregory struggles to control his anger and disdain. He says, "When I was a priest in the Roman Church—before I founded my own—I was her confessor. Divulging her name would violate the code of my faith." He glances at the gold cross around Scully's neck. "And yours, I see."

Scully swallows hard and reflexively touches the cross. Mulder steps forward.

"You say you wanted to protect Paula," he says. "From what?"

Father Gregory ignores the question. "Whatever your intentions," he says, "your secular prejudices blind you from seeing what's really happening here. Two girls are dead not by the hand of man."

The priest's voice rises, becomes more strident. "Unless you accept the truth of God's teachings—that there is a struggle between good and evil for all souls and we are losing that struggle—you are but fools rushing in! You put your own lives in danger as well as the lives of the messengers. I have nothing more to say."

The renegade priest turns to leave. Mulder and Scully watch him silently as does whoever is hiding behind the door.

In the confessional several days later Scully—having told the Catholic priest this part of her story—appears dazed and overwhelmed.

She says, "I brought Agent Mulder on the case to help temper my feelings, to keep them from clouding my judgment. I wouldn't admit it to him, but as I stood there I felt as if Father Gregory were speaking directly to me, in a language only I could understand."

"The 'messengers'?" says the priest.

"Yes," whispers Scully, turning toward him.

At the roadside church immediately after their interview with Father

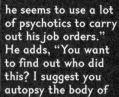

Gregory, Mulder and Scully exit the building.

Mulder says, disgustedly, "Well, people in glass houses shouldn't throw stones, blah, blah, blah, but that guy is *paranoid*."

"You're a little extreme in your judgment, aren't you Mulder?" says Scully,

"No," he replies. "All that crap about the fight for all souls, the literature we saw in there, the performance we just witnessed—it all fits. He thinks he's doing God's laundry."

"He said this wasn't done by the hand of man," says Scully. "Do you think he believes that, too?"

"If he does," says Mulder, "He's even more dangerous than he appears. Even if he's not your killer, he is hiding something."

"What?"

"He said he knew the mother, but he won't give up her name. Maybe she's still alive. I think you have enough to bring him in for questioning, if not make an arrest."

Scully hesitates for a moment, then forces out the next question.

"So basically," she asks hesitantly, "you're ruling out any elements of the supernatural?"

Mulder studies Scully for a moment as if suspecting a trick question. "What do you mean?" he says.

"Well, Dara Kernof was baptized on the day of her death," says Scully. "She was sanctified by the ritual sacrament. Submerged in the spirit."

"Then why would God allow this to happen?" says Mulder. "Why do bad things happen to good people?" He adds, impatiently, "Religion has masqueraded as the paranormal since the dawn of time—to justify some of the most horrible acts in history."

Scully replies, "I was raised to believe that God has his reasons, however mysterious."

Mulder says, skeptically, "He may well have his reasons, but he seems to use a lot of psychotics to carry out his job orders." He adds, "You want to find out who did this? I suggest you autopsy the body of Paula Koklos before it's interred. Before the man who killed her has the chance to find her sisters."

Later that day Scully is in the county morgue, standing over the body of Paula Koklos. She dictates her case notes into a microphone hanging from the ceiling.

"The victim is Paula Koklos, age sixteen, cause of death unknown. I'll begin with the external examination. Victim has signs of congenital physical defects, including four supernumerary digits. The only indications of external trauma are the burning—by means unknown—of both globes of the eyes."

Scully is shaken by this sight. She gathers herself, glances down, and frowns quizzically.

"I'm noting something on the shoulder. A bony process of some kind, possibly a tumorous mass. No indication of surgical procedure."

She turns to a set of X rays tacked onto a wall-mounted lightbox.

"The mass appears on both the right and left clavicle."

Scully turns back to the body and closes her eyes in horror at what she sees. It is Emily, her daughter, looking at her with sad, pleading eyes.

Scully opens her eyes again and sees the eyeless face of Paula Koklos.

"Oh God," she says, turning away.

"Mommy?"

Scully braces herself to turn back. She sees the face of Emily once more.

"Mommy. Please!" says the little girl.

At the ragged edge of hysteria, Scully clutches her mouth and forces herself to turn away again. When she turns back for the last time the corpse of Paula Koklos has returned.

In the confessional Scully continues her painful account.

"I told myself it

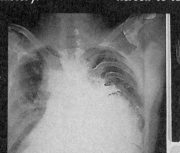

was all in my head," she says, crying. "A hallucination brought on by my emotional connection to the case."

"That would seem to be a reasonable explanation," says the priest, carefully.

"But that's not what it was, Father! I was meant to see Emily. For a purpose!"

"Which was?"

"To save these girls," says Scully, choking back more tears.

At the county morgue after her autopsy Scully—under control now—continues examining Paula's X rays while taking a call on her cell phone.

"Hey, Scully, it's me," says Mulder. "I did a little more digging on those adoption records. I think I got a lead on that third sister."

Mulder is in his car, driving through a rough neighborhood.

"Apparently," he adds, "she wandered into a teen crisis center here in D.C. last week. Homeless. This guy over at Social Services, Starkey, is helping me canvas the area."

Mulder parks his car and exits. At the morgue, Scully takes another look at the X rays.

She says, "But, Mulder, if she shares anything with her sister she wouldn't be walking anywhere far. There's evidence of a progressive degenerative bone disease." She hesitates, and adds, "And, uh, I know you're going to think I'm crazy, but I swear I found evidence of something winglike."

"Well, then, maybe she flew here, Scully," says Mulder.

Trailed by Starkey, with his cell phone at his ear, Mulder checks out the parked cars in the neighborhood. One of them has a cross hanging from its rearview mirror—upside down.

Scully says, "Mulder, there's something else—"

"Why don't you hold that thought," says Mulder, "and tell it to Father Gregory and me when you see us."

He clicks off the phone and sees Starkey disappear past a chain-link fence and into an abandoned building.

Down a decrepit hallway scurries a teenage girl—identical to Dara and Paula. She collapses in a deserted bedroom. She is followed by a man in black, whose footsteps echo through the hall. The girl gasps, looks up, and sees a dark figure standing before her. The man is surrounded by a blinding light. She raises her hands in supplication.

A few seconds later Mulder enters the same hallway. He sees a dark figure, and draws his gun.

"Stop right there!" he yells. "Move into the light! Hands where I can see them!"

Father Gregory's face is illuminated. "We're too late," he says, dazed.

Mulder throws him against the wall.

"Where's the girl!?" he yells.

"She's dead," says Father Gregory.

"Where is she!?"

"In there."

Slowly and carefully, Mulder enters the deserted bedroom. He holsters his gun. The third quadruplet, her six-fingered hands outstretched, sits slumped in a corner. Her eyes are gone. Mulder glances upward at a sudden noise. A dark bird, wings fluttering, flies upward and through a skylight.

Seated in the interrogation room of a D.C. police station, Father Gregory prays softly. The two FBI agents watch him.

"What are you asking for, Father?" says Mulder. "Mercy? Or forgiveness?"

Father Gregory says nothing.

Mulder says, "You know, they say when you talk to God it's prayer, but when God talks to you, it's schizophrenia." He adds, "What is your God telling you, Father?"

Father Gregory looks up.

"I pray for the girls' souls," he says.

"Oh! You pray for their souls now," says Mulder. "That's convenient."

"I'm immune to your mockery," says Father Gregory. "You're not interested in the truth."

"I'm *only* interested in the truth!" says Mulder, angrily. "I would like to know *why* you did what you did to three defenseless, helpless young girls! What in your sick mind would possess you to burn their eyes out! Did they see you for who you are? Like *I* do?"

Mulder places the inverted cross—from Father Gregory's car—on the table in front of him.

"What does this mean, Father?" demands Mulder.

Father Gregory smiles thinly at Scully, who has been standing, silently, against the back wall.

"Tell him what it is," he says.

Scully says nothing.

"St. Peter," says Father Gregory, gently. "You know the story. St. Peter on the cross."

"St. Peter would only be crucified upside down," says Scully reluctantly. "Out of humility toward Christ."

Father Gregory closes his eyes.

"I've risked my life to protect their precious souls," he says. "Which the Devil has sought to claim for his own. He took two before I could reach them. I was too late to save the third."

The door opens and a District police sergeant enters. He beckons Mulder and Scully out of the room. As they turn to leave, Father Gregory catches Scully's eye. She lingers.

"You know," says the priest. "You've already guessed what they are." He adds fervently, "The last one is still out there. The Devil is here and if he finds her, his victory will be complete."

Mulder reenters the interrogation room and leans toward his partner. "Scully, they think they've found the fourth girl," he whispers.

Mulder exits. Scully lingers, shaken.

"As long as I'm in here there's no one to protect her," says Father Gregory. "Let me go. Or she will die."

In the confessional the priest sits, considering this. "You believed him?" he asks.

"Yes," says Scully.

"But you didn't tell your colleague."

Scully says, "He believed that he'd find the last girl. But I already knew that I was meant to save her."

"From what?"

"I wasn't sure. Father Gregory said that the Devil claimed the life of the first three girls."

"You don't believe that?"

"I know now," says Scully, "that Father Gregory was mistaken. The Devil didn't take their souls. But the threat to those girls was real. And Father Gregory gave his life to protect them."

In the police station after their interview with Father Gregory, Mulder shows Scully a file: the social services records of Roberta Dyer, the fourth quadruplet. He tells her that she has been in several foster homes, and that her current guardian has been investigated several times after allegations of child abuse.

Scully pulls out a photo of the fourth girl and is startled. The teenager is in a pose vaguely similar to that of her dead sisters. A faint nimbus of light surrounds her head.

"What? What's wrong?" asks Mulder.

"Father Gregory called them messengers," says Scully,

Mulder grimaces, and looks his partner in the eye. "Scully, you can't let this guy get into your head," he says. "That's the last thing you want. Sometimes the most twisted ones are the most persuasive."

"Mulder, he knows where she is," says Scully.

Mulder smiles. "Well, that's okay. As long as he's locked up here, it doesn't matter."

Scully shakes her head. "You're not going to find her. I think you're being misled."

"By who?" asks Mulder.

Scully looks away.

"Scully, I think you're the one who's being misled," says Mulder. "And not just willingly, but willfully." He adds, "I've never seen you more vulnerable or susceptible or more easily manipulated. And it scares me, because I don't know why."

Scully looks up at her partner.

"I saw Emily," she says, sadly.

Mulder gazes at her with what might be sympathy.

"She came to me in a vision," adds Scully, hesitantly.

Mulder leans forward and places his hand on his partner's shoulder.

"I think you should step away," he says softly. "Personal issues are making you lose your objectivity and clouding your judgment."

Scully considers this for a moment. "You go," she says. "Go find the girl. I'm going to finish up with Father Gregory."

Mulder nods, gently takes the file from Scully, and moves away. Scully stares at the photo of the fourth girl.

In the locked interrogation room Father Gregory, alone in prayer, clutches the inverted cross. He hears a male voice call out his name, and looks up at Aaron Starkey, who has inexplicably appeared before him.

"Where is she, Father?" asks Starkey.

"How did you get in here?" says Father Gregory, startled.

Starkey speaks with an affectless rumbling authority that he hasn't shown before. "I will not be denied this time, Father," he says.

The priest's confusion changes to fear. "But you took the others," he says.

Starkey says, with chilling calm, "The others were taken from me. I will not allow that to happen again. *Where is the fourth girl?*"

In response Father Gregory begins praying, but his hands, still clutching the crucifix, become red hot. The skin starts to bubble and blister. He tries to keep praying, but the pain is too intense. He drops the cross and screams in anguish.

"Tell me, Father," says Starkey, his voice echoing hollowly. "Save yourself."

Wisps of smoke rise from Father Gregory's eyes and mouth. He says nothing, his agony escalating. Outside the interrogation room sits the D.C. sergeant, reading a magazine. Scully arrives and asks him to let her in the room. The cop tries his key. It doesn't work. Scully knocks frantically on the door.

"Father Gregory?" shouts Scully.

Inside, the priest lies dead on the floor. His skin is hideously blistered and burned.

At a house nearby—Roberta Dyer's current address—a police car comes to a screeching halt in the driveway. A squad of cops jump out. They run—with Mulder alongside them—to the front door.

A shifty-looking middle-aged man answers their knock.

"Yeah?" he says.

Mulder pushes past him, waving a piece of paper. "Mr. Dyer, we have a warrant to search the premises for your daughter."

"She's not here, I tell ya," says Dyer, sullenly. "She's out. She's at school."

Mulder briskly searches the house's first floor.

"No. We checked the school. She hasn't been there for a week," he says, evenly. "We have reason to believe that her life may be in danger. If you know something—"

Mulder spots a small locked door beneath a stairwell. "What's behind this door?" he asks.

"It's the basement," says Dyer, sullenly.

"Well, can you unlock it?"

"I don't have the key."

Mulder stares at Dyer with pure contempt for a second, then kicks the door open. He aims his flashlight down the basement stairs and sees a filthy, cell-like living area.

"Is this her room?" shouts Mulder angrily. "Where is she, Mr. Dyer? Where is she!?"

Dyer stands nervously, at the top of the stairs.

"They're gonna cut off the check, aren't they?" he says.

"Where is she?"

"He said he'd take her off my hands, but I could keep the disability," says Dyer.

"Who?" shouts Mulder.

"The priest."

"Who?!"

"Father Gregory."

At 9:52 that evening Scully leaves the D.C. police station and heads for her car in the parking lot. She chooses a key from her key ring and sticks it in the door lock. It doesn't work. She fumbles for another one. Her cell phone rings. It is her partner, returning her call.

"He's dead, Mulder," says Scully.

"Who?"

"Father Gregory. They found him alone in the interrogation room. No one can figure it out. There was a guard sitting right outside the room."

Scully drops her keys. She sighs, and kneels down to pick them up.

Mulder says, "We didn't find her. The fourth girl. She was here."

Still kneeling, Scully looks up to see a man in black, standing before her. A nimbus of bright light appears behind his head.

"Scully?" says Mulder. "Scully!?"

She is too awed and frightened to answer. The man's face begins to rotate slowly—turning into a lion, then a bird of prey, then a bull. The light behind the man's head grows even brighter until all is obliterated.

The next morning Scully enters Father McCue's office. He gazes at her expectantly.

Father McCue says, "I understand you found the man responsible for the deaths of those girls. I'm sure the Kernofs will be relieved."

"I'm not sure if they should be," says Scully.

"Why not?"

Scully says, "I've seen things. Things that have made me question whether there aren't . . . larger forces at work here."

"What have you seen?" asks Father McCue.

"Visions," says Scully, "of my daughter Emily, for one."

Father McCue smiles and nods reassuringly. "I'm sure that's understandable," he says. "I'm sure you identified with the loss—"

"I considered that," says Scully, slowly. "But then I saw something last night which I—which I can't explain. I saw a man in dark clothes. But he had four faces. They weren't human."

Father McCue considers this.

Without a word, he rises and walks to a bookcase. He removes a leather-bound volume and places it in front of Scully.

"Is this what you saw?" he asks.

Scully looks down. It is a reproduction of a medieval text, depicting a four-faced winged being, brandishing a sword.

"It's a seraphim," says the priest. "An angel. With four faces. Those of a man, a lion, an eagle, and a bull." He adds, "In the story, the angel descends from Heaven and fathers four children with a mortal woman. Their offspring are the Nephilim—'the fallen ones.'

"They have the souls of angels, but they weren't meant to be. They're deformed, tormented. So the Lord sends the seraphim to Earth, to bring back the souls of the Nephilim. To keep the Devil from claiming them as his own."

"How did he bring back their souls?" asks Scully.

"They were 'Smote with the brightness of his countenance,'" recites Father McCue. "'To look upon the Seraphim, in all his glory, is to give up one's soul to him.'"

Scully asks, "You think that's what I saw?"

Father McCue smiles gently.

"No," he says. "I think what you saw was a figment of your imagination. A half-remembered story from your childhood that surfaced because of this case."

"But I saw it, Father," insists Scully.

Father McCue shakes his head. "Dana, the Nephilim is a *story*, the text in which it appears isn't even recognized by the Church."

Scully looks at the priest. She struggles with her uncertainty. She asks, "Father, do you believe that God has His reasons?"

"Yes," says Father McCue. "I'm certain of it. It's how He rewards our faith."

A few minutes later Dana Scully walks slowly down the church steps. Aaron Starkey hurries toward her from the parking lot.

Starkey says, "I can't believe I found you. Agent Mulder's been trying to reach you. He's been down at the station house."

"Trying to reach me for what?"

"The fourth girl. She's at Father Gregory's church. Come on. I'll drive you."

Starkey drives Scully to the Church of St. Peter the Sinner. She enters; it is deserted. Starkey hangs back, standing in the doorway.

"There's no one here," says Scully, suspicious.

"They must be on their way," says Starkey.

Scully stares back at the social worker. She glances at the man's feet and at his shadow. It is not the shadow of a man, but of a demon.

Scully recoils.

"She's here," says Starkey, ominously. "I know it."

Looking for a way out, Scully spots a staircase leading to a door. She climbs it, and turns the knob. The door is locked. She looks down. She can see that someone is looking at her through a crack in the staircase.

"Agent Scully?" asks Starkey. "Did you find her?"

Scully glances toward Starkey, but doesn't answer. She heads for the door that leads to the crawl space beneath the stairway. She lifts a latch and opens the door just a crack.

"Agent Scully!" shouts Starkey.

Scully peers at the fourth girl, huddled in the crawl space.

"My name is Dana," says Scully, as calmly and reassuringly as she can manage. "I'm going to get you out of here, okay? I'm not going to hurt you. I'm going to take you someplace safe."

Scully takes the girl's six-fingered hand in hers. She gently leads her out of the crawl space. Starkey still stands in the doorway, silhouetted by the light behind him.

"Where are you going?" he demands. "Where are you taking her?"

Scully says quietly to the girl, "Everything's going to be fine."

The light behind Starkey flares into a blinding brilliance. Scully squints and throws up her hand to shake herself. The fourth girl stares into the light.

"Bring me the girl!" says Starkey. "BRING ME THE GIRL!"

The girl—Roberta—struggles to walk toward the doorway. Scully, still holding her hand, struggles to pull her back.

"Bring her out to me," says Starkey, his voice echoing hollowly.

Scully turns to the girl and sees her daughter Emily instead. She is at once terrified, deeply moved, and struck speechless.

"Mommy!" says Emily, tugging at Scully's hand, as had the girl. "Mommy, let me go. Mommy, please. Let go."

"AGENT SCULLY! GET HER OUT OF THERE!" says Starkey.

"Mommy, please!"

Gently, and with infinite sadness, Scully lets go. Emily smiles, turns, and walks into the light.

Scully regains her voice.

"Emily!" she cries, desperately. "Emily!"

The light fades. Both Starkey and Emily are gone. Roberta Dyer kneels on the floor in front of her, dead. Her eyes are gone and her hands are raised in supplication.

In the confessional several days later, Scully agonizes over the memory.

The priest says, "You believed you were releasing her soul to Heaven."

"I felt sure of it," says Scully, crying and shaking her head slowly.

The priest says gently, "But you still can't reconcile this belief with the physical fact of her death."

"No. I thought I could, Father. But I can't."

"Do you believe," he asks, "there is a life after this one?"

"Yes," whispers Scully.

"Are you sure? Has it occurred to you that maybe this, too, is part of what you were meant to understand?"

"You mean accepting my loss?"

The priest pauses.

"Can you accept it?" he asks.

Scully considers his question for a moment. Much depends on her answer.

"Maybe that's what faith is," she says, finally.

back story:

Touched by an Angel: The Lost Episode?
Not quite. This is a tale of loss and rebirth;
of false starts and missteps; of big risks and
incredible changes at the last minute. In brief:
it's an almost typically atypical *X-Files* adventure.

In its initial stages, "All Souls" was considerably different than the tale that viewers finally
saw. Originally, it was the brainchild of Billy
Brown and Dan Angel, two story editors who
left *The X-Files* around Christmas 1997.

"They had this story about Mulder and
Scully and angels, but it never quite worked
the way it was originally conceived," says
co-producer John Shiban. "So (co–executive
producer) Frank Spotnitz and I were given the
task of rewriting it. And so we decided to bring
in the 'Emily' element."

In making 5X17 the unofficial third part
of the "Christmas Carol" (5X05) and "Emily"
(5X07) two-parter, the writing team refocused
the episode on Scully and the "very universal"
aspect of her relationship with her dead child.
In pulling Scully, much against her will, into
the spiritual and supernatural aspects of the
story—and at the same time making Mulder
the unconvincible skeptic—they underlined
the Mulder-Scully crisscross that had been
a major theme of the entire fifth season.
"And in the end," says Shiban, "we were really
happy about the story."

The only trouble, adds Shiban, was that
the writers found themselves far from the end
when they viewed the initial edit of the episode.
"After we came out of the cutting room,"
he says, "we decided there were aspects of
Scully's journey that just were not coming
through."

The remedy for that, Shiban and Spotnitz
decided, was to place Scully in a church
confessional, then interpolate her anguished
dialogue with the action of the story. Screen
time for this additional footage—seven script
pages worth—had to be carved out, scene by
scene and line from line, from the rest of the
episode. It was a painful and expensive task,
but deemed essential by all concerned.

The newly written part of Scully's Father
Confessor was given to—or, rather, claimed
by—Vancouver-based producer J. P. Finn, who
offered to smooth the reentry of the film crew
into his parish church—where the new scenes
were shot—in exchange for stardom. Due to
scheduling difficulties (see below) Finn never
once actually performed the scene with Gillian
Anderson, but his hushed delivery and map-of-

Ireland features were considered by one and all
to be just what the writers ordered.

The location for "St. John's Church" was
a real church, St. Augustine's in Vancouver,
but Father McCue's study, complete with
stained-glass window, was designed by production designer Graeme Murray and art director
Gary Allen. "We looked at old books of medieval
stained glass for inspiration," says Allan. "The
director, Allen Coulter, wanted an 'ascension
mood,' so we included an angel figure heading
up toward heaven." Father McCue's book containing the story of the Nephilim was designed
and drawn by assistant art director Vivien Nishi,
with the guidance of Frank Spotnitz.

Creating four different "looks" for the
four anguished quadruplets (all played by
actress Emily Perkins) proved a different kind
of challenge for makeup artist Laverne Basham
and hairstylist Anji Bemben, as was their
assignment to make Jody Racicot, the actor
who played Father Gregory, appear older. "We
couldn't give him gray hair because he didn't
have any hair," says Bashem. "And it was hard
to give him any wrinkles or sags, because he
had the tightest skin of any thirtysomething guy
I'd ever seen. In the end, we couldn't age him
as much as the producers would have liked."

Additionally, all special effects involving
the angels—especially the four-headed angel—
were extremely difficult. Visual effects supervisor Laurie Kallsen-George wasn't finished until
literally hours before airtime.

And, finally—and most dramatically—
the scheduling of Gillian Anderson's confessional scenes, carved out of the production time
for a succeeding episode—produced what
passes at *The X-Files* for a cast uprising.

"After principal photography wrapped,"
recalls Anderson, "I was told that we needed to
shoot a new scene. I said okay. I was told that
it was going to take place on a Wednesday
morning. Fine. I asked for some sides (script
pages), and they sent me two and a half pages,
and I had enough time to work on it. Great.

"Then, the night before—at 10 o'clock on
Tuesday—I get revised sides. And all of a sudden it's five and a half pages and they still want
me to shoot the next morning. And I called
them up and I said 'You know what? I've never
done this before, but this is impossible. It's
absolutely impossible—especially because of
the nature of this scene—for me to have this
ready by tomorrow morning.'"

Shocked silence.

"And you know what?" concludes Anderson.
"They had to scramble around, but they moved
it a day and we ended up doing it a day later.
And I'm glad that we did it that way, because
I was pleased with the outcome. It was a very
strong episode, altogether."

the pine bluff variant

Playing a dangerous double game, Mulder infiltrates a gang of domestic terrorists.

EPISODE: 5X18
FIRST AIRED: May 3, 1998
EDITOR: Lynne Willingham
WRITTEN BY: John Shiban
DIRECTED BY: Rob Bowman
GUEST STARS:

Mitch Pileggi (AD Walter Skinner)
Daniel Von Bargen (Jacob Haley)
Michael MacRae (August Bremer)
Sam Anderson (Leamus)
Armin Moattar (Goatee Man)
Kate Braidwood (Usherette)
Trevor Roald (Martin)
Kett Turton (Brit)
Douglas Arthurs (Skinhead Man)
John B. Lowe (Dr. Leavitt)
J. B. Bivens (Field Agent)
Dean McKenzie (Army Tech)
Ralph Alderman (Motel Manager)
Michael St. John-Smith (CIA Operative)
Marek Wiedman (Bank Manager)
Brian Drummond (Teller)
Darcy Kirkpatrick (Teller #2)
Zoltan Buday (Bank Robber/Frankenstein)
Don Thompson (Bank Robber/Ghoul)

PRINCIPAL SETTINGS:
Washington, D.C.;
Gabels Corner, Ohio;
Angola, Delaware;
Alexandria, Virginia;
Atlanta, Georgia;
Harrisburg, Pennsylvania

In Washington's Folger Park, Fox Mulder, wearing jogging clothes, runs smoothly along a tree-lined walkway. In a nearby FBI surveillance van—containing Scully and Skinner, among others—his progress is monitored by several long-range video cameras.

Mulder is wearing a hidden radio transceiver. "North perimeter clear. No sign of him," he says.

"South access clear," reports another agent.

Skinner radios Mulder to head toward the west entrance. Other agents, disguised to blend in with the park patrons, report no contact. The agents in the van call up the video feeds from numerous other remote cameras.

"There," says Scully, pointing to a monitor. "The bus."

On the screen a D.C. city bus pulls up to a curb. The camera operator zooms in; an intense-looking middle-aged man, wearing a leather jacket and gloves, gets off.

"Stay close, Mulder," orders Skinner.

The AD glances at another monitor—it displays a mug shot bio of the man. Skinner reads that the man's name is Jacob Haley; that he's wanted on suspicion of bombing, treason, and domestic terrorism; and that he should be considered armed and extremely dangerous.

"We have Alpha, off an eastbound Metro bus," radios Skinner to the entire surveillance team.

Mulder jogs toward the suspect, who—watched closely by undercover agents—is walking briskly toward a park bench. He sits down next to another man.

"Beta contact made," reports a field agent.

"All right, hold your positions," says Skinner.

Haley and the other man begin a hushed conversation. After a few seconds Haley leans forward and peers into the distance as if he's spotted something that bothers him.

"What's he looking at?" asks Scully.

The camera pans left to find the object of his curiosity—Mulder—jogging in place nearby.

"Mulder, he's watching you," radios Scully.

Mulder glances surreptitiously in Haley's direction. The target has resumed his conversation with his contact. Haley reaches into his jacket pocket, pulls out a white envelope, and hands it to the second man, who opens it and studies its contents.

"Take it slowly," says Skinner, staring intently at the monitor. "Slowly. Wait for it. Wait. Wait. Wait for it."

The second man places the envelope in his jacket pocket, then grimaces in pain, and collapses onto the ground.

Scully and Skinner watch this, astonished.

"What just happened? What's happening" asks Scully?

"I don't know what the hell happened," says Skinner.

Haley leaps to his feet and begins calling loudly for a doctor. Other park dwellers rush toward him; a knot of Good Samaritans conceals him from the camera lens. Skinner orders the surveillance team to converge on the spot. They break cover and rush toward the park bench.

Scully scans the monitors and spots Haley running away. "There he is!" she says. "He's heading west! He's on the move! He's on the move!"

"I'm on him," radios Mulder.

The agent runs after Haley. At the park bench, other FBI men surround the downed second man and find him mercifully unconscious. The flesh on his hands and face is being slowly eaten away as if acid were spreading over him.

"Oh my God!" says an agent hovering over him. "How the hell did he do that?"

Skinner says, "Haley must be carrying something lethal."

"Where's Mulder?" shouts Scully, terrified for her partner.

Skinner realizes the awful consquences also. "Mulder was on him!" he says. "There's no way he couldn't catch him!"

Scully radios a warning to Mulder. There is no answer. In another area of the park, Mulder is rapidly catching up to Haley.

"Mulder! Damnit!" says Scully.

She leaps to her feet, and—disobeying Skinner's shouted orders to stop—bolts out the back door of the surveillance van. She runs after Mulder and, after a brief chase, sees a strange vignette. A silhouetted figure—Mulder—stands beside a black BMW sedan. As Mulder watches, the car, with Haley in the driver's seat, pulls out and roars away. Scully watches this scene, bewildered. Mulder comes up behind her.

"What happened?" asks Scully.

"I lost him," says Mulder.

"What do you mean?" says Scully, half-accusingly.

"He got away," says her partner, curtly, before jogging away toward the other agents.

In her basement office the next morning Scully carefully reviews a few seconds of videotape. It shows two shadowy figures—quite possibly Mulder and Haley. The Mulder figure runs up to the Haley figure, hands him something, then runs away.

The door to the office opens, and Mulder enters. Scully freeze-frames the video.

"I came in early," she says to her partner. "I wanted to take a look at the surveillance tapes to make sure I wasn't crazy."

Mulder looks at her, but says nothing.

"What happened out there, Mulder?" Scully asks.

Mulder walks quickly to his desk. "What happened?" he says, stonefaced.

"There were twelve agents in the park yesterday," says Scully. "We had ownership of the suspect. We were in position to make the capture. And you let him get away." She adds, "And from what I see now, you may have aided in his escape."

Mulder looks at her blankly and says he doesn't know what she's talking about.

"It's on the video, Mulder," says Scully. "I can't prove it was you, but I know

what I saw. This man is a murderer. He's a terrorist."

Mulder has no response. He merely rummages through some papers on his desk.

Scully says, insistently, "I hav a report to give this morning. I expect you to give me an answer. I expect you to tell me the truth!"

Mulder looks up. "We're late for the hearing," he says.

In a large conference room at FBI headquarters sit dozens of FBI agents, CIA operatives, and lawyers from the Justice Department. It is a joint FBI/CIA Counter-Terrorist Council meeting. Walter Skinner presides.

"Fifteen hours ago," says the assistant director, "a joint FBI/CIA task force assembled to capture Jacob Steven Haley, second in command of the militia group known as 'New Spartans.' Intelligence revealed Haley was to make an exchange of money for a quantity of automatic weapons to conduct domestic terrorist activities, and to further their expressed goal of overthrowing the federal government. Due to reasons that are still under review, our operation failed. Jacob Steven Haley remains at large, whereabouts unknown."

Seated in the room are Mulder and Scully. Scully glances at Mulder, but he doesn't return her gaze. The next speaker is a tough-looking, middle-aged U.S. Attorney. His name is Leamus.

"What about the weapons?" he asks.

Skinner says, "An arms dealer named Kadri, who died at the scene, received from Haley a fifty thousand dollar bearer bond. Presumably payment for weapons delivered."

Leamus says, "In other words Haley not only got away, he got away with fifty-thousand dollars worth of guns?"

Skinner nods grimly. Leamus pauses, and asks the big question. "Have we determined the cause of death—how Haley killed this man?"

Scully answers him. "He was killed by means of a highly toxic biological agent."

"What kind of toxin are we talking about?"

"We don't know," says Scully. "Its effect on the dermis and soft tissues, the rapidity of its action—it is not a disease known in nature. It would seem to be genetically engineered. A bioweapon."

Leamus nods. "How the hell did he get it?"

"The former Soviet Union," says a CIA operative, reading from a file folder. "Security on the Siberian Vector lab is lax. It's conceivable it was stolen. Though we have no confirmation from Moscow."

"So," asks Leamus, "is this in the ozone now? Is this stuff floating through Folger Park?"

Scully says, "Level Four decontamination procedures were undertaken immediately. Our best indications are that exposure was limited, and that the toxin is directly transmitted and not contagious."

Leamus asks, skeptically, "How do you know that?"

Mulder has the answer to this one. "We're not all dead," he says.

Scully stares at Mulder for a moment, then continues. "At this point we can only guess that the toxin was transmitted by liquid or gas, touch or injection."

Leamus grimaces, and addresses the room. "Anybody care to tell me how this guy Haley eluded us?"

Scully glances again at Mulder, who shifts uncomfortably in his seat.

Skinner says, "Video recon indicates Haley had an accomplice at the park. We've yet to identify who he was or how Haley knew he was under surveillance."

An FBI field agent who was at the park the day before—suggests that Haley must have recognized one of the agents.

Leamus turns to Skinner. "Could he have?"

Skinner says, "Every member of this task force was chosen for their lack of exposure in terrorist circles."

Mulder says, "Haley's extremely suspicious to the point of paranoia. He's got military training and a guerrilla mentality."

Skinner says, "Second only to this man."

The AD snaps on an overhead projector. "August Bremer. He's the group's mastermind, however, there are reports that he and Haley are vying for control. This destabilization makes Arthur Bremer our primary threat."

"Well, this is it," says Leamus, summing up. "This is the scenario we've all

been worried about, people. Now, I need maximum control of information. Nothing leaves this room. The media gets a sniff, we're going to disavow. We're going to stop these men. We're going to make it all go away."

The meeting breaks up, and as the participants leave Scully calls out to Mulder. He leaves the room without saying a word.

In Gabels Corner, Ohio, a goateed, middle-aged man—August Bremer—approaches the Dunbar Theater, an old-fashioned small town movie house. The movie playing is *Die Hard with a Vengeance*. Bremer pushes a crisp ten-dollar bill at the bored usherette in the ticket booth.

"The show's almost over," says the girl.

Bremer smiles. "One, please," he says.

The usherette punches out an old-fashioned paper-roll ticket. Bremer takes the ticket and his change, walks inside the theater, and stops in front of the unmanned snack bar.

"I'd like some popcorn, please," he says, politely.

The usherette leaves the ticket booth, enters the theater, and walks behind the snack bar.

"Do you want large, extra large, or jumbo large?" asks the usherette.

Bremer asks, "Could I get some *fresh* popcorn, please? The sign says 'fresh popcorn.'"

The girl looks at him blankly. "This is fresh popcorn."

"*Fresh*, fresh," says Bremer. "Hot. Out of that machine back there? Please. A large."

The usherette turns and reluctantly walks toward an industrial-sized corn popper chugging away in a service room behind her. She tells him that it will take a minute to make a fresh batch. While her back is turned to him, Bremer pulls on a pair of black gloves and removes a small aerosol can from his coat pocket. He removes the cap and places his gloved finger on the nozzle.

That night a rented sedan pulls into the Aaron Burr Motor Court in rural Delaware. Mulder parks the car and enters the motel office. Another car pulls up a few dozen yards behind. At the wheel, watching Mulder surreptitiously, is Scully.

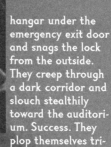

Mulder leaves the office and drives to his room. A few minutes later his room phone rings.

"Yeah?" says Mulder.

"You set me up," snarls a male voice at the other end.

It is Jacob Haley, speaking from a converted farmhouse.

"I saved your ass," says Mulder.

"Well, why wasn't I told?" asks Haley, angrily.

"I didn't know about the operation," says Mulder.

"It was your operation," says Haley,

"No, no," says Mulder. "The Justice Department got an anonymous tip. I found out about half an hour before it went down. I did what I could."

Haley says, "You'll have to do better than that, Mulder."

"What else can I say?" says the agent. "I've got as much to lose here as you do. They catch you, they'll flip me." He adds, "Look. I believe in your ideals, your goals. The only reason I tolerate your methods is because the government's are worse."

"Wow," says Haley, sarcastically. "What a ringing endorsement."

"Hey! You came to me, remember?" says Mulder, angrily. "I mean, what more do you want from me? I've risked everything. I've given you information. My partner is seriously suspicious and if that's not enough for you, that's all I've got."

Mulder slams down the phone. Haley hangs up, too, deep in thought.

In Gabels Corner two teenage boys—their names are Martin and Brit—sit on the curb across the street from the movie theater. The ticket booth is empty.

"There ain't nobody home," says Martin.

"Aw, she's in there," says Brit. "She's just hiding or something."

Martin says, "We could break for it. Right through the front doors."

"Why? I got us front-row seats," says his friend.

Brit grins and holds up a wire coat hanger. He and his friend stand and walk across the street. Brit sticks the wire

hangar under the emergency exit door and snags the lock from the outside. They creep through a dark corridor and slouch stealthily toward the auditorium. Success. They plop themselves triumphantly in the front row and sneak a peek behind them.

"She see us?" asks Brit. "She coming?"

Martin takes a long, hard look at the patrons sitting behind them.

"Hey, man . . ." he says, suddenly frightened.

His buddy takes a good look, too. In the flickering light reflected off the movie screen, they see that the patrons are all dead. Their flesh is eaten away, leaving nothing on their skulls but patches of skin, hair, and musculature. Their eyeballs remain, however, staring out of lidless sockets.

At the Aaron Burr Motor Court, Scully stands at the counter in the motel office. She rings the manager's bell loudly. He sticks his head around the corner.

"Maybe you can tell me what's going on," says Scully, impatiently.

"What?" says the manager.

"There seems to be a problem. A man just told me you gave him the keys to my room. Room 130."

"Who are you?"

"Who am I? Who is he?"

"Mr. Kaplan."

"Mr. Kaplan?"

"Yes."

"Thank you," says Scully.

She turns on her heel and heads for the door.

"Are you the wife?" asks the motel manager, confused.

"Not even close," replies Scully, exiting.

In Room 130—Mulder's room—the phone rings again. The agent picks it up. It is Haley.

"We'll proceed as planned," says the militia leader.

Mulder hangs up the phone without speaking. He leaves his room and is spotted by Scully, who hurriedly ducks behind a parked car to avoid being seen herself.

A black BMW pulls into the motel parking lot, and Mulder enters the passenger side. Scully bolts for her car, gets in, and follows. She tails the BMW down a dark country road. A car in the other lane approaches her, its high beams blazing.

Scully squints into the headlights, but they get brighter and brighter. As it nears her, the other car—a black Lincoln—swerves suddenly into her lane, sliding to a stop. Scully slams on the brakes, missing a collision by inches. Two black-suited men get out of the Lincoln and head toward her. Frantically, she throws her car into reverse and tries to back up. Another big Lincoln pulls up behind her, cutting off any escape.

A black-suited man raps loudly on her window and orders Scully to get out of her car. She is out of options.

In a nondescript government office building sometime later Scully is escorted down a long corridor.

"Exactly what agency are you guys from?" asks Scully.

No response.

"Obviously not the Office of Information," she says.

She is led through an unmarked door. Behind it sit Skinner and Leamus, the U.S. Attorney, who asks her calmly to take a seat.

"What the hell is going on!?" asks Scully, angrily.

Leamus says, "I apologize for our methods."

"They may well have saved Agent Mulder's life," adds Skinner.

Scully is far from placated. "What about my life? I don't appreciate being run off the road."

Leamus says, blandly, "We had our reasons."

Skinner looks at Scully. "You're suspicious Agent Mulder has betrayed his country," he says.

"I have no idea what you're talking about," she replies.

"Your discretion is understandable," says Leamus. "In point of fact, Agent Mulder's actions are entirely honorable. What you've stumbled into is a classified action. A deep cover assignment."

Skinner adds, "Until now, Agent Mulder's true mission was known only to the U.S. Attorney and myself."

"His true mission?"

"The council we sat on was a front," says Leamus. "To make the New Spartans believe we're unaware of Agent Mulder's complicity."

"Why him?" demands Scully. "Why chose Agent Mulder?"

Skinner says, "We didn't choose him. They did."

Leamus explains that Mulder spoke at a UFO conference in Boston (in 5X13) where he apparently broadcast his feelings about the government and its conspiracies against the American people.

"Somebody from the organization was listening," adds Leamus. "The man who escaped, Haley, sent out feelers in hopes that Agent Mulder was a man whose politics were in line with his own. Someone on the inside he could use."

"To what end?" asks Scully.

Skinner says, "That we don't know."

Scully faces the AD. "You've put Agent Mulder's life in danger by not telling me."

"Agent Mulder came to me," replies Skinner, testily. "I advised him not to tell you. He's at a very delicate point. Everything he does now must work to build trust."

"Including letting this man Haley get away with murder?" asks Scully.

No reply. Scully leans forward.

"Sir," she says, "we know nothing about this bioweapon. We don't know what they want to use it for. We don't even know if they have the capacity to store it safely. Putting Agent Mulder in this situation is extremely risky."

Skinner listens, not unsympathetically. "They want something from him," he says. "We have no way of knowing what."

At this moment the door opens and the field agent enters.

"Movie theater in Ohio," he says. "Whatever they're using, they've used it again."

That night the black BMW pulls up to a farmhouse. The driver—a rough-looking, skinheaded man—leads the passenger, who has a black hood over his head, inside. The hooded man is seated and his hands are strapped to the wooden table in front of him.

"Is this the Pepsi Challenge?" asks the hooded man, who is, of course, Mulder.

The skinhead yanks Mulder's hood off. Jacob Haley sits across the table from him.

"Welcome, Agent Mulder," says Haley.

"Okay. Deal me in," says Mulder, facetiously.

The skinhead steps forward, leans over the table, and grips the little finger of Mulder's left hand in his fist.

"This is just a little method," says Haley, "to learn the truth."

Mulder says, "Well, you might want to put that hood back on, man, unless you want to see a grown man cry."

Haley is stone-faced. "What happened at the park?" he asks.

"I told you on the phone," says Mulder, evenly.

The skinhead yanks Mulder's finger back. The agent cries out in pain.

"I was set up," says Haley.

Mulder tries to refocus through the pain.

"I'm telling you the truth!" he says.

The skinhead obviously doesn't believe him.

"Wait! Wait! Wait!" shouts Mulder. "I let you go!"

"You're spying on us, aren't you?" says Haley, calmly.

"No, no, no!" says Mulder.

The skinhead yanks Mulder's finger again—much farther this time. Mulder cries out.

"You want me to lie and say yes?"

Another pull. Mulder's knuckle makes a cracking sound. He screams defiance at his captor.

"You sonofabitch! I'm gonna kill you! If I set you up, do you think I'd even get into the car with this Nazi piece of sh—"

The skinhead yanks his finger again before Mulder can finish cursing him. Mulder bends forward and head-butts the man, forcing him to let go of his finger and causing him to fall backward to the floor. Haley watches all this impassively.

Mulder shakes his head clear and turns to Haley. "I risked everything!" he rages. "If I were lying there'd be federal agents descending on this place like the wrath of God right now!"

The skinhead staggers to his feet.

"You touch me again, you'd better kill me!" shouts Mulder.

The skinhead moves fast, lunging for Mulder's injured finger once again. The agent clenches his fist tightly, but the man succeeds in prying it open.

"A war is going on, Agent Mulder," says Haley. "Either you're on the right side, or the wrong."

Haley reaches into his pocket and produces a small aerosol container. He points the nozzle at Mulder's face.

"You've seen the effects of this?" he says.

"Yeah," gasps Mulder.

"Would you like to see them again?"

"No!" shouts Mulder. "I didn't set you up! If you were set up, it was one of yours."

Haley thinks this over for a second, then nods curtly to the skinhead, who breaks Mulder's little finger with a sudden, sure motion. Mulder nearly passes out, his head flopping onto the tabletop. Haley stares down at his captive.

"You know what?" he says. "I believe you."

At the Dunbar Theater in Gabels

Corner, Scully arrives in the midst of a Haz-Mat quarantine. An Army technician tells her that there are no traces of the bioweapon inside. She joins up with Skinner, who escorts her through the lobby.

The AD tells her that there are a total of fourteen victims, including patrons, a projectionist, and employees. Scully walks behind the snack bar counter, looks down, and sinks to her knees in horror.

"That's the usherette," says Skinner.

Flashlights shining, the pair enter the darkened auditorium. The dead patrons—each wrapped in clear plastic—sit like ghostly mounds among the red seats.

Skinner says, "How does it happen that those two kids survived?"

"I don't know," says Scully, still shaken. "But it's going to help us establish a method of delivery."

Scully leans over and peers into the eyes of one of the victims.

"It's doubtful the pathogen was airborne," she says. "They found no atmospheric traces. So it's got to be something everybody touched."

She reaches down and, with a gloved hand, lifts a red ticket stub off the floor.

That evening a battered and stressed-out Mulder enters his apartment in Alexandria. He examines his broken finger. Scully emerges from the shadows.

"Don't be alarmed," she says.

Mulder grimaces in dismay. "Scully, get out of here," he says.

"Mulder—"

"GET OUT OF HERE!"

"—I know what you're doing," says Scully. "Skinner told me everything."

Mulder shakes his head. "I don't know what you're talking about."

"What happened to your hand?" asks Scully.

"Nothing."

Scully reaches for his finger gently, and examines the injury. "What did they do to you?" she asks. "This needs to be set. You're in pain."

Mulder grumpily sits down so Scully can treat him. He comments on her methods. "You keep pulling it around like that," he complains.

Scully goes to the kitchen, wraps some ice in a towel, and presses it against the swelling on Mulder's hand.

"They've killed again, Mulder," she says. "Fourteen people in a movie theater in Ohio. Same toxin they released in the park."

"Fourteen people?" says Mulder. "It doesn't make any sense."

"Unless it was a test," says Scully, "of something bigger."

Unseen by the agents, a thin red light beam is shooting through Mulder's window, the one still bearing traces of the masking-tape "X" signal. The beam leads to a car parked outside. Inside it, someone is eavesdropping, via a laser listening device, on the agents' conversation.

Mulder says, "They're testing me, too. Haley's paranoid. And spooked. I was sure he was going to kill me."

"What stopped him?" asks Scully.

Mulder says, "He still needs something from me. And I'm sensing that there's someone Haley trusts even less. The man giving him his orders. Someone I haven't met yet. A guy named August Bremer."

In the parked car the man conducting the laser surveillance sits calmly in the driver's seat, smoking a thick cigar. It is August Bremer.

At FBI headquarters at 3:14 that morning, Mulder—his finger now neatly splinted—trudges through an empty corridors. He enters the large conference room, where Skinner and Leamus are waiting for him.

"What happened to your hand?" asks Skinner.

"Terrorist lie detector," says Mulder.

"Well, did you pass?" asks Leamus.

"Well, I must have. I'm still here," says Mulder. "They told me what they want.

Documentation from the Federal Reserve Bank. Fund-transfer schedules for the eastern seaboard. Cash money."

"They're gonna hit a bank. Or an armored car," says Leamus.

Skinner says, skeptically, "That's it? That's all?"

Mulder nods. "Now, I think I convinced Haley," he says, "that the near-miss in Folger Park was due to a mole inside his own group. He wants surveillance files on them."

"How soon?" asks Skinner.

"They're waiting for my call," replies Mulder.

Skinner says that he needs time to redact, to dummy up some fake information. Leamus says that he's anticipated this and has some files ready for use. At this, Mulder shoots a skeptical glance at Skinner, who is also disturbed by Leamus's prescience.

The AD says, "You know, I'm getting a bad feeling about this. I want a tail on him."

"No tail," declares Leamus, flatly.

Skinner says, angrily, "Once they get what they want from Mulder, what's to keep them from killing him?"

Leamus glares back at Skinner. "If they spot a tail on him," he says, "they're going to shoot him on the spot." He adds, "We have no other way of learning what they want past this. What the big picture is."

Unhappy, Skinner turns to Mulder. "You may not have another chance to contact us."

Mulder turns to leave. "If you don't hear from me by midnight," he says, "feed my fish."

At the Centers for Disease Control in Atlanta, Scully gazes at a rapidly multiplying microorganism on a video screen attached to a microscope. Standing next to her is a middle-aged microbiologist, whose name is Dr. Leavitt.

"That's it," he says. "That's your bug."

"It's a bacterium," says Scully.

"An especially virulent one," says Leavitt. "We isolated it from the bearer bond."

Scully asks him if the bacterium was also found on the ticket stub.

"Actually, no," says Leavitt. "Barring the usual particles and dust mites, the ticket stub was clean."

Scully is surprised at this. "Well, then how was the biotoxin spread at the theater?"

"I don't know," says Leavitt.

Scully glances again at the video monitor. "It looks like streptococcus," she says.

"A strain of streptococcus," says Leavitt. "But one that has been genetically altered to make it extraordinarily lethal."

Scully frowns. "But strep wouldn't be able to survive any exposure to the environment."

"Normally," says Leavitt. "But whoever produced this has cleverly coated the bacterium with a synthetic protective covering." He adds, "The covering gives it an adhesive quality. It's like scratch-and-sniff. Dermal contact activates the contagion. Ingenious in its own evil way."

"Developed by the Russians?" asks Scully, also appalled.

"I've seen everything in the Russian arsenal," says Leavitt. "They've got nothing this sophisticated."

"Well, then, by whom?" asks Scully.

Dr. Leavitt shrugs.

At the Aaron Burr Motor Court that day Mulder parks his sedan, enters his room, and flicks the light switch. The light does not go on.

The skinhead switches on a lamp. He is standing in a corner of the room. As he moves menacingly toward Mulder, Jacob Haley walks in through the bathroom door.

"Do you have what we need?" asks Haley.

Mulder glares—not altogether fearlessly—at the skinhead. "Tell the gimp to back off," he says.

After a few tense seconds Haley nods curtly at his henchman, who retreats.

Mulder hands him a role of microfilm. Haley examines it cursorily.

"I'll need that back tomorrow," says Mulder.

"Lies within lies," mutters Haley.

Haley opens up a briefcase and pulls out the black hood. "Put it on. You're coming with us," he says.

Fear showing in his eyes, Mulder picks up the hood.

"No," he says, finally.

"You put it on, or the gimp puts it on for you," says Haley.

In Skinner's office at FBI headquarters the AD's desk phone rings. He hits the speaker button. It is Scully.

She says, "The biotoxin was applied to the bearer bond with an aerosol spray. But there was no evidence whatsoever of it on the theater tickets. I have no idea how these kids were unaffected."

Skinner asks her if she's identified the toxin. Scully seems troubled by this question.

"Scully?"

"Sir, are you alone?" she asks.

He is not. Sitting across the desk from him is Leamus.

"No," says Skinner. "Why?"

"I'd like to speak to you in private."

Skinner glances at the peeved Leamus,  then picks up the receiver. "We're off the speaker."

"Thank you," says Scully. She adds, "Now, CIA intelligence suggested this biotoxin was stolen from the Russians, but my research indicates that it was almost certainly developed domestically."

"The United States has no bioweapons, Agent Scully," replies Skinner. "President Nixon dismantled that program in 1969."

Hearing this, Leamus stiffens.

"Yes, sir," says Scully. "That's what we've been told. But the CDC database contains evidence of a streptococcus bacterium being developed by the Army's Pine Bluff facility in the 1960s. It appears to be a very primitive strain of what we're seeing here."

"What are you saying?" asks Skinner. Leamus is listening intently.

"I'm saying," says Scully, "that the bioweapons program may have continued in secret, that someone may be sending Agent Mulder on a suicide mission."

Skinner glances at Leamus.

"Right. Thank you," he says evenly. Skinner hangs up, troubled.

"What is it?" asks Leamus.

Battling with his doubts, Skinner stares at the U.S. Attorney. "She's just concerned for her partner," he says.

At the New Spartans' farmhouse, a hooded Mulder climbs out of the black BMW and is escorted inside. Haley and Bremer are there, as are five other militia members toting short-barreled assault rifles. Mulder's hood is removed. Bremer has a tense, *sotto voce* conference with Haley.

"You put us all at risk bringing him here," says Bremer.

"We took the usual precautions," says Haley. "Besides, he came through for us. Federal Reserve schedules for tomorrow."

He hands Bremer the microfilm. Unimpressed, Bremer turns to Mulder.

"You a believer?" he asks.

"I have my beliefs," says the agent.

"Are you willing to die for them?"

"I'd rather it didn't come to that."

Bremer smiles thinly and turns back to Haley. "We've got a job to do," he says.

He reaches into a cardboard box, pulls out something rubbery, and tosses it across the room. Mulder catches it with his good hand. It is a Dracula mask, of the Halloween variety.

Later that day Scully sits in her car outside Mulder's motel room. She watches a maid leave the room carrying dirty linen. A sudden thought hits her, a painful realization.

"Oh, damn. The money," she whispers.

She quickly starts her rental car and speeds away.

In the back of an armored car the New Spartans—plus Mulder—head for the First Sovereign Bank of Pennsylvania in Harrisburg. Haley, wearing a Wolfman mask, hands Mulder an automatic rifle. The skinhead dons a skeleton mask.

Arthur Bremer is the Creature from the Black Lagoon. "Make sure you point that the right way," he tells Mulder menacingly.

The armored car backs up to the bank's loading dock. A Federal Reserve cash transfer is taking place; bags of bundled banknotes are being wheeled out. The bank manager takes a set of keys from a coworker, opens the door connecting the bank's vault room to the loading dock, and walks outside.

The back door to the armored car opens and the gun-toting militiamen spill out. Bremer sticks a pistol in the bank manager's face.

"You do what I say, or I'll shoot you!" he yells.

Haley says, calmly, "Three minutes."

They frog-march the manager into the bank lobby. Customers and employees, spotting the robbers, scream and drop to the floor in panic.

"Don't be foolish!" shouts Bremer. "Give us the money, and we'll be gone!"

Another militiaman—disguised as Frankenstein's monster—disarms the bank guard. Bremer motions to Mulder to cover the tellers. He obeys. Haley rushes along the teller windows, shouting orders to each teller as he passes.

"Step away from the counter!" he shouts. "Open the doors! Put your hands up against the windows! Now! Now! Do it!"

"Two minutes," says Haley.

Bremer marches the bank manager to the vault. "Let's open it," he says. "Open it!"

The bank manager spins the combination lock frantically. In the lobby, a male teller makes a move toward the alarm button. Both Mulder and the skinhead notice him.

"I got it—" says Mulder.

The skinhead fires. The teller falls to the ground, bleeding from a gunshot wound in his side. Mulder stands over him, anguished.

Haley growls at Mulder from across the bank. "Is he dead?"

"No," says Mulder. "He's still alive."

"Finish him!" orders the terrorist.

Mulder shoulders his rifle, and—watched closely by the other gang members—points it directly at the head of the helpless man. He cannot pull the trigger.

"One minute, buddy!" shouts Haley.

The bank manager opens the vault. Two gang members start scooping cash into empty carryall bags.

Haley glances at Mulder. "What are you waiting for?" he says. "Do it!"

Mulder aims the rifle again. Again, he is unable to fire. Bremer pulls a small aerosol can out of his pocket and begins methodically spraying untouched stacks of bills.

Haley shouts to Mulder, "I told you to finish him! FINISH HIM!"

Mulder aims yet again. The wounded man stares up at him in terror.

A hand reaches out and pushes Mulder's rifle away. It is Bremer.

"That weapon is traceable," he says. "Go!"

Mulder turns and starts to move off. Bremer fires at the helpless teller, killing him.

At the New Spartans' farmhouse later that day the gang members stand around a small wood fire in the backyard. Bremer appears and drops bundles of money into the fire.

"What are you doing?" says Mulder. "What are you doing!?"

"The bills could be traced," says Bremer.

Mulder stares at him for a second, realizing the awful truth.

"The bank heist was a decoy," he says, quietly. "To contaminate the money you didn't take!"

"No more tests, Mr. Mulder," smirks Bremer. "This is the real deal. You've been a real help."

Bremer pulls out his pistol and aims it at Mulder. Haley steps forward.

"Put that down!" he says.

"He's a liability now," says Bremer.

"To who? You?" says Haley. "If you think you're going to kill Mulder to protect your secret, it's too late. I already know your secret."

Haley turns and addresses the other gang members.

"Agent Mulder provided us with FBI surveillance reports," he says. "Files which contain a name. A source who's been leaking information on us for a period of two years. Charles Bogard."

He adds, "'Bogard' is an alias—an old one—for Arthur Bremer."

Mulder stares at Bremer in genuine surprise. Bremer, however, is unfazed. He says, "Agent Mulder knows my alias, just as he knew a false report would feed your ambition and pit you against me."

"Mulder risked his life for us!" protests Haley.

"Are you sure of that?"

Bremer pulls out a small tape recorder and switches it on. The scratchy voices of Mulder and Scully—their conversation in his apartment several days ago—are audible.

Mulder says, once again, *"They're testing me, too. Haley's paranoid. And spooked. I was sure he was going to kill me."*

Scully says, *"What stopped him?"*

Mulder says, *"They still need something from me. And I'm sensing there's someone Haley trusts even less."*

As the terrorists listen, their looks shift to Haley, whose expression is one of total incredulity.

He turns to Mulder. "What the hell is this?" he asks.

In the conference room at FBI headquarters dozens of agents sit at video monitors, screening surveillance tapes. Scully enters and walks hurriedly over to Skinner.

"Director Skinner, you've got to get to Mulder," she says, frantically. "You've got to find the bank that they hit!"

"That's what we're trying to do," says Skinner, calmly.

Scully fights for control. "Agent Mulder's life is in danger. And anybody else who touches the currency at that location. They're putting the biotoxin on the money!"

Skinner immediately realizes the urgency of the situation. Leamus appears next to him, but makes no comment.

Skinner says, glancing at the U.S. Attorney, "We've got no way of contacting him. Not without blowing his cover."

"You've got no choice!" says Scully.

Leamus finally speaks. "We've had surveillance tapes satellited to us. There have been twenty-seven robberies in seven eastern states, all this morning."

Skinner adds, grimly, "There's been no sign of Mulder."

Scully is not willing to accept that. She walks quickly from monitor to monitor, looking at each surveillance tape in turn. She glances at a freeze-frame of a man—disguised by a Dracula mask, brandishing an assault rifle—and moves on.

At the New Spartans' farmhouse Haley and Mulder kneel on the ground. Bremer stands behind them, holding a pistol in his gloved hand.

"We've made some decisions," he says.

He places a leather key holder on the top of Haley's head. "Take it and get out of here," he says. "I don't want to see your face again."

Haley grabs the key holder. Without questioning his good fortune he rises, enters the black BMW, and drives away.

Bremer pokes the gun into the back of Mulder's neck. "On your feet," he says.

Mulder says, "I don't need a car. You can just call me a cab. That would be fine."

"Let's go," says Bremer, unamused.

"Go where?"

The skinhead grabs Mulder by the

shoulders and drags him roughly to his feet. Bremer gestures to the other militia members.

"Witnessing the murder of a federal agent will make these men accessories to the crime."

Mulder turns to the skinhead. "You hear that?"

The skinhead jabs his gun into Mulder's back. "I wouldn't miss it for the world!" he hisses.

He pushes Mulder forward, out of sight of the others and into a dilapidated greenhouse. Bremer brings up the rear.

"Stop there," says Bremer. "Down on your knees. Hands behind your back."

Mulder turns around, takes a final look at his executioner, and kneels. Bremer moves toward Mulder. A single shot rings out.

The skinhead falls forward, dead. Mulder, badly shaken, opens his eyes.

Bremer whispers urgently in Mulder's ear. "There's a car for you just over the rise. Head south until you get to the highway."

"Who are you?" gasps Mulder.

"Go on," says Bremer, urgently. "They come out here and find us, they'll kill us both. Go!"

Mulder rises unsteadily to his feet and staggers into the underbrush.

Later that day he arrives at the Harrisburg bank—now under Haz-Mat quarantine. He spots Scully in the loading area.

"The money!" he says. "They sprayed the money!"

Scully says, quickly, "We got here an hour ago, before any of the funds were touched or transferred. The cash supply is being isolated. It's being locked down in the vault."

Mulder catches his breath. "How did you know it was this bank?"

"I recognized you from the surveillance tape. Your finger," says Scully.

Mulder glances at his splinted finger. Skinner joins the agents.

Mulder says, "August Bremer—whatever his real name is—is working with us."

Scully interrupts him. "Mulder, before you go any further, you should know that the biotoxin they used may have come from government labs. Our government."

Mulder is staggered. "You're saying I was set up?"

Skinner shakes his head. "We have no definitive information to justify that," he says.

Mulder turns to Scully. "I was being used? The whole operation—the people who died in that theater?"

"Agent Mulder!" says Leamus, who has been standing nearby, unseen. "Our government is not in the business of killing innocent civilians."

"The hell they aren't!" says Mulder. "Those were tests on us to be used on someone else."

Leamus looks Mulder in the eye. "Those bills have been analyzed," he says coolly. "The money in the vault gave no readings. There's absolutely no evidence of any biotoxins. So before you jump on any bandwagons—"

Scully is in Leamus's face immediately. "You knew this all along!" she shouts. "You knew about this the whole time!"

Mulder says, grimly, "I want that money rechecked."

"That money has been cleared," says Leamus. "It's being used as evidence in a federal crime."

Mulder shakes his head. "That money is as dirty as you are, isn't it?" he says. *"Isn't it?"*

Leamus stares the agent down, unflinching.

"Say that that were true," he says. "Then what would you hope to accomplish, Agent Mulder, as a whistle blower? To mobilize a civil rights action? To bring down the federal government? To do the very work that the group you've been a part of is bent on doing?" Leamus speaks with barely contained fury. "What do you want?" he asks. "Laws against those men? Or laws protecting them?"

Mulder says, intensely, "I want people to know the truth."

"Sometimes our job is to protect those people from it," says Leamus, spitting out the words. "Excuse me."

He turns and walks quickly toward

the street. Mulder, Scully, and Skinner share an uneasy silence.

In Delaware, the black BMW drives down a country road. Its horn blares, and it swerves slowly into a ditch and stops. Inside the car, Jacob Haley lies slumped against the steering wheel, dead, the flesh on his face eaten away by the biotoxin. Below the car's ignition switch, the leather key case swings innocently from its key ring.

back story:

Alec Leamas, a disillusioned former British intelligence officer, "defects" to East Germany as part of an elaborate plan to sow disinformation and uncover a mole inside the spy organization's London headquarters. Once in place, Leamas gradually realizes that he has been deceived: that he is merely an expendable cog in a larger, infinitely more convoluted scheme. His struggle to save himself, and his soul, becomes his prime mission.

Sound vaguely familiar? The above is a fair account of the plot of *The Spy Who Came In From The Cold*, John le Carré's seminal Cold War spy novel, later made into a 1965 movie starring Richard Burton. Both the book and movie are particular favorites of *X-Files* co-producer John Shiban, who, for much of the fifth season, had an index card pinned to his bulletin board that read simply MULDER UNDERCOVER.

"I always wanted to do something like that," says Shiban. "It always seemed to fit to me—putting Mulder in a situation where he has to lie; so that they don't know his allegiance and eventually we don't know his allegiance. It seemed to work especially well this season, because we've played with who Mulder is and what he actually believes. So I kept saying to Frank (Spotnitz), 'I want to do this to Mulder.' And finally, we found the right time and right way to do it."

One reason that the time was right, according to the producers, was that Mulder's initial deception of Scully highlighted the growing, season-long alienation between the partners. Another was that, the Cold War being over, Shiban had the opportunity to introduce a more up-do-date bogeyman: the domestic terrorist/militia movement.

"We hadn't really planned to do it," says Shiban, "but it was a fortunate opportunity to open up that subject, to start the ball rolling. It worked out nicely."

To come up with his main plot device the writer had only to dip down into the current controversies, suspicions, and fears swirling around Saddam Hussein's alleged production

and concealment of biological weapons; the near-nightly TV news reports of "flesh-eating" bacteria; and the fact that the Pine Bluff Arsenal, thirty-five miles from Little Rock, Arkansas, is indeed a real Army base—and contains a major stockpile of U.S. chemical weapons.

To play the part of terrorist "allies" Jacob Haley and August Bremer, the producers chose Daniel Von Bargen, a veteran character actor who'd played supporting roles in films like *The Postman, Amistad, Broken Arrow,* and *Crimson Tide*; and Michael MacRae, who during the first season played Ranger Peter Brullet in "The Jersey Devil" (1X04).

To play the part of "The First Sovereign Bank of Pennsylvania," the production team rented and renovated an abandoned Canadian government money depository—complete with a 4,900-square foot bank vault and 8,000-pound steel door—in downtown Vancouver. For the bank robbery scenes they assembled more than $15,000 in U.S. currency and were promptly chided by the Royal Canadian Mountain Police for creating a security risk.

"When the place was an actual bank it held about five billion dollars," notes art director Greg Loewen. "One day during the shoot, we sat outside and wondered how many of these buildings Bill Gates would need to stash all his cash in."

The episode was not one of the season's highest-rated (nor was it one of the lowest). But afterward, to John Shiban's surprise and pleasure, he got considerable feedback on "The Pine Bluff Variant," both in person and on the Internet.

"People told me it was very scary because it sounded real," he says. A few even asked him if he believed that, just as our government claims, the U.S. has stopped all research on biological and chemical weapons.

"Personally, I can't believe we would do that," says Shiban. "I have no evidence. But it just seems since so much of that has gone on in the past that has been kept from our eyes, that you have to wonder."

(X)

Kate Braidwood, who played the movie theater usherette, is the daughter of *X-Files* first assistant director Tom "Frohike" Braidwood.

(X)

When Scully asks for "Mr. Kaplan" at the Aaron Burr Motor Court, it is John Shiban's sly homage to the Alfred Hitchcock masterpiece *North by Northwest*. In that film, George Kaplan is the CIA-assigned pseudonym to an imaginary secret agent registered at hotels all around the country.

folie à deux

A giant buglike creature is sucking the life out of humans. Or so says one gun-toting, apparently mentally ill man, who holds a group of his coworkers, plus Mulder, hostage.

EPISODE: 5X19
FIRST AIRED: May 10, 1998
EDITOR: Casey O Rohrs
WRITTEN BY: Vince Gilligan
DIRECTED BY: Kim Manners
GUEST STARS:
Mitch Pileggi (AD Walter Skinner)
Brian Markinson (Gary Lambert)
John Apicella (Greg Pincus)
Cynthia Preston (Nancy Aaronson)
Roger R. Price (Agent Rice)
Owen Walstrom (Mark Backus)
Dmitry Chepovetsky (Supervisor)
Leslie Jones (Gretchen Starns)
Nancy Kerr (Nurse)
Brenda McDonald (Mrs. Loach)
Time Bissett (Medical Assistant)
Steve Bacic (SWAT Commander)
Grant Gladish (SWAT Teamer)
Robert Luft (Male Telemarketer)
Norma Jean Wick (Newscaster)
Cheryl McNamara (Hostage #1)
Biski Gusushe (Hostage #2)
Karin Title (Hostage #3)
Stacee Copeland (Hostage #4)
PRINCIPAL SETTINGS:
Oak Brook and Chicago, Illinois;
Washington, D.C.;
Quantico, Virginia;
Camdenton, Missouri

At a generic office building in Oak Brook, Illinois, dozens of telephone salesman—each in his or her tiny cubicle—make cold calls to prospective customers. One of them, a balding thirtyish man named Gary Lambert, looks like he's made a few pitches too many.

He speaks in a lackluster near-monotone voice. "Hello, may I speak to Mr. Zachary Llosa?"

"It's 'yo-sa.' Not 'lo-sa.' Speaking."

"Hello, Mr. Yosa," says Lambert. "I'm calling on behalf of the VinylRight Corporation, which would like to put a crisp one hundred dollar bill into your hand by five o'clock tomorrow evening."

"Okay, yeah. Listen," says Mr. Llosa, interrupting him. "I'm not really interested at this time—"

Lambert isn't really listening. He reads his spiel from his computer monitor as it scrolls down the screen.

"Yes, sir, one hundred dollars," he says. "All for allowing us the privilege of introducing you to VinylRight siding—the thousand-year siding that never needs painting or maintenance—"

"Look, man! I'm really not interested."

"Manufactured in America from space-age polymers. It beautifies while it protects while it adds to the resale value of your home."

"Look, I said I'm not interested. I have to go now. I have to go. Sorry."

Click. Dial tone.

Robotlike, Lambert hits a button on his keyboard. His screen now reads CALLING: LOACH, EDITH R. The autodialer goes to work. As it does, Lambert hears a faint chirping—like a cricket's sound. He pushes a button to pause the autodialer and peeks Kilroy-style over the low wall of his cubicle. He sees nothing except a vast sea of telemarketers' cubicles. He's startled by a male voice in his ear.

"Yo, Gary! Dial and smile" says a young supervisor, standing next to his cubicle, smarmily. "See if you're not smiling, they can hear it."

Lambert nods nervously. The salesman's next-cubicle neighbor—a pretty young woman named Nancy Aaronson—pops her head above the partition.

"'If you're not smiling, they can hear it!'" she says, mimicking their supervisor sarcastically.

She chuckles derisively. "Jerk!" she adds.

Lambert smiles and unfreezes the autodialer. Then he hears something; the chirping sound.

"Hello?" says a voice in his headset.

"M-Mrs. Edith Loach?"

"Yep, that's me," says a sassy-sounding elderly lady.

"Hello, Mrs. Loach," says Lambert. "I'm calling on behalf of the VinylRight Corporation, which would like to put a crisp one hundred dollar bill into your hand by five o'clock tomorrow evening."

"You want to give *me* a hundred dollars?" says Mrs. Loach, delighted. "Why?"

Lambert hears the chirping sound. He looks up abruptly and catches a glimpse of something very strange moving behind a translucent partition in the distance.

"Hello?" says Mrs. Loach. "Did I win something?"

Now Lambert is clearly frightened. He stares at the partition. Sweat breaks out on his forehead.

"Yes, ma'am," he says, on autopilot. "One hundred dollars. All for allowing us the privilege of introducing you to VinylRight siding—the thousand-year siding that never needs painting or maintenance. Manufactured in America from—"

A shadowy black figure flits—with a jerky, abrupt rhythm not seen in nature—behind the partition. Now Lambert is terrified.

"Hello?" says Mrs. Loach.

"Manufactured in America from space-age polymers! It beautifies while it protects while it—"

Another chirp, louder now. Lambert sees a hideous buglike creature, man-size, flitting right through the honeycomb of cubicles. Two supervisors standing nearby should be able to see it, but don't.

Lambert starts hyperventilating, in sheer panic.

"Hello? Hello?" says Mrs. Loach.

"Mrs. Loach, listen very carefully," Lambert whispers frantically. *"It's here!"*

In Washington sometime later Mulder and Scully are ushered into Skinner's office. He asks them to take a seat, and

tells them he needs them to go to Chicago as soon as possible to conduct a threat assessment.

"A threat assessment for whom?" asks Scully.

"VinylRight," says Skinner. "They make siding. Their telemarketing hub in Oak Brook was the focus of an anonymous audiotaped manifesto. One which threatened violence."

He adds, "Apparently, several years back they had an incident in another office—a disgruntled employee with a gun. They feel they can't be too careful."

Mulder looks at Skinner quizzically. "Why can't the Chicago field office take care of this?" he says.

Skinner says, evenly, "Because I prefer that you did."

Mulder stares at his boss, catching on. "Because the manifesto contains bizarre overtones?" he says, a bit annoyed, "Claims of a paranormal nature?"

Skinner replies in a similar tone, "It speaks of a monster stalking employees," he says. "Your insight into such claims should aid in assessing the threat, if any, posed by this person."

Mulder grimaces. "Monsters," he says, nodding. "I'm your boy."

The meeting breaks up, and Mulder and Scully head down the hallway. Mulder shakes his head.

"I must have done something to piss him off," he says.

"What do you mean?" asks his partner.

Mulder stops and turns toward Scully. "To get stuck with this jerk-off assignment," he says. He adds, "Or have I finally reached that magic point in my career where every time someone sees Bigfoot, or the Virgin Mary on a tortilla, I get called out of my basement warren to offer my special 'insight' on the matter?"

Now Scully is annoyed, also. "You're saying 'I' a lot," she says. I heard 'we.' Nor do I assume that this case is just a waste of our time."

"Not yours, anyway," says Mulder. "There's no reason both of us should go to Chicago. I'll take care of it."

He starts to walk away.

"Mulder!" says Scully, calling after him.

"I'm Monster Boy, right?" says Mulder, disgustedly.

At the VinylRight building in Oak Brook later that day Mulder sits in the office of the telemarketing office manager, a fortyish man named Greg Pincus. Pincus slips an audiocassette into a tape player on his desk.

"Whoever sent it," says Pincus, "wanted them to play it over and over again, twenty-four hours a day." He smiles briefly. "They elected not to."

The manager presses the PLAY button, and in a second a voice fills the room. It is the voice of Gary Lambert, electronically altered. He says, "Attention, people of Illinois. This is a warning of the utmost urgency. At VinylRight, 12340 Wabash Terrace in Oak Brook, there is a monster. An evil one that preys on the people there. But they can't see it, because it hides in the light.

"I see it. I know where to look. I can't be the only one. We all must hunt it down and kill it. Because if we don't, it will take us all."

The message ends. Pincus hits the STOP button. Mulder turns to him.

"You recognize the voice?" he asks.

Pincus rolls his eyes. "We have ninety-six employees," he says. "And, anyway, I'm hoping it's not one of our people. Though I don't know who else it could be."

Mulder says, "Your company had a violent incident in it's recent history?"

Pincus nods. "We have a plant in Kansas City. Back in '94, one of the warehouse guys came in with a gun and threatened everybody. I think it was over a woman."

Mulder rises wearily. "May I borrow the tape?" he asks.

"Keep it," says Pincus. "I know our home office has to call you guys for insurance reasons, but this is probably just a crank, right? Some guy making a joke?"

Mulder says, "It wouldn't hurt to err on the side of caution. Can you hire security for the building?"

"If you think we need to," says Pincus. He tells the agent that he's also conducting an internal investigation, interviewing employees to see if they're happy.

"Use your best judgment," says Mulder, exiting. "I'll be in touch."

On his way out Mulder walks through the cavernous telemarketing room. He pulls out his cell phone, calls Scully, and tells her he needs her to check on something.

"What?" says Scully.

"It's a phrase," says Mulder. "'Hiding in the light.' It's on this tape that I'm looking into."

"On this case that's a total waste of time?"

"Yes," says Mulder, testily, "and I didn't say that it wasn't." He adds, "'To hide in the light,' 'hiding in the light'—some form of that. I think it's in an old case file somewhere that I've got hidden away."

Scully can't believe her ears. "Which one?" she says. "There's hundreds."

"I'm not sure," says Mulder. "But I'd appreciate it."

Click.

Scully rises reluctantly from her desk to begin the search.

Mulder pockets his phone and leaves. He's eyed by Gary Lambert, seated in his cubicle. At that moment Pincus's voice floats over the intercom.

"Nancy Aaronson," says the manager. "Come to my office, please."

Lambert's eyes widen with fear. He turns to his neighbor, who casually stands up behind him.

"Uh-oh," says Nancy, smiling playfully. "Now I did it."

She heads up the aisle past Lambert, who rises quickly and follows her.

"Nancy!" he whispers urgently.

She turns to face her terrified coworker. "Yeah?" she says, puzzled

"Nancy Aaronson, come to my office, please," announces Pincus, again.

"What, Gary?"

Lambert is breathing faster now—he can't get the words out. He manages a slight shake of his head.

"Don't!" he says, finally.

"Don't *what?*" asks Nancy, impatiently.

Gary is paralyzed with fear. Nancy chuckles.

"Gary, I love you, buddy," she says, smiling and turning to go, "but you're really, really weird."

Nancy enters Pincus's office. Lambert hears a shrill woman's scream, which nobody else in the office reacts to. Horrified, he walks toward the office. The young supervisor, annoyed, appears in front of him.

"Dial and smile, Gary!" he says menacingly.

Lambert returns to his cubicle. He breathes deeply and squeezes his eyes shut. Pincus gets on the horn again.

"Mark Backus," he says. "Come to my office, please."

Lambert looks up to see Nancy leaving the manager's office. Her face is blank. It is also a zombielike gray. Her hair is lank; her eyes dead. She steps inside her own cubicle and turns to Lambert.

"See?" she says. "Nothing to it."

Nancy turns away and slips on her headset. Now—at least to Lambert— her face and skin are normal.

"He just wants to say 'Hi,' to everybody," she says, cheerily.

Then her face is ghoulish again.

"He's going alpha-betically."

Shaking with terror, Gary stands up and bolts for the door. The supervisor calls after him, but the traumatized salesman doesn't look back.

At the FBI's Chicago field office later that day Mulder listens again to the threatening tape—now transferred to a large reel-to-reel recorder. He takes notes on a legal pad, writing down several phrases: "Hides in the light"; "Formality of phrasing"; "Desire for authority"; and "To be taken seriously."

In his apartment Lambert clicks open the clasps to a suitcase.

Mulder writes: "Exactness of performance indicates delib. mind." and "Tape likely recorded many times until perfect."

A long row of rifle rounds stand on the edge of Lambert's dresser. He carefully loads them one by one into a rifle magazine.

Mulder writes: "Paranoia. Exclusion."

Lambert slams the magazine into an assault rifle.

Mulder's cell phone rings. It's Scully, at her desk.

"'Hiding in the light,'" she says. "That was a phrase spoken by one Jerrold Resnick to a Lakeland, Florida police investigator on August 9, 1992."

"What was he describing?" asks Mulder.

"Well, Mr. Resnick was a deacon of his local church. And apparently he was concerned that there was an evil presence among his fellow parishioners and that he alone was aware of that fact."

"He was trying to warn them?"

"Not as such. He showed up for mass one Sunday with four handguns. He began wounding people, saying 'the afflicted ones wouldn't bleed.' He committed suicide a week later in his cell."

Mulder says, "Scully, at the risk of you telling me 'I told you so,' I think it's time for you to get down here and help me."

Scully says, "I told you so."

With a click, she hangs up on him. Mulder packs up his cell phone and heads for the door.

At 12:14 that afternoon the cubicles at VinylRight are empty and silent. Mulder enters the telemarketing room.

"Hello?" he says.

No answer. A woman's head peeks out around a cubicle wall. It is Nancy Aaronson, looking terrified, mouthing silently for him to get down.

A rifle is cocked behind him. Mulder freezes at the sound.

"Who are you?" says Lambert, pointing his weapon at Mulder's head.

A short while later Scully drives up in a rental car outside the VinylRight building. The area is swarming with FBI agents, SWAT team members, and TV news crews. Helicopters circle overhead.

Scully jumps out and heads for the agent in charge, a man named Rice. He's conferring with the SWAT commander.

"I'm Scully, Agent Mulder's partner," she says. "What can you tell me?"

"Not much," says Rice. "TV news got the call. A man's voice told them they were needed to broadcast a 'stunning revelation.' Since then, we keep ringing the phones, but nobody answers."

"Who's inside?" asks Scully.

"We can't be sure of the total. It happened over lunch hour, so it could've been

worse. The lot's only got eighteen cars. One of them is a rental registered to Agent Mulder."

The SWAT commander turns to Scully. "We're about to try him on his cell phone," he says.

"No," says Scully, firmly. "Not until we get a clear idea of the situation."

It's obvious from their expressions that the two men disagree with her.

The SWAT commander says, "There's a small cafeteria in the building. We figure our guy's got everyone barricaded there. He couldn't have picked a better spot. One door, no windows." He adds, pointedly, "We're not gonna get a clear idea of the situation unless someone in there talks to us."

Scully says, just as strongly, "If you make a phone call right now, you may compromise Agent Mulder." She turns to the agent in charge. "Sir," she says, "we need to find another way."

Inside the VinylRight cafeteria the panicked hostages are crying and whimpering. Lambert has formed a human barricade by zip-cuffing three employees to the panic bar of the exit door. The rest of the hostages—including Mulder—are kneeling in a circle, their hands laced behind their heads.

Lambert brandishes his rifle. "Everybody stop crying!" he shouts. "JUST SHUT UP!"

Things get quieter. Lambert walks over to Greg Pincus, who is bleeding from a slight head wound. He says, "Everybody needs to be afraid of *him!* He's the one who's out to get you! I'm protecting you!"

Nancy Aaronson, kneeling near Pincus, speaks up, her voice quavering with fear. "Gary, what are you talking about?" she asks.

"SHUT UP! I'm not addressing you!" shouts Lambert. "I'm addressing the actual people over here, okay?"

He points to several other hostages. "I'm not talking to you, or you, or you!"

Mulder speaks for the first time. "Why should we be afraid of Mr. Pincus?" he asks, calmly. "I'd really like to hear what you have to say."

Lambert looks at Mulder, puzzled. "Who are you, anyway?" he asks.

"My name is Mulder."

"You said that already. What are you

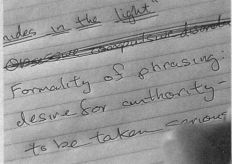

[handwritten note:] ...nides in the light"
~~class issue: computer disorder~~
Formality of phrasing:
desire for authority —
to be taken serious

doing here?"

"Applying for a ~~clas~~ job."

Lambert cackles. He can't help but laugh at this remark.

"Man, did you come to the wrong place!" he says.

"I get that," says Mulder, looking right into his captor's eyes. "Why should we be afraid of Mr. Pincus, Gary?"

Lambert sneers. "Because he's a monster," he says, turning to face his boss. "Only, you can't see that because he's clouded all your minds! But he means to take us all. One by one. Harvest our souls! Make us into zombies. Robots made out of meat."

Lambert jacks a round into the chamber. Slowly, carefully, Mulder unbuttons his suit jacket.

"Dear God almighty!" moans Pincus.

Mulder says, even more calmly, "Gary, I want to believe that you're protecting us, but I'm kind of afraid of that rifle. It makes it hard for us actual people to concentrate on what you're saying."

Lambert's eyes narrow on Mulder. "Why are you talking to me like I'm a three year old?" he demands angrily. "Don't act like you understand what I'm talking about! Because you don't. But you will."

Lambert turns away. Mulder releases the safety clasp on his shoulder holster. Lambert cocks his head and looks up toward the ceiling.

"Shhhh," he says. "Everybody hold their breath."

It becomes very quiet very quickly. A faint noise—a drilling noise—is coming from an air vent. A small amount of dust sprinkles down.

"Oh, you sons of bitches!" says Lambert.

He hauls Nancy to her feet and, using her as a human shield, looses a burst of automatic fire into the ceiling. On the roof directly above, two SWAT cops make a mad dash off the top of the building and onto a waiting rescue ladder. The SWAT commander yells into his radio for everyone to hold their fire. Crouched down behind his car, Agent Rice turns to Scully.

"We gotta find out what the hell's going on in that building," he says. "I'm calling your partner."

Scully shakes her head, adamant.

"No! If it was safe to do so, he would have called us already."

Rice says, already dialing, "Agent Scully, we don't have a lot of options here."

Inside the cafeteria Lambert stops firing and flings Nancy to the floor. He stares expectantly at the ceiling and Mulder sees his chance. He eases his gun hand slowly, carefully, toward his weapon until his cell phone rings. Lambert whirls around, leveling his rifle at Mulder.

"Just my cell phone," says Mulder. "Let me get it."

"Put your hands behind your head!" says Lambert.

He reaches into Mulder's inside jacket pocket with his free hand, revealing the holstered pistol as he does so. Lambert yanks the gun out and delivers a backhand blow to Mulder's face. Mulder sprawls backward. A male hostage takes the opportunity to rush Lambert. The gunmen whirls and cuts the hostage down with a burst of bullets to the chest.

After a few seconds—an eternity—he stops shooting. Amid the screams and cries of the hostages, Mulder's cell phone is still ringing. Lambert reaches inside Mulder's jacket again and pulls out the agent's ID.

"FBI!?" he says. "You happy now? You wanna mess with me some more?"

Lambert pulls out Mulder's cell phone, clicks it on, and holds it to his ear. At the other end Agent Rice speaks urgently.

"Hello? Hello? Is anybody on the line?" he says. "We heard gunfire. Is everybody all right?"

Lambert answers him. "I just shot a zombie. Everybody thinks I killed him, but I didn't!"

"Who am I speaking to?" says Rice.

"The guy who's gonna start killing actual people IF YOU DON'T PUT ME ON THE DAMN TV!"

Click. Lambert hangs up. The worried field agent does, too.

"I think he just shot a hostage," says Rice.

"Who?" says Scully.

Rice shakes his head. "He's still asking for his fifteen minutes of fame," he says.

Scully says, "Give it to him."

In the VinylRight cafeteria two hostages drag Backus's body—trailing a thick smear of blood—into a corner. Lambert faces Mulder.

"You wanna know why it jumped at me like that?" he says.

"It's not an 'it,' Gary," says Mulder. "It's a 'he.' What was his name?"

Another hostage—Lambert's supervisor—briefly comes out of his shock. "Mark Backus," he says.

"WRONG!" screams Lambert.

The telemarketer turns toward Pincus. "It stopped being Mark Backus when he turned it into a zombie. Then he instructed it by means of mental telepathy to attack me." He turns back toward the hostages. "And so I shot it! I had no choice. But it doesn't matter because it was already dead. He wants us all like that: insects, not people. Mindless drones!

"He wants to take away who we are! To control us! So we'll be his eyes and ears. And spy on each other! And help him do our dirty work!"

"Gary?" says Pincus, barely forcing out the word.

The VinylRight executive screws up his courage. "If I'm the monster," he begs, "why do you need these people for? Wh-why don't you let them all go?"

Lambert smirks at his boss. "You just wait until I put you on TV," he says. "Then they'll see what you are."

At this moment Mulder's cell phone—

in Lambert's shirt pocket—starts to ring once more.

"Answer the phone, Gary," says Mulder, softly.

Lambert fishes it out. "Dial and smile!" he says, throwing an extra smirk in Pincus's direction.

It is Rice on the line. "Okay. I'm sending in the cameraman," he says. "Just stay calm."

"Fine then," says Pincus. "Do it."

A few minutes later a nervous TV cameraman has arrived in the cafeteria. As he hoists a wireless news camera to his shoulder, a portable television in the room shows a newscaster previewing the approaching live feed. Lambert pushes the hostages against the door, creating an even stronger human shield.

The cameraman switches on. Lambert holds his rifle on Mulder.

"See who's getting hurt," he says, "if you bust down the door?"

Outside, at the parking lot command post, Scully watches live video of Lambert and Mulder. "Is he getting this?" she asks.

"Yeah," says Rice. "Closed-circuit's bouncing it right back into the building. He thinks he's going to be a star."

Next to them stands the SWAT commander, who is transmitting instructions into the earpiece of the cameraman—actually a SWAT team member. He tells him to swing around and show the room. The SWAT man does a jerky 360, showing the disposition of the hostages.

"What are you doing?" shouts Lambert.

"My battery cable's twisted," explains the cop.

"Well, untwist it!"

Rice points excitedly to his TV screen. "Right there!" he says. "The exterior wall's clear."

"Entry team—into position," says the SWAT Commander, leaping to his feet.

Scully turns around. She sees a small, tanklike armored vehicle rolling quickly toward the building. Inside, Lambert shoves Mulder roughly to the ground. Rifle cradled in his arms, he looks into the camera.

"People of America," he says, nervously. "A monster walks among you."

He motions to the cameraman. "Go, pan over," he says.

The camera swings right to show a beaten-down Pincus, sitting forlornly in the corner. Lambert points his rifle at him.

"Now I'll show it to you," he says, taking dead aim.

Pincus gasps in fright. Mulder scrambles to his feet and stands between the gunman and Pincus.

"No, Gary!" says the agent.

"Get out of the way!" says Lambert.

"Don't do this, Gary."

The lights in the room flicker off.

"Get out of the way!"

"Put down the rifle."

"GET OUT OF THE WAY NOW!"

Lambert takes aim, ready to blow both Mulder and Pincus away. There is a slight chirping noise.

"There!" hisses Lambert, to Mulder. "Look at it!"

Mulder swivels around toward Pincus and sees the hideous face of the monster. Shocked, he turns back around into Lambert's gun barrel.

"See?" says Lambert, at the same moment he hears a faint rumbling noise.

Behind him, the SWAT tank crashes through the wall of the building. Chunks of masonry fly and sunlight streams in. A SWAT cop emerges from the turret of the tank, rifle at the ready. Lambert turns and aims at him—and is cut down by two well-placed police bullets.

The hostages scream, then flee, as the rest of the SWAT team enters the cafeteria en masse. Lambert, dying, is relieved of his weapon. Dazed, Mulder turns and stares at Pincus, who has seemingly returned to normal. Then he kneels over Lambert. The gunman managers a hoarse whisper.

"Now you know," he says.

Shortly afterward the SWAT team is almost finished securing the crime scene. Lambert's remains are zipped into a body bag, placed onto a gurney, and rolled away.

Scully turns to her partner and urges him gently to leave. But Mulder doesn't seem to be listening.

"Mulder?" she says.

Mulder crosses the room to speak with Pincus, who is having his wound bandaged.

"I can't begin to thank you," says the manager, gratefully. "I owe you my life. We all do."

Mulder is unmoved by this tribute. "Do you have any idea why he fixated on you as he did?" he asks.

"No. None at all. I feel like I barely even knew the man. I mean I try to be a good guy to work for."

Mulder studies the manager for a second. "You mentioned another incident with another employee at a plant in Kansas City in 1994."

"Yes," says Pincus.

"Were you at that plant at that time?"

Pincus appears puzzled by the question.

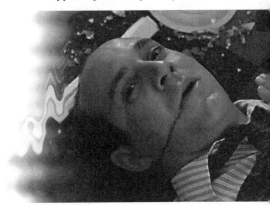

"Well, I wasn't there when it happened, but yeah. Didn't I mention that?"

"What about Lakeland, Florida?" asks Mulder. "You ever lived there?"

"I've been there. I have relatives there."

Pincus seems even more confused. "Is there anything else?" he asks.

Scully steps in. "Uh, no, Mr. Pincus," she says. "Thank you very much for your patience."

The executive leaves. Scully approaches Mulder, deep concern in her eyes.

"What's going on?" she asks.

"I don't know," whispers Mulder, moving away from her.

At FBI headquarters next morning Mulder is at his desk, working on a large map of the U.S. Six cities are highlighted in red marker—Oak Brook and Lakeland among them—and red lines connect the cities.

Scully enters and is astonished to see

her partner. "Mulder? Why didn't you take the day off?" she says.

"Close the door," says Mulder, abruptly.

He looks up at his partner. He looks very tired.

He says, "There was a reason the phrase 'hiding in the light' seems so familiar to me. I found it, or variations of it, in five other X-Files."

He glances down and reads, "'Hiding in plain view,' 'hiding in the open,' 'lurking in the open.'" He looks up. "All to describe some sort of manifestation of evil, which goes unnoticed by everyone except the claimant in each case."

Scully reacts worriedly to this. "Mulder, have you slept?" she asks.

Mulder ignores her. "Seven cities in all," he adds. "Dating back ten years. VinylRight has offices within fifty miles of four of those cities.

"Greg Pincus has worked for VinylRight guess for how long? Ten years."

Scully's expression doesn't change. "What exactly is it you think you have here?"

Mulder sighs. "What if Gary Lambert was right?"

Scully stares at him for a second. "Mulder, you're not serious," she says.

He is. "Just bear with me for a moment. I mean, what if such a creature existed that could camouflage itself by clouding the minds of its victims. There are antecedents for it in nature, right? In the insect world. Mantids, for instance. They're said to be able to hypnotize their prey."

Scully shakes her head. "No," she says.

Mulder says, "What if it could induce a visual hallucination? A sort of temporary conversion disorder?"

Scully says, "What you're describing would be more like some kind of a visual agnosia—an inability to recognize what's before one's eyes."

"Only Gary Lambert," says Mulder excitedly, "could see through it somehow. As could the others. Maybe because of some heightened adrenaline level. Or maybe because they knew where to look somehow."

Scully says, "Mulder, he was disturbed."

"Yeah," says Mulder. "But did he see it because he was disturbed? Or was he disturbed because he saw it?"

"He was *mentally ill.* This monster was a sick fantasy, a product of his delusions."

Mulder nods grimly. "I saw it, too," he says. "Does that make me disturbed? Demented? Does that make me sick, too?"

"No," says Scully, quickly and nervously. "No," she adds. "This kind of thing is not uncommon. You—you went through a terrible ordeal. And sometimes people in close associations, under tense conditions, the, uh, the delusions of one can be passed on to the other."

Mulder shakes his head. *"Folie à deux,"* he says. "It's not that, Scully, not Helsinki Syndrome either. What I saw was real. And there may be a way to prove it."

"How?"

"Lambert pointed out certain individuals he said had been victimized by Pincus—turned into zombies. The man he shot, Backus, was one. If you autopsy the body—"

"No. No. Absolutely not," says Scully.

Mulder says, "Scully, if this is all in my mind, as you say it is, I would be very grateful if you prove that."

Scully says, "Mulder, I am not going to serve the delusions of Gary Lambert—a madman—by giving credence to them."

Mulder stands. "Then I'll prove it without you," he says.

Later that day Mulder and Agent Rice enter Gary Lambert's apartment in Oak Brook. "What are we looking for?" asks Rice.

"I'll know it when I see it," says Mulder.

On a wall of Lambert's bedroom is a large map of the U.S. marked almost exactly the same way as the one in Mulder's office.

Rice stares at it, baffled. "What's this about?"

Mulder says, "Lambert was tracking his boss's movements over the years."

"Stalking him?"

"Gathering evidence."

Mulder walks across the room and looks out the window. Standing directly below, looking up at him, is Nancy Aaronson—her face as dead and gray as

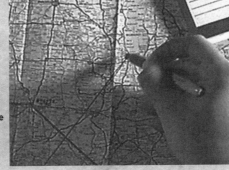

Lambert saw it. To Rice's astonishment, Mulder runs out the front door and into the street. But by the time he gets there, she is gone.

"You see her?" Mulder asks. "You see where she went?"

"Who?" asks Rice. "You mind telling me what's going on here?"

Just up the block a late-model sedan starts up and pulls out of its parking space. Mulder runs after it, followed by the baffled Rice. At the wheel of the car is Greg Pincus. Next to him sits Nancy Aaronson. Their faces are now normal, but eerily expressionless. The car speeds away, and Mulder breaks off his hopeless chase.

Later that day Scully enters Skinner's office at FBI headquarters. "You wanted to see me?" she asks.

"Yes," says Skinner. "I was hoping you could give me some insight into Agent Mulder's recent behavior."

"Sir?"

"Why is he back in Illinois?" asks Skinner. "I thought that case was closed."

Scully speaks carefully. "Agent Mulder believes that there may be a connection between the Oak Brook incident and several other cases."

Skinner says, "But you elected not to join him." He adds, "The Chicago field office has been in contact with him. They describe his behavior as being erratic."

Scully hesitates before replying. "To the best of my knowledge," she says, "Agent Mulder is currently working on a legitimate investigation. I will join him in Illinois immediately."

"Don't you have an autopsy to do first?" asks Skinner.

Scully looks at him, confused.

"This body Mulder sent to Quantico," Skinner adds. "Mark Backus, the shooting victim. You're scheduled to do an examination. Or didn't you know that?"

Scully frowns and gets the picture. "I'll get right on it, sir," she says, and heads toward the door.

Skinner stops her. "Is there something you want to tell me, Scully?" Skinner asks.

"No, sir," says Scully, who then exits.

At the FBI Forensic Pathology Lab at Quantico, Scully and a male assistant stand over the body of Mark Backus. Scully tells him that her autopsy will be restricted to an external examination and photos.

"Well, this guy came an awful long way just to have his picture taken," he replies.

"Knock yourself out," says Scully, sourly.

Scully pulls off her latex gloves and retrieves her cell phone. The assistant pulls down an overhead microphone. Snapping photographs as he goes, he says:

"Case number 98–6522. Mark Backus. Thirty-five-year-old Caucasian male. There are three one-centimeter gunshot entry wounds on the left anterior chest wall with some burn stippling present."

Scully dials; the call goes through but no one answers. "C'mon, Mulder," she says.

The assistant continues:

"Judging from the corpse's resolved rigor and fixed lividity, as well as the decompositional bloating, I'd place the time of death between forty-eight and seventy-two hours."

Scully hears this, hangs up the phone, and turns around.

"No," she says. "This man died late yesterday afternoon."

"Are you sure?" asks the assistant.

"Absolutely."

"It sure looks to me," he says, "like he's been dead longer than that."

In Oak Brook that night a familiar sedan pulls up to a two-story frame house. Greg Pincus gets out, alone. He heads up the walk toward the front door. Just up the street a black sedan comes to a halt. Mulder gets out.

Pincus turns and walks along the side of the house. Mulder sees this and runs after him. By the time he gets to the alley the man has disappeared, but TV sounds—an old Shirley Temple musical—are coming from a first-floor window.

Mulder peers inside. A fortyish woman

is sitting on a couch. Behind her is the monster, ready to pounce. Mulder draws his gun and uses it to shatter the window. The woman screams, and the monster disappears.

Mulder sprints around to the front door, kicks it open, and enters the living room. The woman still sits before her TV, alive and calm; in fact, oblivious. Mulder scans the room, but does not see the monster, which is escaping by crawling upside down across the ceiling behind him.

Gun still drawn, Mulder searches the rest of the house. Nothing. He pokes his head out of a back room window and hears a scratching sound, and looks up. The monster is scurrying up the sheer outside wall of the house. Before Mulder can react, it is onto the roof and gone.

The next morning the woman who was stalked sits in Greg Pincus's office at VinylRight. She speaks to Pincus and Walter Skinner.

"Suddenly," she says, "I became aware of this . . . presence. And I could feel it creeping toward me. It was terrifying. The next thing I knew, this madman was inside my house."

She turns to face Mulder, who is slumped silently in a chair in the corner of the office.

She adds, angrily, "He breaks my window, kicks in the door, and the whole time he's screaming about monsters. I mean, worse than Gary."

Skinner, looking extremely uncomfortable, rises. "Ms. Starns," he says, "I apologize for the incident. I assure you it will receive my utmost attention."

Ms. Starns gets up to leave.

Pincus says, "Why don't you take the rest of the week, Gretchen?"

"Thank you, Mr. Pincus," she says. She turns to Skinner and says, "That man has no business carrying a gun, if you ask me."

She exits. Mulder looks Pincus in the eye and speaks firmly, but very quietly.

"You got to her, too, didn't you?" he says.

"Agent Mulder!" warns Skinner.

"I was too late. You changed her somehow. You infected her!"

"Agent Mulder!" says Skinner, more forcefully this time. "Think very carefully about the next words that come out of

your mouth." The AD turns to Pincus. "Again, I apologize," he says.

Pincus says, evenly, "There's no need. I'm well aware of the stress Agent Mulder has been under. I still consider him a hero. Which is why I want to handle this privately."

Mulder frowns and shakes his head. Skinner does his best to ignore this.

"We appreciate that," he says.

Pincus says, "For my part, I'm happy to let this entire matter drop. I'm sure I can persuade Ms. Starns to do the same, provided Agent Mulder is amenable."

Mulder is anything but amenable. He ignores Pincus and turns to Skinner.

"You don't see what's going on here," he says.

"I'm afraid I do," says Skinner.

Frustrated, Mulder turns toward Pincus. "Lambert knew your secret," he says. "He knew you were sucking the humanity out of these people! Feeding on them!"

"Agent Mulder, that's enough!" says Skinner, leaning forward. "I don't want to hear another word out of you! If you care about your career, you'll knock this crap off! Because I guarantee I'll not stand for another second of this—"

As Skinner speaks, Mulder looks over his shoulder and sees Pincus, standing behind Skinner, turn into the monster. The creature slowly approaches his unwitting target.

"GET OUT OF THE WAY!" yells Mulder.

The agent rises, pulls out his gun, and draws a bead on the monster. Reacting instantly, Skinner hits Mulder's gun hand, brushing it away, and pins the agent to the floor. Helpless, Mulder swivels his head to see Pincus—who is normal again and staring down at him impassively.

At Calumet Mercy Hospital in Chicago that day Scully enters a private room and looks down at Mulder, who is tied down with wrist restraints to his bed. Scully takes her partner's hand gently.

"Five years together, Scully," says Mulder, with a wry smile. "You *must* have seen this coming." He adds, "Did you examine Backus's body? What did you find?"

"More or less what we thought we'd find," says Scully, frowning.

"'More or less'? What is that supposed to mean?"

Scully says, reluctantly, "The body showed signs of decomposition beyond what I expected to find. Which in of itself means nothing, really. Time of death is notoriously hard to quantify."

"Or that Lambert was telling the truth," says Mulder. "And that man was dead before he was gunned down."

"No. Mulder—"

"Scully, when that monster—Pincus, whatever the hell you want to call it—when he attacked that woman last night, he did something to the back of her neck. He bit her there, injected something in there. There's got to be evidence of that. You've got to check for that."

"Mulder, the case is over," says Scully. "There's no more evidence to be gathered. There's only my hope that you'll be able to somehow see past this delusion."

Mulder looks his partner in the eye. "You have to be willing to see."

"I wish it were that simple," says Scully, sadly.

Her partner says, "Scully, you have to believe me. Nobody else on this whole damn planet does or ever will. You're my one in five billion."

Later that night Scully is back in the forensic pathology lab at Quantico. Backus's body lies atop a transport cart.

"Well, you just made it," says the assistant. "I was just about to ship him."

Scully stares down at the corpse.

"Full autopsy this time?" asks the assistant.

"No," says Scully. "Let's flip him."

They turn the body over on its stomach. Using a magnifier, Scully examines its upper back. She notes some bruising, then uses a small electric razor to shave off the body hair. She blows away the loose hairs and reaches again for her magnifier. In the shaved swath, at the base of the skull, are three distinct puncture marks.

In his hospital bed Mulder watches a nurse prepare a large hypodermic of sedative. He gestures toward his wrist restraints.

"We can do without these," he says. "What do you say?"

"Sorry," says the nurse, smiling and plunging the needle into his arm. Mulder stares forlornly out the closed window opposite him.

"Sleep tight!" says the nurse, cheerily, drawing a translucent privacy curtain around his bed.

She switches off the room light as she exits. Mulder lies awake in the dark and hears a familiar faint chirping sound. A giant buglike shadow appears on the curtain.

"Nurse?" shouts Mulder. "Nurse! NURSE! NURSE!" He strains against his wrist restraints. "IT'S HERE!"

The curtain moves. The nurse's face appears before him.

"Nurse!" says Mulder. "It's here! It's at the window."

The nurse stares at Mulder. "What's here?" she asks.

Mulder fights for calm.

"There is something—there is something at the window, trying to get in here. Please unstrap me—"

"Sir!"

"—so that I can stop it."

"Sir, we're three floors up!" says the nurse, firmly. "There's nothing at the window."

Mulder smiles and chuckles—somewhat hysterically—at the absurdity of the situation. It's a game attempt to prove he's not stark raving mad. He fails.

"Just undo my straps so I can check," he says.

The nurse replies, "I can show you mysel—"

"No, no. NO!" says Mulder. "Don't! Please!"

The nurse switches on the light, zips the curtain all the way open, and raps on the window pane. There is no sign of any monster.

"See?" she says. "Nothing's gonna get you."

"Okay," says Mulder. "Just untie me anyway, please?"

The nurse flips the window latch and opens the window half way.

"What are you doing?" asks Mulder, alarmed.

"You just need some fresh air," says the nurse, her expression becoming oddly blank.

She walks toward Mulder—a slight stream of blood dripping from a wound on the back of her neck. She reaches down to Mulder's wrist restraints and tightens them.

"I can't be running in here all night," she says, chillingly. "Okay?"

She zips closed the privacy curtain, flips off the light, and leaves. Mulder is in the dark again. He hears the chirping sound. The giant bug's shadow is again on the curtain. This time the monster crawls inside, up the wall, and onto the ceiling above Mulder's head. He snaps out of his horrified trance.

"HELLLLP! SOMEBODY HELP!" he screams.

At the nurse's station outside, the nurse is turning away a visitor.

"I'm very sorry," she says politely, "but it is after hours, and Mr. Mulder is resting. We'll have to ask you to come back in the morning."

Scully flashes her FBI ID. "Well, I've come a long way, and I know he wants to see me," she says, firmly. "So what do you say?"

The nurse smiles ruefully. "I'm sorry. Really. It's hospital policy."

Scully opens her mouth to protest, then stares, horrified, at the nurse's face. It is pale white-gray, her eyes blank. She is a zombie.

Scully dashes into Mulder's room, gun drawn, and sees the monster about to attack her screaming, panicked partner. She fires. The monster lets out a terrifying squeal and skitters toward the window. Scully fires again, hitting it just as it smashes its way out through the glass.

Scully runs to the window and looks down, scanning for any signs of the monster. There are none. She turns back toward Mulder, stunned.

Sometime later Scully sits in Skinner's office. The AD is holding her report in his hands.

He says, "Agent Scully, I have to say I'm at a bit of a loss here. Do I infer correctly from this that you believe that there's some merit to Mulder's claims?"

Scully takes a deep breath. "I believe that Agent Mulder is mentally sound and fit for duty," she says. "Aside from that belief, I can only present to you the few hard facts that I've been able to gather. That, as per Agent Mulder's assertions, a toxin has been found to have been injected into the spine of the shooting victim, Mark Backus. As of yet we have been unable to identify it.

"Furthermore, Gregory Pincus has apparently disappeared without a trace along with half a dozen key witnesses integral to this investigation. Among them, Agent Mulder's nurse at the hospital and several VinylRight employees."

"Men and women described by Mulder as 'zombies,'" says Skinner, puzzled.

Scully sighs. "I personally vouch," she says, "for the fact that there was an intruder in Agent Mulder's hospital room."

"Describe this intruder," says Skinner.

Scully pauses, then says, simply, "It was dark."

Skinner frowns. "You must have gotten a glimpse," he says. "What did you see?"

A few moments later Scully leaves Skinner's office and meets Mulder in the hallway. They wait for the elevator together.

Mulder asks, "What did you tell him?"

Scully says, "The truth as well as I understand it."

"Which is?"

The elevator arrives. They enter. The doors close in front of them.

Folie à deux," she says. "A madness shared by two."

At a large warren of cubicles in Camdenton, Missouri, scores of telemarketers sit in cubicles making their sales pitches. One of them, a man in his early twenties, seems nervous. There are sweat beads on his forehead.

He says, "Mr. Jaycox, may I take a few moments to tell you about the advantages of WeatherRight replacement windows? They keep down high heating and cooling costs. They beautify—they beautify and add value to your home as well as—"

The telemarketer pauses. He hears a familiar chirping sound. He stares at something in the distance, his expression growing panicked. Hopeless.

"Mr. Jaycox?" he whispers, hoarsely. "It's here!"

back story:

It's not easy to frighten a veteran *X-Files* staffer, but at least one of them found himself becoming "unhinged" at his first encounter with the awful "Folie à Deux" monster.

"I saw it the first day we were shooting the hostage scene," reports Brian Markinson, who played the tormented telemarketer Gary Lambert. "The monster walked on the set. It was a short woman wearing a bug suit. She had some kind of breathing apparatus stuck in her throat. I thought, 'This is what's driving me crazy?'

"Then I looked up and I saw (director) Kim Manners. He had absolutely lost it. He just kept saying, 'Oh, my God! My career—it's over!'"

Similar expressions of horror—mixed with bursts of hysterical laughter—were heard in the offices and editing suites of the show's L.A. production base. Even worse was the fact that the season was almost over; there would be little spare time to somehow make the "bug" legitimately scary.

"I guess it was just one of those things," says supervising producer Vince Gilligan, the writer of 5X19. "We're usually on such a short schedule that there has to be a weak link somewhere. Part of it, I guess, was that (make-up/special effects supervisor) Toby Lindala did too good a job. If anything, the bug suit was a little overengineered; the eyebrows moved and all those little antennas wiggled and stuff. If it had been a little lighter and a little less engineered it would have been easier to move in a believable fashion."

Gilligan adds, "As it was, the suit weighed something like seventy pounds, and the female stuntperson had a hard time moving in it. And because she had a hard time moving, her movements made the whole thing look sort of ridiculous. In fact, it looked like someone standing on the side of the road in a big costume, saying, 'Eat at Subway.' You know what I mean?"

In fact, it meant that a tense, taut stand-alone episode was in real danger of becoming a comedy, which, although Gilligan has written some of *The X-Files*'s most memorable comedic episodes, was nobody's intention.

"The idea that there's a monster around that only you can see—the clinical definition of madness—has always seemed scary," says Gilligan. The notion that one's boss is secretly a demon also resonates widely, he adds. In making the tormented protagonist a telemarketer, his intention was to funnel some of the torment generated by these intrusive, dinner-wrecking pitchmen.

In playing Lambert, Markinson—last seen in the series as corrupt cop Tony Fiori in "Born Again" (1X21)—drew on a soul-draining experience, during his starving-actor period, of selling auto insurance over the phone. "I was awful at it," says Markinson. "My supervisor in the episode was Cinderella compared to the ones in the real world. They were in your face all day. I ended up a sobbing mess."

To film the exterior portion of the hostage scenes, locations manager Todd Pittson rented a building in an industrial park in Richmond, near Vancouver International Airport. In contrast, the interior of the VinylRight building was constructed on a sound stage so that an armored personnel carrier, rented by picture car coordinator Nigel Habgood from a local military vehicle aficionado, could knock down the office wall on cue.

To allow the monster to skitter over Gretchen Starns's living room ceiling, art director Greg Loewen designed an upside-down ceiling fixture that rested on the floor. The bug lady crawled over it; thus giving the illusion—after the filmed image was rotated 180 degrees—that she was defying gravity.

And, finally, to keep the sandwich shop monster from wreaking total havoc, the whole mess was dumped—at the last possible moment, of course—in the lap of visual effects supervisor Laurie Kallsen-George. With frequent input from the show's producers, she finished her work at 7:30 on the morning of the day "Folie à Deux" aired.

"Basically, the stuff she did was amazing," says Vince Gilligan, smiling wryly. "She took the footage with the monster in it, erased the monster completely, took the monster to a different screen or whatever, animated it, and added speed blur."

And in the end, concedes Gilligan, the monster is barely visible on screen at all.

"You never really see it that closely, but that's okay," he says. "There's a long, noble history to that kind of thinking. The truth is, your imagination can be much more effective than real life."

the end

A child chess prodigy has the ability to read minds. If Mulder and Scully can protect him, he could be the answer to the mysteries they've long been exploring. If the rulers of the Syndicate capture him, he could be the key to world hegemony and the final destruction of the X-Files.

EPISODE: 5X20
FIRST AIRED: May 17, 1998
EDITOR: Heather MacDougall
WRITTEN BY: Chris Carter
DIRECTED BY: R. W. Goodwin
GUEST STARS:
Mitch Pileggi (AD Walter Skinner)
Mimi Rogers (Agent Diana Fowley)
Jeff Gulka (Gibson Praise)
William B. Davis
(The Cigarette-Smoking Man)

Chris Owens
(Special Agent Jeffrey Spender)

Nicholas Lea (Alex Krycek)
John Neville
(The Well-Manicured Man)

Tom Braidwood (Frohike)
Dean Haglund (Langly)
Bruce Harwood (Byers)
Don S. Williams (First Elder)
George Murdock (Second Elder)
John Moore (Third Elder)
Martin Ferrero (Shooter)
Michael Shamus Wiles
(Federal Guard)

Orest Blajkevitch
(Anatole Klebanow)

Patrick Phillips (Clinician #1)
Paul Moniz De Sa (Clinician #2)
John Trotter (Clinician #3)
PRINCIPAL SETTINGS:
Vancouver, British Columbia;
Laurentian Mountains, Quebec;
Washington, D.C.;
Fort Marlene, Maryland;
Centerville, Virginia

Inside a large indoor stadium in Vancouver, a packed house watches raptly as two chess players—one a Russian grand master, the other a startlingly young boy—face off. They sit across from each other at a simple table, in a pool of white light, dead center on the arena floor. Their moves are relayed to the crowd on giant video screens.

The Russian man—his name is Anatole Klebanow—is playing black. He scans the chessboard, concentrates, and moves his king one square to the right. His young opponent—whose name is Gibson Praise—counters immediately by checking the black king with his rook.

Klebanow winces slightly, trying hard to control his dismay. On a catwalk above the highest balcony, a middle-aged man—lean and hardened-looking—watches all this grimly. He opens a black suitcase and pulls out a sniper's rifle.

Wide-eyed with apprehension, Klebanow captures the white rook with his king. Gibson pushes his queen across the board. Check again.

Klebanow doesn't react. His young opponent leans back in his chair, cocking his head slightly. Inside the boy's mind is a cacophony of vaguely human sounds. Gibson turns around and scans the crowd behind him. He looks up at the spot where the shooter is loading a cartridge into his weapon.

Klebanow eyes his opponent, slightly puzzled, and looks down at the board for salvation. The shooter rests his rifle on the catwalk railing and aims carefully at the back of Gibson's head. Klebanow moves his king out of check. The shooter's finger tightens on the trigger.

Gibson stands, reaches down, and moves his queen. The shooter keeps the boy in his crosshairs.

"Checkmate," says Gibson.

Klebanow looks up in disbelief. Gibson leans backward slightly at the same instant as the shooter fires. A single bullet rips into Klebanow's chest. The grand master slumps to the floor, killed instantly, as the thousands of witnesses react with horror. Gibson Praise turns, expressionless, and looks up directly at the fleeing assassin.

In a remote area high in the Laurentian Mountains, two black-clad parachutists—their faces covered by black balaclavas—land silently in the snow.

They alight near a small, isolated cabin. Inside it, a lone middle-aged man— the Cigarette-Smoking Man—is boiling water for tea. He is haggard, unshaven; he buttons his flannel shirt over a long, thin scar on his chest. An electronic chirp attracts his attention. One of the parachutists has walked past a miniature motion detector, attached unobtrusively to a fallen log.

Guns drawn, the parachutists cautiously approach the cabin. One man creeps slowly to the front door, turns the knob, and is blown away by a shotgun blast fired from inside. The second gunman scurries around to where the dead body lies, and sees red-tinged footprints leading into the woods.

The surviving gunman dashes off in pursuit of the Cigarette-Smoking Man, who is running headlong down a narrow path. The younger man catches up quickly, mounts a small rise overlooking the path, and fires a warning shot over his quarry's head. The Cigarette-Smoking Man stops, his eyes betraying his certain fate.

The gunman carefully aims his pistol, then whips off his balaclava, revealing himself to be Alex Krycek (last seen in 5X15). The Cigarette-Smoking Man's expression changes to what might be smug satisfaction.

"Take your shot, Alex!" he shouts.

He turns and walks calmly away. Krycek brandishes his pistol in his remaining hand.

"Right there!" he shouts, bringing the Cigarette-Smoking Man again to a halt. "I was sent to bring you back."

Inside the X-Files office in the bowels of FBI headquarters, Walter Skinner stands alone. He scans the memorabilia and detritus pinned to the bulletin board; them scans the X-File—file number X–491679—in his hands. Absorbed in his reading, he doesn't notice Mulder standing in the doorway behind him.

"Wow," says Mulder, smiling. "You know you're going places in the Bureau when the Assistant Director tidies up your office for you. What's up?"

"I was just, uh, looking," says Skinner, sheepishly.

"For anything special?"

"I came down to ask you something,"

says Skinner, distractedly. "I guess I was, uh, nosing around. Wondering about you, your long-term plans."

"My long-term plans?" says Mulder, nodding at the X-File Skinner is holding. "You've got them right there in your hands."

Skinner's expression softens. He stares into space for a moment, then turns back to Mulder.

"What do you hope to find?" he asks. "I mean, in the end."

Mulder takes the file from his boss. "Whatever I hope to find is in here," he says. "Maybe I'll know it when I find it." He places the folder in his filing cabinet. "Is that what you came to ask me?"

"No," says Skinner. "There's a case. Nothing I'd send you normally."

The AD briefly outlines the circumstances of Anatole Klebanow's murder. "The shooter is former National Security Agency," he adds. "One of ours. It's got a lot of people upset. This kid Jeffrey Spender—Special Agent Spender—he's been given the case. He's running it."

"Did you give it to him?" Mulder asks.

"No," says Skinner, tight-lipped. "It came as an order from somewhere outside the Bureau. He's got his team assembled upstairs right now. He was very specific that you be excluded."

A few minutes later Jeffrey Spender (last seen in 5X15) addresses two dozen or so agents in a medium-sized operations room. On an overhead projector a slow-motion tape of Klebanow's last milliseconds is shown. He tells his attentive audience that the Russian was shot with a weapon registered to a U.S. intelligence agency; and that the gunman fired one kill shot before being captured, without incident, a short distance from the scene. He adds, "No motive has been established. Nor has the shooter offered up a statement or accomplice."

At this, Spender looks up to see Mulder and Skinner standing in the doorway. An agent sitting in the front row—Scully—swivels around and exchanges glances with her partner. Spender frowns, irritated, and loses his train of thought.

"Please continue," says Mulder, evenly.

He stares past Spender's head at the video screen. Spender turns away.

"The trajectory of the kill shot," says Spender, "suggests the shooter acted alone. We cannot yet rule out an accomplice or conspiracy. A single bullet was fired from a catwalk at a steep angle, striking the target just right of the solar plexus."

Mulder points at the screen.

"I'm sorry," he says. "Can you rewind the tape?"

Spender stares daggers at Mulder.

"Please," says Mulder. "I'll tell you where. Just take it back."

Spender says, seething, "Let me get through this. If you have any questions, we can talk later."

"I don't have any questions," says Mulder. "No. I just think you're wrong."

Embarrassed, Scully looks at her partner. "Mulder, what are you doing?" she asks softly.

Mulder says, "I don't think the Russian was the target. It was his opponent."

"His opponent, Agent Mulder, was a twelve-year-old boy," says Spender.

"And a good chess player," says Mulder. "Here, let me show you his best move."

Spender fumes for a moment and silently winds back the tape.

"Stop it there," says Mulder. "Look what the kid does right here, right before the kill shot. Play. See what he does? He just pushes back. You see that?"

Spender says, angrily, "He just completed a checkmate. He was pushing back because the game was over."

"No, no," says Mulder. "You described a steep trajectory of the kill shot. If the kid doesn't push back at that precise moment, he catches the bullet in the back of the neck. Not the Russian."

"Can we move on here?" says Spender.

"I think Agent Mulder is right," says a voice from the back of the room.

It comes from an attractive female agent in her mid-thirties. Her name is Diana Fowley.

"It looks like the boy sensed the shooter precognitively," she says. "Now, if you rewind the tape you'll see it."

Mulder turns toward Fowley with a look of surprised recognition.

Spender says, skeptically, "There's no way. It's impossible."

Skinner says, with steel in his voice, "Let's rewind the tape so we can all see for ourselves."

Spender nods grudgingly, rewinds, then freeze-frames it. The boy's quick glance toward the catwalk is easily visible. Mulder looks again at Fowley, who returns his gaze knowingly.

That night, somewhere in the D.C. area, Krycek and the Cigarette-Smoking Man walk slowly across a deserted parking lot. At the other end are the men they've come to meet: several familiar-looking envoys from the Syndicate.

The Cigarette-Smoking Man faces the First Elder. "You look surprised," he says. "Is it that I'm here or that I'm alive?"

The First Elder says, stone-faced. "When we heard you were shot, we assumed the worst," he says.

The Second Elder, standing nearby, says, "There were reports you lost too much blood to survive."

"Obviously, you underestimated me," says the Cigarette-Smoking Man. "More obviously, you overestimated the man you sent to do the job."

The First Elder is silent. The Cigarette-Smoking Man lights up, takes a deep drag, and exhales.

"Well, let's say all is forgiven," he says. "Now you have a job for me."

The Well-Manicured Man, also present, speaks up. "There's been an incident. An unfortunate mistake."

The Cigarette-Smoking Man smiles thinly. "Yes. I've seen. I've heard. I've read."

"The boy is a problem for us," says the Second Elder.

"What would you like me to do?" says the Cigarette-Smoking Man, coldly. "Shoot him dead? Splatter his brains?"

"Dear God!" says the Well-Manicured Man, appalled.

The Cigarette-Smoking Man turns toward him, frowning. "What's the matter?" he says. "Does this sort of business offend you?"

"It's in your interest," says the First Elder. "As in ours."

"You think you know my interests?" demands the Cigarette-Smoking Man.

The First Elder ignores this. "Can we count on you?"

Yes," says the Cigarette-Smoking Man.

He takes a final drag, turns on his heel, and walks back in the direction from which he's come.

That evening Mulder is at the wheel of an FBI sedan. Scully sits beside him; Diana Fowley rides in the backseat. Scully asks her how long she's been with the Bureau.

"Since '91," says Fowley. "I took an assignment in Europe after the Wall came down. When the Director stepped up foreign terrorism concerns."

"And they brought you on this because of a terrorist angle?" asks Scully.

"No," says Fowley. "I requested a reassignment. There were things at home I decided I wanted to get back to."

Mulder looks at Fowley in his rearview mirror. Fowley notices this and catches his eyes in the mirror, also.

Scully turns to Mulder. "Nineteen ninety one," she says. "That's about when you started working on the X-Files."

Her partner says, "More or less, yeah."

At Inget Murray Psychiatric Hospital in Maryland, Gibson Praise sits alone on the floor of a large empty dayroom, watching *The Simpsons* on a television set. Mulder, Scully, and Fowley enter. Mulder walks over to the boy and squatting down to his eye level.

"Gibson? My name is Fox. This is Dana and Diana. How ya doin'?"

"I don't mind it here," says Gibson.

"They get all the good TV shows. Where I live in the Philippines, all we get is *Baywatch*."

"What's wrong with *Baywatch*?" asks Mulder, with a smile.

Gibson says, "You've got a dirty mind."

Mulder turns to Scully and shrugs.

Scully says, "Your parents are going to pick you up on Friday, Gibson, to take you back home."

Gibson turns back toward the TV. "I don't want to play any chess," he says.

"How do you know I want to?" asks Mulder.

"'Cause you got that cheapo chess computer in your hand."

"Not so cheap," protests Mulder. "You wanna see how fast you can beat it?"

"No."

"Maybe because you can't."

Gibson says nothing. Mulder reaches for the remote control and turns off the TV.

"I'm right, aren't I?" says Mulder. "You know what I'm talking about. You knew the moment I came in."

Silence.

"That's how you win, isn't it?" he adds. "How you know what your opponent's going to do. You get inside his head. You read his thoughts. That's how you knew the man was going to shoot you. Isn't it?"

Gibson says, "I know what's on your mind. I know you're thinking about one of the girls you've brought. And one of them's thinking about you."

"Which one?" asks Fowley.

Gibson replies, "He doesn't want me to say."

Mulder rises, smiling wryly, and heads toward the door. "This kid's going to need round-the-clock protection," he says.

A few seconds later Scully catches up with Mulder in the hallway. "What was that all about?" she asks.

"The kid's no chess master," he says. "Under con-

trolled conditions, I could probably beat him."

"Mulder, he's recognized internationally as a prodigy," says Scully. "He's beaten grand masters."

"With the most unfair advantage. What he's doing amounts to a kind of parlor magic trick."

"Mulder, he was goofing on you! He was playing along. What you're positing is that this kid can read minds."

Mulder says, "We've seen a number of these case before, Scully."

Scully says, "We have seen cases, Mulder, of fakers and lucky guessers. But no one who has ever been able to stand up to any kind of rigorous testing. And no one who has gone so far as to claim they can zero in on the mind of one person in a crowd of thousands."

"Maybe," says Mulder, "that's why they want him dead."

"Who?" says Scully. "Who are you talking about?"

"I don't know," says Mulder. "I'm not the mind reader."

Scully says, "Say that what you're suggesting is even possible. Who would want to kill a kid whose abilities would offer you the ultimate advantage? In business, in war, in anything."

Fowley has left Gibson's room and walked up behind Scully. "Maybe somebody whose business is to keep secrets," she says.

Scully turns, staring searchingly at Fowley. Then she turns back to Mulder, who is looking intensely at Fowley, too.

"Let's test him," he says. "I think the kid will stand up. Let's run a brain scan and a psych evaluation on him. You know what to do, Diana."

With that he turns and walks down the long hallway. Scully is left alone with Fowley.

"So you two know each other," she says.

Fowley says, "It was a long time ago."

Later that night at a nearby federal detention facility Jeffrey Spender exits a door and locks it behind him. Mulder approaches from the other end of the hallway; Spender is chagrined, to say the least, to see him.

"What are you doing here?" asks Spender.

"I want to talk to the shooter," says Mulder.

Spender steps between Mulder and the cell door. "I just spent the last six hours talking to him," he says. "He's not been what I'd call forthcoming."

Mulder says, "Okay, let me see what I can do—"

Spender steps in front of him again. "I'd prefer you stay out of there. In fact, I'd prefer you stay out of this thing altogether."

Mulder levels Spender with his gaze. "You know, when I first met you I figured you were just ambitious," he says. "This morning my opinion changed, and I thought you were arrogant. Now I'm beginning to wonder what you're protecting."

Spender bristles. "I'm just trying to run this thing right. Not like some ridiculous paranormal free-for-all."

"You're insulting me when you should be taking notes," says Mulder. He adds, "Somehow you got the big assignment, but just because you're wearing the suit doesn't mean it fits. You're lucky you're not busy defusing an international incident, kissing some serious Russian ass, and sending a whole lot of agents barking down a whole lot of bad leads. Now, the kid is the key to this. And the shooter knows why. Excuse me."

Mulder steps past Spender and into the cell. Fuming, Spender follows behind him. The shooter slouches on his bunk, eyeing Mulder with the confidence of a man who's been trained for just such an encounter.

"What's it take to kill a kid?" asks Mulder. "Money? Or just evil stupidity?"

"I didn't kill a kid," says the shooter, softly.

"No. Thanks to the kid," says Mulder.

"Can we talk about heartlessness?" says the shooter. "Your squeaky friend there hasn't given me any food or water for sixteen hours."

"I won't tolerate that," says Mulder.

He turns to face the younger agent. "Spender, you gotta get this guy some food," he says.

Spender realizes the game they're playing, but glares at Mulder all the same. He exits, and Mulder turns back to the shooter. The assassin tells him smugly that he has nothing to say.

"Yeah," says Mulder. "I read your bio. You've been trained. Special Forces, Granada, Zaire; you were inside Saddam's palace with a hit squad when they started raining bombs down over it. Yet you failed to kill him as well."

"Like I said—" says the shooter.

"Yeah, I know. You've got nothing to say. That's okay, I'm a pretty good guesser. The kid reads minds, how's that?"

The shooter smiles faintly.

Mulder says, "Why don't I tell them you told me that and see how safe and snug you feel in here?"

The shooter's smile fades. "What can you do for me?" he says.

"I don't know," says Mulder. "I might be able to get you immunity, or get you into the witness protection program."

"Never happen," says the shooter.

"Think about it," says Mulder.

He leaves the cell, just as Spender and a federal guard are returning with some food on a cafeteria tray.

"What did you get? Anything?" asks Spender.

"Just his attention," says Mulder, smiling.

He grabs a bag of chips and a bottle of Coke off the tray before heading off. He doesn't look back.

At the psychiatric hospital the next morning Scully leads Gibson Praise down a long hallway. "How're you doing?" asks Scully.

"I didn't like those tests," says

Brandon. "I didn't like being on the machine."

Scully nods sympathetically. "They were a little scary, weren't they?" she says.

Gibson says, "You're wondering, aren't you?"

"About what? About you?"

"About that other girl."

Scully looks up to see Diana Fowley, standing in a doorway at the other end of the hall.

"She's wondering about you, too," says Gibson.

In an observation room at the hospital a few minutes later, six clinicians sit in a semicircle facing Gibson. Scully and Fowley watch in an adjacent room through a large window.

One of the clinicians says, "We're going to show you a group of cards and as we look at them, we want you to tell us what we're thinking. Now, take as much time as you need."

The clinician holds up a card, blank on Gibson's side. On the clinician's side there is a picture of a chair.

"Chair," says Brandon.

The clinician next to him sees a picture of a piano.

"Piano.

"Piece of pie.

"Light bulb.

"Smiley face.

"Statue."

The boy is correct each time. Scully and Fowley watch him in astonishment.

"It's amazing," says Scully. "It's hard to believe."

Fowley says, "I've witnessed clairvoyants who were over ninety percent accurate, and seen telepathy being demonstrated, but I don't know I've ever witnessed anything quite like this."

"Where did you see that?" asks Scully.

"Agent Mulder and I spent some time in psychiatric hospitals. There were some patients serving criminal sentences who we felt had been misdiagnosed."

In the observation room Brandon is gazing at each of the clinicians in turn.

"Omelet," he says.

"Coffee and a cruller."

"A non-fat latte."

"An English muffin."

"Grand Slam number two with double hash browns and a side of Canadian bacon."

The clinicians break into laughter, then applause. The first clinician turns around and addresses Scully and Fowley.

"He just told us what we all ate for breakfast," he says.

Scully says, softly, to Fowley, "I have to disappear a bit."

At the federal detention facility that night the guard we've seen before walks down the long hallway to the door of the shooter's cell. He slides open a small viewing slot at eye level.

"I was handed a note," says the guard. "Now I'm handing it to you."

He pushes a folded piece of paper through the slot. The shooter takes it. The guard closes the slot. The shooter unfolds the paper. A handwritten note reads YOU'RE A DEAD MAN.

The shooter turns over the paper. It is actually the front side of a package of cigarettes: Morleys.

At the Lone Gunmen's headquarters later that night there is an insistent buzzing at the front door. Frohike—buckling a flak jacket over his pj's—looks into a security monitor and sees Scully standing in the entryway.

"Is somebody gonna let me in?" asks Scully, over the intercom, impatiently.

"Yeah. Coming. Coming!" says Frohike. He unlocks half a dozen or so door locks and latches and opens up. "Sorry," he says. "You caught me getting ready for bed."

Scully enters. Frohike is puzzled and delighted.

"To what do we

owe the pleasure of this late-night hour?" he says.

"I need your help," says Scully.

"With what?" says Langly, stepping forward.

A toothbrush protrudes jauntily from the corner of Langly's mouth. In another corner of the cluttered room, Byers—in pajamas and bathrobe—watches quietly.

Scully says, "You've all heard of Gibson Praise, the chess wunderkind?" She opens a file. "These are a series of scans and neural electrical outputs of his brain and brain processes. There seems to be some suspicion that he's a fraud."

Byers takes Gibson's brain scans and places them on a light table. "Dorf on chess?" he says.

"Well, apparently," says Scully, "he wins by reading his opponents' minds."

Frohike says, "I love it!"

"And you want us to what?" asks Langly.

Scully frowns, and hesitates. "Analyze the data with an eye to the parapsychological."

"Ooh!" says Frohike. "A walk on the wild side!"

Scully switches off the light table. "But first I want you guys to tell me who Diana Fowley is."

"Diana Fowley?" says Byers. "Geez, we haven't heard that name in a while."

"Then you know her?"

"Well, yeah," says Byers, hesitantly.

Frohike says, "She was Mulder's chickadee when he just got out of the Academy. Good lookin'. "

Scully says, "Well, she claims she worked closely with him for a while."

Langly says, quickly, "She was there when he discovered the X-Files. She has some kind of background in para-science."

"She got a LEGAT appointment a while back," says Langly. "In Berlin. I always wondered why they split up."

Scully swallows hard and flips on the light table again. "How about you boys see what you can find?" she says.

In the dayroom of the psychiatric hospital Gibson Praise watches a *Silver Surfer* cartoon. Diana Fowley watches the boy from the adjacent observation room. Mulder enters the room behind her.

"How's little Karnac holding up?" he says.

Fowley says, "Put a TV in front of him and he turns right into a normal kid. But he's the real deal, Fox." She adds, "We tested him with Zener cards, random numbers, a variety of ESP tasking. He's got ability to not just focus on a thought, but a multitude of thoughts at once."

"There's something else," says Mulder. "There's something we're missing here."

Fowley says, "That was a good catch on the videotape. I was impressed."

"You would have caught it eventually."

Fowley shakes her head. "No. It's been too many years trying to get inside the head of too many Arab terrorists. I'm out of practice with this stuff. But you seem at the top of your game."

"It's all I do. It's all I've been doing for the last five years. It's been my life such as it is."

Fowley says, "Sometimes I hear about you, about the work you've been doing. I think how it might have been if I had stayed."

Mulder says, "How we'd all have been blown up by some terrorist bomb, huh?"

Fowley says, "I sense you could have used an ally, though. Someone who thinks like you. With some background."

"You mean Scully?"

"She's not what I'd call an open mind on the subject."

Mulder laughs softly. "She's a scientist. She just makes me work for everything."

"Yes, but I'm sure there were times when two like minds on a case would have been advantageous."

Mulder says, "I've done okay with her."

"Hey," says Fowley, softly. "I'm on your side."

At that moment Scully walks through the corridor at the hospital, has a passing glance through the glass door in the observation room, sees Mulder and Fowley in close conversation, does a slight double take, doubles back, glances at them again, and leaves the building. She gets into her car and sits, thinking. She pulls out her cell phone, sighs, and hits the speed dial.

"Mulder."

"Mulder, it's me," she says.

"Where are you?"

"I'm, uh, I'm on my way to work. I was

hoping I could show you something. Something about the boy."

"Well, I'm at the psych facility with him right now. Why don't you come by and show me?"

"No, I'd prefer to show you at work, if that's okay," says Scully.

"Okay. What is it?" says Mulder.

"I think you'll be surprised," says Scully. "Very surprised."

"I'm on my way," says Mulder.

Scully starts her car, puts it in reverse, and swivels around to see Jeffrey Spender in his own car, looking for a parking space and passing directly behind her.

Scully pulls away. Spender parks his car and gets out. He hears a voice behind him.

"Agent Spender," says the Cigarette-Smoking Man, standing in the dim recesses of the garage, "I need to speak with you."

"Who are you?" says Spender.

"Somebody who's taken an interest in you. In this case of yours. This case I gave you."

Spender cautiously approaches the Cigarette-Smoking Man. "Who are you? CIA? NSA?"

"You're a bright boy," says the Cigarette-Smoking Man.

"You said you had information," says Spender, impatiently.

"Control the board," says the Cigarette-Smoking Man. "Know which men to sacrifice, and when."

"I don't know what you're talking about," says Spender.

"Don't become part of someone else's cause or crusade. Pursue your own self-interest. Always."

Spender gives the Cigarette-Smoking Man a look of puzzled annoyance. An access door opens on the far side of the garage behind him. It is Mulder.

"Agent Spender!" shouts the agent, running toward him. "Agent Spender!"

Spender turns toward Mulder. When he turns back, the Cigarette-Smoking Man is gone.

"Agent Spender! Who were you talking to?"

"I don't know," says Spender.

"You don't know who you were talking to? You're lying!"

"What's your deal?" says Spender, angrily.

"I was told he was dead!" says Mulder.

"Well, obviously, whoever he is," says Spender, "he's not."

In Skinner's office the next day most of the FBI task force is assembled. Mulder, Scully, Spender, and Fowley sit across from the AD.

"You're here to tell me a story," says Skinner, to Scully.

Mulder turns to his partner. "Tell him exactly as you told me," he says.

Scully says, "I've conducted some tests on Gibson Praise and have come up with some rather unexpected conclusions. Ones which I myself have difficulty reconciling with what I know."

"These are?" says Skinner.

"Neurological tests. Mapping of brain functions, using very high-resolution EKG."

"What did you find out?"

"The tests revealed something peculiar in an area of the brain we are only beginning to understand. An area of the temporal lobe that neurophysicists are calling the 'God Module'."

Skinner frowns. "I hope I'm not going to hear that this kid is the next Christ child," he says.

Scully says, "All of the boy's brain processes are showing extraordinary activity in exactly this part of the brain, which is not just abnormal or anomalous, but from what I know, absolutely unheard of."

"There are corollaries," says Mulder, "individuals who've been responsible for great leaps forward in understanding and science. Newton, Galileo, Einstein.

Stephen Hawking: all these men exhibited modes of thinking that are suggestive of access to special brain centers."

"All right, so this kid is a human oddity," says Skinner, impatiently. "Would someone please tell me why anyone would go to such great lengths as to kill him?"

Mulder says, "This kid may be the key. Not just to all human potential, but to all spiritual, unexplained, paranormal phenomena. The key to everything in the X-Files."

The others in the room are stunned by this assertion. Finally Spender speaks.

"Let me get this right," he says. "We're supposed to believe that this boy was going to be killed because of the X-Files?"

"No," says Mulder. "It's bigger than that."

"Uh-huh," says Spender, skeptically. "Explain it to me. To us."

"I can't. But the shooter can. The assassin that you have locked up. In exchange for immunity from prosecution."

Spender is irate. "You want to give a murderer a free ride for the secrets of the pyramids? This is crazy. This is nuts."

Scully turns to him. "You've mischaracterized what I've said. This would be quantifiable, scientific proof of everything that Agent Mulder and I have investigated over the past five years."

Fowley speaks up. "How do you quantify the spiritual?" she asks. "It can't be done." She adds, "If you ask for immunity for a killer on that basis, the attorney general is going to go off."

She turns to Mulder. "You're allowed to investigate the X-Files as an indulgence. But draw the wrong kind of attention, and they'll close you down. Put an end to all your work—something I happen to have an interest in myself."

Mulder nods. Through all this, through a rush of barely identifiable emotions, Scully has been staring at him intently.

Sensing an impasse, Skinner asks everyone to step out into the hall except Mulder. Alone with the agent, Skinner addresses him in as personal a manner as he possesses.

"She's right, you know," he says. "The risk you're taking. The long-term plans you and I talked about."

Mulder says, "If what Agent Scully's found is true—and I have every reason to think that it is—then the answers I might have spent a lifetime searching for may fall together like a million puzzle pieces."

"You'd risk the X-Files?"

Mulder says, "How soon can you call the attorney general?"

At the federal detention facility that night Mulder opens the shooter's cell door, jolting the gunman awake. Spender enters the cell behind Mulder, who tells the shooter that the attorney general has heard his request for immunity.

"Heard it?" says the shooter, incredulously. "You said that you could get it."

"She needs something more," says Mulder. "Something to convince her that you're not just playing games. Something that I can corroborate. I need answers from you."

The shooter looks Mulder in the eye. "The kid is a missing link," he says.

"To what?" asks Mulder

The shooter says nothing.

"He's genetic proof, isn't he?" says Mulder.

The shooter nods.

"Genetic proof of what?" asks Spender.

There is no reply from either man.

"Genetic proof of *what*?"

"The kid's not superhuman," says Mulder, finally. "He's just more human than human."

He turns and leaves the cell. Spender follows him angrily.

"He's what?" the young agent demands angrily.

"Most of us have genes we don't use," says Mulder. "They lie there dormant. Turned off. Science doesn't know what they're for, why they're there, or where they came from."

"Right. And you think this has something to do with that?"

"There's a long-held but unpopular theory tied to prehistoric evidence of alien astronauts," says Mulder.

Spender says, "You're not going to go out there and say the kid's part alien."

Mulder says nothing. He walks past the angry agent and toward the exit. Spender calls after him.

"You think that's what you heard?" he says. "You led him, Agent Mulder! Now you're letting yourself be led!"

The next day, in a low-rent neighborhood in Washington, the Cigarette-Smoking Man exits a fleabag motel and stands, waiting, on the sidewalk. A sedan pulls up to the curb in front of him. At the wheel is Krycek. In the passenger seat is the Well-Manicured Man. His window slides down. He is very unhappy.

"We entrusted you," he says. "You failed!"

"Failed? Failed who?" asks the Cigarette-Smoking Man, mockingly.

"Mulder has gone to the Justice Department. He has testimony about the boy."

The Cigarette-Smoking Man eyes the Well-Manicured Man coolly.

"That's just part of the game," he says.

"It's not a game, for God's sake!" snaps the Well-Manicured Man.

"Sure it is," says the Cigarette-Smoking Man. "It's all a game. You just take the pieces one by one until the board is clear."

The Well-Manicured Man glares at him and the window rolls back up. The car speeds away; the Cigarette-Smoking Man calmly lights another Morley.

In a nondescript motel room in Centerville, Virginia, that night, Gibson Praise watches *King of the Hill* on a television set. Scully sits in an armchair nearby, watching him.

"Gibson?" she says.

"This is a great show," says the boy. "I wish we got this where I live."

"I'd like to ask you something," says Scully, pulling over a chair to where he's sitting. "How do you do it?"

"I just hear you thinking. Like on a radio. And sometimes there are lots of radios, and I want to shut them off and watch some TV."

"Is that why you like chess? Because it's just one thought that you hear?" says Scully.

"Yeah. But that's not why I like it all the time."

"Why else do you like it?" asks Scully.

"Because there's no talking. Just thinking," says Gibson. "It's nothing like real life, where people think one thing and say something else."

Scully smiles. "Is that what people do?"

"They're worried about what people are thinking, when the people they're worried about are worried about the same thing," says Gibson, solemnly. "It makes me laugh."

"Why?"

"They make up all this stuff to believe, but it's all made up. Some people try to be good people, but some people just don't care. Like you."

"You think I don't care?"

"No. You don't care what people think. Except for her. The other one."

At that moment Diana Fowley arrives to relieve Scully.

Scully sees her, and turns back to Gibson.

"We'll talk about this later, okay?" she says.

She rises to leave. Gibson looks up at her, still solemn.

"They want to kill me, you know," he says.

"Nobody's going to do anything to you, Gibson," says Scully. "I promise."

"I know you do," he says.

At the federal detention facility the guard slides open the viewing slot to the shooter's cell. "I've been handed another note," he says.

He slides it through the opening. The shooter takes it—another Morleys package. He turns it over. It is blank.

He looks up to see the guard aiming a pistol with a silencer through the slot. The guard fires one shot.

At the Centerville motel Fowley dozes in the armchair. Her eyes open, and she notices that the television is off and the bed is empty. She snaps fully awake.

"Gibson!" she says.

The boy is kneeling at the window, peering out.

Fowley sighs with relief. "What are you doing?" she says.

"There's a man with a gun," he says.

Fowley gets up and moves quickly to the window. She shoos Gibson away and looks outside.

"He didn't come here to kill me," says Gibson. "He's aiming at you."

"What?"

A single shot rings out. The window shatters. Fowley falls backward, severely wounded.

Early the next morning Mulder and Scully arrive at the crime scene. The guard who had been stationed at the door of the motel room is dead; two paramedics carry Diana Fowley into a waiting ambulance. Mulder stares down at the unconscious agent, and squeezes her hand. Skinner briefs him.

"They worked on her here for an hour," says the AD. "They couldn't get a chopper in, so they're in radio communication with the hospital. She's got weak vitals and a hole in one of her lungs, so they're not optimistic."

"What about the boy? Is he here?" asks Scully.

Skinner shakes his head.

"Where's Spender?" she asks.

"He's gone over to Federal Detention," says Skinner. "We found the shooter shot dead in his cell early this morning. We also found this."

He hands Mulder the flattened package of Morleys. The agent takes this evidence, and without a word strides toward his car.

In the parking lot where they'd met before, the Well-Manicured Man approaches the Cigarette-Smoking Man, who this time has Gibson Praise with him. As always, the boy appears calm and unafraid.

The Well-Manicured Man bends down and smiles. "Hello, young man," he says.

"Hello," says Gibson.

The Well-Manicured Man says, "There's nothing to be afraid of."

"You're a liar," says Gibson. "Just like him."

The smile disappears from the Well-Manicured Man's face. The Cigarette-Smoking Man is amused at his discomfort.

"You've never had the stomach for our business," he says.

"Just not for your practices," says the Well-Manicured Man, contemptuously.

The Cigarette-Smoking Man doesn't flinch.

"I'm a necessity," he says, with a touch of anger. "The compliment to your cowardice."

The Well-Manicured Man snarls, "Your work is done now."

The Cigarette-Smoking Man, turning to leave, says, "My work is just beginning."

The Well-Manicured Man places his hand on Gibson's shoulder, leads the boy into the backseat, and seats himself up front. Again, the driver is Krycek.

"I've got a nice straight shot," says the younger man, eyeing the Cigarette-Smoking Man's retreating figure.

"No," says the Well-Manicured Man. "He's useful. And you may need him in the future."

Krycek shifts into gear, stomps on the accelerator, and aims the car directly at the Cigarette-Smoking Man, who hears it behind him but does not turn around. Krycek swerves aside at the last possible second. The Cigarette-Smoking Man smiles—almost imperceptibly—and takes another drag on his cigarette.

At FBI headquarters Spender stands in a corridor, briefing other members of his task force. As he issues orders directing the search for Gibson, Mulder rounds the corner of the corridor, furious. He rushes up behind Spender, grabs him by the shoulders, and spins him around.

"Who do you work for!?" he demands, grabbing him by the necktie and pushing his face against the wall.

"Do you work for him!? You and Old Smokey—is that who put this together?"

The other agents drag Mulder away. He twists out of their grasp.

"YOU'RE GOING DOWN FOR THIS, SPENDER!" he shouts. "I'M GOING TO SEE YOU PROSECUTED FOR MURDER! YOU WATCH ME! WATCH IT HAPPEN! YOUR DAYS ARE NUMBERED!"

He turns and strides angrily away. Spender watches him go.

"You're wrong, Agent Mulder," he says, quietly. "It's your days that are numbered."

In Mulder's apartment that night Scully sits at his desk. She is on the phone with Skinner.

"We knew there were risks going to the attorney general," she says.

"You know what's coming down here?" says Skinner.

"Yes, sir."

"They're serious about this, Scully."

"I understand."

"I assume you'll make Agent Mulder aware of this?"

"Yes," says Scully, "I'm here with him now."

Skinner says, "I'm making the case that his personal involvement clouded his judgment, but I don't know if the attorney general is listening."

Scully says "I'll communicate that to him. Is there anything else? Any other news?"

"You should know that Agent Spender's going after Mulder full bore," says Skinner. "He's been reciting some line about 'alien astronauts' that makes you both look pretty bad."

"Right," says Scully, grimly. "Well, I'll be here if you need to reach me."

She hangs up and turns to Mulder, who has been lying on his couch, his eyes closed.

"Any news on Diana?" he asks.

Scully sighs. "They have her on maximum pressers, but she's barely maintaining her pressure."

"What did Skinner have to say?"

"There are talks going on right now about reassignment."

"For who?"

"Both of us. These talks include instructions from the Justice Department to close down the X-Files."

Mulder turns away.

"This was all strategized. Every move," he says, softly. "I just couldn't see it. It was all part of a plan."

Scully shakes her head.

"Mulder, whatever you believe," she says, "this time they may have won."

In Mulder's office later that night the Cigarette-Smoking Man stands alone in the darkness. He flicks his lighter, lights up, and scans the room slowly. His gaze falls on Mulder's file cabinet. He thumbs through the files, stopping at the one marked MULDER, SAMANTHA T. He removes it, takes one last drag on his Morley, and stares at its glowing tip.

A few moments later he emerges from an elevator, carrying a large white envelope in his hand. Coming from the opposite direction is Jeffrey Spender, who looks up, startled, as he sees him.

"Can I help you?" says Spender, tensely.

"Actually," says the Cigarette-Smoking Man, with surprising gentleness. "I can help you."

"How did you get in here?" asks the agent.

"Access, Agent Spender," says the Cigarette-Smoking Man. "It's about access." He adds, "It's what I can give you. It's what can make you. It's why I'm doing this for you."

"Who are you?" demands Spender.

The Cigarette-Smoking Man, a slight tremor in his voice, says, "I'm your father."

"What?"

At that moment an alarm bell rings. The Cigarette-Smoking Man turns and walks away. In the X-Files office Mulder's file cabinet is totally engulfed in flames. The flames are leaping toward the ceiling, turning the entire area into an inferno.

Sometime later the FBI basement is swarming with agents and firemen. Mulder arrives on the scene, Scully trailing apprehensively behind him. He walks into the X-Files office. It is a blackened shell. The cabinet containing the X-Files is a melted, twisted, skeleton.

Scully enters, stops, and stares at the devastation in disbelief. She turns, walks slowly toward Mulder, and lays her head on his shoulder.

Mulder stares into the distance, into the darkness.

back story:

"The End" is the 117th—and final—episode of *The X-Files* to be filmed in Vancouver, British Columbia. This bittersweet milestone is marked in several ways: the first and most visible being Chris Carter's siting of the opening scene in Vancouver. This is the first—and only—time that the city has "played itself."

"It was a little bit of a storytelling lie—Canada really isn't within the FBI's jurisdiction—but it was more than worth it," says Carter.

To say good-bye to the citizens of Vancouver—for whom *The X-Files* had become a friend, a neighbor, and even a significant source of jobs and revenue—the producers threw a mammoth, open-to-the-public location shoot. It was held at GM Place, the local arena that on normal days is the home of the NBA's Vancouver Grizzlies and the NHL's Vancouver Canucks. One week-day evening early in the production of the last episode it served as the site of Gibson Praise's chess match. Appreciative Vancouverites served as honored guests/guest stars.

"We thought, hopefully, that five thousand people would show up. That would have let us easily simulate a full house," says producer J. P. Finn, who organized the shoot. "The final count total was over twelve thousand. We could have had two or three thousand more, except for staff and safety reasons."

Most of the "chess fans" seated in the arena during 5X20's opening scene are show biz drop-ins who obtained free tickets through local radio station giveaways. Several stood in line overnight to get front-row seats. Executive producer Bob Goodwin, who was directing the final episode of the season, gave instructions to his "actors" via giant video screens attached to the scoreboard. During the long breaks between shots a festive atmosphere prevailed: concession stands were thrown open for snacks; there was music, videos, and other entertainment; the show's stars—including Gillian Anderson and David Duchovny—took the microphone and answered questions from the crowd; and over $20,000 worth of television sets and other electronic equipment were raffled off.

"It was like a huge farewell party for all of us," says Finn.

In order to be with his Canadian-based crew for their final episode together, Chris Carter directed much of the second-unit filming for "The End." On the last day of shooting, first assistant director Tom Braidwood announced to his crew that the abandoned hospital corridor they were filming in was the identical site of the first scene, of the first day, of the early first-season *X-Files* episode he first worked on.

"And I was so nervous that I yelled 'action' before the director did," he laughed.

And, finally, on April 29, 1998, *The X-Files*'s daily call sheet, for "Day 8 of 8," included several pages of the usual important information about crew and cast schedules and location requirements. Attached to the back of this, however, were two personal letters.

The first one was from producer Joseph Patrick Finn to his crew. It read:

To: The Crew
From: J.P.
I will always remember your indomitable spirit, your tireless stamina, your generosity to one another and your insatiable appetite for fun. Never lose these qualities.
Thanks for all the wonderful memories.

(Signed)

J.P.

The second was from executive producer R. W. Goodwin. It read:

Dear Everyone:
I was going to try to get around to speak to each of you personally, but I realized with my schedule this week it's impossible, so I'm writing this instead.
Thank you all for a wonderful five years. Everyone of you has worked so hard and with such great talent to create the best television show ever made, and it's an experience I'll never forget. Time after time, directors and actors have said to me that they thought you were the best group of people they ever worked with. Of course you are. After all, I'm the one who put you together, and everyone knows how smart I am.
Seriously, you have all performed well above the call of duty, and you've done it graciously and so perfectly it's almost hard to believe. I'll never forget all the struggles and stresses and all of the incredible things we've created, but most of all, I won't forget all the good times and laughs.
I won't say good-bye because I'm not going anywhere and I know we'll be working together soon on something else. So long for now. I love you all.

(Signed)
Bob

awards and honors
1997–98

awards and honors

PRIME-TIME EMMY AWARDS

—Winners, Outstanding Art Direction for a Series—Graeme Murray, Greg Loewen, and Shirley Inget for "The Post-Modern Prometheus."

—Winner, Outstanding Single-Picture Editing for a Series—Heather MacDougall for "Kill Switch"

—Nominee, Outstanding Drama Series

—Nominee, Outstanding Lead Actress in a Drama Series—Gillian Anderson

—Nominee, Outstanding Lead Actor in a Drama Series—David Duchovny

—Nominee, Outstanding Writing for a Drama Series—Chris Carter for "The Post-Modern Prometheus"

—Nominee, Outstanding Directing for a Drama Series—Chris Carter for "The Post-Modern Prometheus"

—Nominee, Outstanding Cinematography for a Series—Joel Ransom for "The Post-Modern Prometheus."

—Nominee, Outstanding Single-Picture Editing for a Series—Casey O Rohrs for "Mind's Eye"

—Nominee, Outstanding Single-Picture Editing for a Series—Lynne Willingham for "The Post-Modern Prometheus"

—Nominee, Outstanding Makeup for a Series—Laverne Basham, Pearl Louie, makeup artists; Toby Lindala, Dave Coughtry, Rachel Griffin, Robin Lindala, Leanne Rae Podavin, Brad Proctor, Geoff Redknap, Tony Wohlgemuth, Wayne Dang, Vince Yoshida, prosthetic makeup for "The Post-Modern Prometheus"

—Nominee, Outstanding Music Composition for a Series—Mark Snow for "The Post-Modern Prometheus"

—Nominee, Outstanding Guest Actress in a Drama Series—Veronica Cartwright as Cassandra Spender in "Patient X" and "The Red and the Black"

—Nominee, Outstanding Guest Actress in a Drama Series—Lili Taylor as Marty Glenn in "Mind's Eye"

—Nominee, Outstanding Sound Editing for a Series—Thierry Couturier, supervising sound editor; Maciek Malish, Jay Levine, Gabrielle Reeves, Michael Goodman, Ira Leslie, Chris Fradkin, Rick Hinson, Michael Kimball, sound editors; Jeff Charbonneau, music editor; Gary Marullo and Mike Salvetta, foley artists

—Nominee, Outstanding Sound Mixing for a Drama Series— Michael Williamson, production mixer; David J. West, Harry T. Adronis, and Kurt Kassulke, re-recording mixers, for "The Red and the Black"

GOLDEN GLOBE AWARDS

—Winner, Best Television Series, Drama

—Nominee, Best Performance by an Actress in a Television Series— Gillian Anderson

—Nominee, Best Performance by an Actor in a Television Series, Drama— David Duchovny

PRODUCERS GUILD OF AMERICA AWARDS

—Nominee, Outstanding Episodic Series

DIRECTORS' GUILD OF AMERICA AWARDS (GOLDEN LAUREL AWARDS)

—Nominee, Outstanding Directing— Chris Carter for "The Post-Modern Prometheus"

VIEWERS FOR QUALITY TELEVISION

—Best Actress in a Quality Drama— Gillian Anderson

worldwide broadcast outlets

During the 1997–98 season,
The X-Files was licensed for broadcast
in the following countries:*

Algeria
Argentina
Armenia
Australia
Azerbaijan
Bahrain
Bangladesh
Belarus
Belgium
Bolivia
Brazil
Brunei
Bulgaria
Canada
  (English)
Canada
  (French)
Chile
China
Colombia
Costa Rica
Croatia
Cyprus
Czech Republic

Denmark
Dominican
  Republic
Dubai
Ecuador
Egypt
El Salvador
Fiji
Finland
France
Germany
Ghana
Greece
Greenland
Guatemala
Honduras
Hong Kong
Hungary
Iceland
India
Indonesia
Ireland (EIRE)
Israel
Italy

Jamaica
Japan
Kazakhstan
Kenya
Kuwait
Lebanon
Luxembourg
Malaysia
Malta
Mauritius
Mexico
Moldavia
Morocco
Namibia
Nassau
Netherlands
New Zealand
Nicaragua
Norway
Panama
Paraguay
Peru
Philippines
Poland
Portugal
Puerto Rico

Romania
Russia
Singapore
Slovak Republic
Slovenia
South Africa
South Korea
Spain
Sri Lanka
Sweden
Switzerland
Taiwan
Tajikistan
Tanzania
Thailand
Trinidad
  & Tobago
Turkey
Turkmenistan
Ukraine
United Kingdom
United States
Uruguay
Venezuela

*Broadcast license windows last up to two years; the series may or may not be on the air at any given time.

ratings: season 5

AIRDATE	EPISODE	RATING/SHARE	VIEWERS (in millions)
11/2/97	Redux	16.1/22	27.34
11/9/97	Redux II	15.0/21	24.84
11/16/97	Unusual Suspects	13.0/19	21.72
11/23/97	Detour	13.2/19	22.88
11/30/97	The Post-Modern Prometheus	11.5/16	18.68
12/7/97	Christmas Carol	12.8/19	20.91
12/14/97	Emily	12.4/19	20.94
1/4/98	Kitsunegari	11.6/17	19.75
1/11/98	Schizogeny	12.9/19	21.37
2/8/98	Chinga	12.7/18	21.33
2/15/98	Kill Switch	11.1/16	18.04
2/22/98	Bad Blood	12.0/17	19.25
3/1/98	Patient X	12.6/19	20.21
3/8/98	The Red and the Black	12.0/18	19.98
3/29/98	Travelers	9.9/15	15.06
4/19/98	Mind's Eye	10.4/16	16.53
4/26/98	All Souls	8.5/12	13.44
5/3/98	The Pine Bluff Variant	11.4	18.24
5/10/98	Folie à Deux	11.0/17	17.63
5/17/98	The End	11.9/18	18.76

Each rating point equals 980,000 homes, or 1 percent of all households in the United States. Share is based upon the percentage of TV sets in use within the time period. Total viewers for each episode is measured by Nielsen's people-meter service, which draws its figures from a small sample designed to represent all televison viewers in the United States.
Source: Nielsen Media Research

appendix

SEASON ONE

PILOT 1X79
FBI Agent Dana Scully is paired with maverick agent Fox Mulder, who has made it his life's work to explore unexplained phenomena. The two are dispatched to investigate the mysterious deaths of a number of high school classmates.

DEEP THROAT 1X01
Acting on a tip from an inside source (Deep Throat), Mulder and Scully travel to Idaho to investigate unusual disappearances of army test pilots.

SQUEEZE 1X02
Mulder and Scully try to stop a mutant killer, Eugene Tooms, who can gain access through even the smallest spaces and awakens from hibernation every 30 years to commit murder.

CONDUIT 1X03
A teenage girl is abducted by aliens, compelling Mulder to confront his feelings about his own sister's disappearance.

THE JERSEY DEVIL 1X04
Scully and Mulder investigate murders thought to be the work of the legendary man-beast living in the New Jersey woods.

SHADOWS 1X05
Mulder and Scully investigate unusual murders committed by an unseen force protecting a young woman.

GHOST IN THE MACHINE 1X06
A computer with artificial intelligence begins killing in order to preserve its existence.

ICE 1X07
Mulder and Scully and a small party in the Arctic are trapped after the unexplained deaths of a research team on assignment there.

SPACE 1X08
A mysterious force is sabotaging the United States space shuttle program and Scully and Mulder must stop it before the next launch.

FALLEN ANGEL 1X09
Scully and Mulder investigate a possible UFO crash site, which Mulder believes the government is covering up.

EVE 1X10
Two bizarre, identical murders occur simultaneously on different coasts, each involving a strange young girl.

FIRE 1X11
Mulder and Scully encounter an assassin who can start fires with the touch of his hand.

BEYOND THE SEA 1X12
Scully and Mulder seek the aid of a death row inmate, Luther Lee Boggs, who claims to have psychic abilities, to help them stop a killer who is on the loose.

GENDERBENDER 1X13
Scully and Mulder seek answers to a bizarre series of murders committed by one person who kills as both a male and a female.

LAZARUS 1X14
When an FBI agent and a bank robber are both shot during a bank heist, the robber is killed but the agent begins to take on the criminal's persona.

YOUNG AT HEART 1X15
Mulder finds that a criminal he put away who was supposed to have died in prison has returned, taunting him as he commits a new spree of crimes.

E.B.E 1X16
Scully and Mulder discover evidence of a government cover-up when they learn that a UFO shot down in Iraq has been secretly transported to the United States.

MIRACLE MAN 1X17
The agents investigate a young faith healer who seems to use his powers for both good and evil.

SHAPES 1X18
Mulder and Scully travel to an Indian reservation to examine deaths caused by a beastlike creature.

DARKNESS FALLS 1X19
Mulder and Scully are called in when loggers in a remote Pacific Northwest forest mysteriously disappear.

TOOMS 1X20
Mulder becomes personally involved when Eugene Tooms, the serial killer who extracts and eats human livers, is released from prison.

BORN AGAIN 1X21
A series of murders is linked to a little girl who may be the reincarnated spirit of a murdered policeman.

ROLAND 1X22
Mulder and Scully investigate the murders of two rocket scientists apparently linked to a retarded janitor.

THE ERLENMEYER FLASK 1X23
Working on a tip from Deep Throat, Mulder and Scully discover that the government has been testing alien DNA on humans with disastrous results.

SEASON TWO

LITTLE GREEN MEN 2X01
With the X-Files shut down, Mulder secretly journeys to a possible alien contact site in Puerto Rico while Scully tries to help him escape detection.

THE HOST 2X02
Mulder stumbles upon a genetic mutation, the Flukeman, while investigating a murder in the New Jersey sewer system.

BLOOD 2X03
Several residents of a small suburban farming community suddenly turn violent and dangerous, prompted by digital readouts in appliances telling them to kill.

SLEEPLESS 2X04
Mulder is assigned a new partner, Alex Krycek, and they investigate a secret Vietnam-era experiment on sleep deprivation that is having deadly effects on surviving participants.

DUANE BARRY (PART 1 OF 2) 2X05
Mulder negotiates a hostage situation involving a man, Duane Barry, who claims to be a victim of alien experimentation.

ASCENSION (PART 2 OF 2) 2X06
Mulder pursues Duane Barry in a desperate search for Scully.

3 2X07
Mulder investigates a series of vampiresque murders in Hollywood and finds himself falling for a mysterious woman who is a prime suspect.

ONE BREATH 2X08
Scully is found alive but in a coma, and Mulder must fight to save her life.

FIREWALKER 2X09
Mulder and Scully stumble upon a deadly life form while investigating the death of a scientist studying an active volcano.

RED MUSEUM 2X10
Mulder and Scully investigate a possible connection between a rural religious cult and the disappearance of several teenagers.

EXCELSIUS DEI 2X11
Mulder and Scully uncover strange goings-on in a nursing home after a nurse is attacked by an unseen force.

AUBREY 2X12
Mulder and Scully investigate the possibility of genetic transferring of personality from one generation to another in connection with a serial killer.

IRRESISTIBLE 2X13
A psycho who collects hair and fingernails from the dead steps up his obsession to killing his soon-to-be collectibles himself.

DIE HAND DIE VERLETZT 2X14
Mulder and Scully journey to a small town to investigate a boy's murder and are caught between the town's secret occult religion and a woman with strange powers.

FRESH BONES 2X15
Mulder and Scully journey to a Haitian refugee camp after a series of deaths, finding themselves caught in a secret war between the camp commander and a voodoo priest.

COLONY (PART 1 OF 2) 2X16
Mulder and Scully track an alien bounty hunter, who is killing medical doctors who have something strange in common.

END GAME (PART 2 OF 2) 2X17
Mulder tracks an alien bounty hunter who has taken Scully prisoner while discovering that his sister may not be who she seems.

FEARFUL SYMMETRY 2X18
Mulder and Scully investigate animal abductions from a zoo near a known UFO hot spot.

DOD KALM 2X19
Mulder and Scully fall victim to a mysterious force aboard a navy destroyer that causes rapid aging.

HUMBUG 2X20
Mulder and Scully investigate the bizarre death of a retired escape artist in a town populated by former circus and sideshow acts.

THE CALUSARI 2X21
A young boy's unusual death leads Mulder and Scully to a superstitious old woman and her grandson, who may be possessed by evil.

F. EMASCULATA 2X22
When a plaguelike illness kills ten men inside a prison facility, Scully is called to the quarantine area while Mulder tracks two escapees.

SOFT LIGHT 2X23
An experiment in dark matter turns a scientist's shadow into a form of instant death.

OUR TOWN 2X24
Mulder and Scully investigate a murder in a small Southern town and its strange secrets surrounding a chicken processing plant.

ANASAZI 2X25
Mulder's and Scully's lives are jeopardized when an amateur computer hacker gains access to secret government files providing evidence of UFOs.

SEASON THREE

THE BLESSING WAY 3X01
With the Cigarette-Smoking Man pursuing the secret files that prove the existence of alien visitation and experimentation, and Mulder still missing, Scully finds her own life and career in jeopardy.

PAPER CLIP 3X02
Mulder and Scully seek evidence of alien experimentation by Nazi war criminals while Skinner tries to bargain with the Cigarette-Smoking Man for their lives.

D.P.O. 3X03
Mulder and Scully investigate a series of deaths related to a teenage boy who can control lightning.

CLYDE BRUCKMAN'S FINAL REPOSE 3X04
Mulder and Scully enlist the help of a man who can see when people will die while searching for a serial killer who prays upon fortunetellers.

THE LIST 3X05
A death row inmate makes good on his promise to return from the dead and kill five people who wronged him.

2SHY 3X06
Mulder and Scully track a serial killer who preys on lonely, overweight women via the Internet.

THE WALK 3X07
A suicide attempt and subsequent murders at a military hospital bring Mulder and Scully into contact with a quadruple amputee veteran who may have the power of astral projection.

OUBLIETTE 3X08
The abduction of a young girl prompts Mulder to seek the help of a woman who was kidnapped by the same man years earlier and who has the ability to feel what the victim feels.

NISEI 3X09
Video of an alien autopsy puts Mulder and Scully on the trail of a conspiracy involving Japanese scientists that may shed light on Scully's abduction.

731 3X10
Mulder is caught on board a speeding train with what might be alien cargo and a government killer while Scully seeks her own solution to the conspiracy.

REVELATIONS 3X11
Mulder and Scully seek to protect a young boy who displays wounds of religious significance from a killer, causing Scully to question her own faith while being cast in the role of the boy's protector.

WAR OF THE COPROPHAGES 3X12
A number of deaths seemingly linked to cockroaches cause widespread panic in a small town.

SYZYGY 3X13
Two high school girls born on the same day are involved in a series of deaths thanks to an odd alignment of planets that causes strange behavior in all the townspeople, as well as Mulder and Scully.

GROTESQUE 3X14
A serial killer maintains that an evil spirit was responsible for his actions, as Mulder's own sanity comes into question when the murders persist.

PIPER MARU 3X15
A French salvage ship finds mysterious wreckage from World War II that unleashes a strange force causing radiation sickness and leading Mulder into a web of intrigue.

APOCRYPHA 3X16
Mulder pursues Krycek and the mystery of the sunken World War II wreckage, while the shooting of Skinner brings Scully new clues to her sister's murder.

PUSHER 3X17
Mulder and Scully investigate a man possessing the power to bend people to his will who engages Mulder in a scary battle of wits.

TESO DOS BICHOS 3X18
The unearthing of an ancient Ecuadorian artifact results in a series of deaths potentially linked to a shaman spirit.

HELL MONEY 3X19
The deaths of several Chinese immigrants missing internal organs leads Mulder and Scully to a mysterious game with potentially fatal consequences.

JOSE CHUNG'S *FROM OUTER SPACE* 3X20
A novelist interviews Scully about a rumored UFO abduction of two teenagers that seems open to a number of different interpretations.

AVATAR 3X21
In the midst of a marital breakup Skinner becomes a murder suspect, while a clue to the case may lie in the form of a strange woman who appears to him in dreams.

QUAGMIRE 3X22
Mulder and Scully investigate a series of deaths that may be linked to a lake monster known by the locals as Big Blue.

WETWIRED 3X23
Mulder and Scully discover a conspiracy involving mind control through television signals that's responsible for a series of murders in a small town and begins causing Scully herself to behave strangely.

TALITHA CUMI 3X24
Mulder and Scully search for a mysterious man with the power to heal, whose existence risks exposing a conspiracy involving the presence of aliens on Earth, while various forces seek a strange weapon that comes into Mulder's possession.

SEASON FOUR

HERRENVOLK 4X01
As Mulder's mother lies dying, he and Scully are given tantalizing glimpses of a plan to secretly catalog—and clone—human beings. Only by putting the pieces together can they hope to save Mrs. Mulder's life.

UNRUHE 4X02
Someone is abducting, mutilating, and murdering the inhabitants of a small town. The primary evidence is a series of photographs depicting the killer's psychotic fantasies.

HOME 4X03
While investigating the death of an infant in a close-knit rural community, Mulder and Scully uncover an even darker family secret.

TELIKO 4X04
African-American men are disappearing. Their bodies, when found, are dead white—drained of pigment. Were they killed by a virulent new disease? Were they murdered? Or does the answer lie elsewhere?

THE FIELD WHERE I DIED 4X05
In an effort to prevent a mass suicide at a fanatical religious cult, Mulder and Scully interrogate one of the wives of the polygamous cult leader. Under hypnosis, her accounts of her past lives—and deaths— are inexplicably tied to the agents' own.

SANGUINARIUM 4X06
At a busy—and lucrative—cosmetic surgery clinic, doctors are murdering patients with the tools of their trade. Several clues point toward demonic possession.

MUSINGS OF A CIGARETTE-SMOKING MAN (4X07)
The secret biography of a sinister, all-powerful conspirator. Some old mysteries are cleared up— and some new ones are created.

PAPER HEARTS 4X08
Prompted by a series of prophetic dreams, Mulder reopens the case of a convicted child killer. The murderer claims to know the circumstances of Samantha Mulder's abduction.

TUNGUSKA 4X09
Diplomatic couriers are bringing a lethal alien life form into the United States. Mulder and Scully's investigation points to a high-level international conspiracy beyond even their comprehension.

TERMA 4X10
Stranded in the gulag, Mulder discovers the effects of the alien toxin—firsthand. In Washington, Scully battles a corrupt U.S. senator to keep their investigation alive.

EL MUNDO GIRA 4X11
Fear, jealousy, superstition, and prejudice converge when a young female migrant worker is killed by a mysterious yellow rain.

KADDISH 4X12
Someone—or something—is killing the members of an anti-Semitic gang. To find the truth, Mulder and Scully delve into the ancient canons of Jewish mysticism.

NEVER AGAIN 4X13
On a solo assignment out of town, a lonely Scully meets Mr. Wrong—a single guy who thinks his new tattoo is talking to him.

LEONARD BETTS 4X14
A headless corpse escapes from a hospital morgue. Mulder and Scully investigate; what they find leads them to the jagged dividing line between life and death.

MEMENTO MORI 4X15
Scully learns she has inoperable cancer— of the same type that killed nearly a dozen female UFO abductees. While she undergoes radical treatment, Mulder works desperately to unravel the conspiracy behind her disease.

UNREQUITED 4X16
A Marine Corps prisoner of war, abandoned in Vietnam by his superiors, returns to the United States with a vengeance—and a special talent for hiding in plain sight.

TEMPUS FUGIT 4X17
A former UFO abductee is killed in a catastrophic plane crash. Mulder suspects a conspiracy—and a cover-up.

MAX 4X18
Mulder and Scully get close to proving alien involvement in the crash of Flight 549. As they do so, they trigger a massive military disinformation campaign—and the deaths of several friends and colleagues.

SYNCHRONY 4X19
For centuries, scientists have debated whether time travel is possible—and if it ever will be. For Mulder and Scully, this age-old conundrum is the key to solving several baffling murders.

SMALL POTATOES 4X20
Mulder and Scully investigate several not-so-blessed events in a small southern town.

ZERO SUM 4X21
Walter Skinner makes a deal with the devil—a.k.a. the Cigarette-Smoking Man—in an effort to prevent Scully from dying of cancer.

ELEGY 4X22
Several young women have been murdered on Mulder and Scully's home turf. Their prime suspect is a mentally disabled man, Harold Spüller, who has been beset by a series of frightening apparitions.

DEMONS 4X23
After experiencing a series of blackouts and seizures— and what might be the recovery of repressed memories—Mulder gains new insights into his younger sister's abduction. However, while taking his inner journey, he may also have murdered two people.

GETHSEMANE 4X24
When a controversial scientist claims to have discovered evidence of extraterrestrial life, Mulder and Scully find their lives—and belief systems—in grave peril.